# Ninja Girls

## 5

### Hosana Tanaka

Translated and adapted by
**Andria Cheng**

Lettered by
**North Market Street Graphics**

KC
KODANSHA
COMICS

*Ninja Girls* volume 5 is a work of fiction. Names, characters, places, and incidents are the products of the author's imagination or are used fictitiously. Any resemblance to actual events, locales, or persons, living or dead, is entirely coincidental.

A Kodansha Comics Trade Paperback Original.



Published in the United States by Kodansha Comics, an imprint of Kodansha USA Publishing, LLC., New York.

Publication rights for this English edition arranged through Kodansha Ltd., Tokyo.

First published in Japan in 2006 by Kodansha Ltd., Tokyo, as *Rappi Rangai*, volume 5.

ISBN 978-1-935-42965-4

Printed in the United States of America.

www.kodanshacomics.com

9 8 7 6 5 4 3 2 1

Translator/Adapter: Andria Cheng
Lettering: North Market Street Graphics

# CONTENTS

# HONORIFICS EXPLAINED

Throughout the Kodansha Comics books, you will find Japanese honorifics left intact in the translations. For those not familiar with how the Japanese use honorifics and, more important, how they differ from American honorifics, we present this brief overview.

Politeness has always been a critical facet of Japanese culture. Ever since the feudal era, when Japan was a highly stratified society, use of honorifics—which can be defined as polite speech that indicates relationship or status—has played an essential role in the Japanese language. When addressing someone in Japanese, an honorific usually takes the form of a suffix attached to one's name (example: "Asuna-san"), is used as a title at the end of one's name, or appears in place of the name itself (example: "Negi-sensei," or simply "Sensei!").

Honorifics can be expressions of respect or endearment. In the context of manga and anime, honorifics give insight into the nature of the relationship between characters. Many English translations leave out these important honorifics and therefore distort the feel of the original Japanese. Because Japanese honorifics contain nuances that English honorifics lack, it is our policy at Kodansha Comics not to translate them. Here, instead, is a guide to some of the honorifics you may encounter in Kodansha Comics books.

- *-san:*    This is the most common honorific and is equivalent to Mr., Miss, Ms., or Mrs. It is the all-purpose honorific and can be used in any situation where politeness is required.

- *-sama:*    This is one level higher than "-san" and is used to confer great respect.

- *-dono:*    This comes from the word "tono," which means "lord." It is an even higher level than "-sama" and confers utmost respect.

- *-kun:*    This suffix is used at the end of boys' names to express familiarity or endearment. It is also sometimes used by men among friends, or when addressing someone younger or of a lower station.

**-chan:** This is used to express endearment, mostly toward girls. It is also used for little boys, pets, and even among lovers. It gives a sense of childish cuteness.

**Bozu:** This is an informal way to refer to a boy, similar to the English terms "kid" and "squirt."

**Sempai/**
**Senpai:** This title suggests that the addressee is one's senior in a group or organization. It is most often used in a school setting, where underclassmen refer to their upperclassmen as "sempai." It can also be used in the workplace, such as when a newer employee addresses an employee who has seniority in the company.

**Kohai:** This is the opposite of "sempai" and is used toward underclassmen in school or newcomers in the workplace. It connotes that the addressee is of a lower station.

**Sensei:** Literally meaning "one who has come before," this title is used for teachers, doctors, or masters of any profession or art.

**-[blank]:** This is usually forgotten in these lists, but it is perhaps the most significant difference between Japanese and English. The lack of honorific means that the speaker has permission to address the person in a very intimate way. Usually, only family, spouses, or very close friends have this kind of permission. Known as *yobisute*, it can be gratifying when someone who has earned the intimacy starts to call one by one's name without an honorific. But when that intimacy hasn't been earned, it can be very insulting.

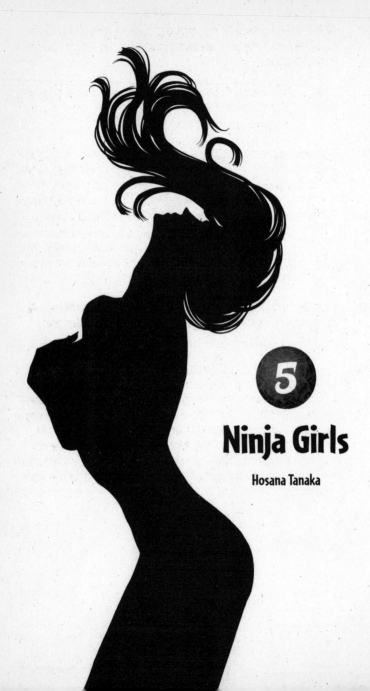

# Ninja Girls

Hosana Tanaka

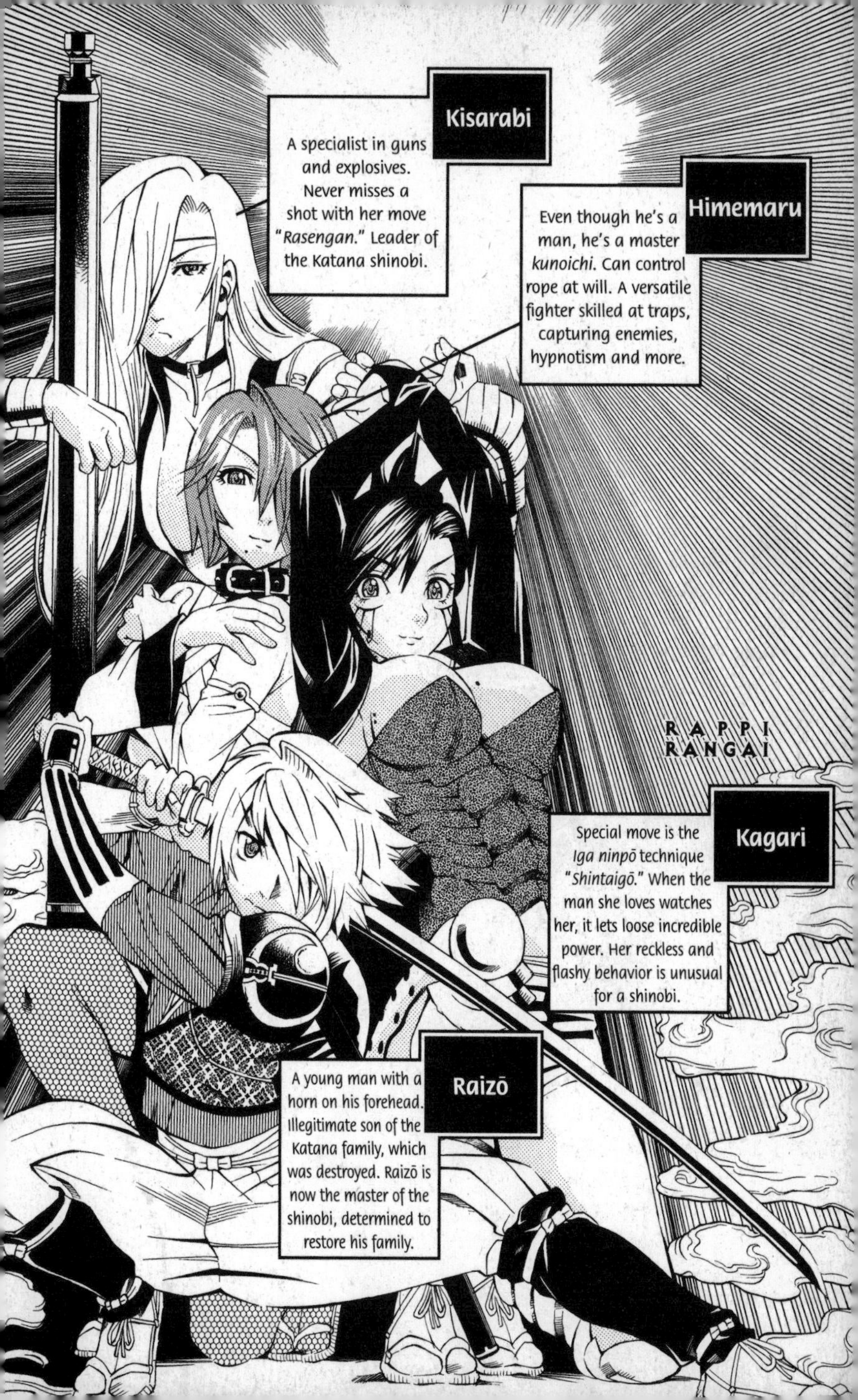
Kisarabi
A specialist in guns and explosives. Never misses a shot with her move "*Rasengan*." Leader of the Katana shinobi.
Himemaru
Even though he's a man, he's a master *kunoichi*. Can control rope at will. A versatile fighter skilled at traps, capturing enemies, hypnotism and more.
RAPPI RANGAI
Kagari
Special move is the *Iga ninpō* technique "*Shintaigō*." When the man she loves watches her, it lets loose incredible power. Her reckless and flashy behavior is unusual for a shinobi.
Raizō
A young man with a horn on his forehead. Illegitimate son of the Katana family, which was destroyed. Raizō is now the master of the shinobi, determined to restore his family.

The only surviving member of the Katana family, Raizō, set off on a journey with the Katana shinobi: Kagari, whose special technique is *Shintaigō*; Kisarabi, a clairvoyant sniper; and Himemaru, a shape-shifting rope-master. Raizō's life is thrown into chaos by these three beautiful yet dangerous *shinobi*. Their goal is to restore the Katana family.

Last time, our heroes met a mysterious woman named Azami, who unbeknownst to them, was actually a minion of their sworn enemy, Kabuki Seigan. Raizō allowed her to join them, which gave her the opportunity to create conflict between the friends. This was Kabuki Seigan's plan in order to get a hold of Kagari. After a tragic end to the battle against Seigan and his minions, the bonds of the group were even stronger. Now they will set sail to Shima…

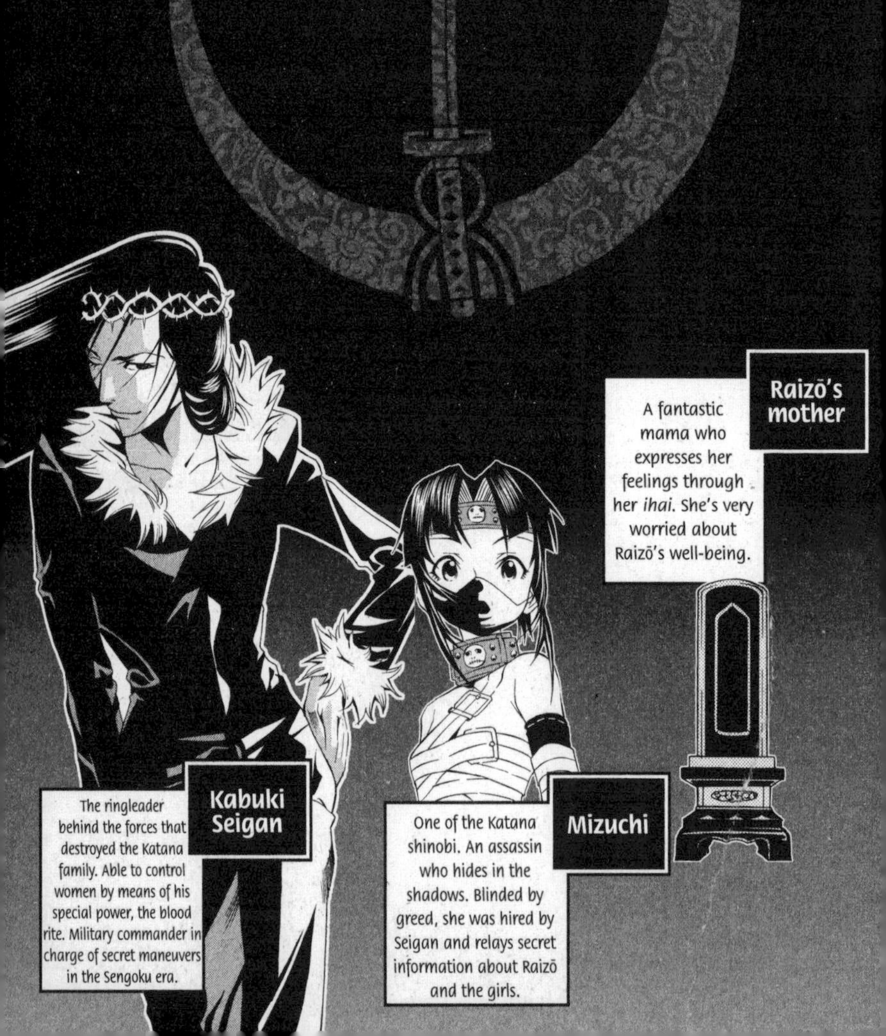
Raizō's mother
A fantastic mama who expresses her feelings through her *ihai*. She's very worried about Raizō's well-being.
Kabuki Seigan
The ringleader behind the forces that destroyed the Katana family. Able to control women by means of his special power, the blood rite. Military commander in charge of secret maneuvers in the Sengoku era.
Mizuchi
One of the Katana shinobi. An assassin who hides in the shadows. Blinded by greed, she was hired by Seigan and relays secret information about Raizō and the girls.

# Ninja Girls
## Volume 5

## Contents

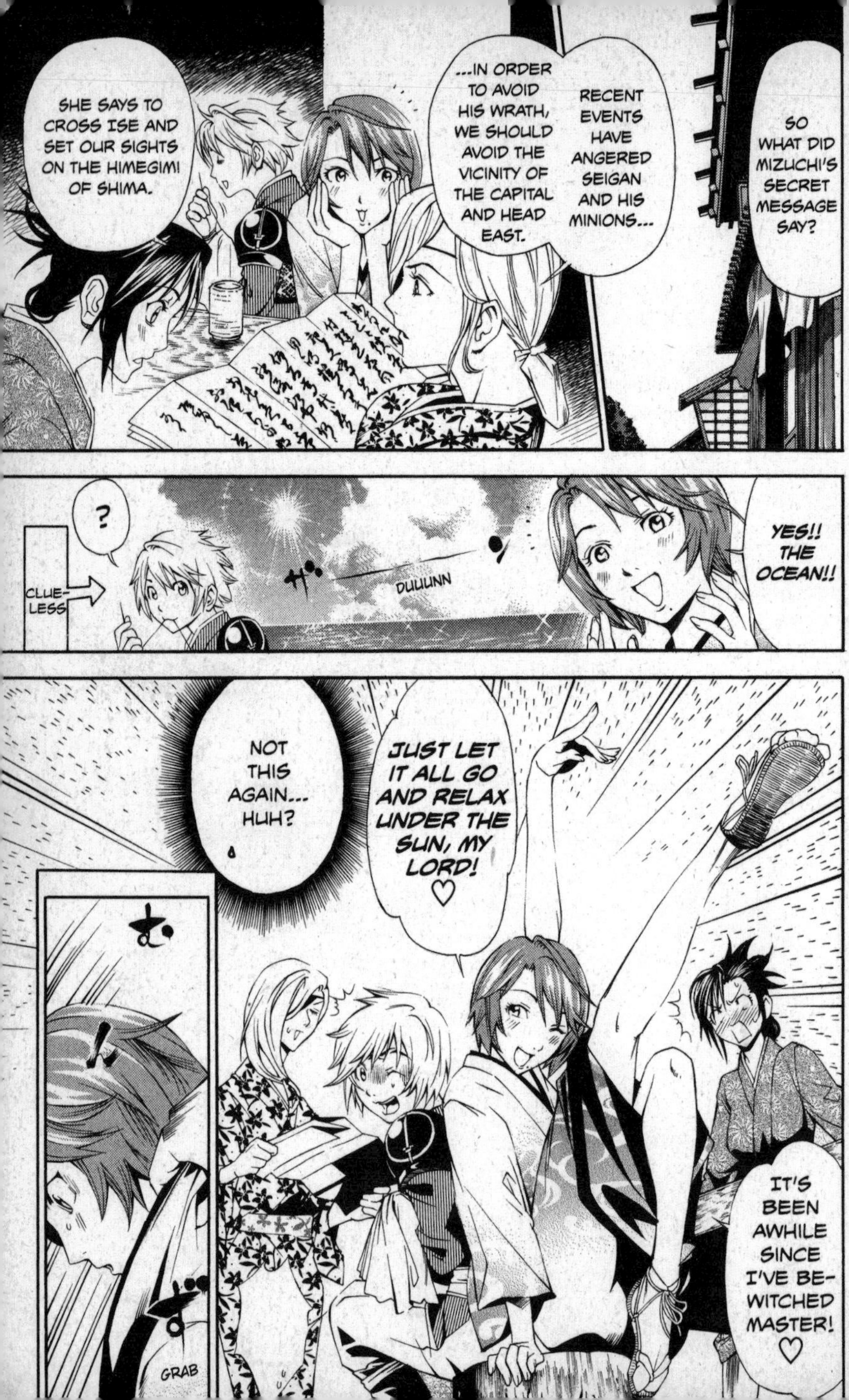
SO WHAT DID MIZUCHI'S SECRET MESSAGE SAY?
RECENT EVENTS HAVE ANGERED SEIGAN AND HIS MINIONS...
...IN ORDER TO AVOID HIS WRATH, WE SHOULD AVOID THE VICINITY OF THE CAPITAL AND HEAD EAST.
SHE SAYS TO CROSS ISE AND SET OUR SIGHTS ON THE HIMEGIMI OF SHIMA.
YES!! THE OCEAN!!
DUUUNN
?
CLUE-LESS
IT'S BEEN AWHILE SINCE I'VE BE-WITCHED MASTER! ♡
JUST LET IT ALL GO AND RELAX UNDER THE SUN, MY LORD! ♡
NOT THIS AGAIN... HUH?
GRAB

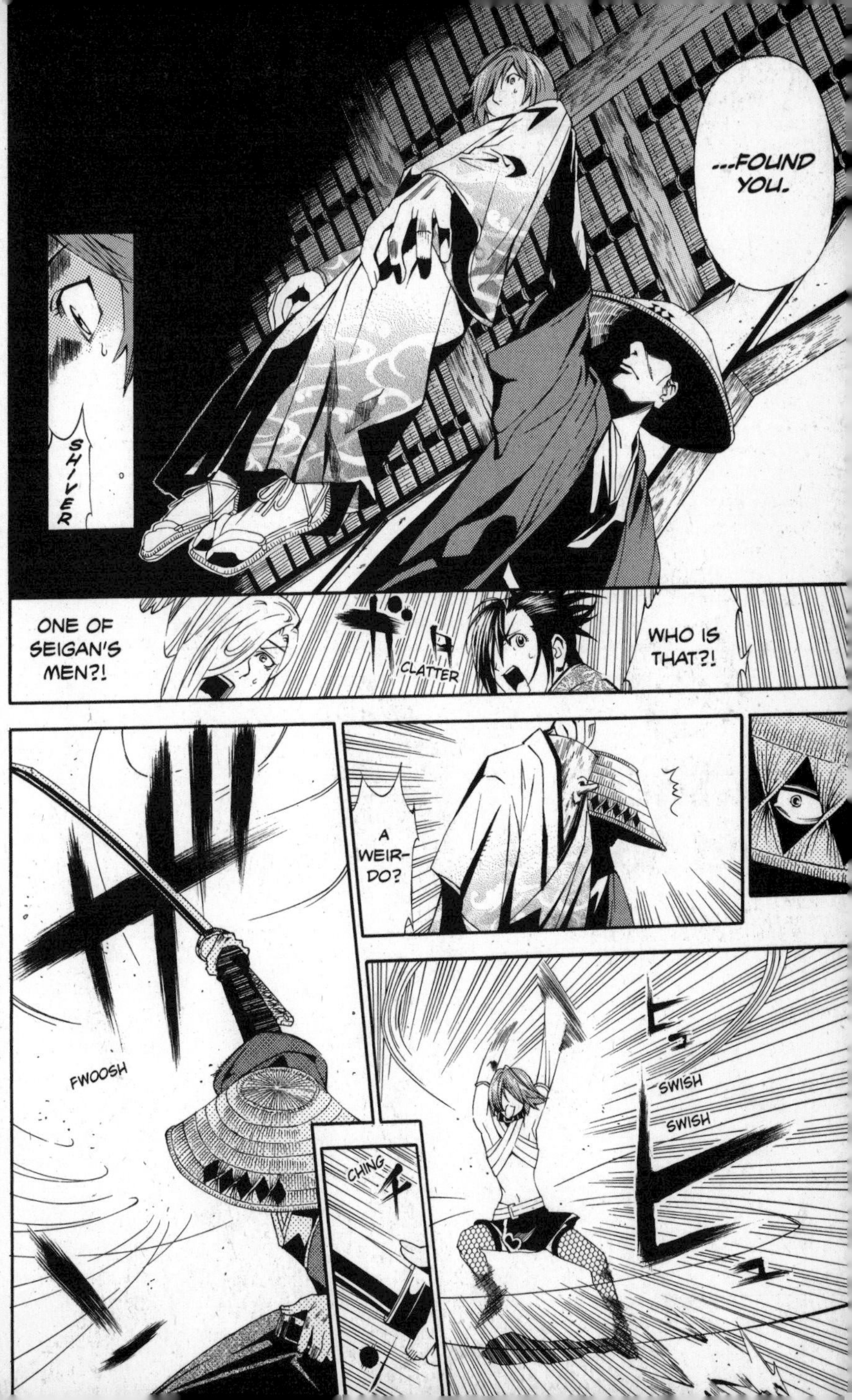

...FOUND YOU.
SHIVER
WHO IS THAT?!
CLATTER
ONE OF SEIGAN'S MEN?!
A WEIRD-DO?
SWISH
SWISH
CHING
FWOOSH

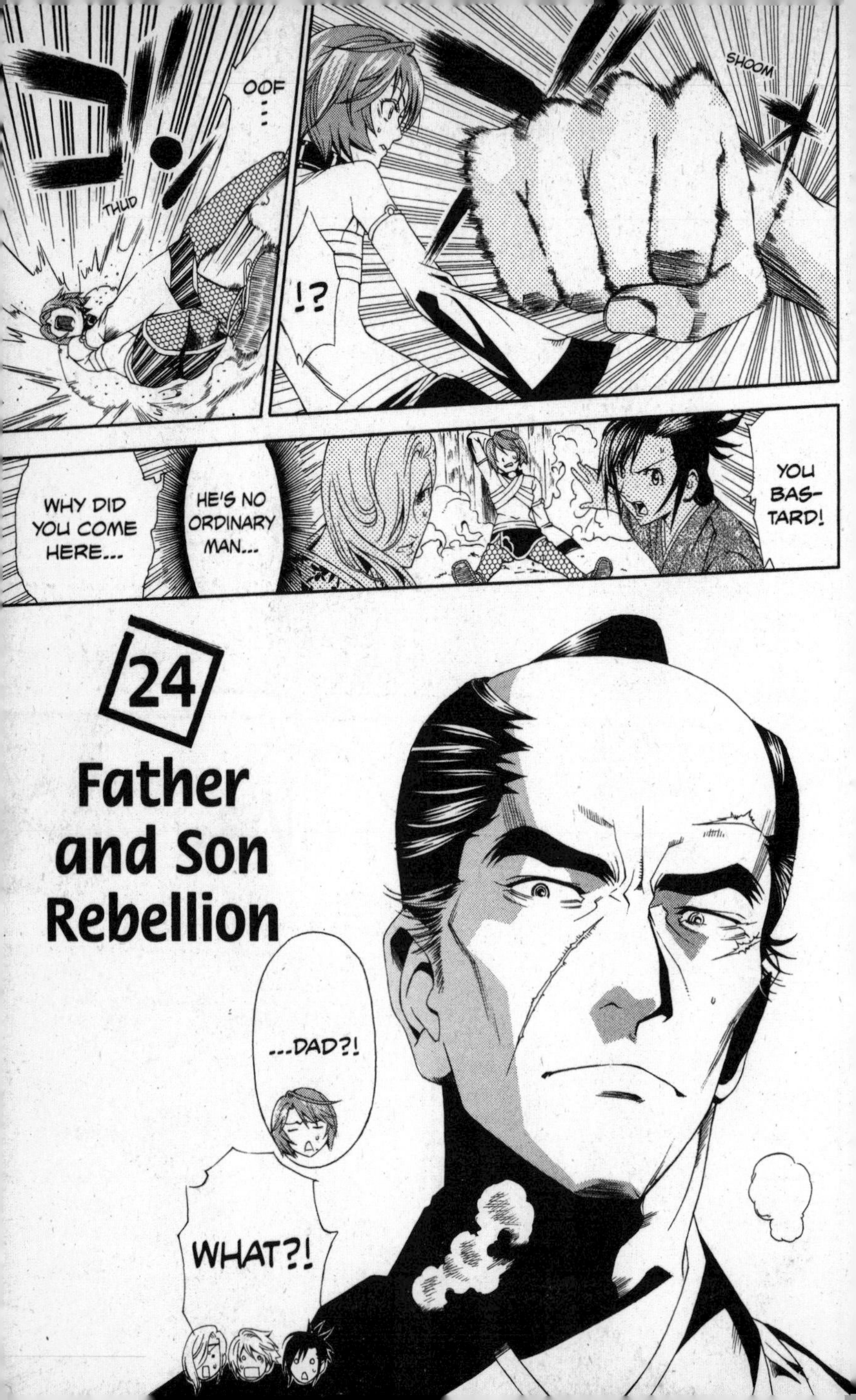
SHOOM
!?
OOF...
THUD
YOU BAS-TARD!
HE'S NO ORDINARY MAN...
WHY DID YOU COME HERE...
24
Father and Son Rebellion
...DAD?!
WHAT?!

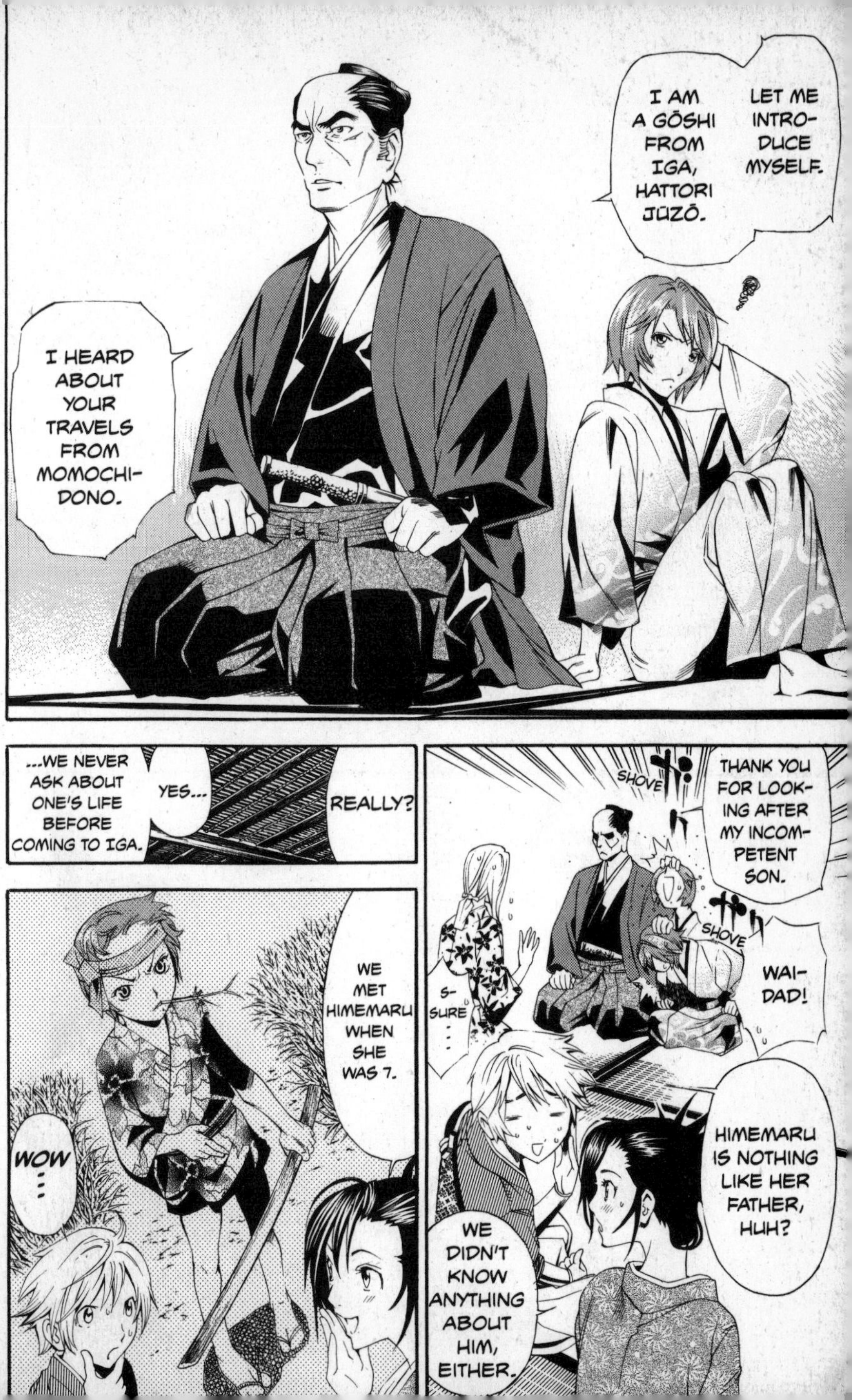
LET ME INTRODUCE MYSELF.
I AM A GŌSHI FROM IGA, HATTORI JŪZŌ.
I HEARD ABOUT YOUR TRAVELS FROM MOMOCHI-DONO.
SHOVE
THANK YOU FOR LOOKING AFTER MY INCOMPETENT SON.
SHOVE
WAI- DAD!
S-SURE...
HIMEMARU IS NOTHING LIKE HER FATHER, HUH?
WE DIDN'T KNOW ANYTHING ABOUT HIM, EITHER.
REALLY?
YES...
...WE NEVER ASK ABOUT ONE'S LIFE BEFORE COMING TO IGA.
WE MET HIMEMARU WHEN SHE WAS 7.
WOW...

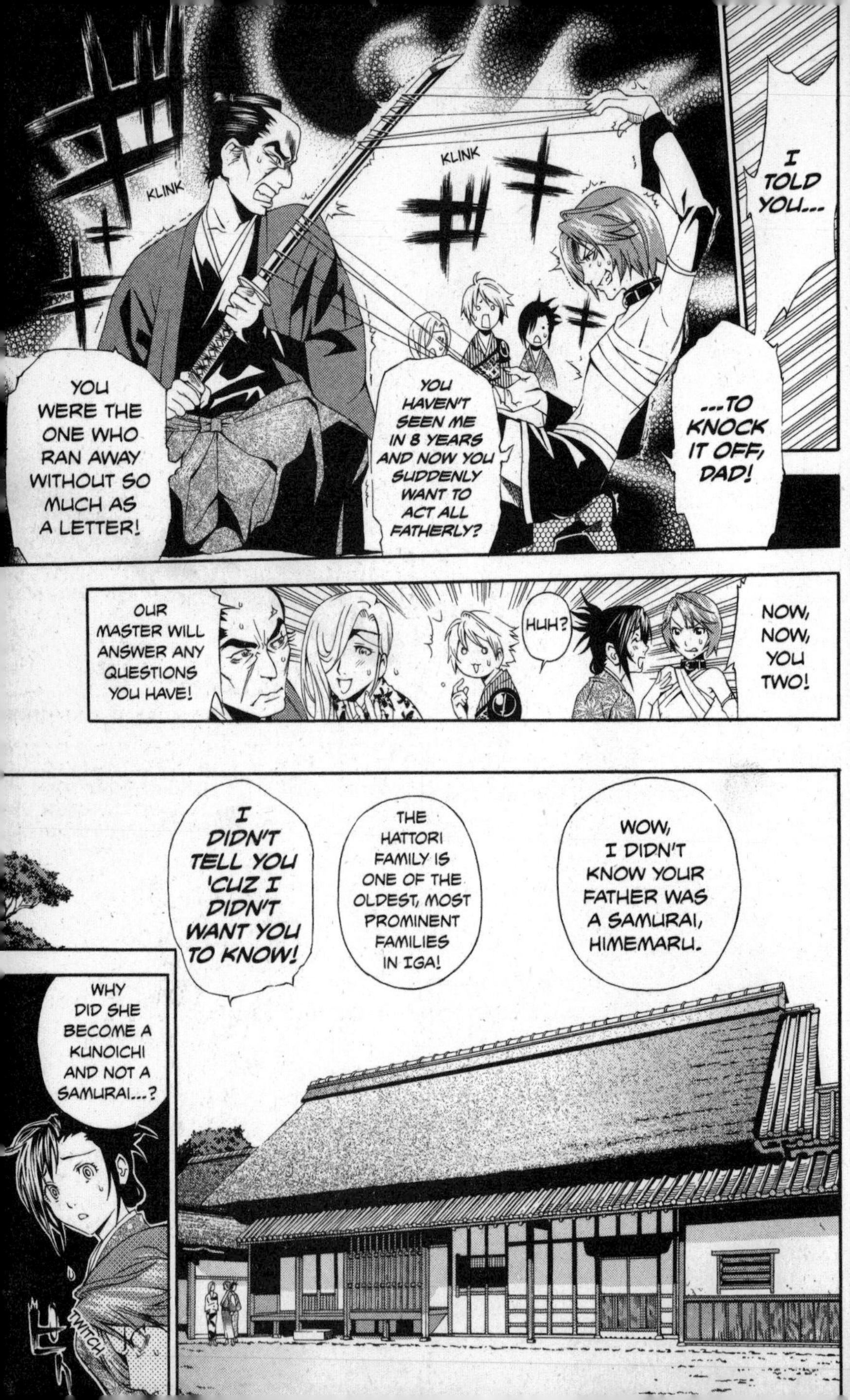
I TOLD YOU...
...TO KNOCK IT OFF, DAD!
KLINK
YOU HAVEN'T SEEN ME IN 8 YEARS AND NOW YOU SUDDENLY WANT TO ACT ALL FATHERLY?
KLINK
YOU WERE THE ONE WHO RAN AWAY WITHOUT SO MUCH AS A LETTER!
NOW, NOW, YOU TWO!
HUH?
OUR MASTER WILL ANSWER ANY QUESTIONS YOU HAVE!
WOW, I DIDN'T KNOW YOUR FATHER WAS A SAMURAI, HIMEMARU.
THE HATTORI FAMILY IS ONE OF THE OLDEST, MOST PROMINENT FAMILIES IN IGA!
I DIDN'T TELL YOU 'CUZ I DIDN'T WANT YOU TO KNOW!
WHY DID SHE BECOME A KUNOICHI AND NOT A SAMURAI...?
TWITCH

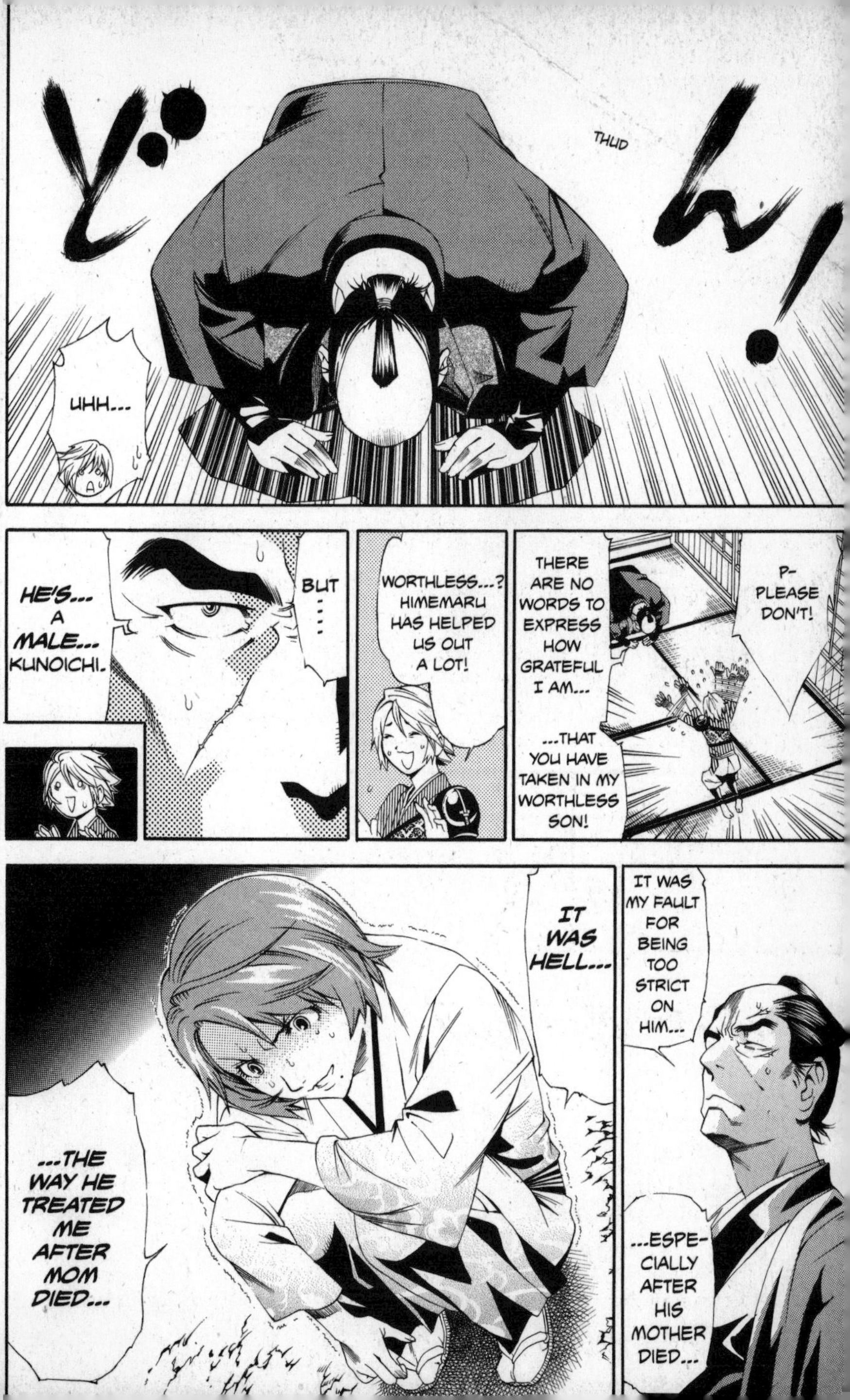

ど
ん!
THUD
UHH...
P-PLEASE DON'T!
THERE ARE NO WORDS TO EXPRESS HOW GRATEFUL I AM...
...THAT YOU HAVE TAKEN IN MY WORTHLESS SON!
WORTHLESS...? HIMEMARU HAS HELPED US OUT A LOT!
BUT......
HE'S... A MALE... KUNOICHI.
IT WAS MY FAULT FOR BEING TOO STRICT ON HIM...
...ESPECIALLY AFTER HIS MOTHER DIED...
IT WAS HELL...
...THE WAY HE TREATED ME AFTER MOM DIED...

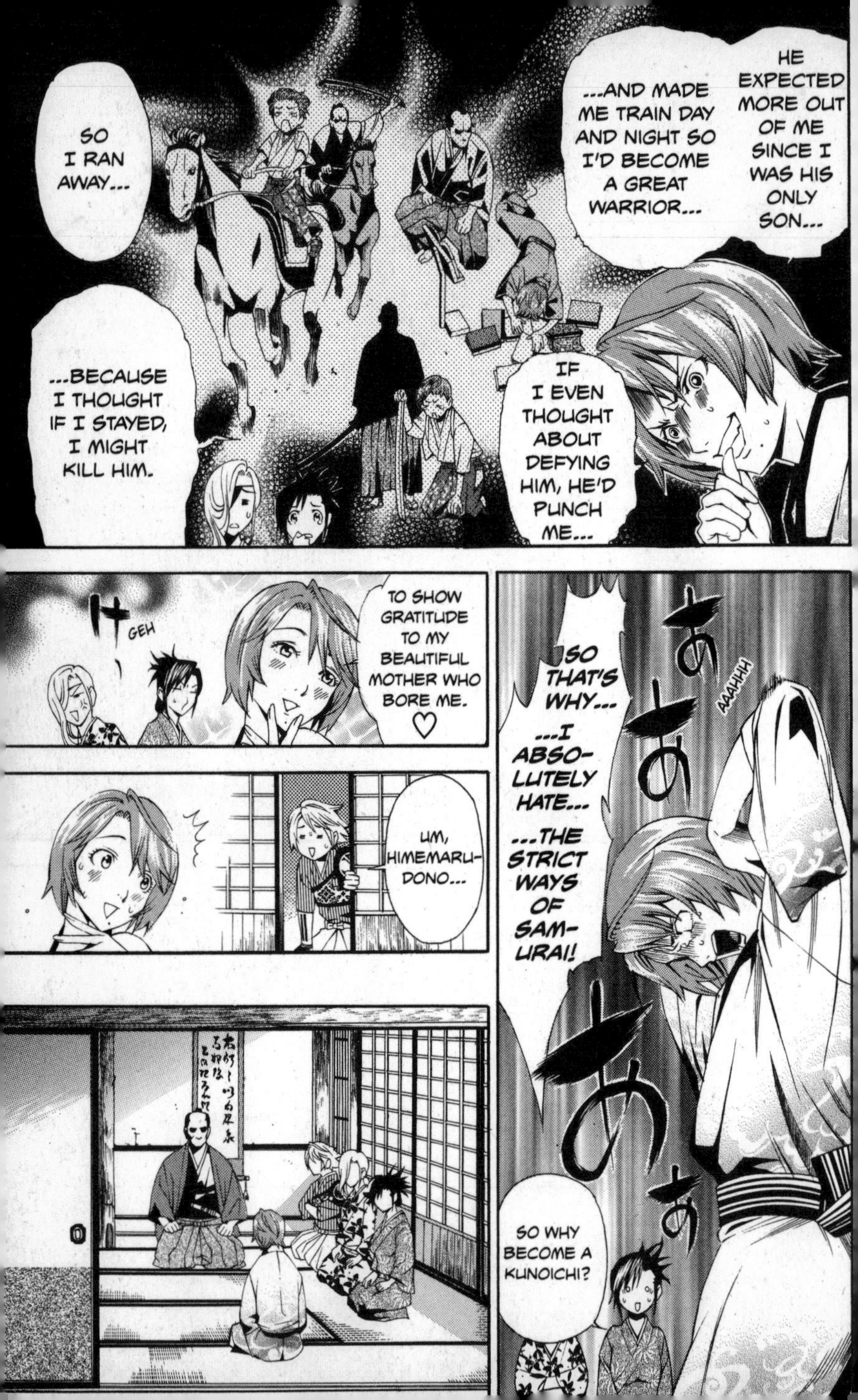

HE EXPECTED MORE OUT OF ME SINCE I WAS HIS ONLY SON...
...AND MADE ME TRAIN DAY AND NIGHT SO I'D BECOME A GREAT WARRIOR...
IF I EVEN THOUGHT ABOUT DEFYING HIM, HE'D PUNCH ME...
SO I RAN AWAY...
...BECAUSE I THOUGHT IF I STAYED, I MIGHT KILL HIM.
AAAHHH
SO THAT'S WHY...
...I ABSO-LUTELY HATE...
...THE STRICT WAYS OF SAM-URAI!
SO WHY BECOME A KUNOICHI?
TO SHOW GRATITUDE TO MY BEAUTIFUL MOTHER WHO BORE ME. ♥
GEH
UM, HIMEMARU-DONO...

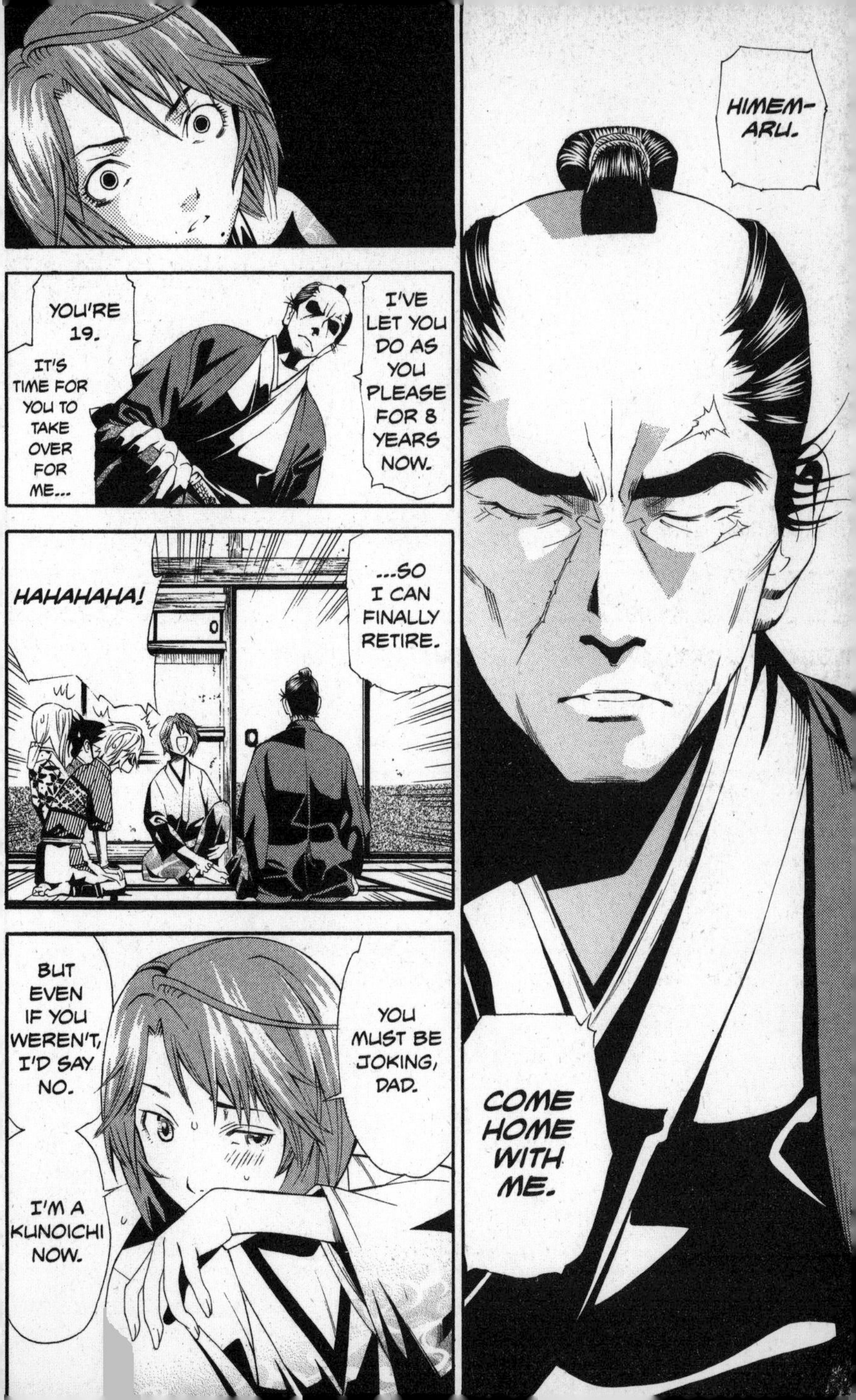
HIMEM-ARU.
COME HOME WITH ME.
I'VE LET YOU DO AS YOU PLEASE FOR 8 YEARS NOW.
YOU'RE 19.
IT'S TIME FOR YOU TO TAKE OVER FOR ME...
...SO I CAN FINALLY RETIRE.
HAHAHAHA!
YOU MUST BE JOKING, DAD.
BUT EVEN IF YOU WEREN'T, I'D SAY NO.
I'M A KUNOICHI NOW.

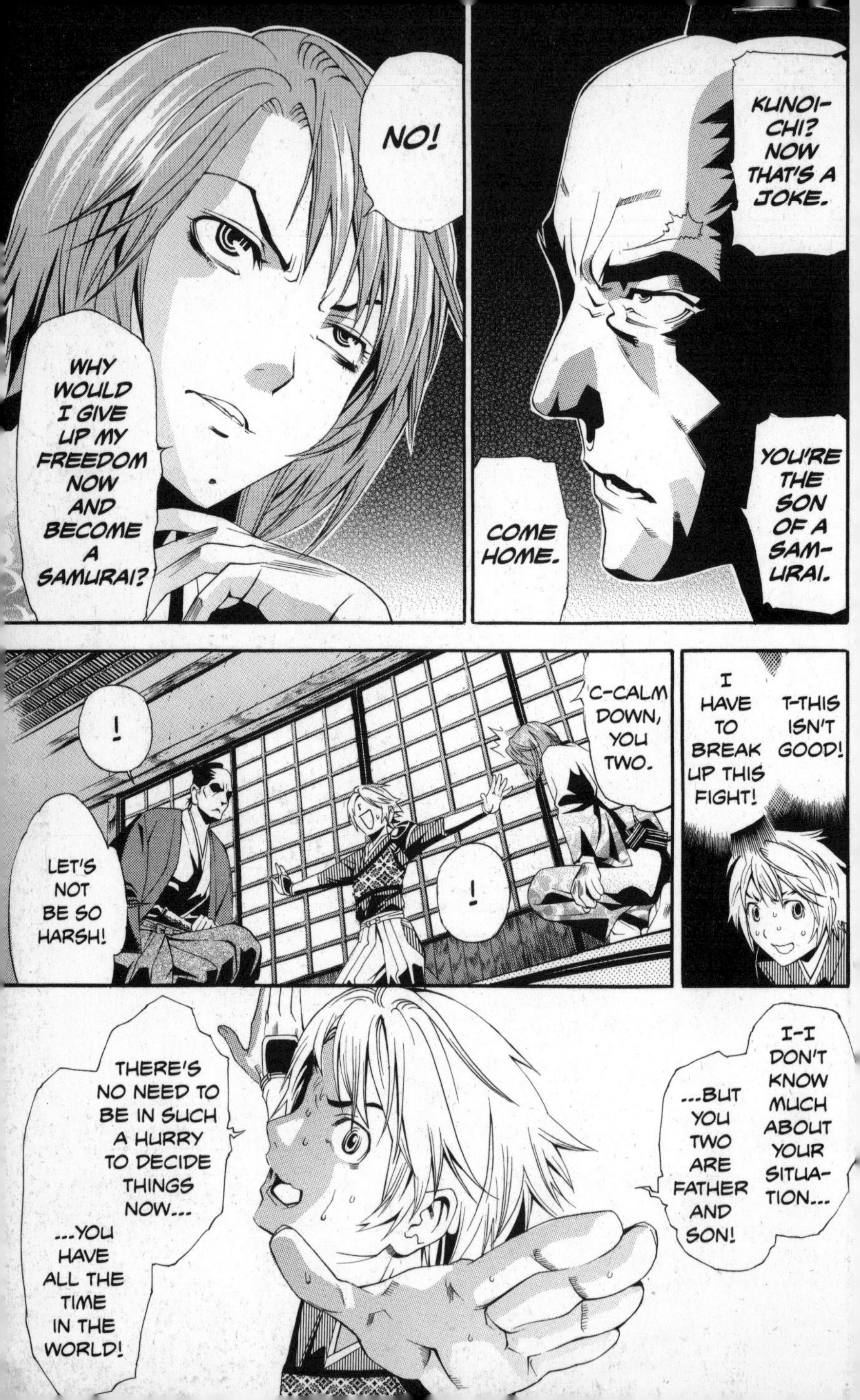
KUNOI-CHI? NOW THAT'S A JOKE.
YOU'RE THE SON OF A SAMURAI.
COME HOME.
NO!
WHY WOULD I GIVE UP MY FREEDOM NOW AND BECOME A SAMURAI?
T-THIS ISN'T GOOD!
I HAVE TO BREAK UP THIS FIGHT!
C-CALM DOWN, YOU TWO.
!
!
LET'S NOT BE SO HARSH!
I-I DON'T KNOW MUCH ABOUT YOUR SITUATION...
...BUT YOU TWO ARE FATHER AND SON!
THERE'S NO NEED TO BE IN SUCH A HURRY TO DECIDE THINGS NOW...
...YOU HAVE ALL THE TIME IN THE WORLD!

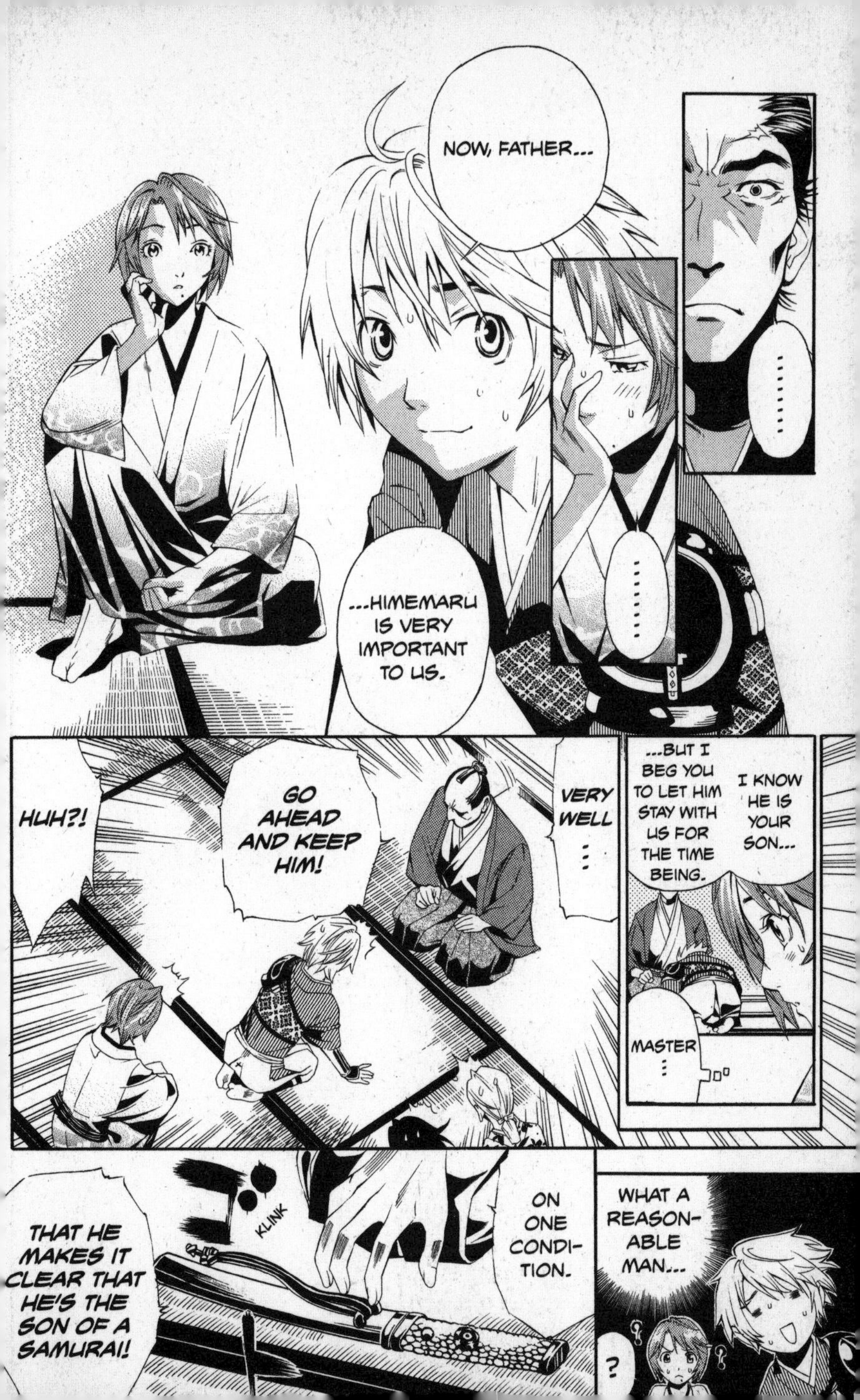
NOW, FATHER...
...HIMEMARU IS VERY IMPORTANT TO US.
......
......
I KNOW HE IS YOUR SON...
...BUT I BEG YOU TO LET HIM STAY WITH US FOR THE TIME BEING.
MASTER...
VERY WELL...
GO AHEAD AND KEEP HIM!
HUH?!
WHAT A REASON-ABLE MAN...
?
ON ONE CONDI-TION.
KLINK
THAT HE MAKES IT CLEAR THAT HE'S THE SON OF A SAMURAI!

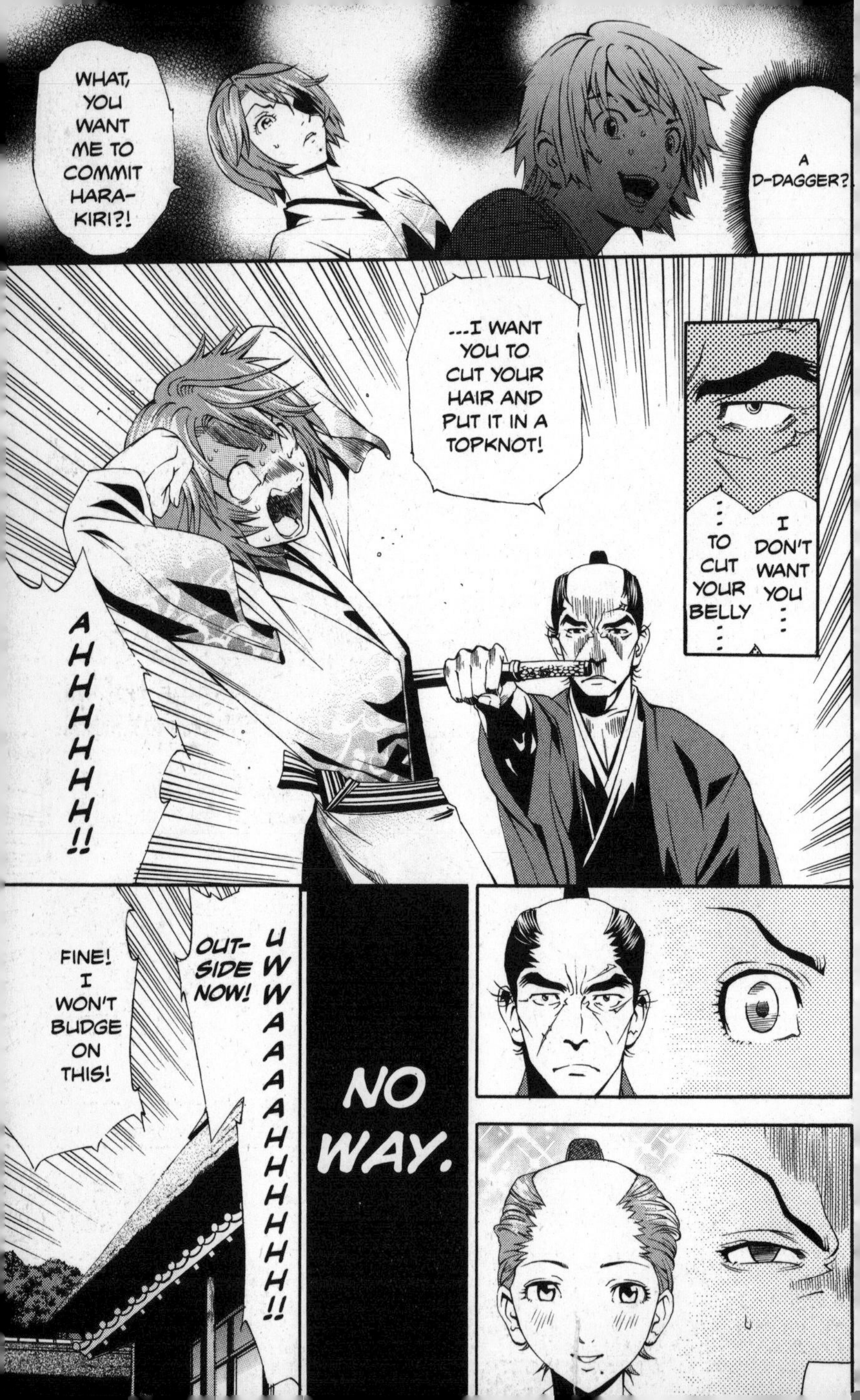
A D-DAGGER?!
WHAT, YOU WANT ME TO COMMIT HARA-KIRI?!
I DON'T WANT YOU...
TO CUT YOUR BELLY...
...I WANT YOU TO CUT YOUR HAIR AND PUT IT IN A TOPKNOT!
AHHHHHHH!!
NO WAY.
UWWAAAAAHHHHHHHH!!
OUT-SIDE NOW!
FINE! I WON'T BUDGE ON THIS!

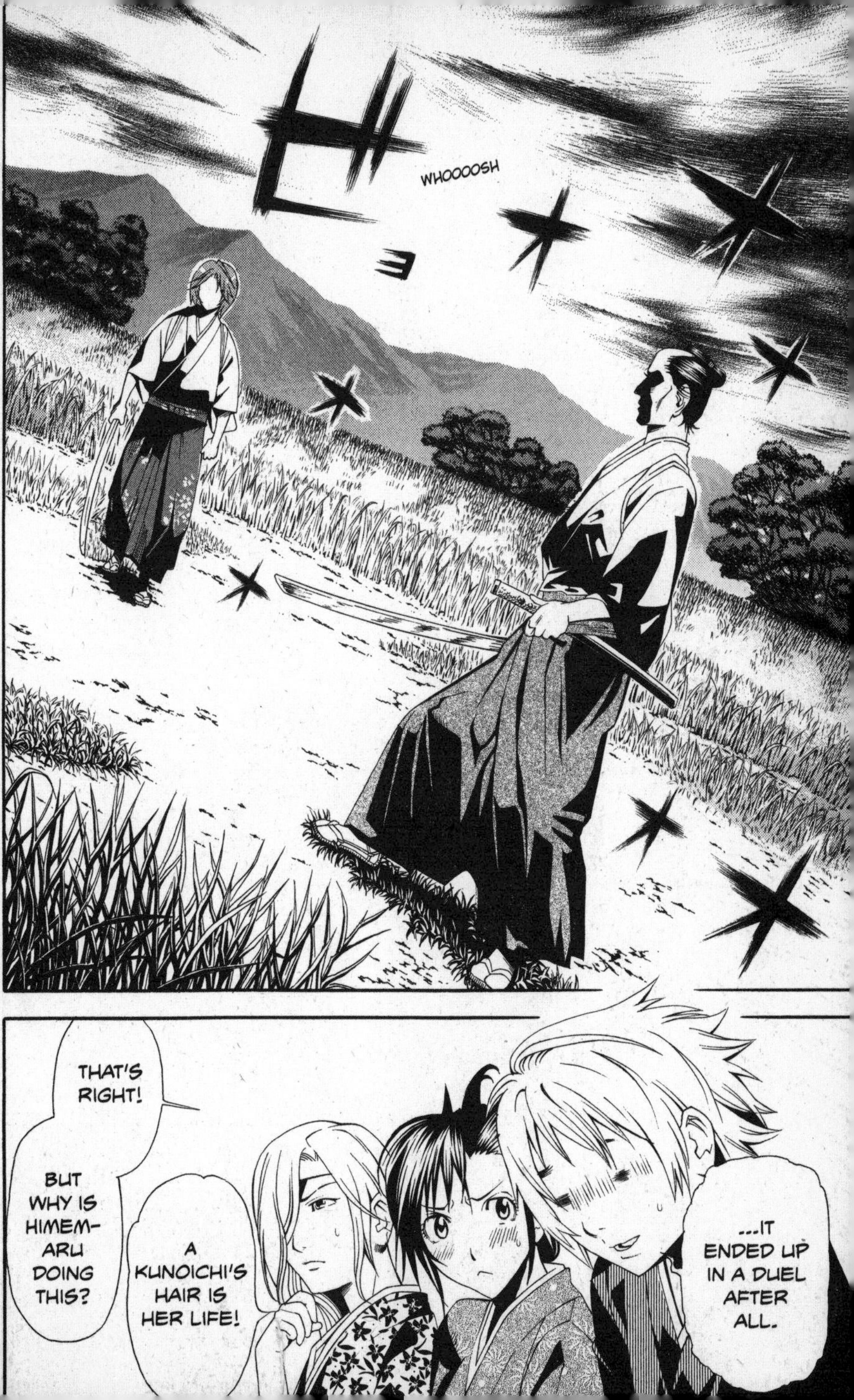
WHOOOOSH
...IT ENDED UP IN A DUEL AFTER ALL.
A KUNOICHI'S HAIR IS HER LIFE!
THAT'S RIGHT!
BUT WHY IS HIMEM-ARU DOING THIS?

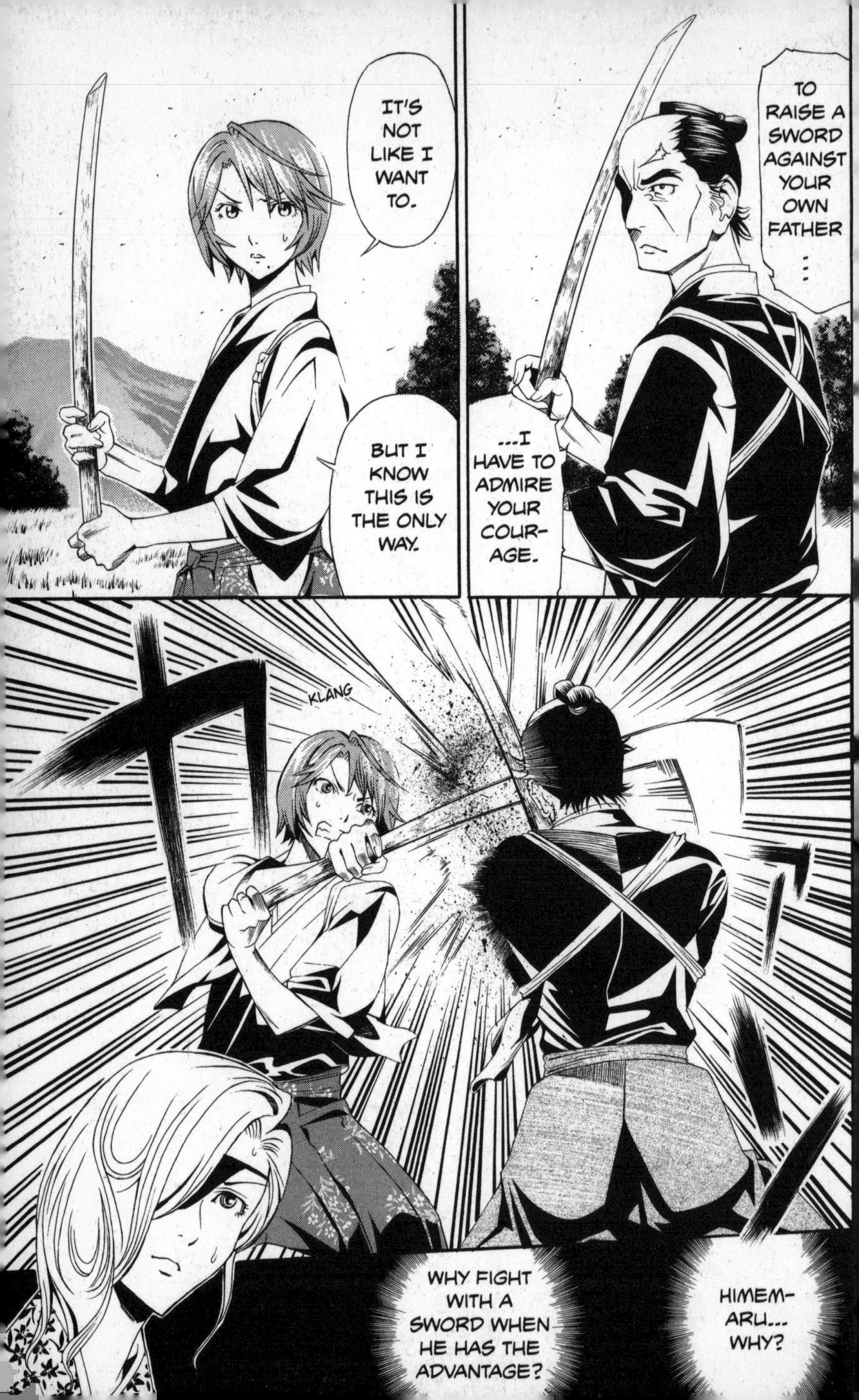
TO RAISE A SWORD AGAINST YOUR OWN FATHER ...
...I HAVE TO ADMIRE YOUR COURAGE.
IT'S NOT LIKE I WANT TO.
BUT I KNOW THIS IS THE ONLY WAY.
KLANG
HIMEMARU... WHY?
WHY FIGHT WITH A SWORD WHEN HE HAS THE ADVANTAGE?

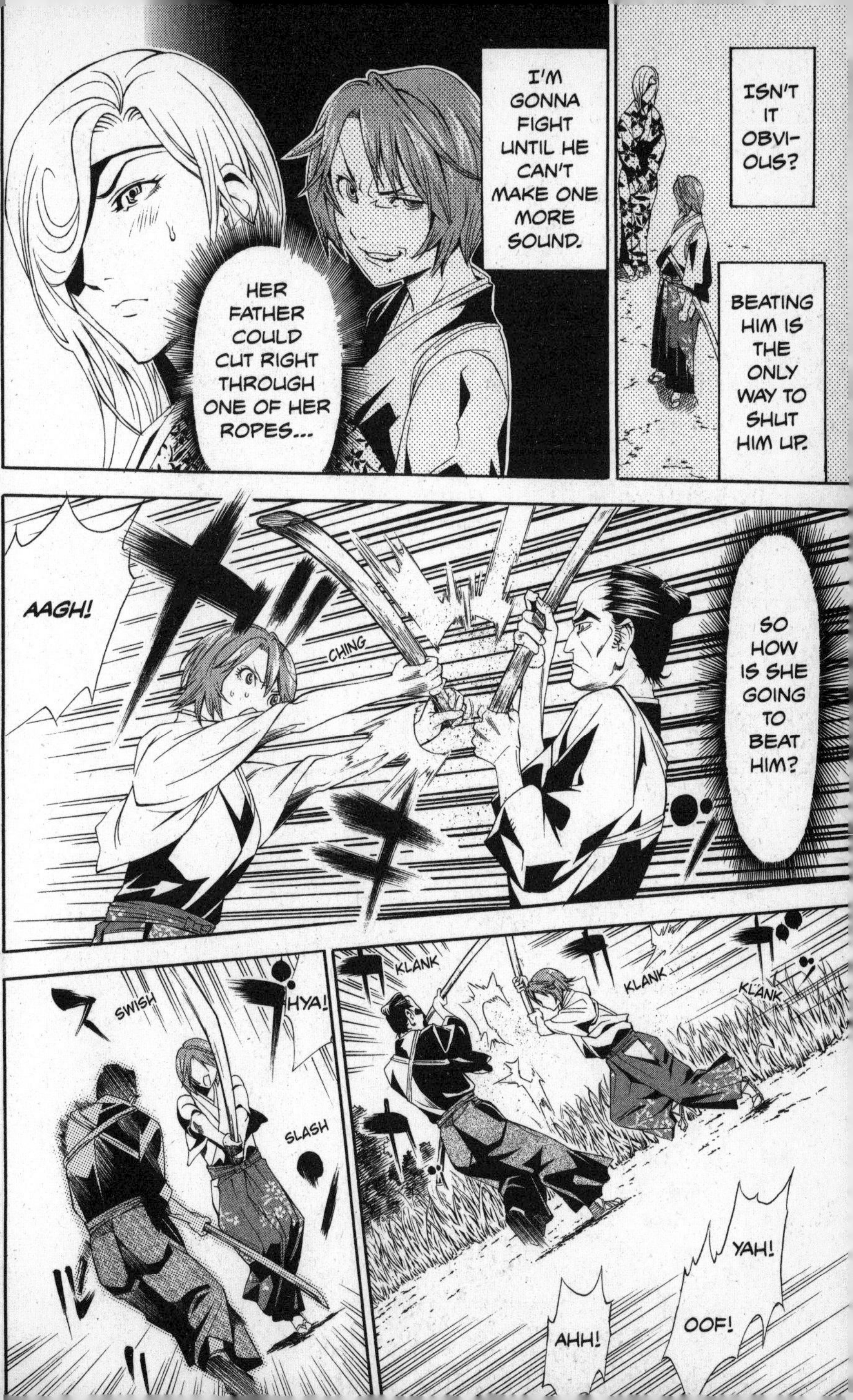
ISN'T IT OBVIOUS?
BEATING HIM IS THE ONLY WAY TO SHUT HIM UP.
I'M GONNA FIGHT UNTIL HE CAN'T MAKE ONE MORE SOUND.
HER FATHER COULD CUT RIGHT THROUGH ONE OF HER ROPES...
SO HOW IS SHE GOING TO BEAT HIM?
CHING
AAGH!
KLANK
KLANK
KLANK
YAH!
OOF!
AHH!
HYA!
SWISH
SLASH

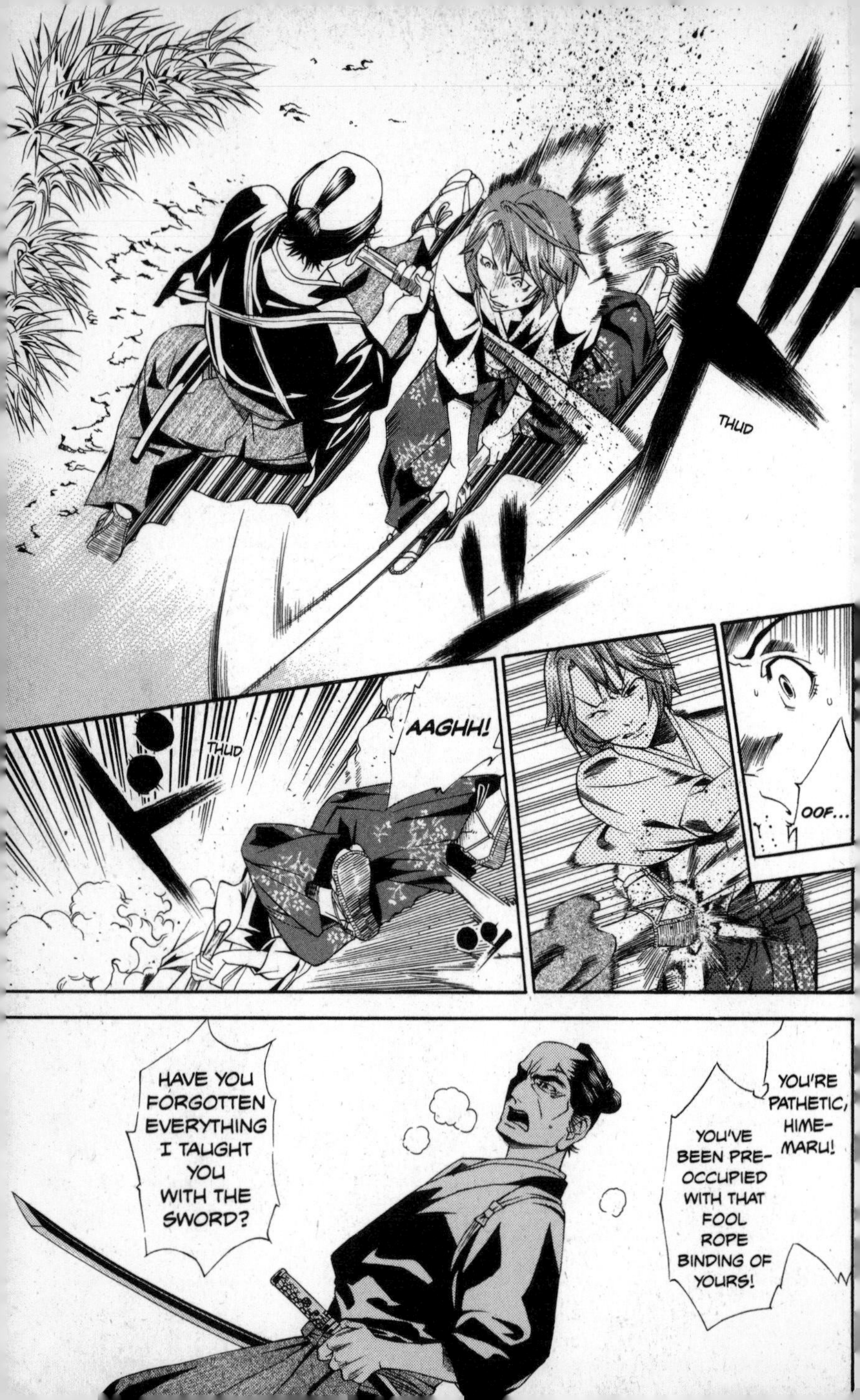
THUD
OOF...
AAGHH!
THUD
YOU'RE PATHETIC, HIME-MARU!
YOU'VE BEEN PRE-OCCUPIED WITH THAT FOOL ROPE BINDING OF YOURS!
HAVE YOU FORGOTTEN EVERYTHING I TAUGHT YOU WITH THE SWORD?

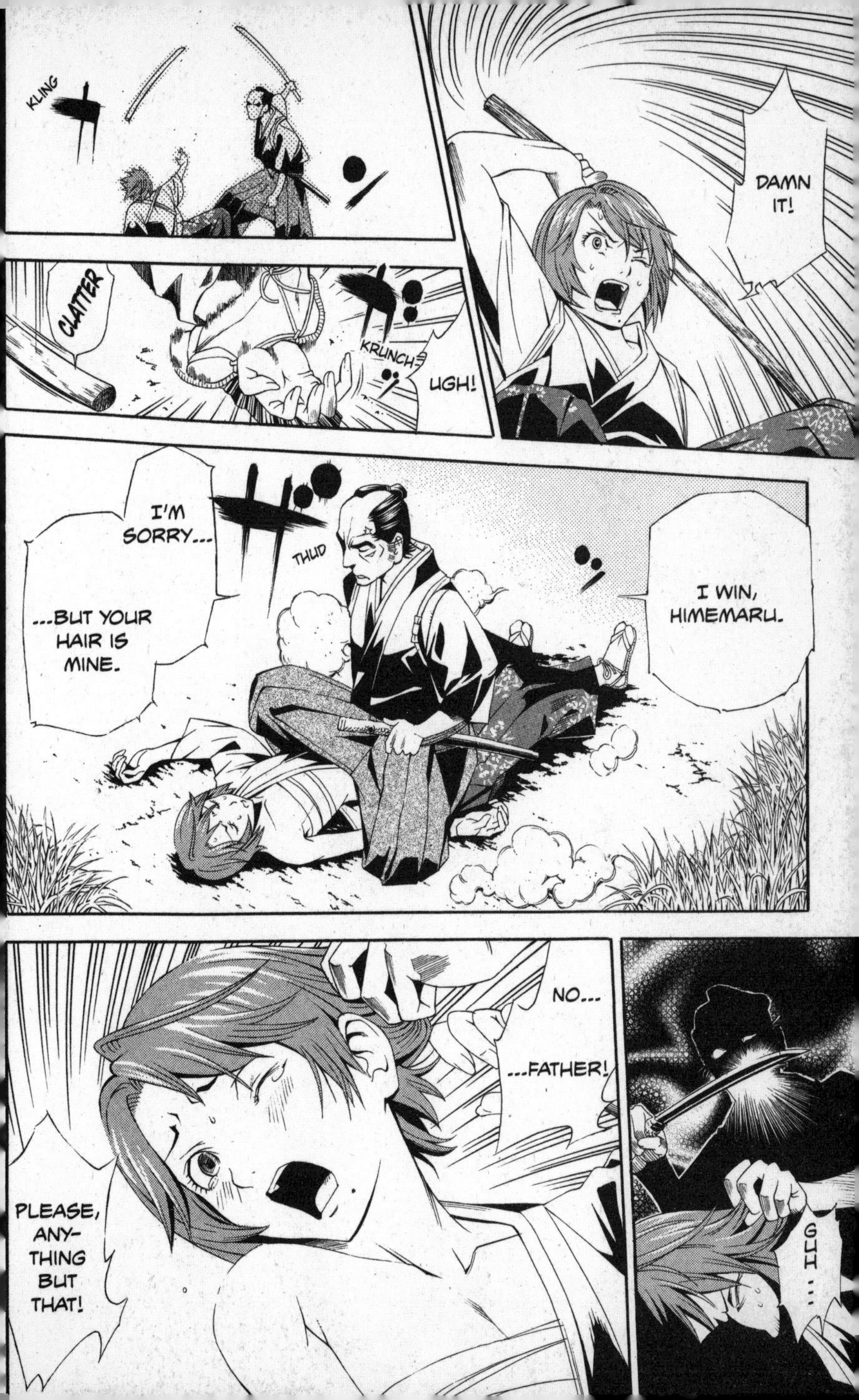
DAMN IT!
KLING
CLATTER
KRUNCH
UGH!
I WIN, HIMEMARU.
THUD
I'M SORRY...
...BUT YOUR HAIR IS MINE.
GUH...
NO...
...FATHER!
PLEASE, ANY-THING BUT THAT!

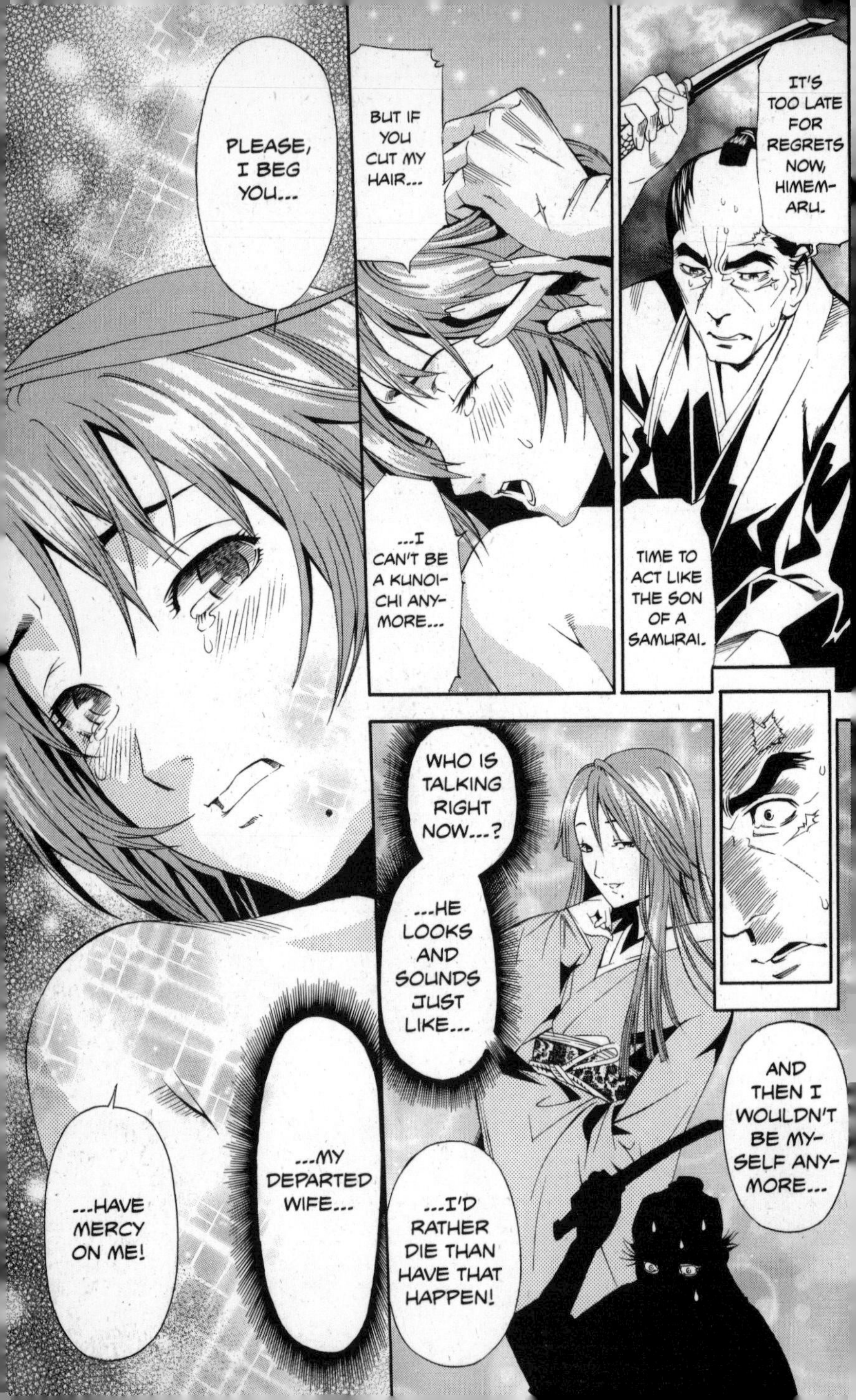
IT'S TOO LATE FOR REGRETS NOW, HIMEMARU.
TIME TO ACT LIKE THE SON OF A SAMURAI.
BUT IF YOU CUT MY HAIR...
...I CAN'T BE A KUNOICHI ANYMORE...
WHO IS TALKING RIGHT NOW...?
...HE LOOKS AND SOUNDS JUST LIKE...
...MY DEPARTED WIFE...
AND THEN I WOULDN'T BE MYSELF ANYMORE...
...I'D RATHER DIE THAN HAVE THAT HAPPEN!
PLEASE, I BEG YOU...
...HAVE MERCY ON ME!

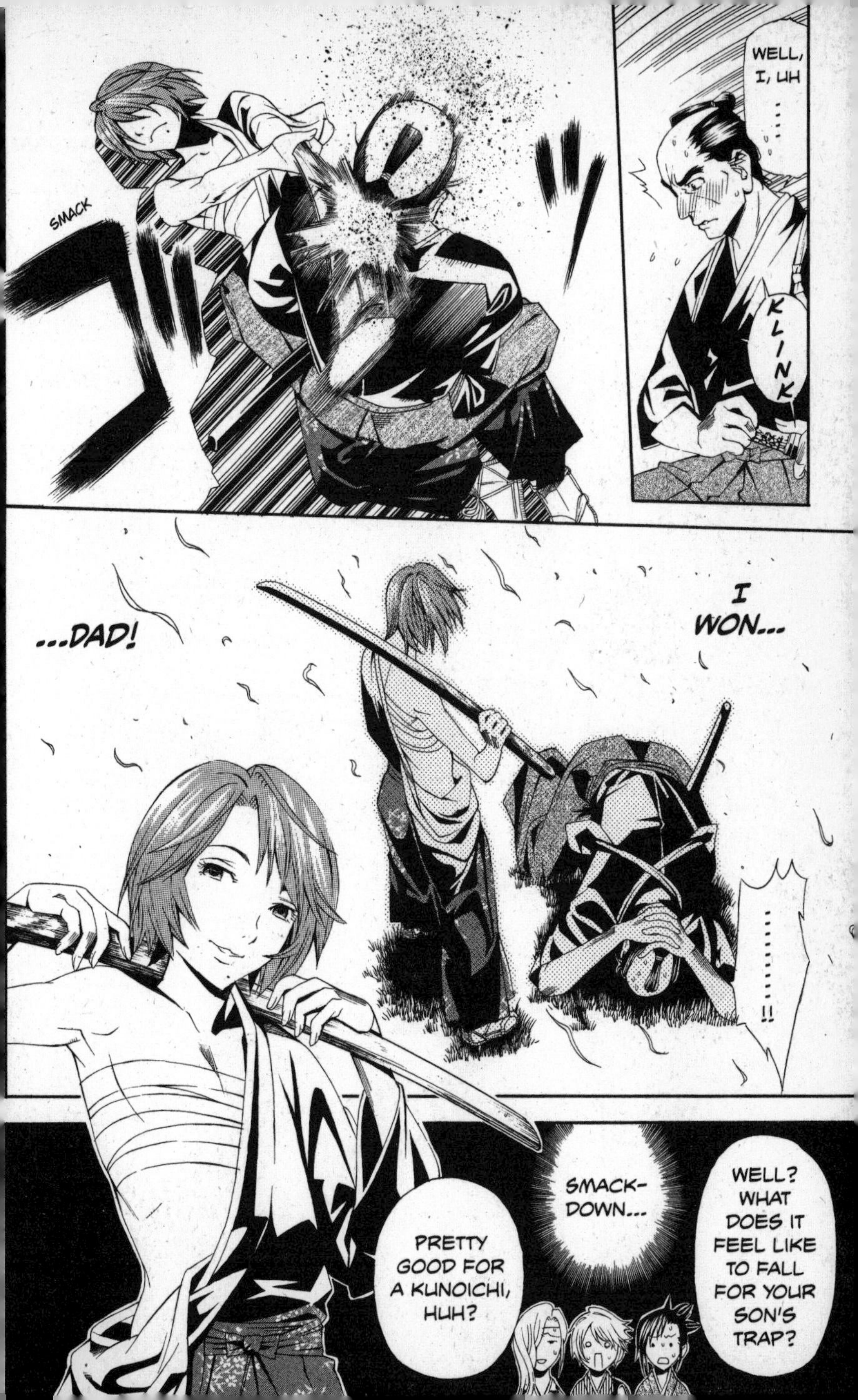
WELL, I, UH ...
KLINK
SMACK
I WON...
...DAD!
......!!
WELL? WHAT DOES IT FEEL LIKE TO FALL FOR YOUR SON'S TRAP?
SMACK-DOWN...
PRETTY GOOD FOR A KUNOICHI, HUH?

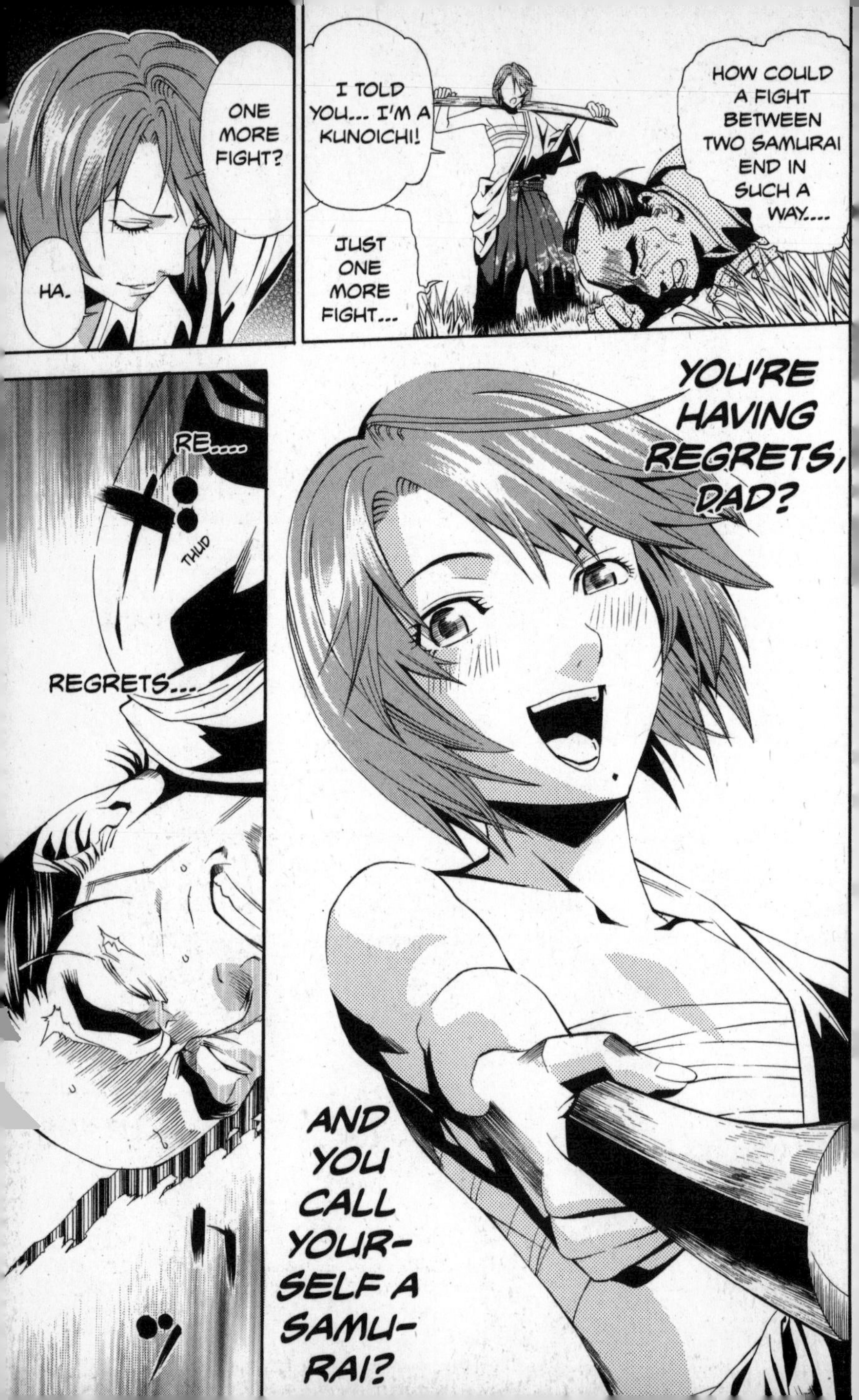
HOW COULD A FIGHT BETWEEN TWO SAMURAI END IN SUCH A WAY....
I TOLD YOU... I'M A KUNOICHI!
JUST ONE MORE FIGHT...
ONE MORE FIGHT?
HA.
YOU'RE HAVING REGRETS, DAD?
AND YOU CALL YOUR-SELF A SAMU-RAI?
RE....
THUD
REGRETS...

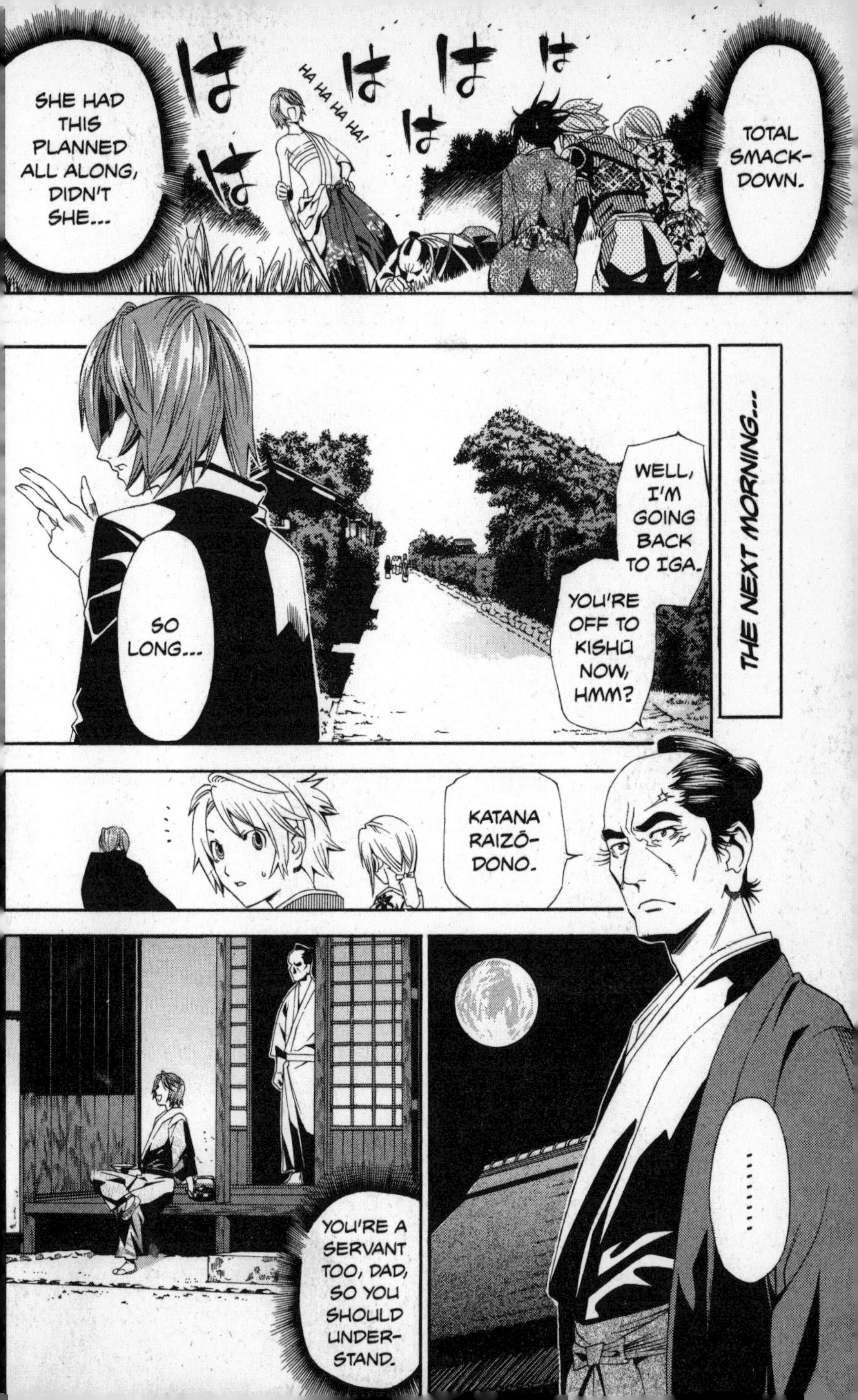
TOTAL SMACK-DOWN.
ははははははは
HA HA HA HA!
SHE HAD THIS PLANNED ALL ALONG, DIDN'T SHE...
THE NEXT MORNING...
WELL, I'M GOING BACK TO IGA.
YOU'RE OFF TO KISHŪ NOW, HMM?
SO LONG...
KATANA RAIZŌ-DONO.
...
......
YOU'RE A SERVANT TOO, DAD, SO YOU SHOULD UNDER-STAND.

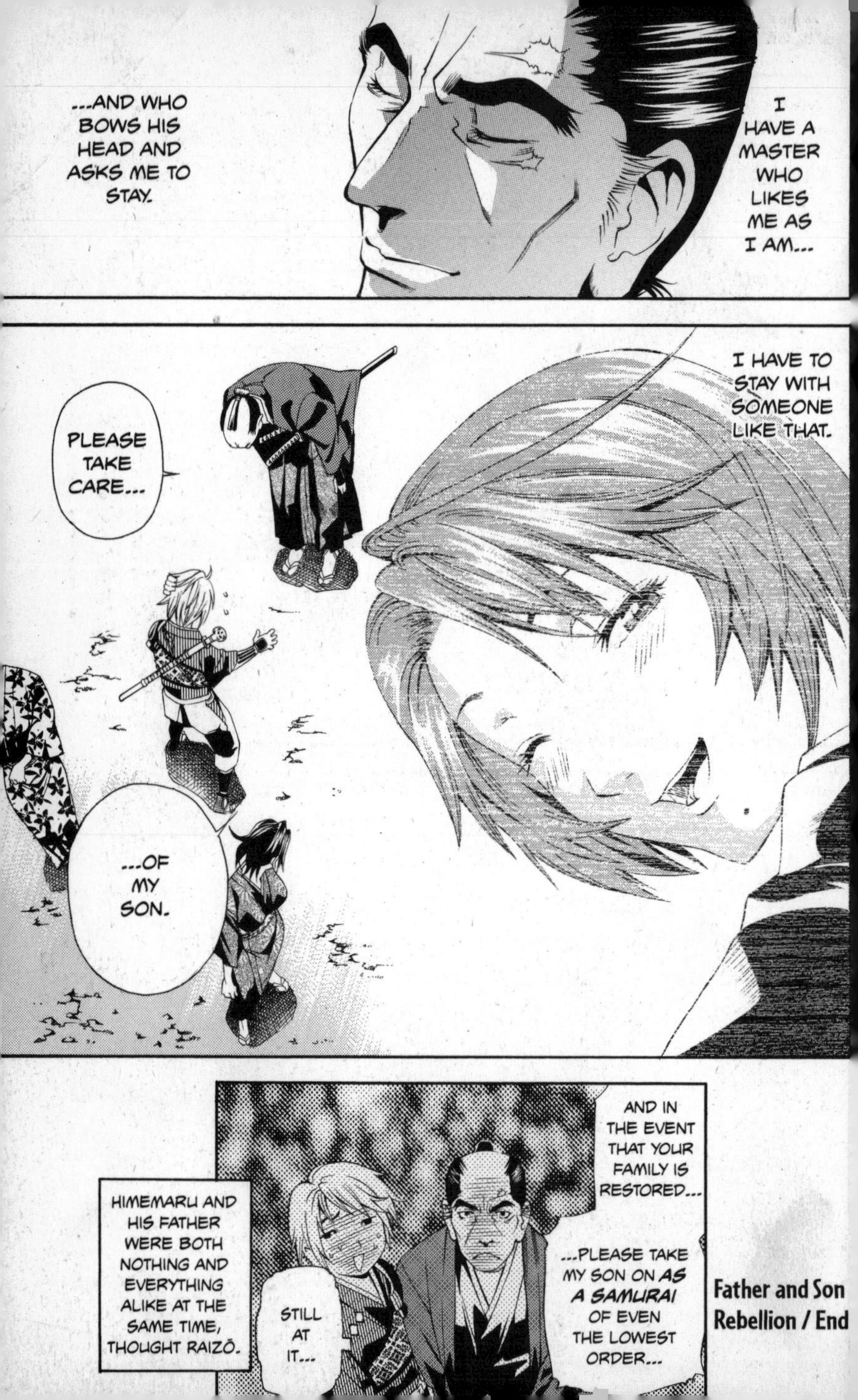
I HAVE A MASTER WHO LIKES ME AS I AM...
...AND WHO BOWS HIS HEAD AND ASKS ME TO STAY.
I HAVE TO STAY WITH SOMEONE LIKE THAT.
PLEASE TAKE CARE...
...OF MY SON.
AND IN THE EVENT THAT YOUR FAMILY IS RESTORED...
...PLEASE TAKE MY SON ON *AS A SAMURAI* OF EVEN THE LOWEST ORDER...
STILL AT IT...
HIMEMARU AND HIS FATHER WERE BOTH NOTHING AND EVERYTHING ALIKE AT THE SAME TIME, THOUGHT RAIZŌ.

**Father and Son Rebellion / End**

Ninja Girls

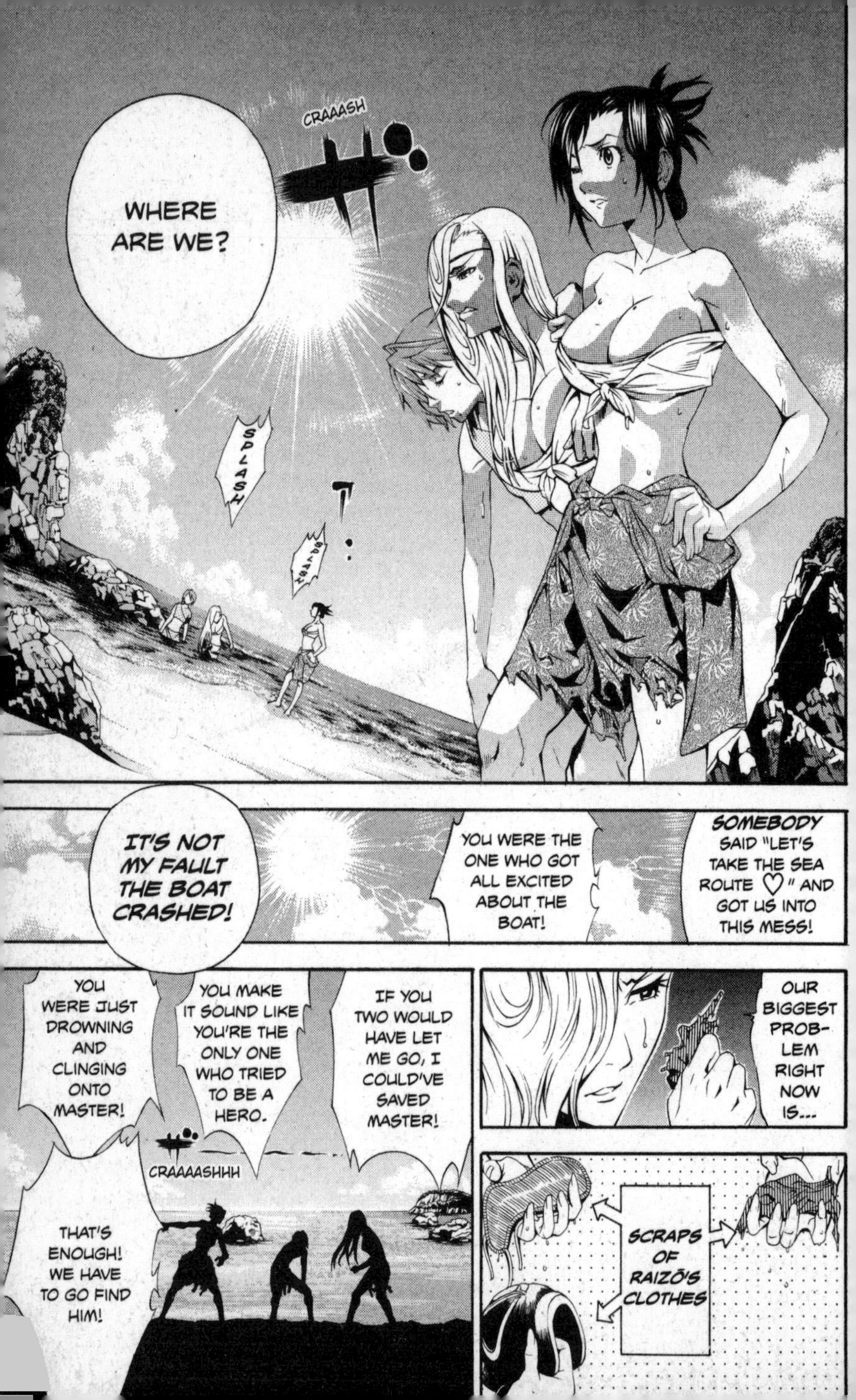
CRAAASH
WHERE ARE WE?
SPLASH
SPLASH
SOMEBODY SAID "LET'S TAKE THE SEA ROUTE ♡" AND GOT US INTO THIS MESS!
YOU WERE THE ONE WHO GOT ALL EXCITED ABOUT THE BOAT!
IT'S NOT MY FAULT THE BOAT CRASHED!
OUR BIGGEST PROB-LEM RIGHT NOW IS...
SCRAPS OF RAIZŌ'S CLOTHES
IF YOU TWO WOULD HAVE LET ME GO, I COULD'VE SAVED MASTER!
YOU MAKE IT SOUND LIKE YOU'RE THE ONLY ONE WHO TRIED TO BE A HERO.
YOU WERE JUST DROWNING AND CLINGING ONTO MASTER!
CRAAAASHHH
THAT'S ENOUGH! WE HAVE TO GO FIND HIM!

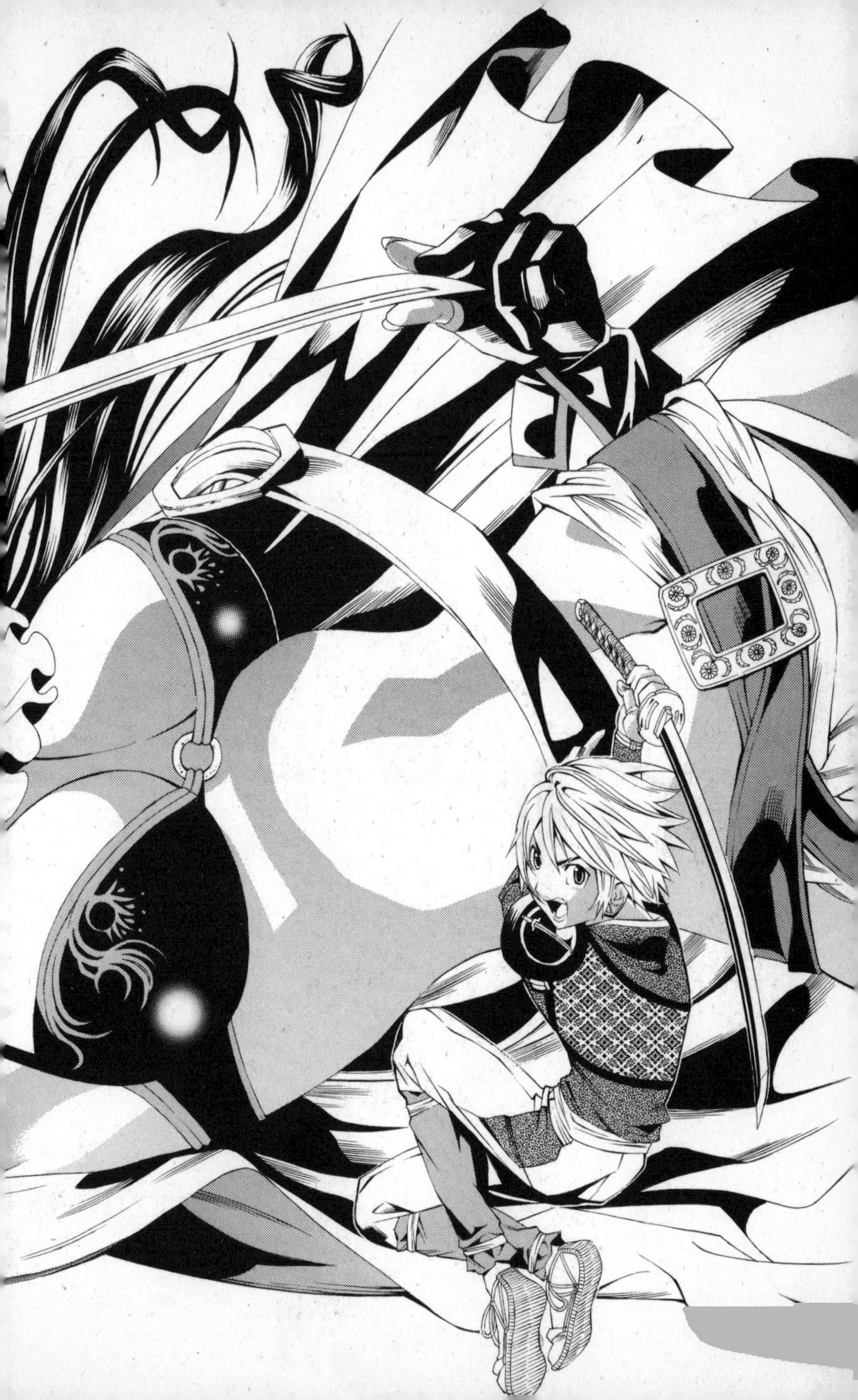

# 25 Pirate Rebellion

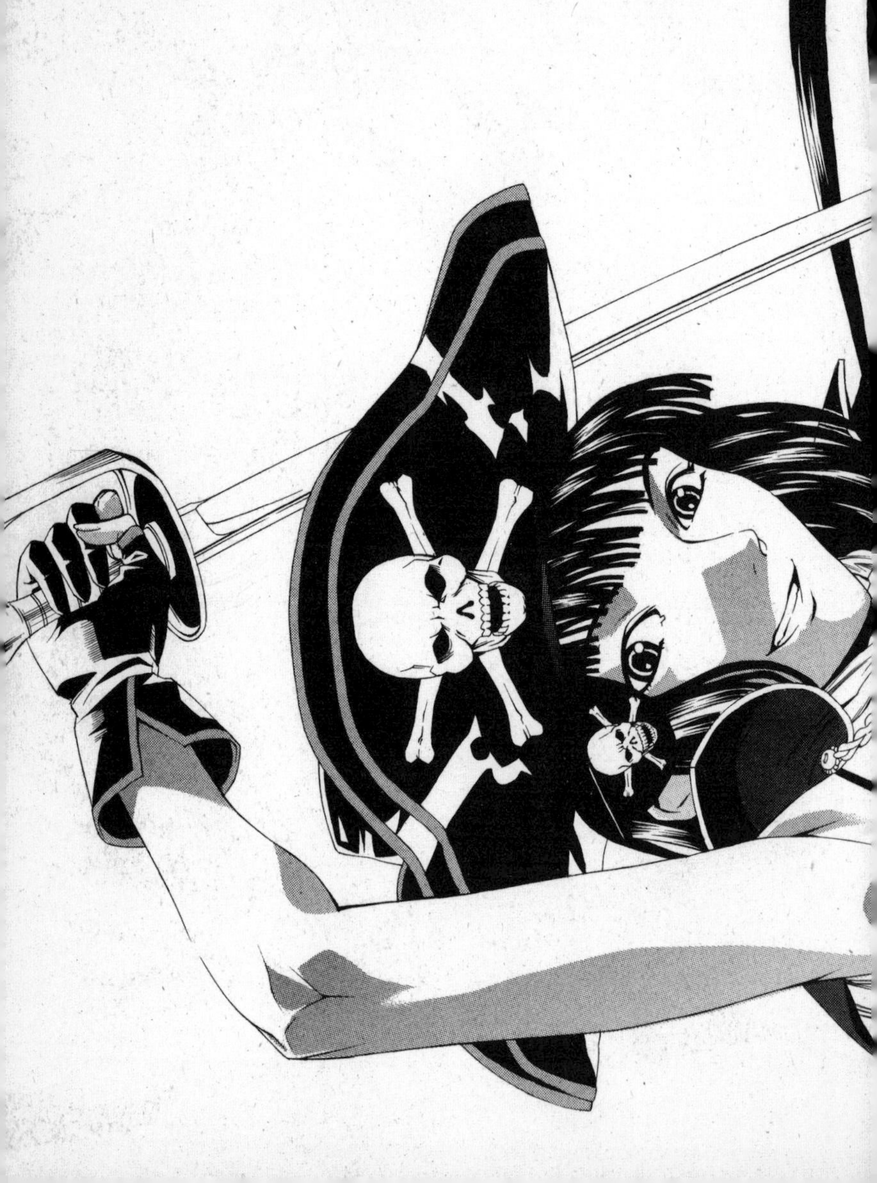

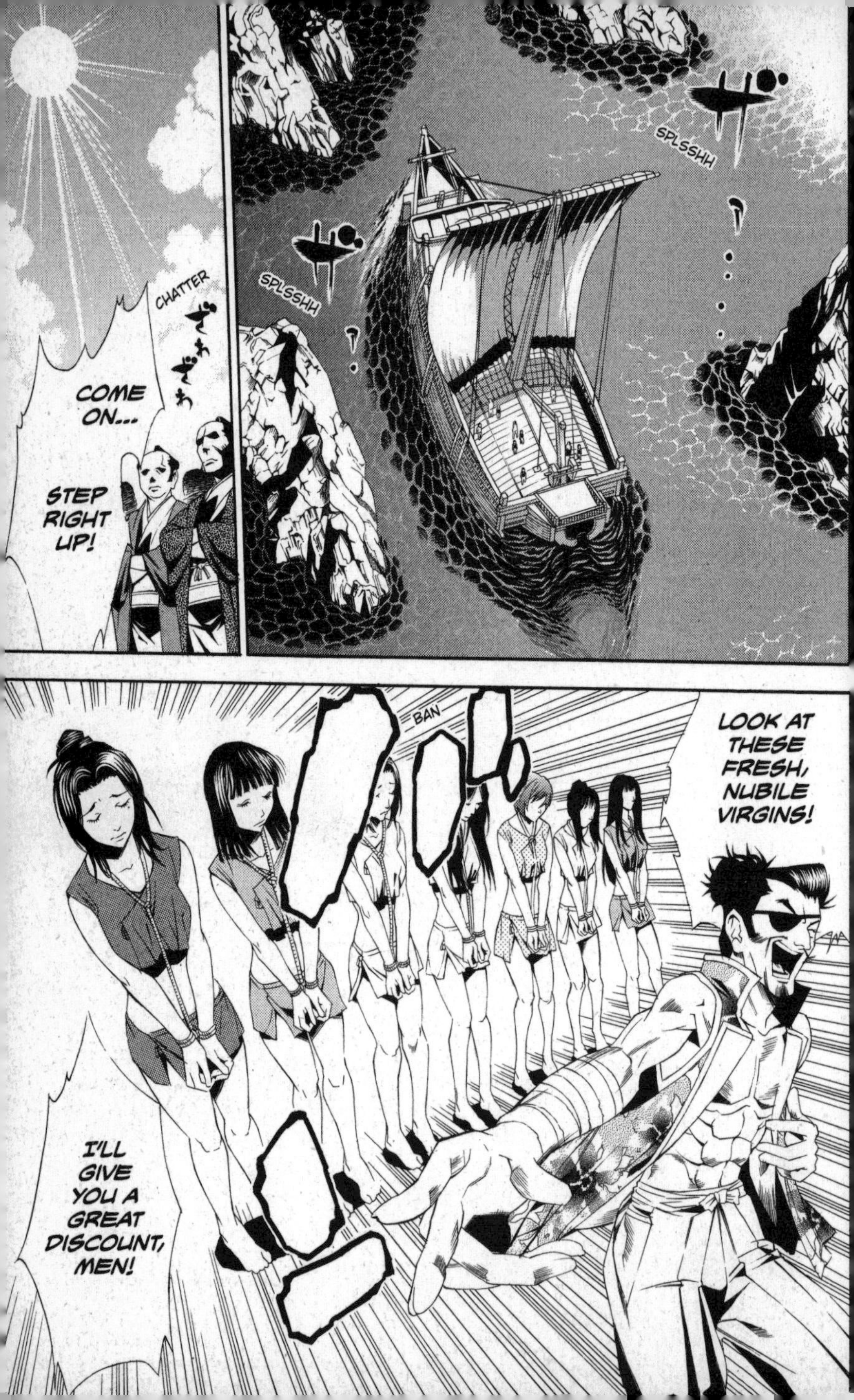
SPLSSHH
SPLSSHH
CHATTER
ざわざわ
COME ON...
STEP RIGHT UP!
BAN
LOOK AT THESE FRESH, NUBILE VIRGINS!
I'LL GIVE YOU A GREAT DISCOUNT, MEN!

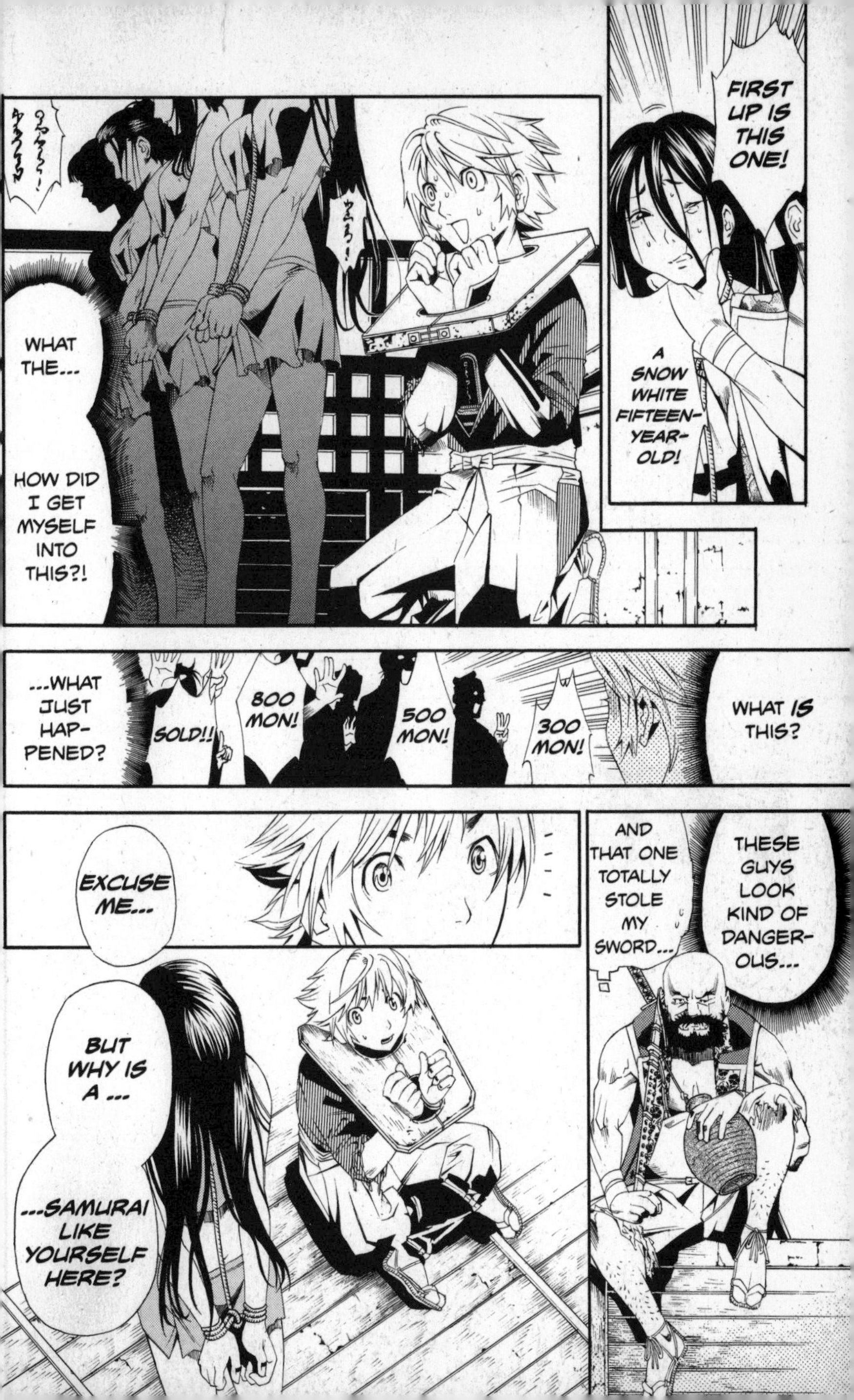
FIRST UP IS THIS ONE!
A SNOW WHITE FIFTEEN-YEAR-OLD!
WHAT THE...
HOW DID I GET MYSELF INTO THIS?!
WHAT IS THIS?
300 MON!
500 MON!
800 MON!
SOLD!!
...WHAT JUST HAP-PENED?
THESE GUYS LOOK KIND OF DANGER-OUS...
AND THAT ONE TOTALLY STOLE MY SWORD...
EXCUSE ME...
BUT WHY IS A ...
...SAMURAI LIKE YOURSELF HERE?

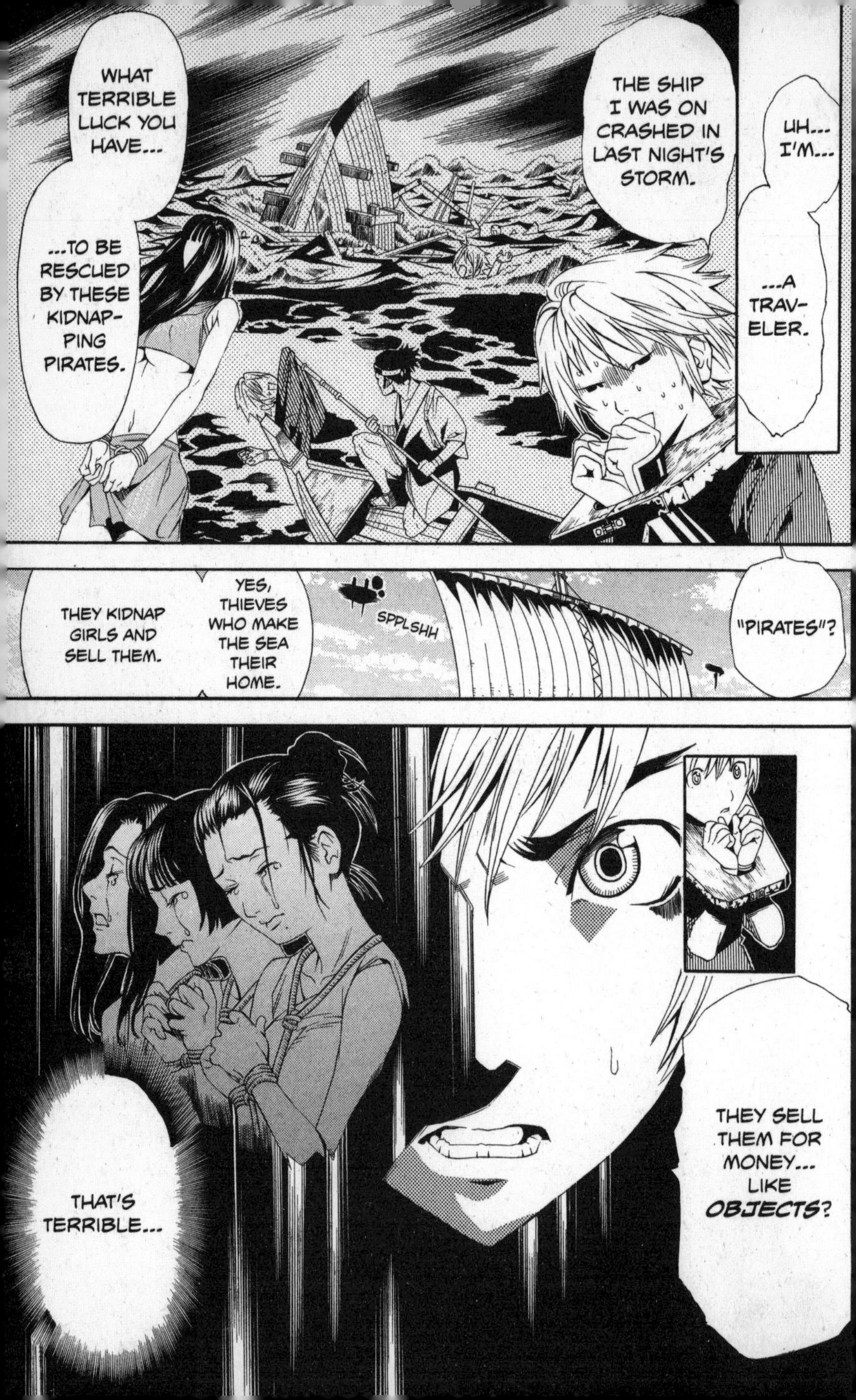
UH... I'M...
...A TRAV-ELER.
THE SHIP I WAS ON CRASHED IN LAST NIGHT'S STORM.
WHAT TERRIBLE LUCK YOU HAVE...
...TO BE RESCUED BY THESE KIDNAP-PING PIRATES.
"PIRATES"?
SPPLSHH
YES, THIEVES WHO MAKE THE SEA THEIR HOME.
THEY KIDNAP GIRLS AND SELL THEM.
THEY SELL THEM FOR MONEY... LIKE OBJECTS?
THAT'S TERRIBLE...

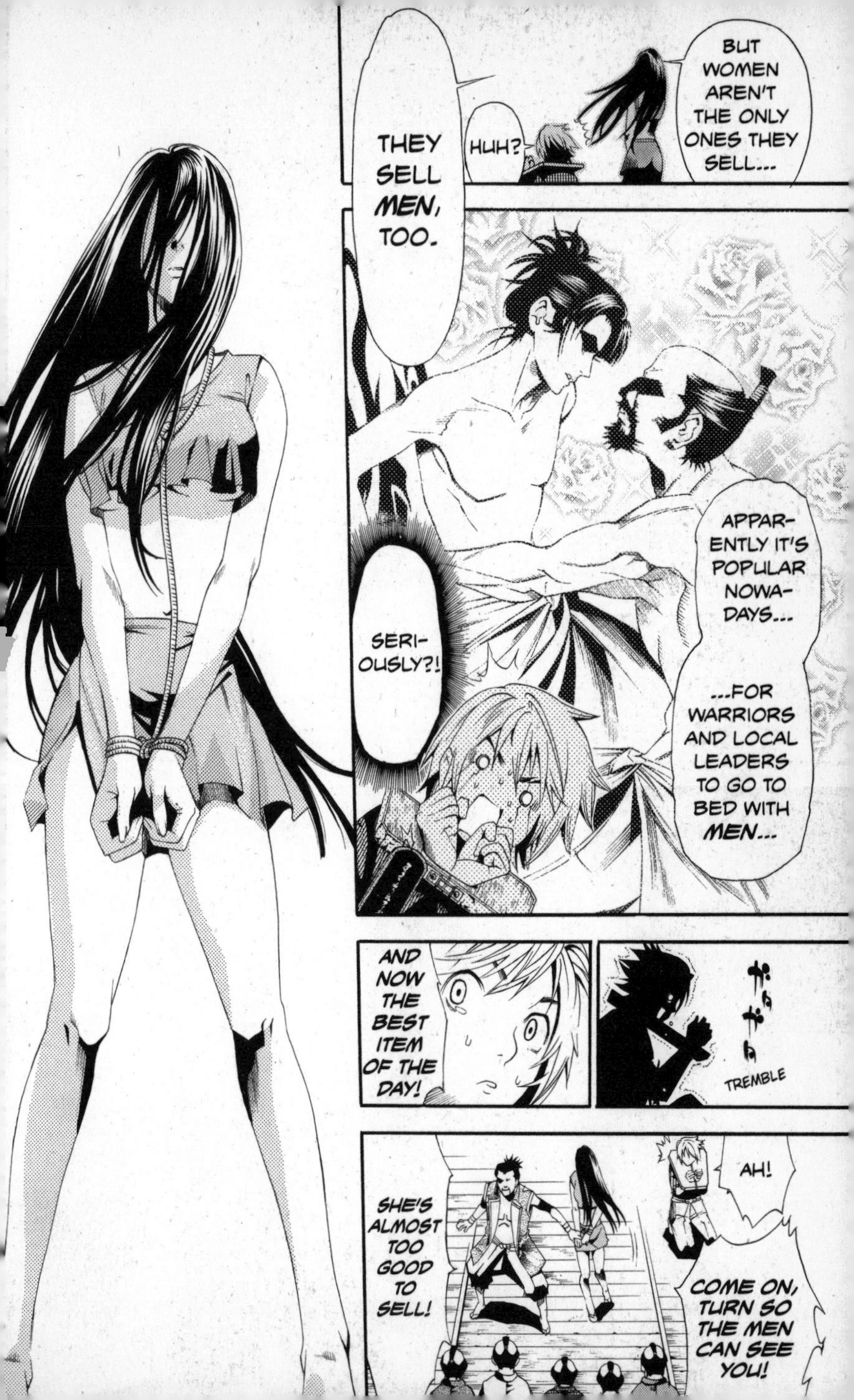

BUT WOMEN AREN'T THE ONLY ONES THEY SELL...
HUH?
THEY SELL MEN, TOO.
APPARENTLY IT'S POPULAR NOWADAYS...
...FOR WARRIORS AND LOCAL LEADERS TO GO TO BED WITH MEN...
SERIOUSLY?!
ガタガタ
TREMBLE
AND NOW THE BEST ITEM OF THE DAY!
AH!
COME ON, TURN SO THE MEN CAN SEE YOU!
SHE'S ALMOST TOO GOOD TO SELL!

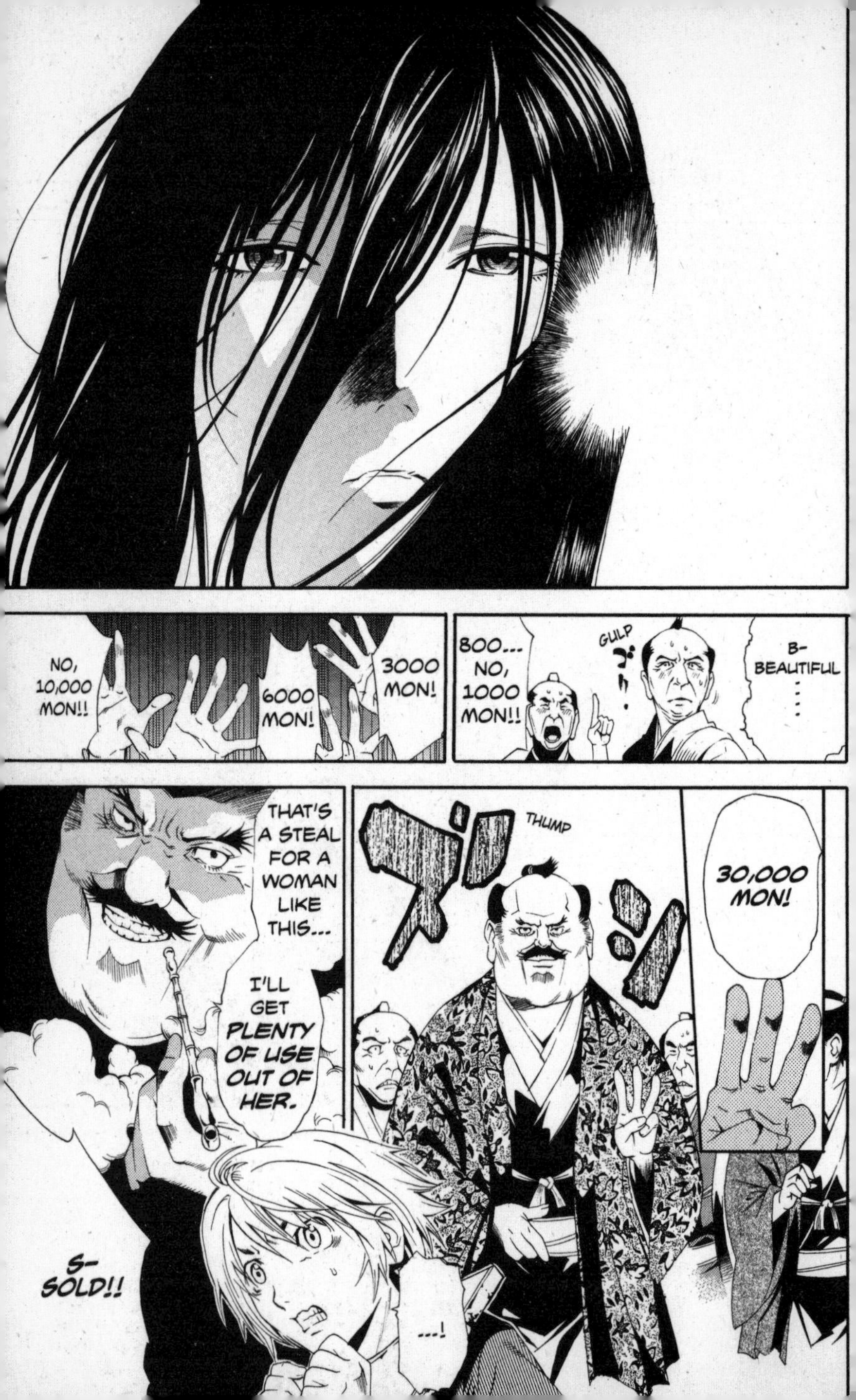
B-BEAUTIFUL ....
GULP
800... NO, 1000 MON!!
3000 MON!
6000 MON!
NO, 10,000 MON!!
30,000 MON!
THUMP
...!
THAT'S A STEAL FOR A WOMAN LIKE THIS...
I'LL GET PLENTY OF USE OUT OF HER.
S-SOLD!!

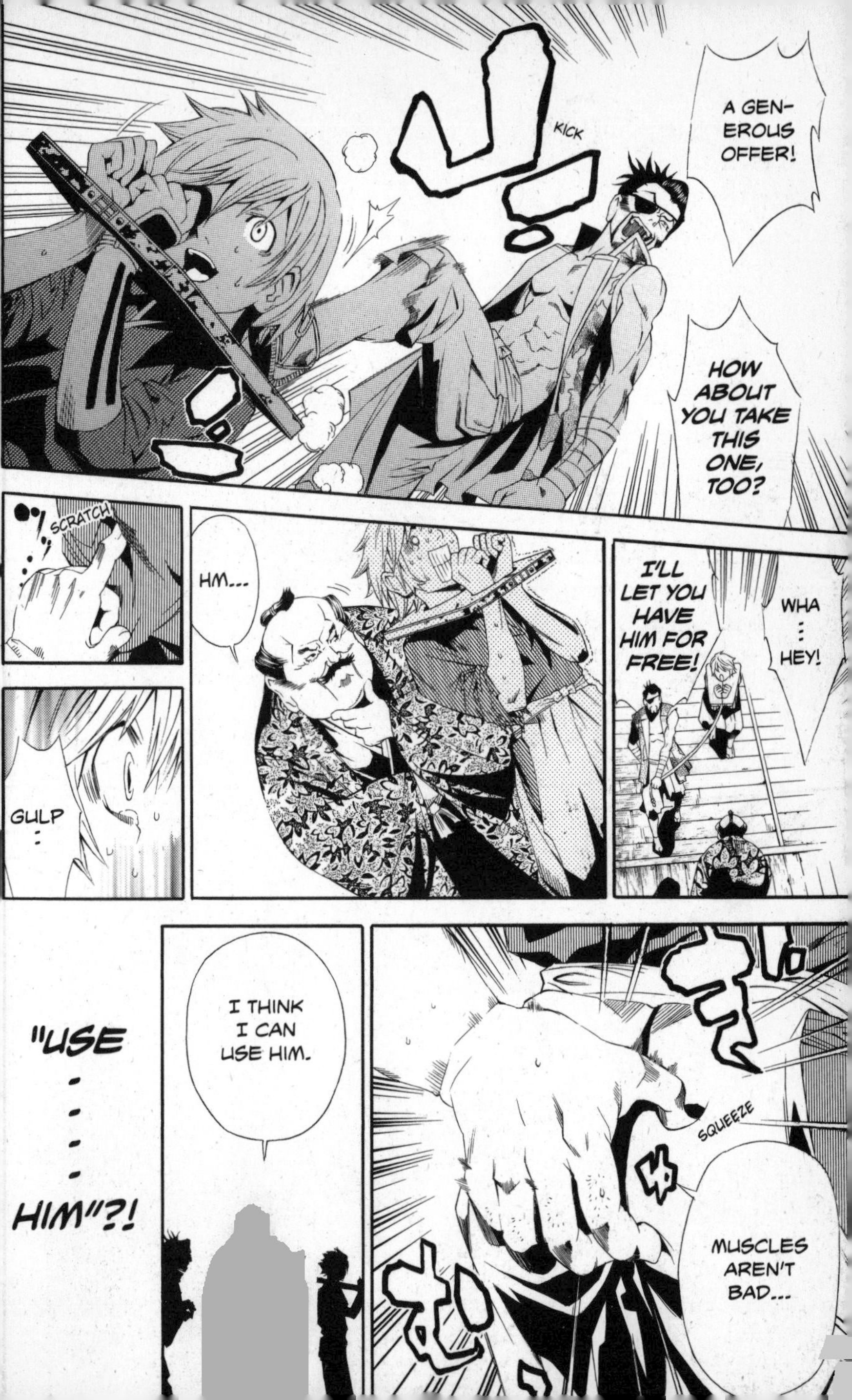
A GEN-
EROUS
OFFER!
KICK
HOW ABOUT YOU TAKE THIS ONE, TOO?
WHA ... HEY!
I'LL LET YOU HAVE HIM FOR FREE!
HM...
SCRATCH
GULP
SQUEEZE
MUSCLES AREN'T BAD...
I THINK I CAN USE HIM.
"USE ... HIM"?!

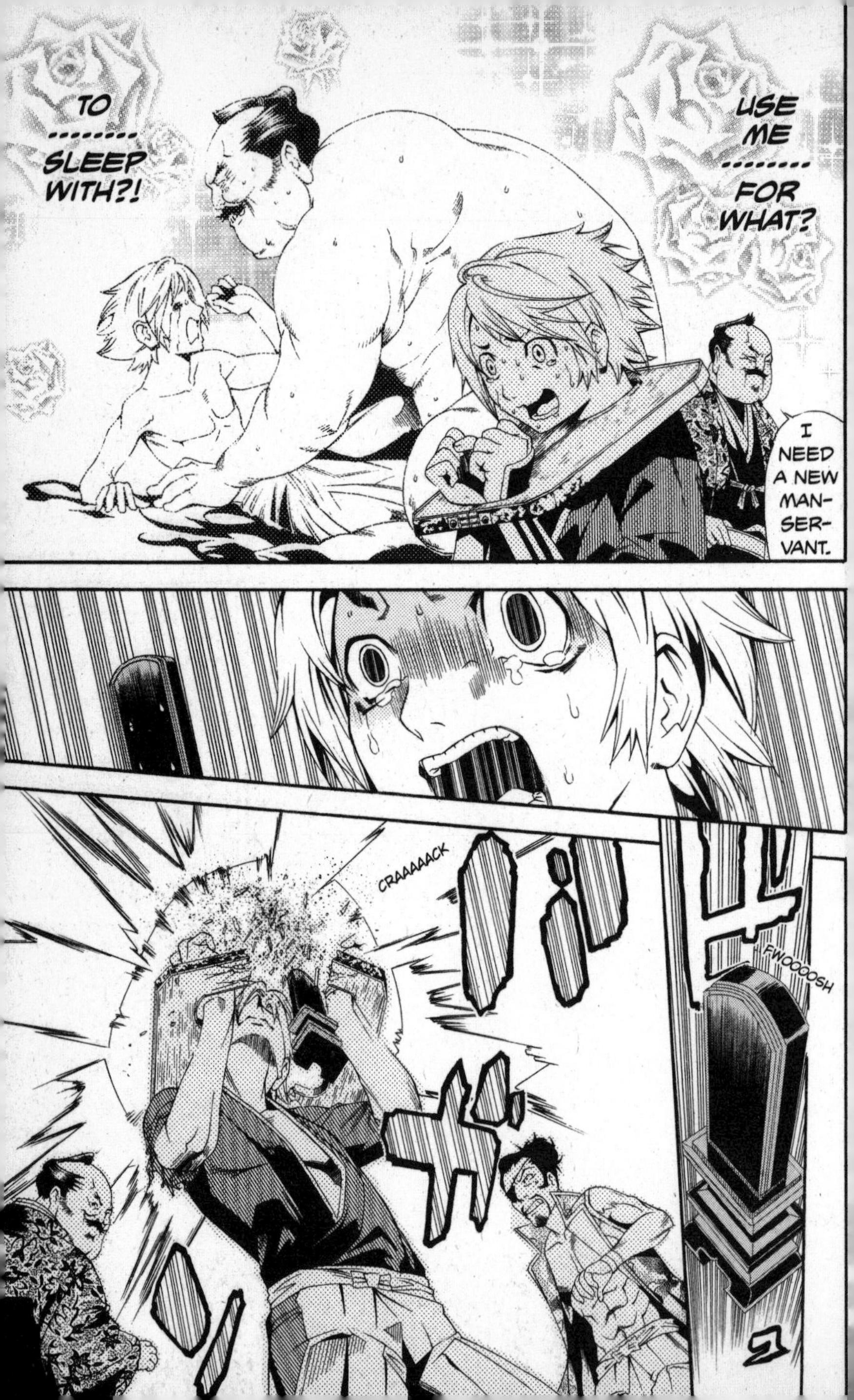
USE ME --------- FOR WHAT?
I NEED A NEW MAN-SERVANT.
TO --------- SLEEP WITH?!
FWOOOOSH
CRAAAAACK

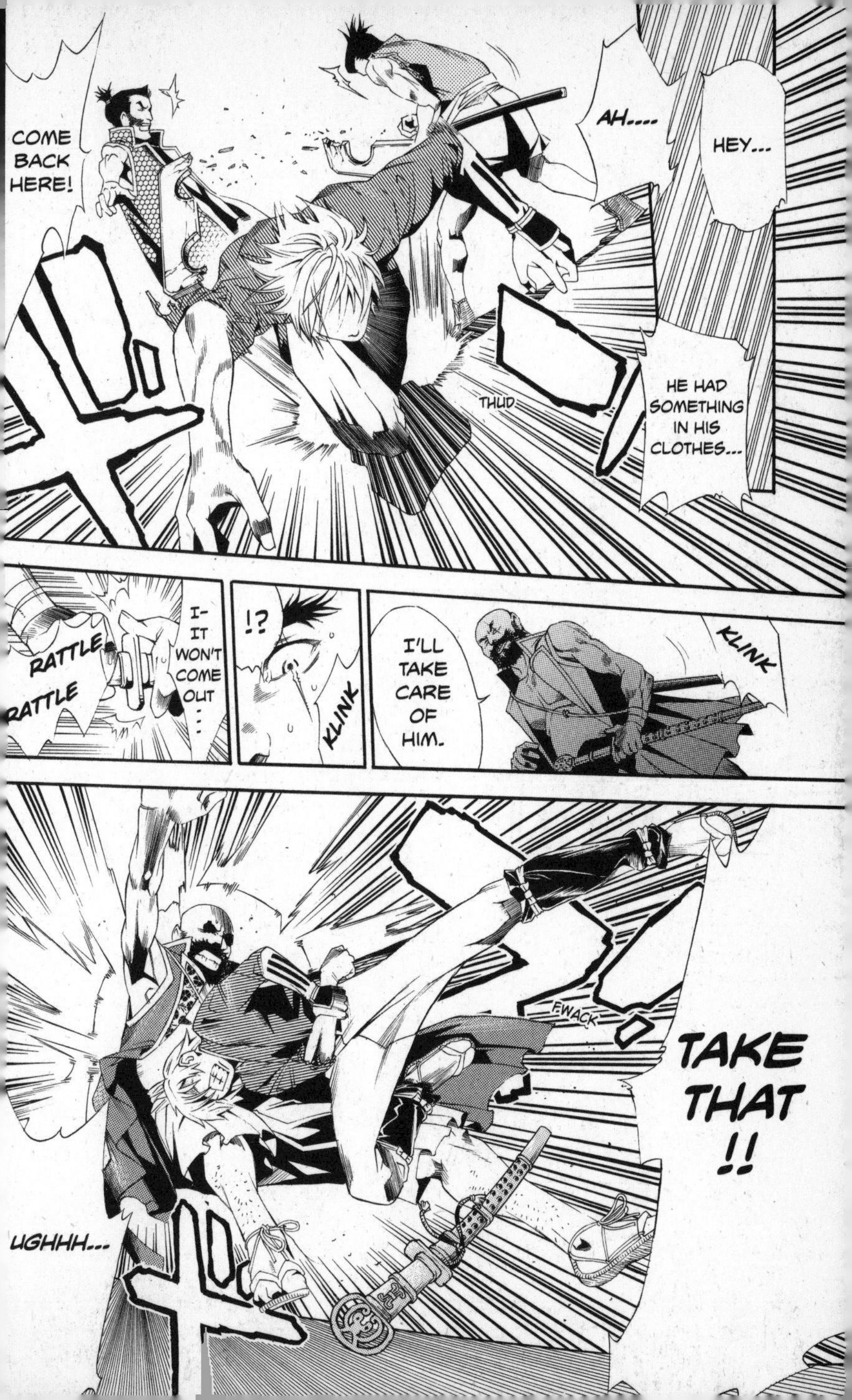
HEY...
AH....
HE HAD SOMETHING IN HIS CLOTHES...
COME BACK HERE!
THUD
KLINK
I'LL TAKE CARE OF HIM.
!?
KLINK
I- IT WON'T COME OUT...
RATTLE
RATTLE
TAKE THAT!!
F.WACK
UGHHH...

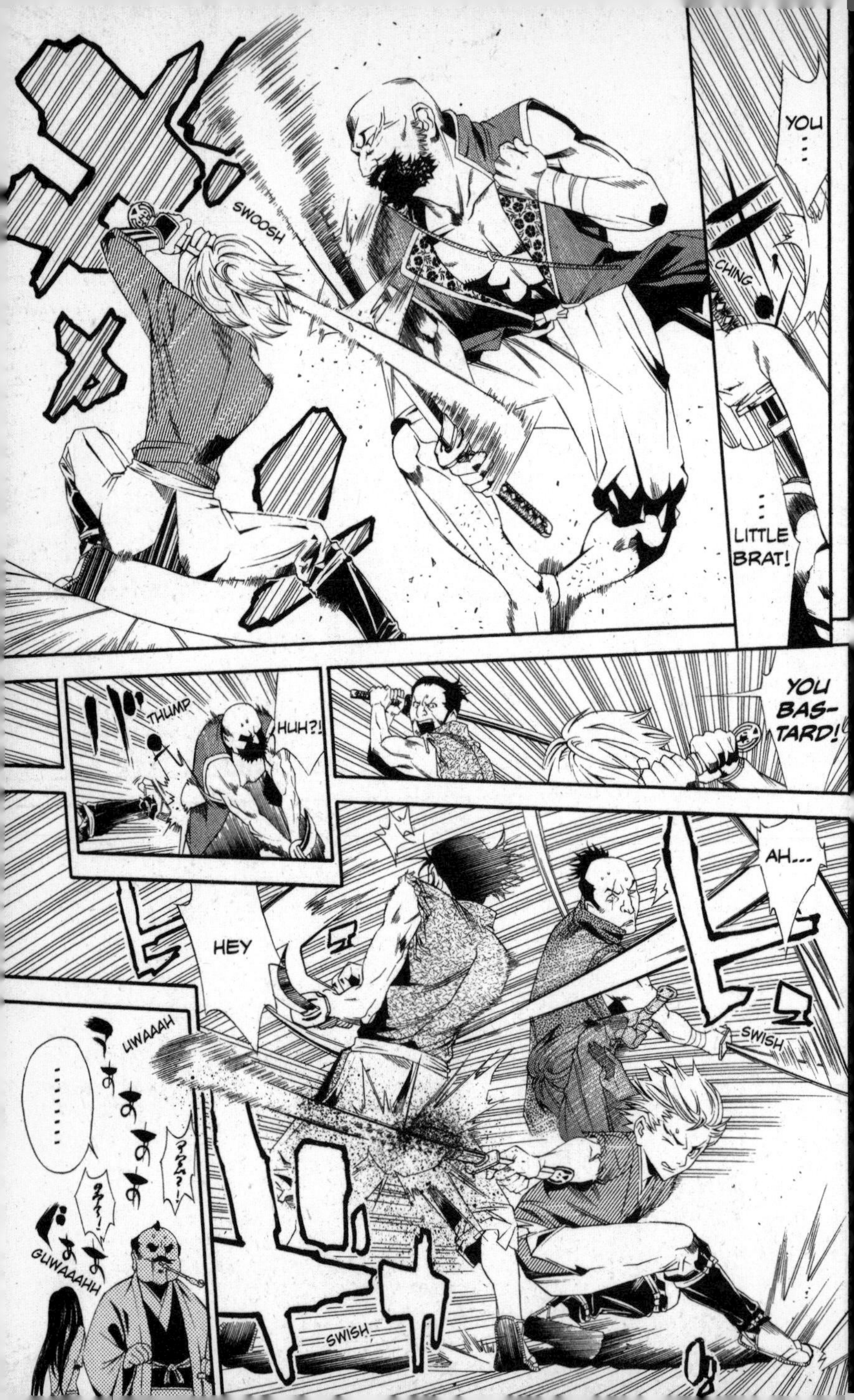
YOU...
CHING
...LITTLE BRAT!
SWOOSH
YOU BASTARD!
HUH?!
THUMP
AH...
HEY
SWISH
UWAAAH
......
GUWAAAHH
SWISH

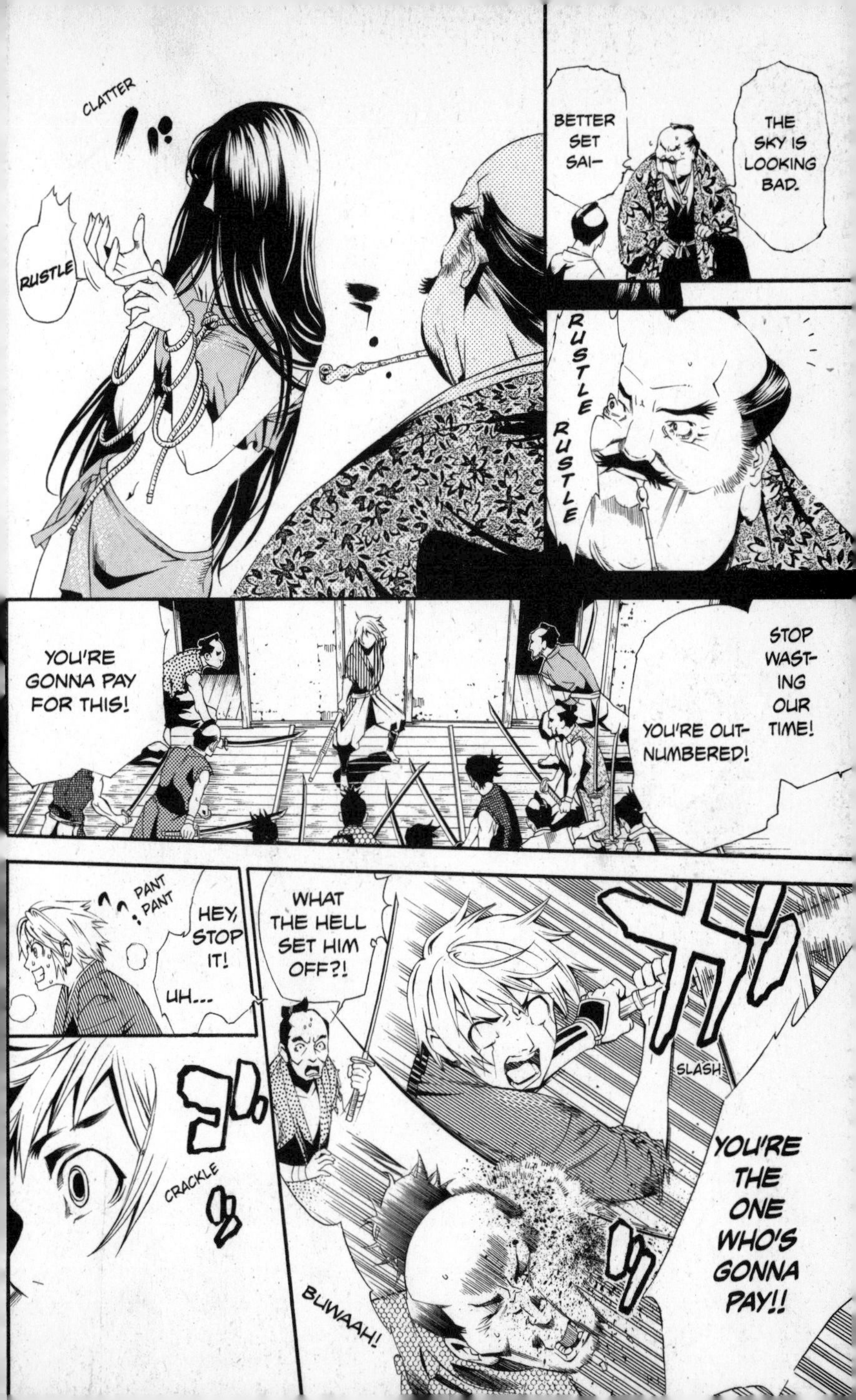
THE SKY IS LOOKING BAD.
BETTER SET SAI—
RUSTLE RUSTLE
CLATTER
RUSTLE
STOP WASTING OUR TIME!
YOU'RE OUTNUMBERED!
YOU'RE GONNA PAY FOR THIS!
WHAT THE HELL SET HIM OFF?!
SLASH
YOU'RE THE ONE WHO'S GONNA PAY!!
BUWAAH!
HEY, STOP IT!
UH...
PANT PANT
CRACKLE

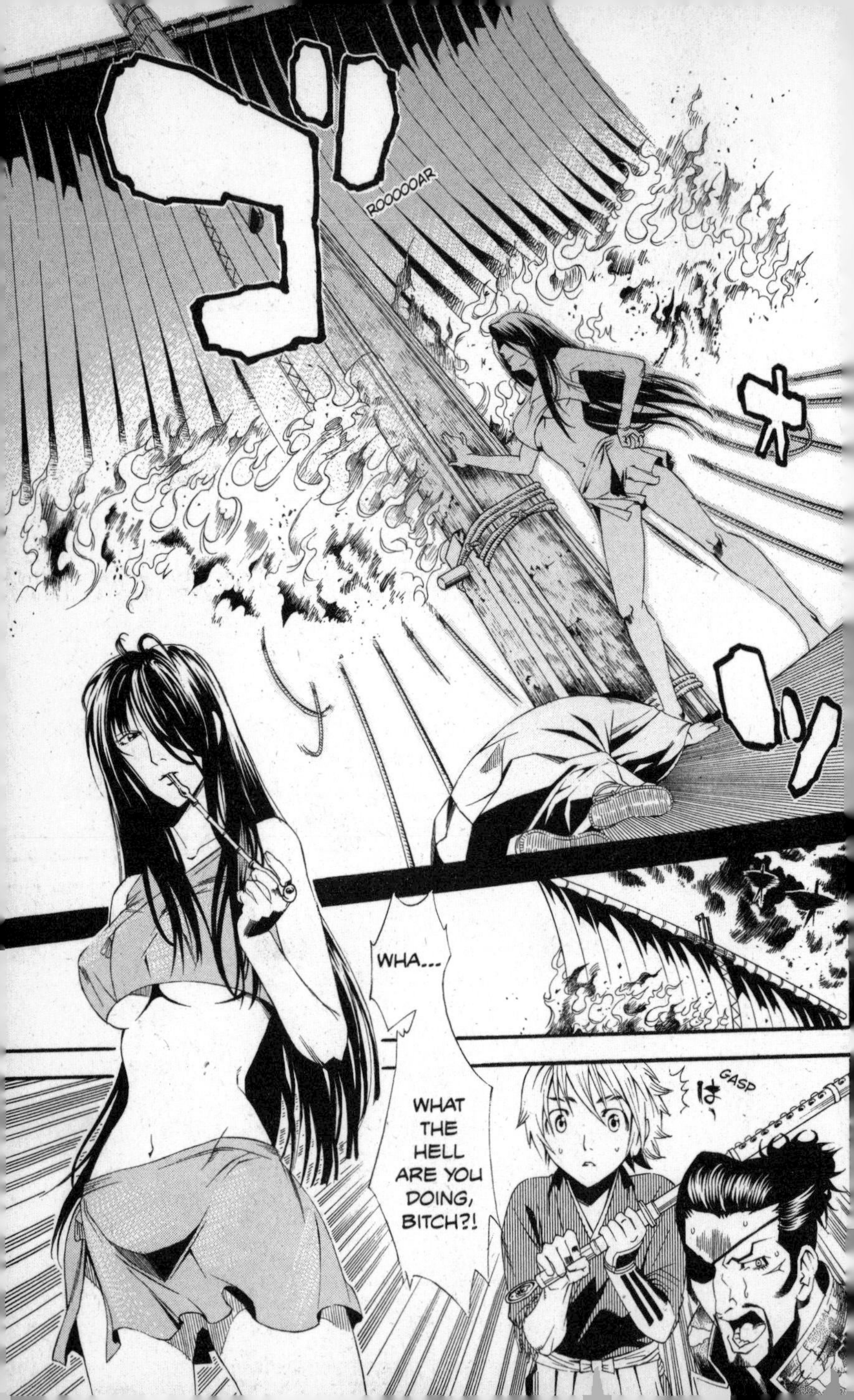

ROOOOOAR
WHA...
は
GASP
WHAT THE HELL ARE YOU DOING, BITCH?!

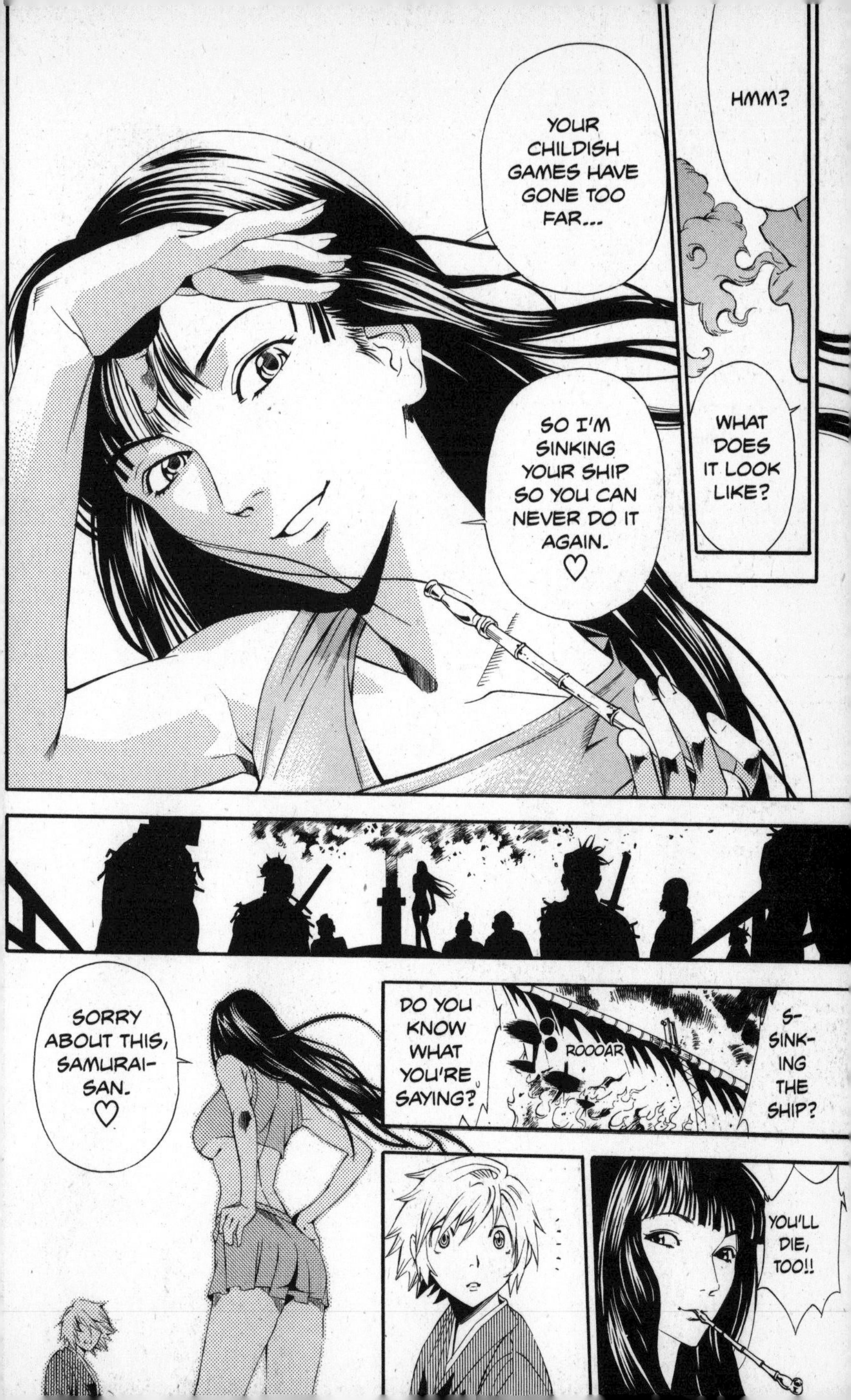
HMM?
WHAT DOES IT LOOK LIKE?
YOUR CHILDISH GAMES HAVE GONE TOO FAR...
SO I'M SINKING YOUR SHIP SO YOU CAN NEVER DO IT AGAIN. ♡
S-SINKING THE SHIP?
ROOOAR
DO YOU KNOW WHAT YOU'RE SAYING?
YOU'LL DIE, TOO!!
SORRY ABOUT THIS, SAMURAI-SAN. ♡

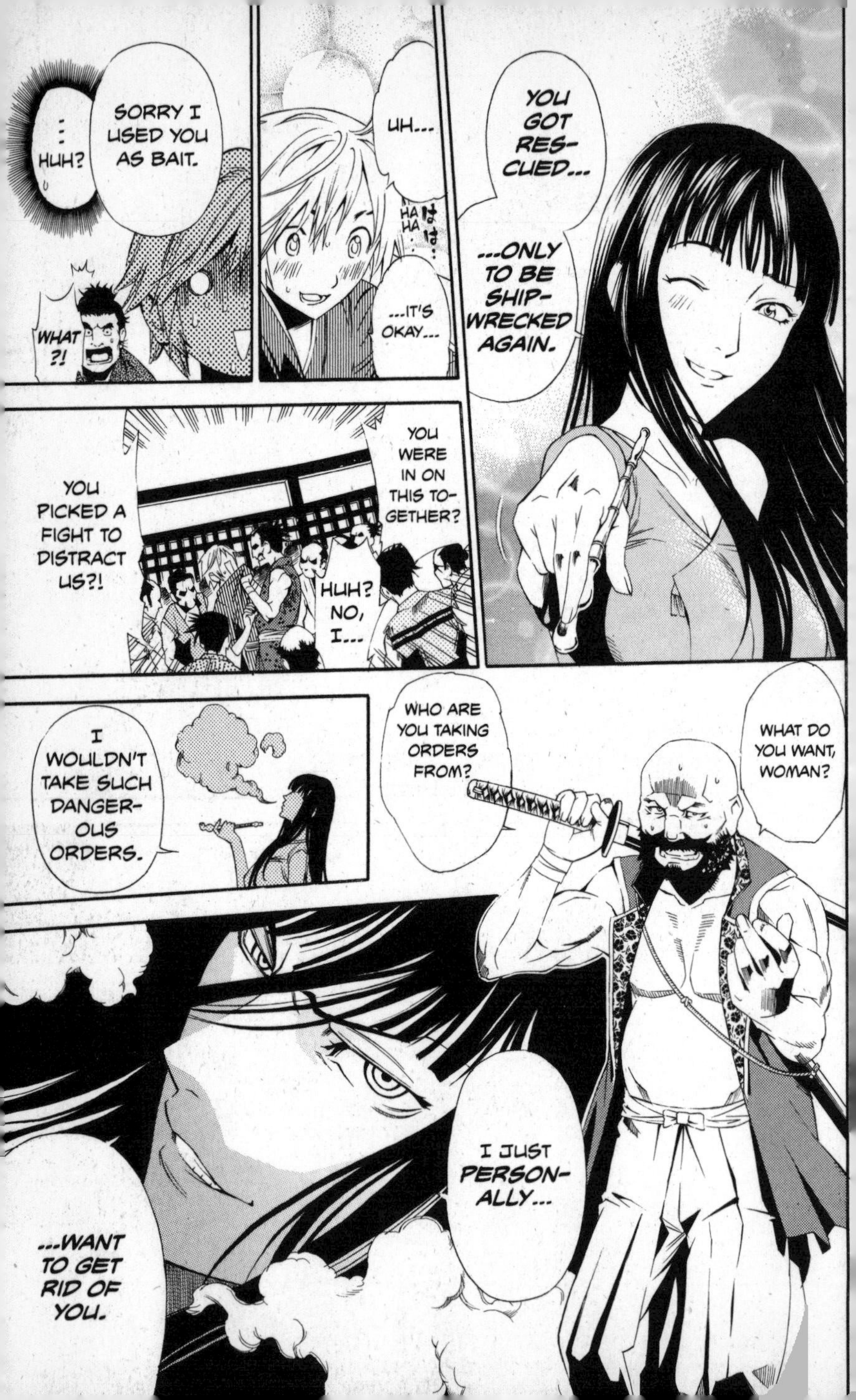
YOU GOT RES-CUED...
...ONLY TO BE SHIP-WRECKED AGAIN.
UH...
HA HA はは...
...IT'S OKAY...
SORRY I USED YOU AS BAIT.
...HUH?
WHAT?!
YOU WERE IN ON THIS TO-GETHER?
HUH? NO, I...
YOU PICKED A FIGHT TO DISTRACT US?!
WHAT DO YOU WANT, WOMAN?
WHO ARE YOU TAKING ORDERS FROM?
I WOULDN'T TAKE SUCH DANGER-OUS ORDERS.
I JUST PERSON-ALLY...
...WANT TO GET RID OF YOU.

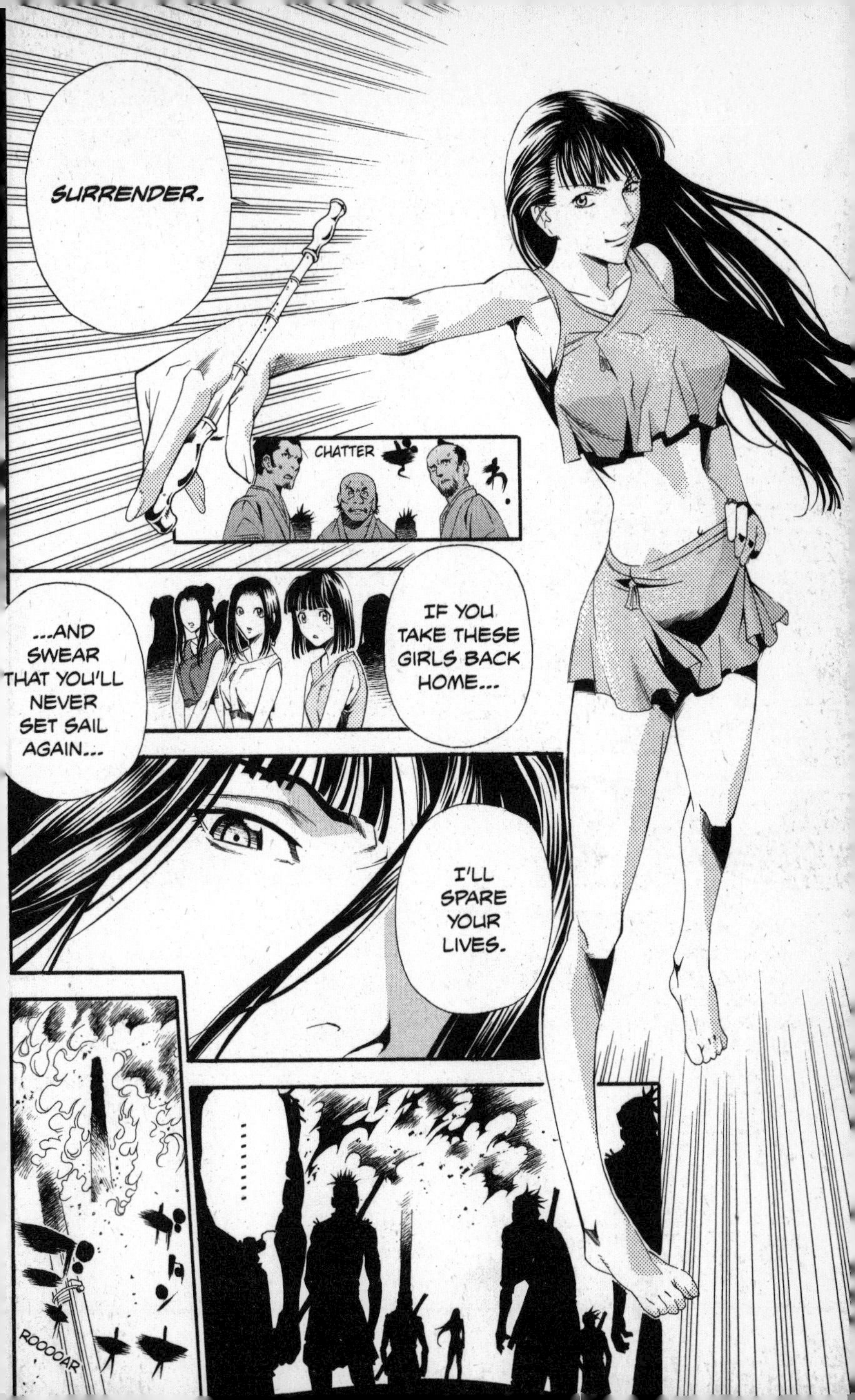
SURRENDER.
CHATTER
IF YOU TAKE THESE GIRLS BACK HOME...
...AND SWEAR THAT YOU'LL NEVER SET SAIL AGAIN...
I'LL SPARE YOUR LIVES.
ROOOOAR

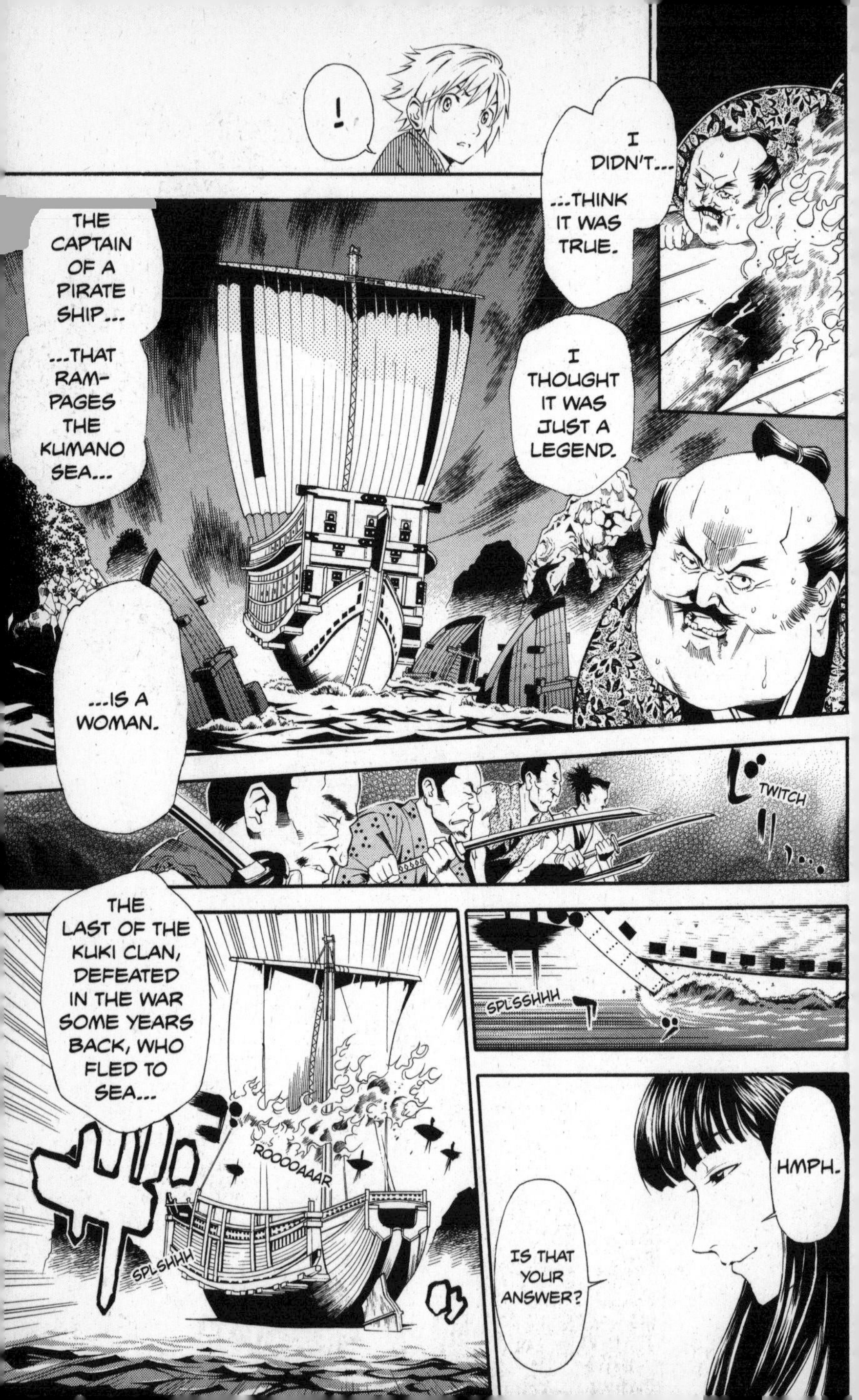

I DIDN'T...
...THINK IT WAS TRUE.
!
I THOUGHT IT WAS JUST A LEGEND.
THE CAPTAIN OF A PIRATE SHIP...
...THAT RAM-PAGES THE KUMANO SEA...
...IS A WOMAN.
TWITCH
SPLSSHHH
HMPH.
IS THAT YOUR ANSWER?
THE LAST OF THE KUKI CLAN, DEFEATED IN THE WAR SOME YEARS BACK, WHO FLED TO SEA...
ROOOOAAAR
SPLSHHH

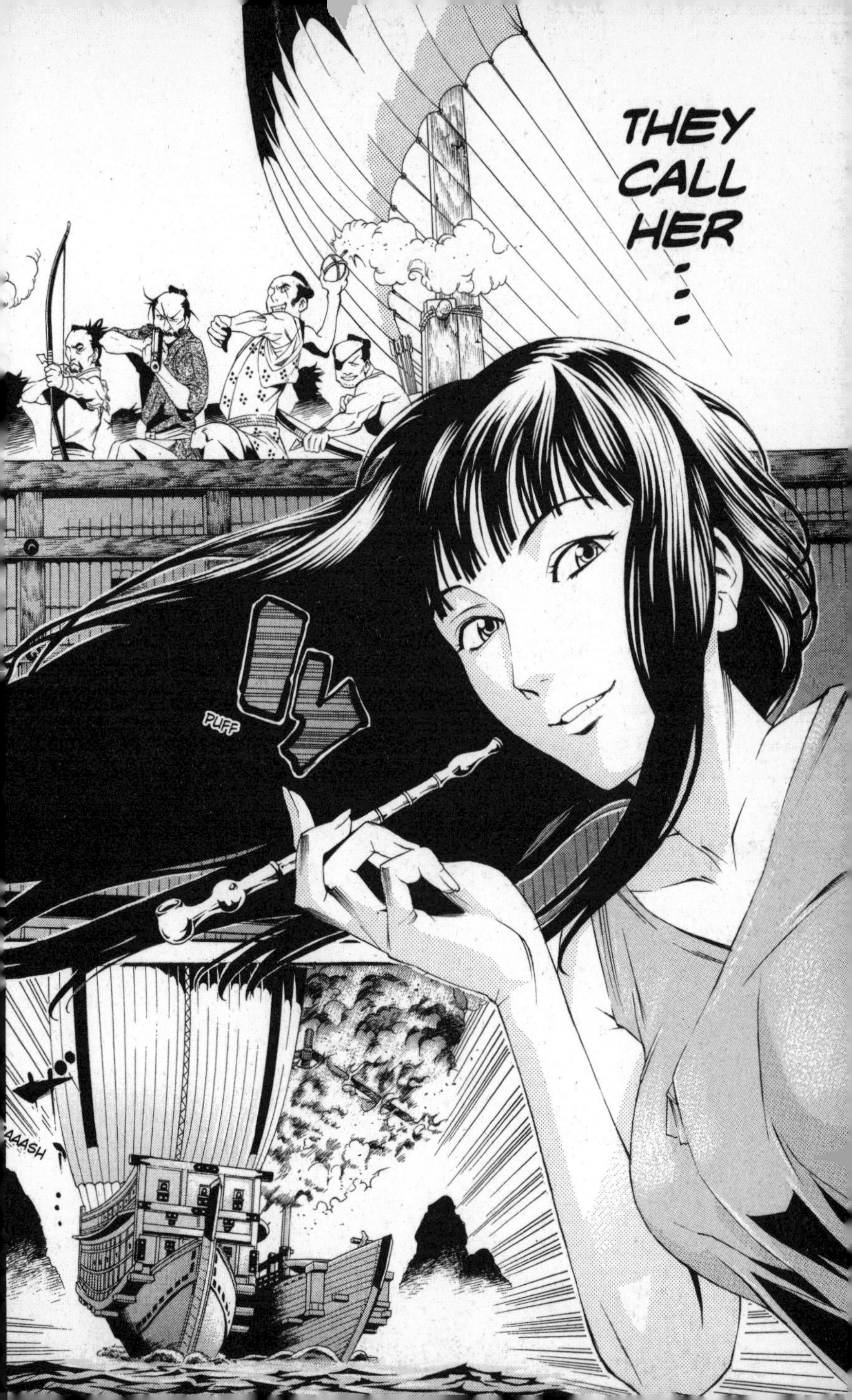
THEY CALL HER...
PUFF
AAASH

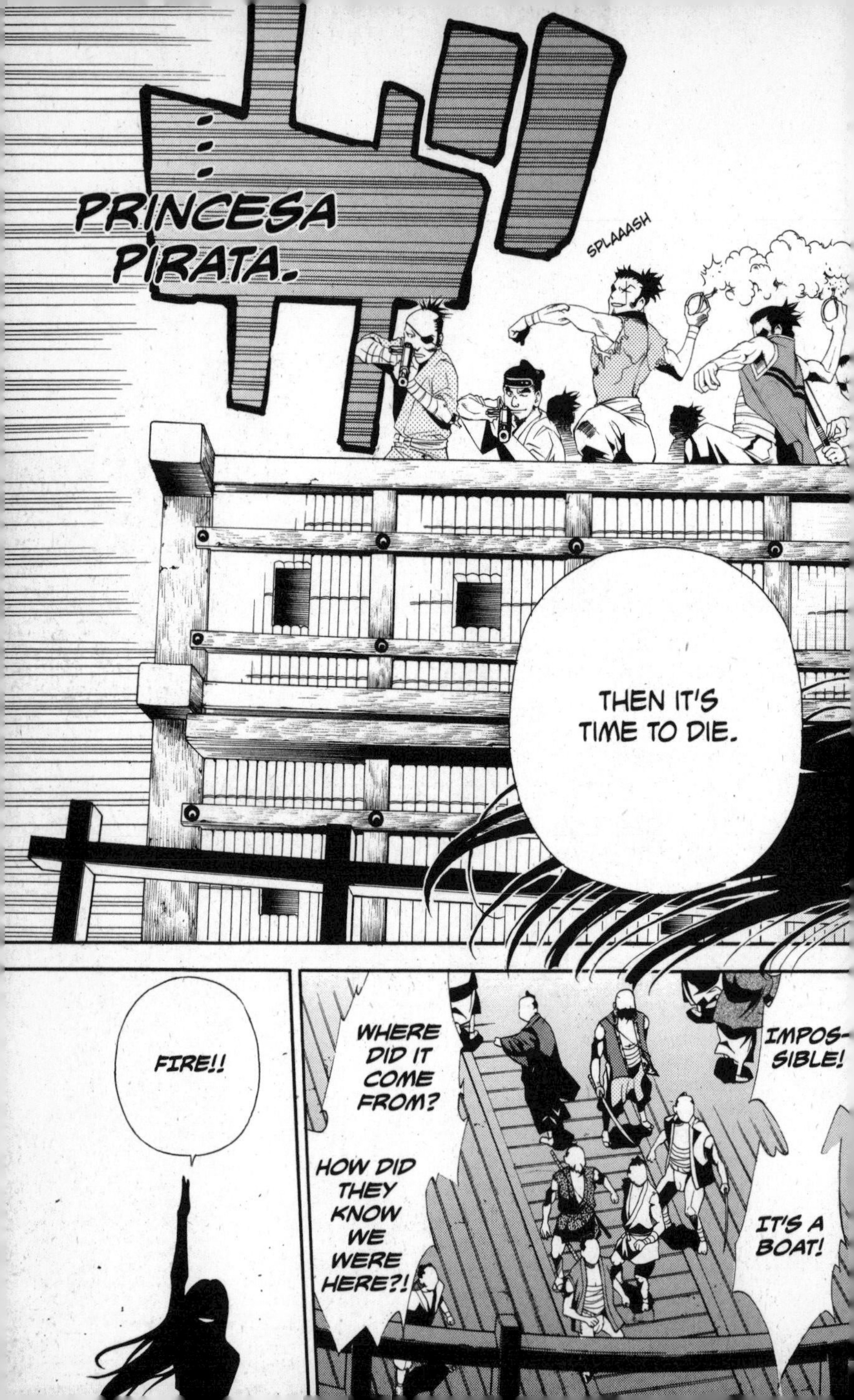
SPLAAASH
...PRINCESA PIRATA.
THEN IT'S TIME TO DIE.
IMPOSSIBLE!
WHERE DID IT COME FROM?
IT'S A BOAT!
HOW DID THEY KNOW WE WERE HERE?!
FIRE!!

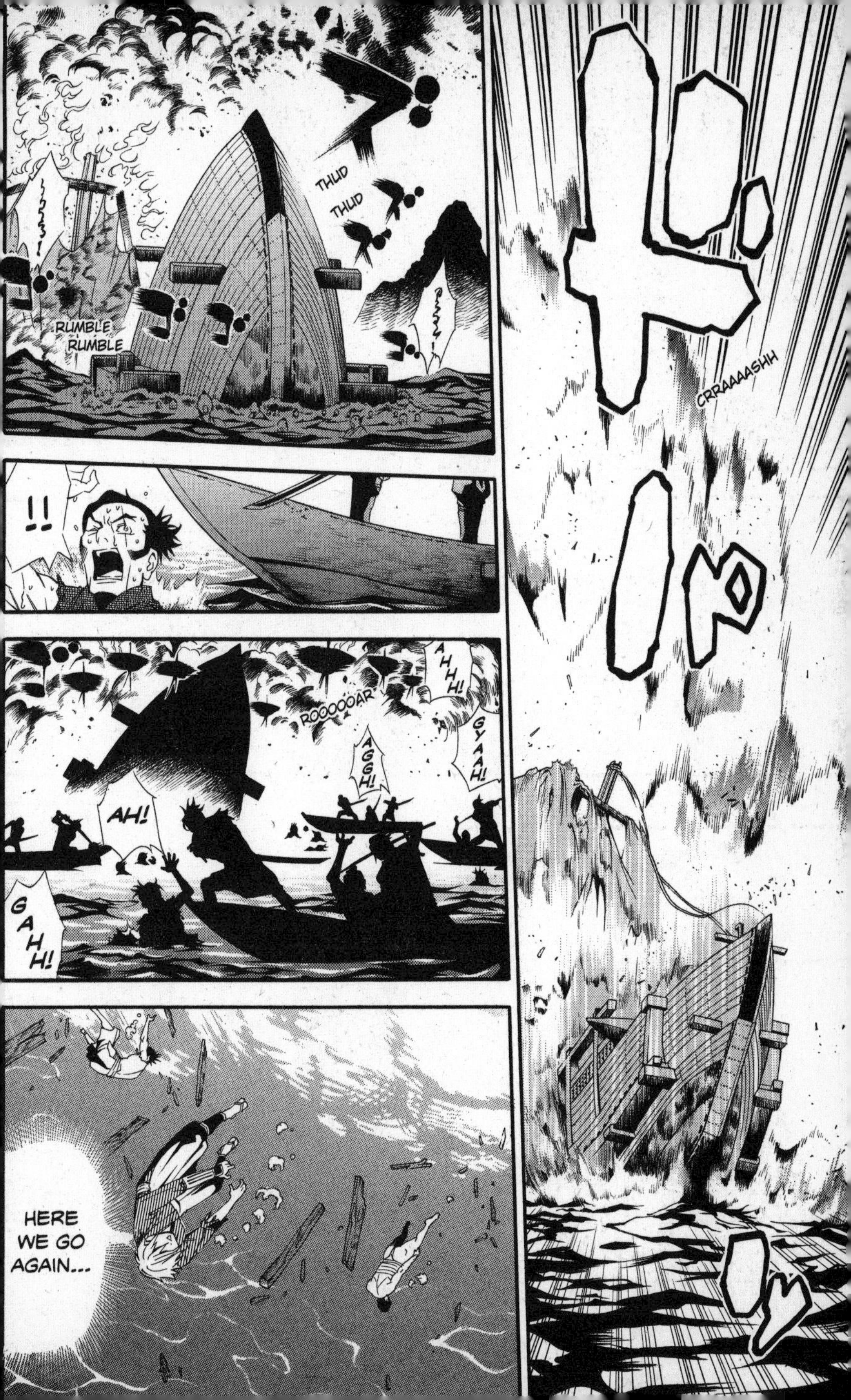
CRRAAAASHH
THUD
THUD
RUMBLE
RUMBLE
!!
AHHH!
GYAAH!
ROOOOOAR
AGGH!
AH!
GAHH!
HERE WE GO AGAIN...

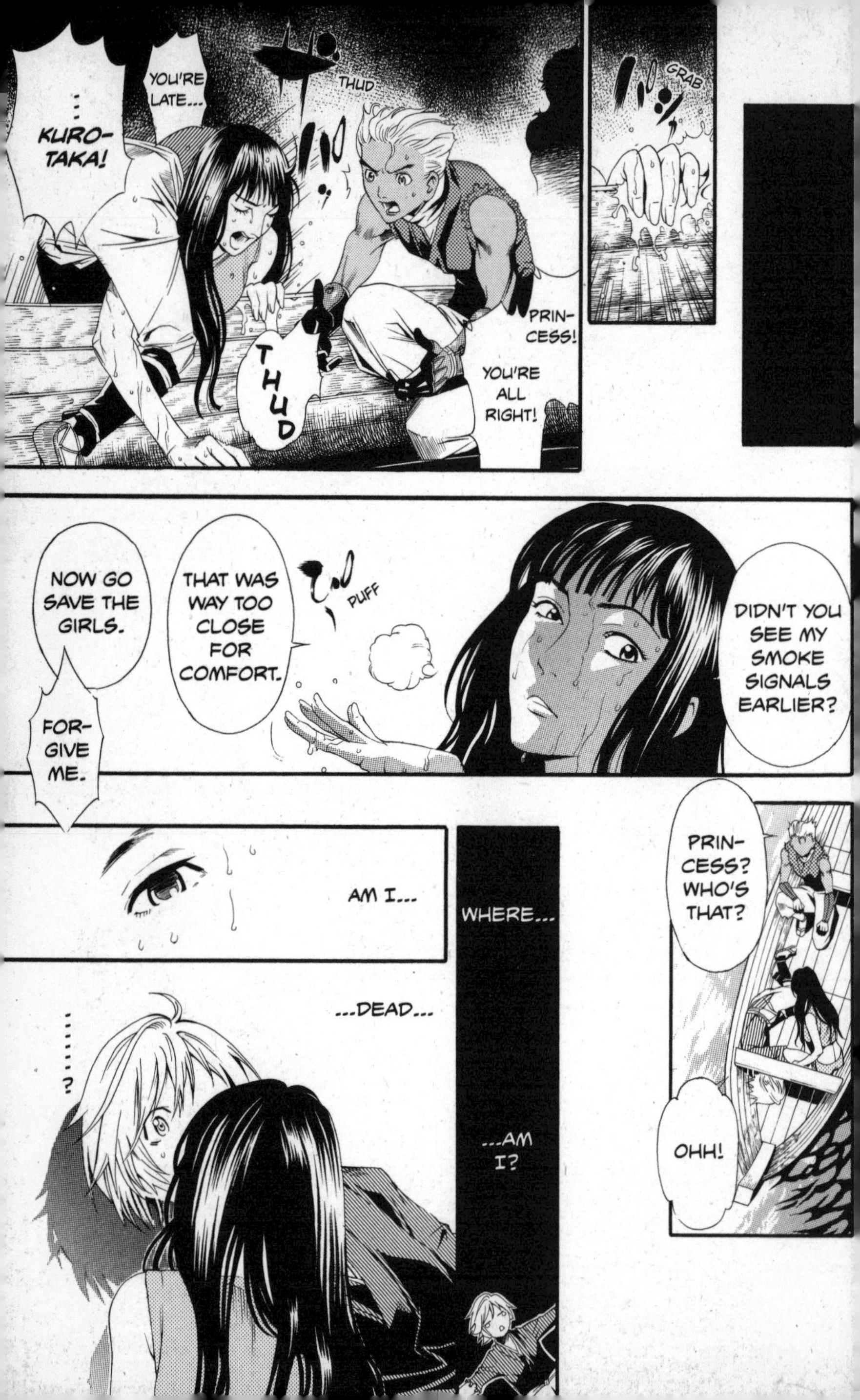
GRAB
THUD
PRIN-CESS!
YOU'RE ALL RIGHT!
YOU'RE LATE...
...KURO-TAKA!
THUD
DIDN'T YOU SEE MY SMOKE SIGNALS EARLIER?
PUFF
THAT WAS WAY TOO CLOSE FOR COMFORT.
NOW GO SAVE THE GIRLS.
FOR-GIVE ME.
PRIN-CESS? WHO'S THAT?
OHH!
WHERE...
AM I...
...DEAD...
...AM I?
......?

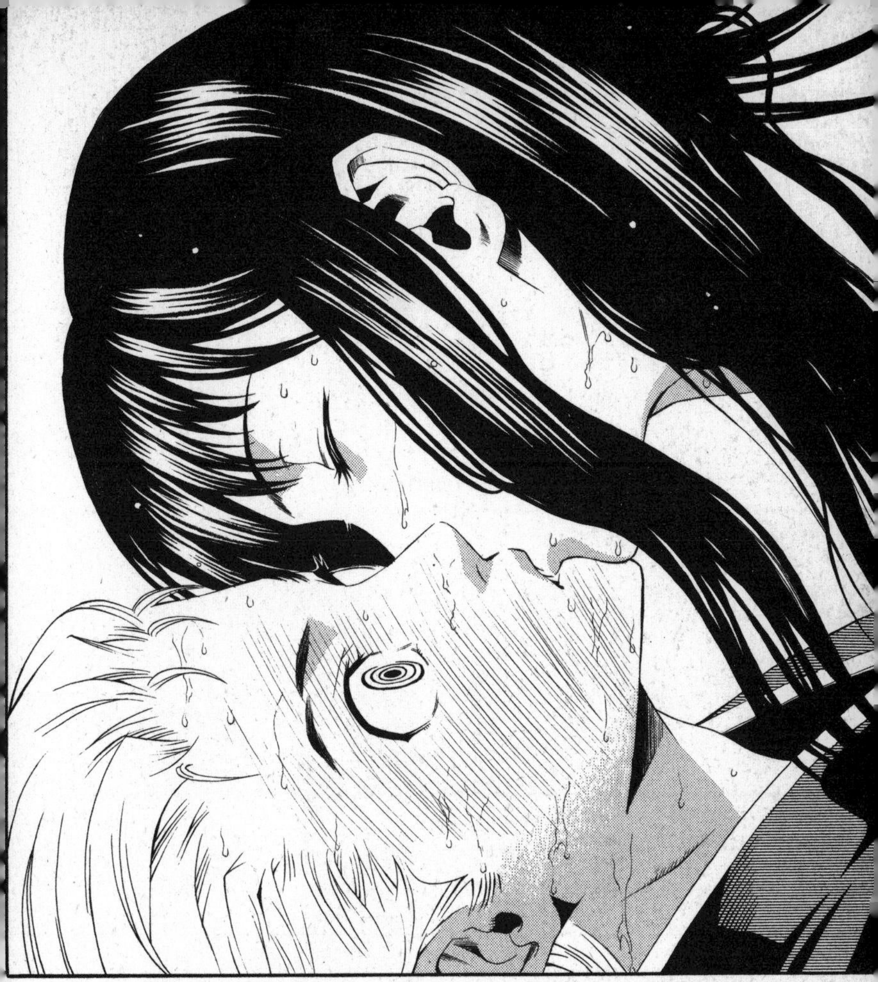

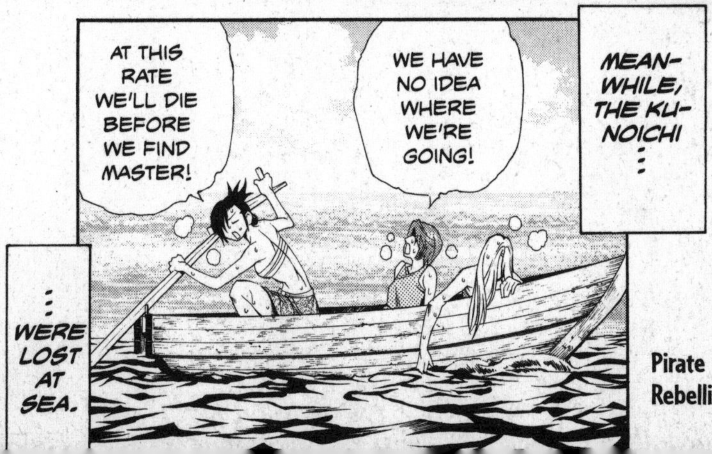
MEAN-WHILE, THE KU-NOICHI …
WE HAVE NO IDEA WHERE WE'RE GOING!
AT THIS RATE WE'LL DIE BEFORE WE FIND MASTER!
… WERE LOST AT SEA.

Pirate Rebellion / End

**Ninja Girls**

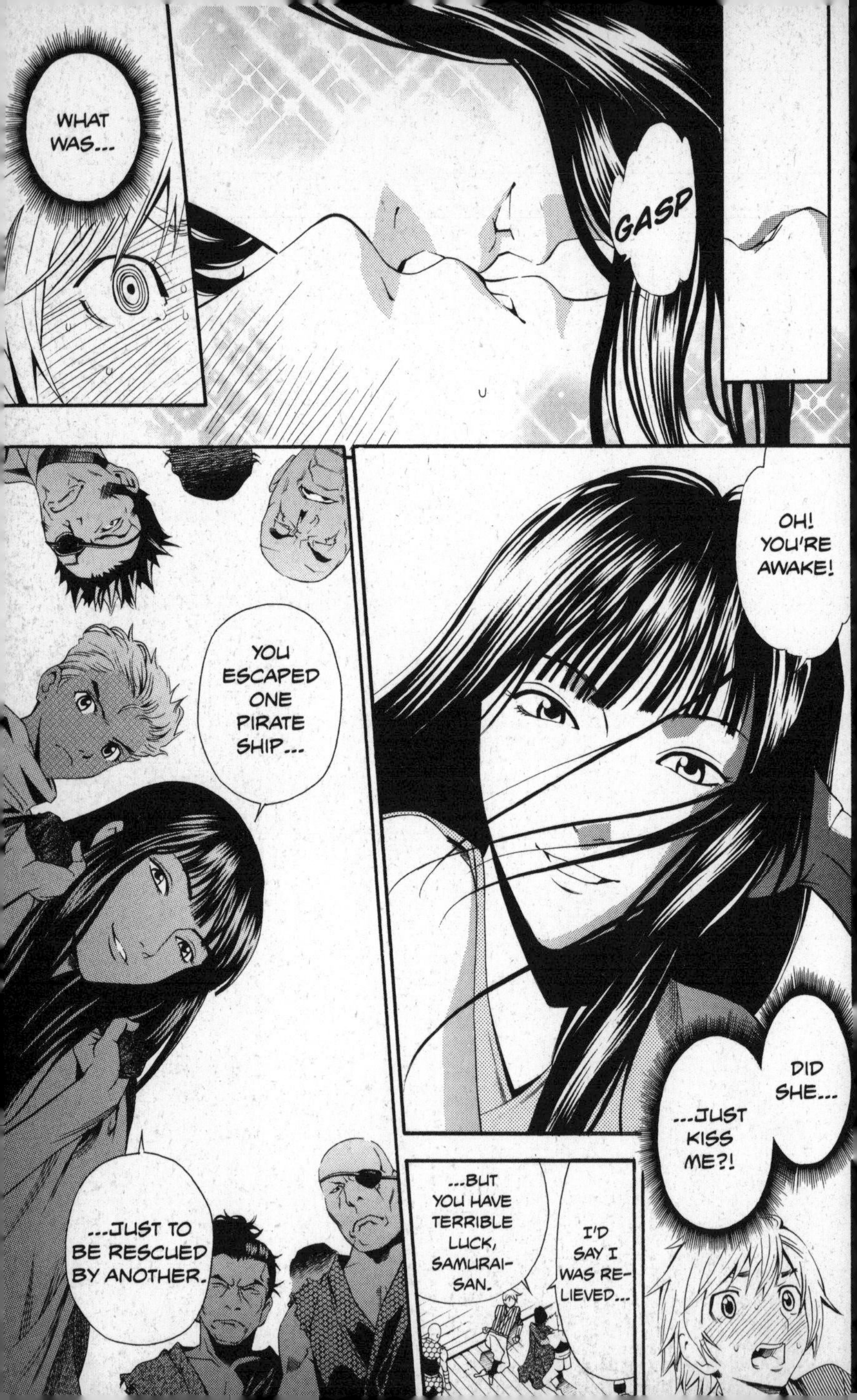
GASP
WHAT WAS...
OH! YOU'RE AWAKE!
DID SHE...
...JUST KISS ME?!
I'D SAY I WAS RE-LIEVED...
...BUT YOU HAVE TERRIBLE LUCK, SAMURAI-SAN.
YOU ESCAPED ONE PIRATE SHIP...
...JUST TO BE RESCUED BY ANOTHER.

# 26 Confession Rebellion

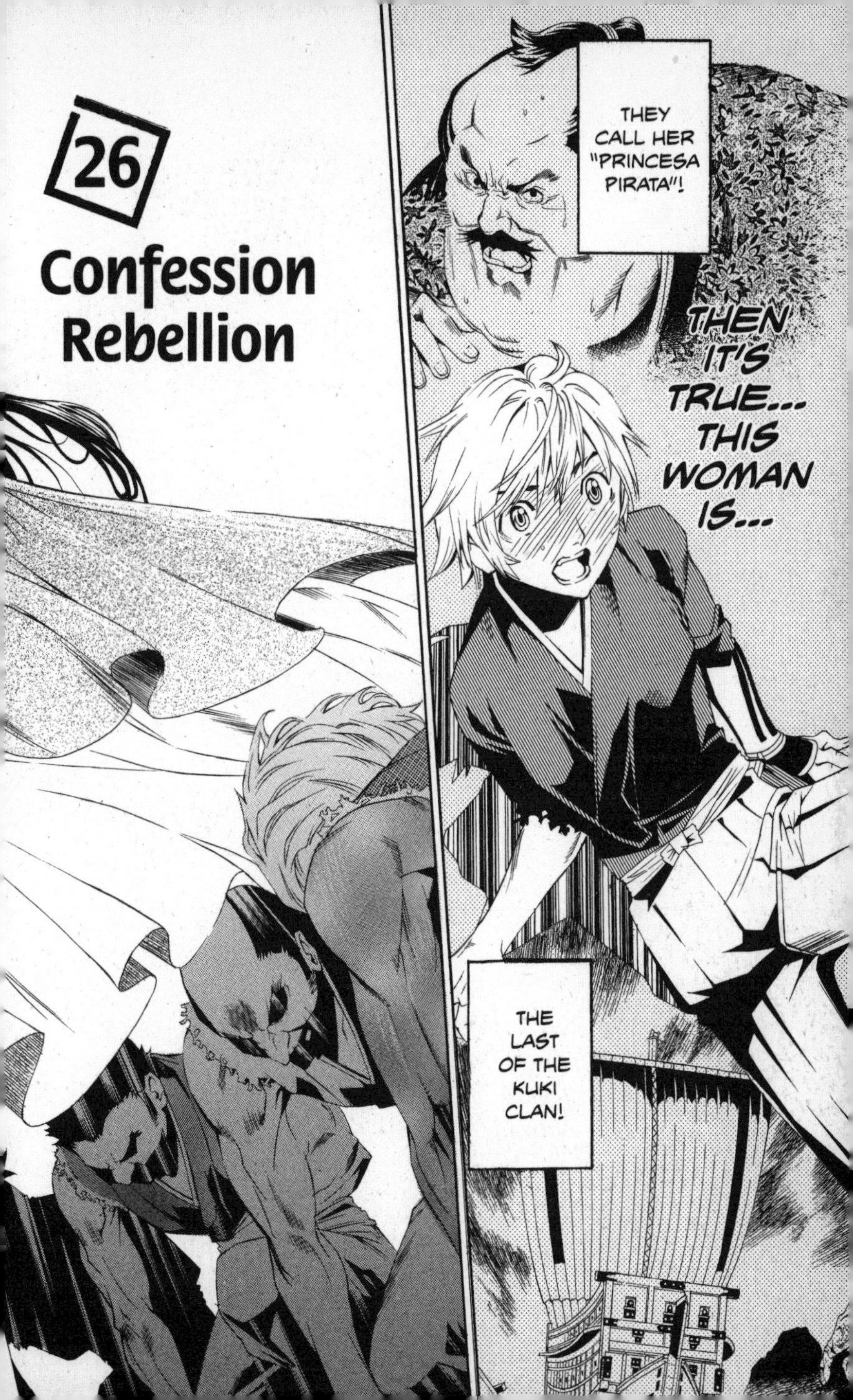
THEY CALL HER "PRINCESA PIRATA"!
THEN IT'S TRUE... THIS WOMAN IS...
THE LAST OF THE KUKI CLAN!

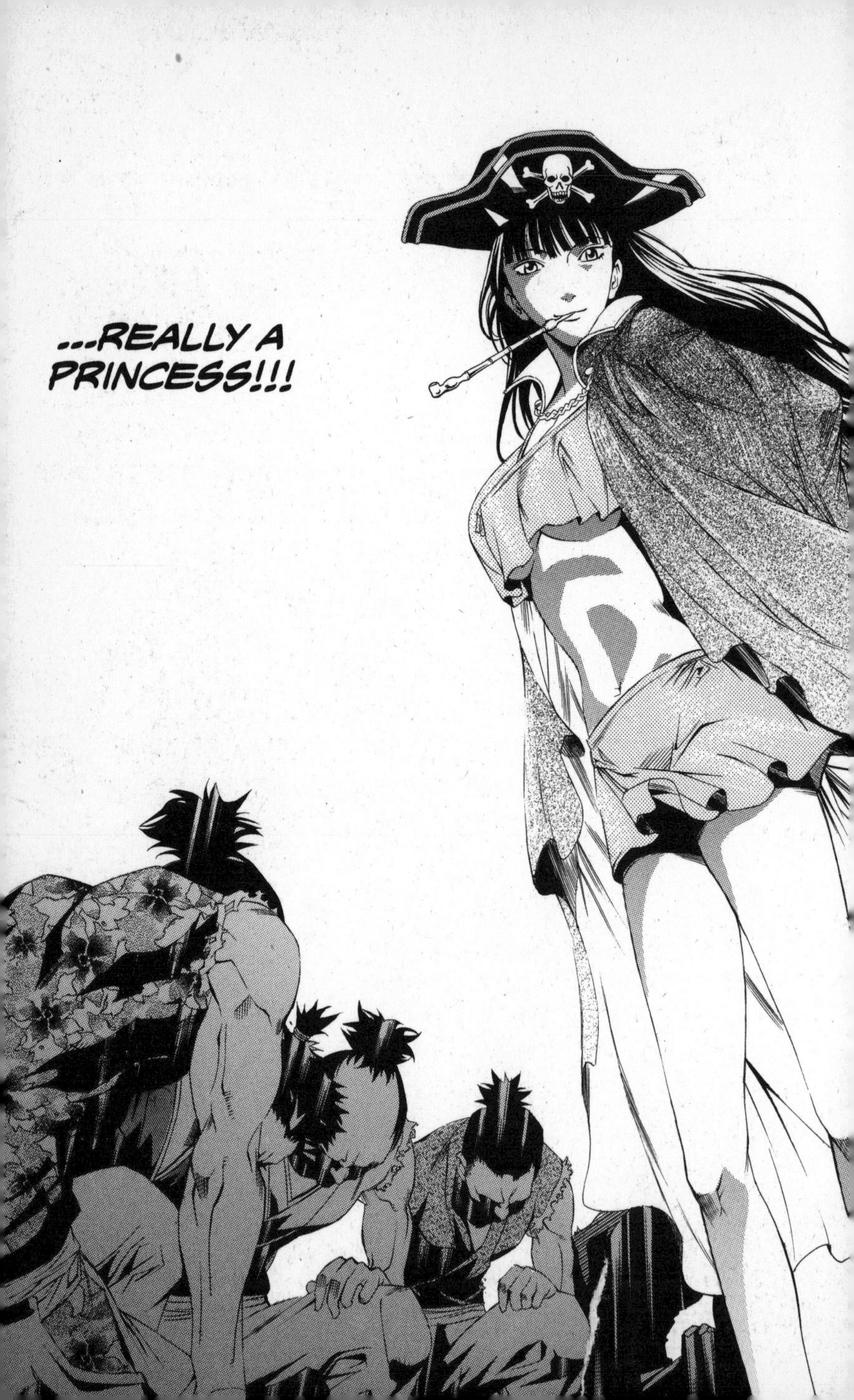
...REALLY A PRINCESS!!!

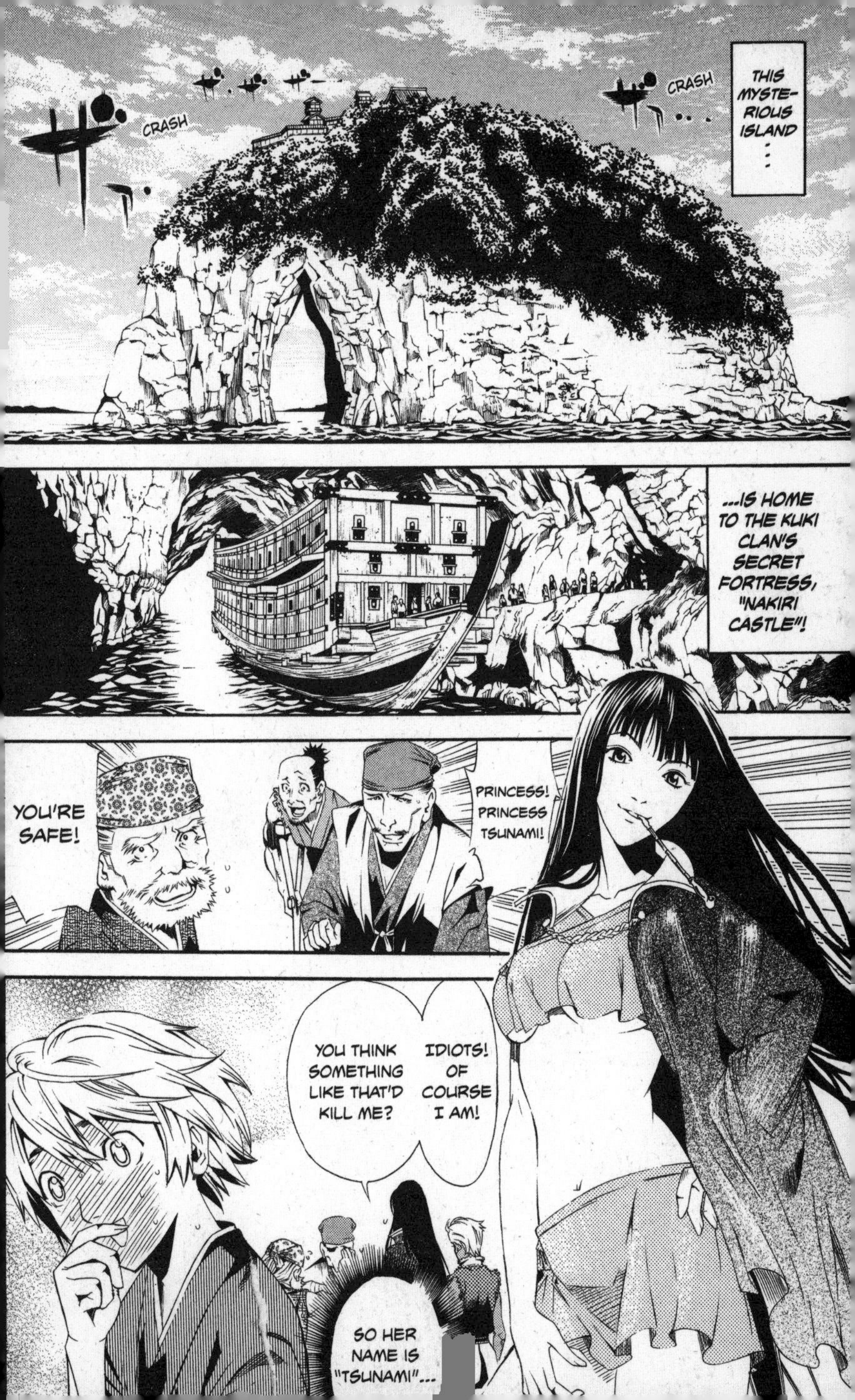
THIS MYSTERIOUS ISLAND...
CRASH
CRASH
...IS HOME TO THE KUKI CLAN'S SECRET FORTRESS, "NAKIRI CASTLE"!
PRINCESS! PRINCESS TSUNAMI!
YOU'RE SAFE!
IDIOTS! OF COURSE I AM!
YOU THINK SOMETHING LIKE THAT'D KILL ME?
SO HER NAME IS "TSUNAMI"...

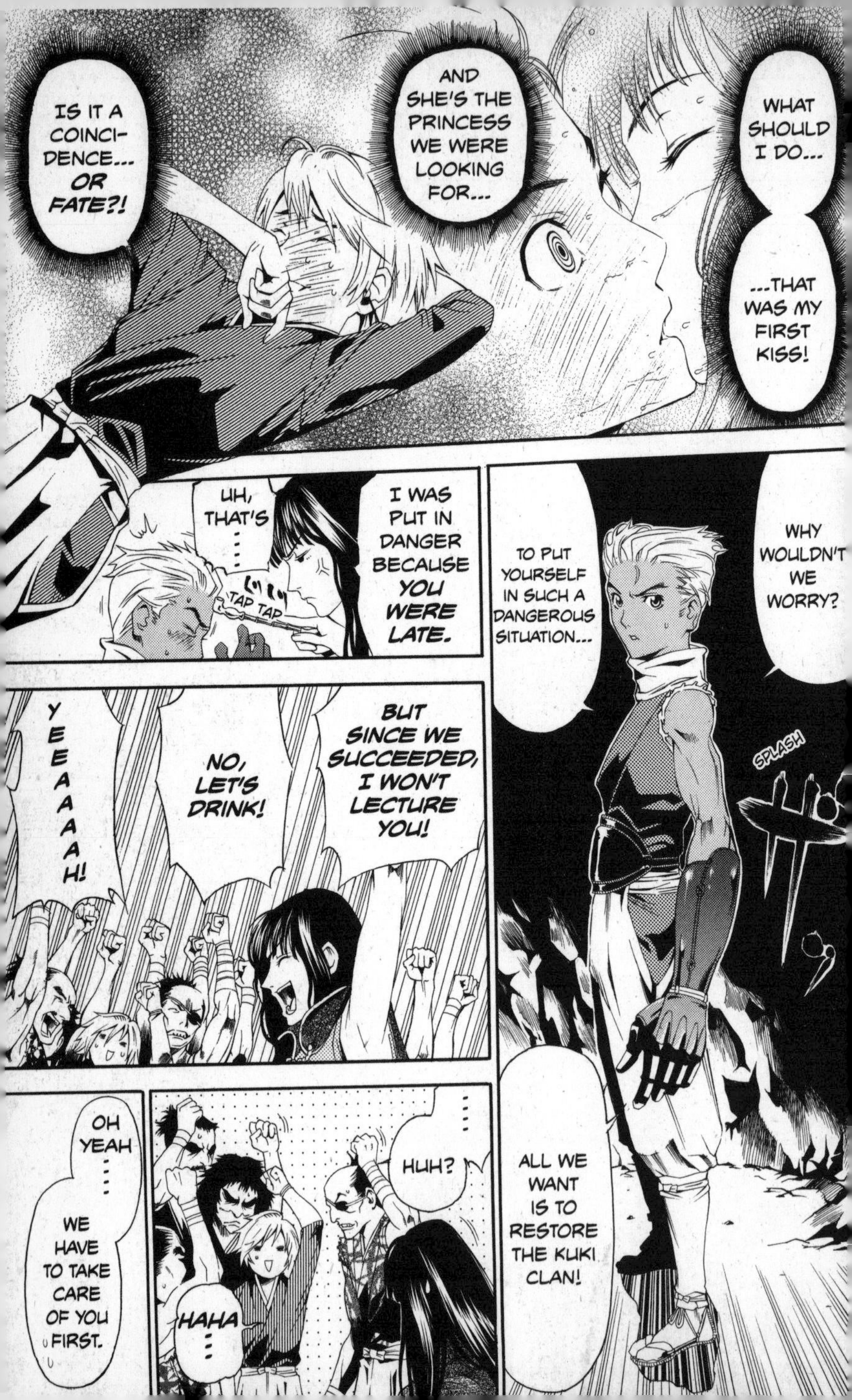
WHAT SHOULD I DO...
...THAT WAS MY FIRST KISS!
AND SHE'S THE PRINCESS WE WERE LOOKING FOR...
IS IT A COINCIDENCE... OR FATE?!
WHY WOULDN'T WE WORRY?
TO PUT YOURSELF IN SUCH A DANGEROUS SITUATION...
SPLASH
ALL WE WANT IS TO RESTORE THE KUKI CLAN!
I WAS PUT IN DANGER BECAUSE YOU WERE LATE.
UH, THAT'S...
TAP TAP
BUT SINCE WE SUCCEEDED, I WON'T LECTURE YOU!
NO, LET'S DRINK!
YEEAAAAAH!
... HUH?
HAHA...
OH YEAH... WE HAVE TO TAKE CARE OF YOU FIRST.

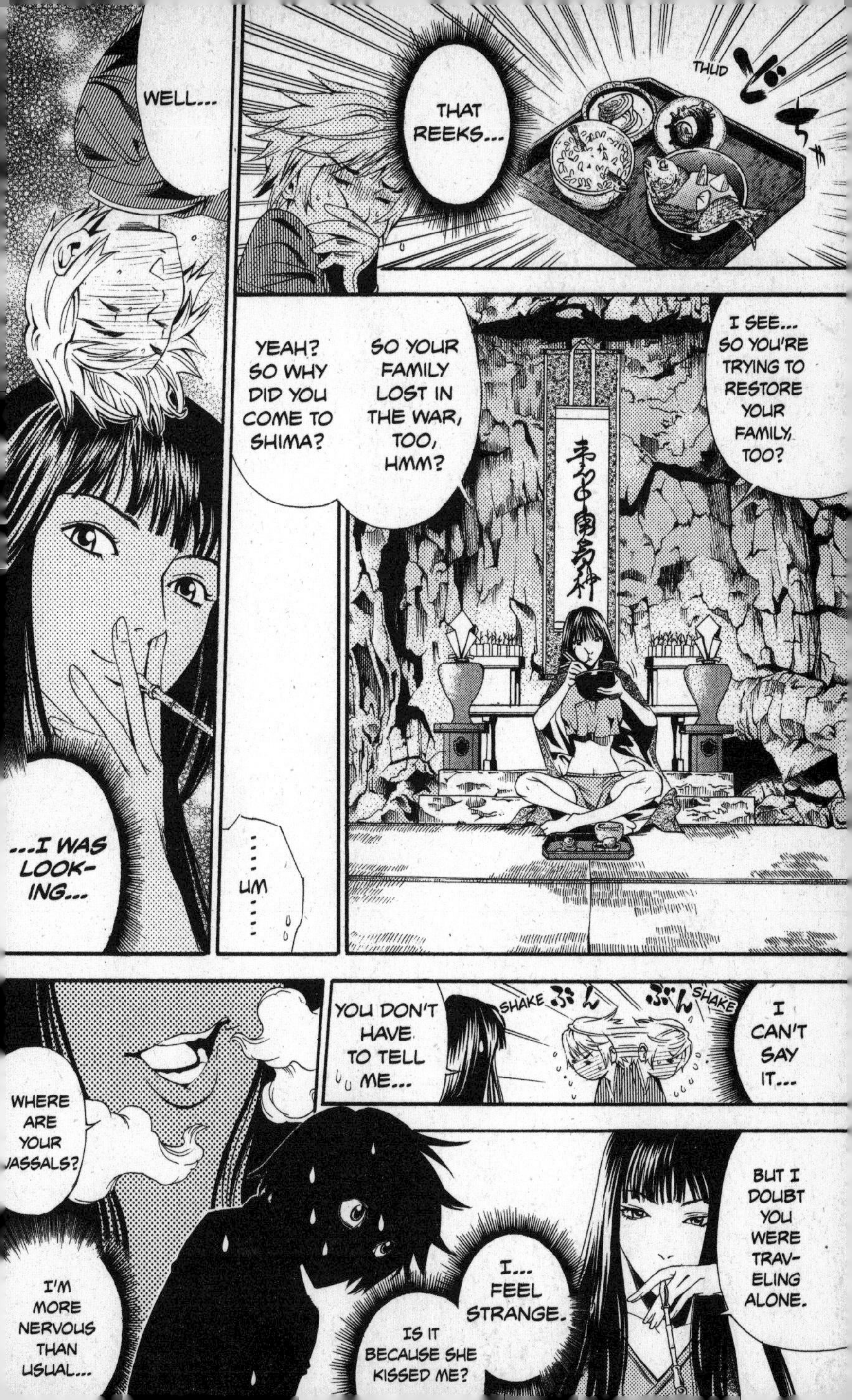
THUD
THAT REEKS...
I SEE... SO YOU'RE TRYING TO RESTORE YOUR FAMILY, TOO?
SO YOUR FAMILY LOST IN THE WAR, TOO, HMM?
YEAH? SO WHY DID YOU COME TO SHIMA?
...UM...
WELL...
...I WAS LOOKING-ING...
I CAN'T SAY IT...
SHAKE
SHAKE
YOU DON'T HAVE TO TELL ME...
BUT I DOUBT YOU WERE TRAV-ELING ALONE.
I... FEEL STRANGE.
IS IT BECAUSE SHE KISSED ME?
WHERE ARE YOUR VASSALS?
I'M MORE NERVOUS THAN USUAL...

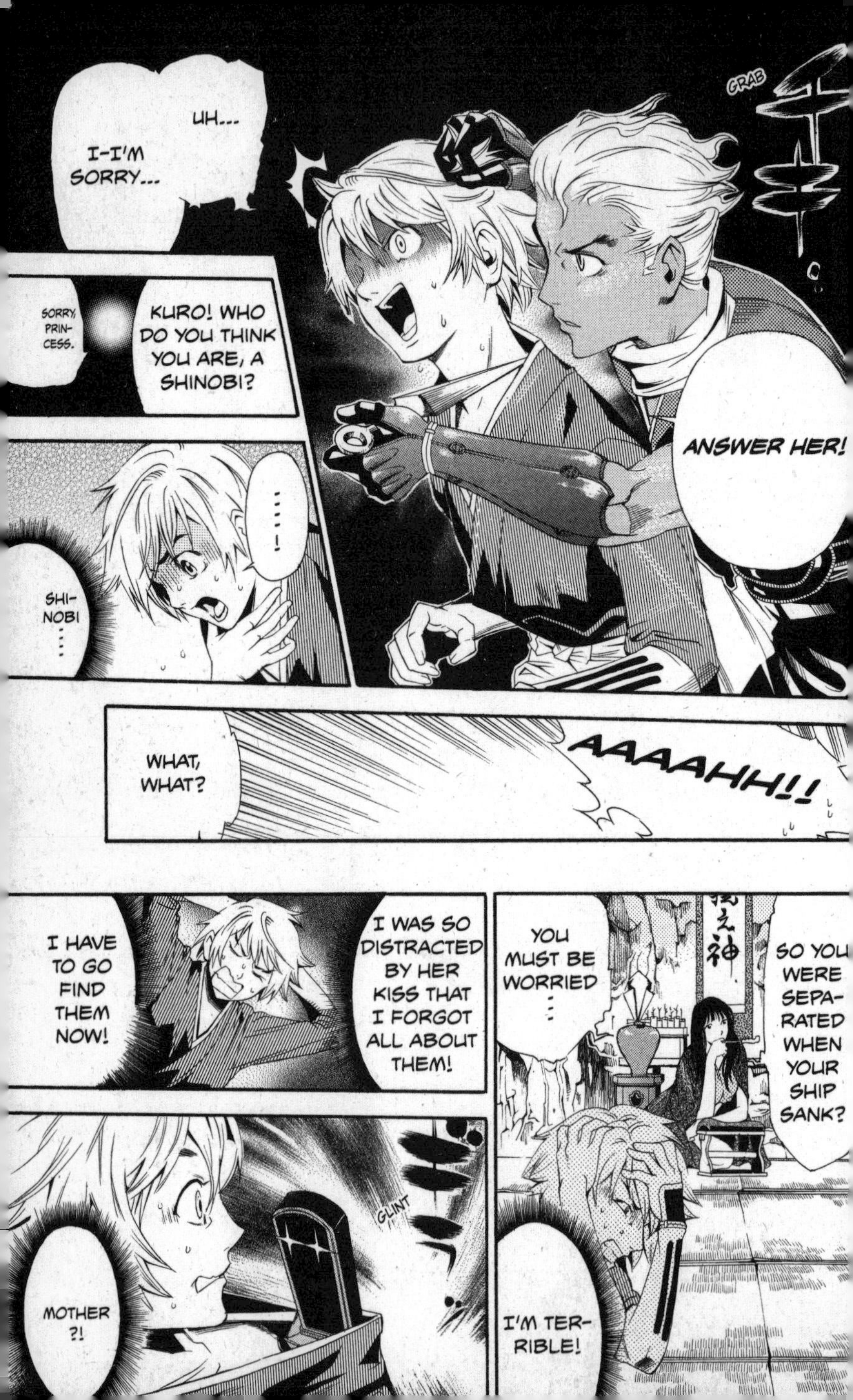
GRAB
ANSWER HER!
UH...
I-I'M SORRY...
KURO! WHO DO YOU THINK YOU ARE, A SHINOBI?
SORRY, PRINCESS.
...!
SHI-NOBI...
AAAAHH!!
WHAT, WHAT?
SO YOU WERE SEPA-RATED WHEN YOUR SHIP SANK?
YOU MUST BE WORRIED...
I'M TER-RIBLE!
I WAS SO DISTRACTED BY HER KISS THAT I FORGOT ALL ABOUT THEM!
I HAVE TO GO FIND THEM NOW!
GLINT
MOTHER?!

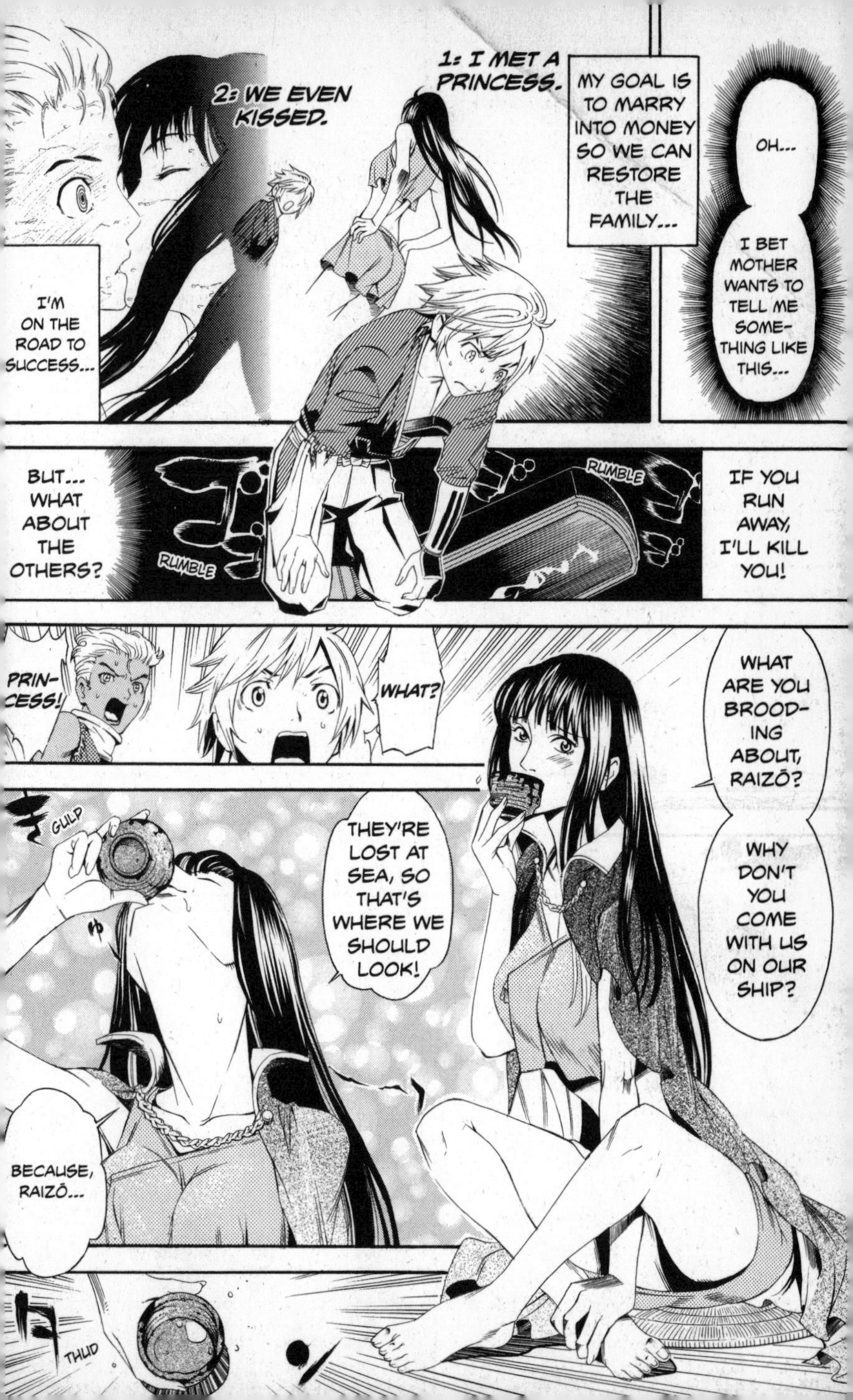
OH...
I BET MOTHER WANTS TO TELL ME SOME-THING LIKE THIS...
MY GOAL IS TO MARRY INTO MONEY SO WE CAN RESTORE THE FAMILY...
1: I MET A PRINCESS.
2: WE EVEN KISSED.
I'M ON THE ROAD TO SUCCESS...
IF YOU RUN AWAY, I'LL KILL YOU!
RUMBLE
RUMBLE
BUT... WHAT ABOUT THE OTHERS?
WHAT ARE YOU BROOD-ING ABOUT, RAIZŌ?
WHY DON'T YOU COME WITH US ON OUR SHIP?
WHAT?
PRIN-CESS!
THEY'RE LOST AT SEA, SO THAT'S WHERE WE SHOULD LOOK!
GULP
BECAUSE, RAIZŌ...
THUD

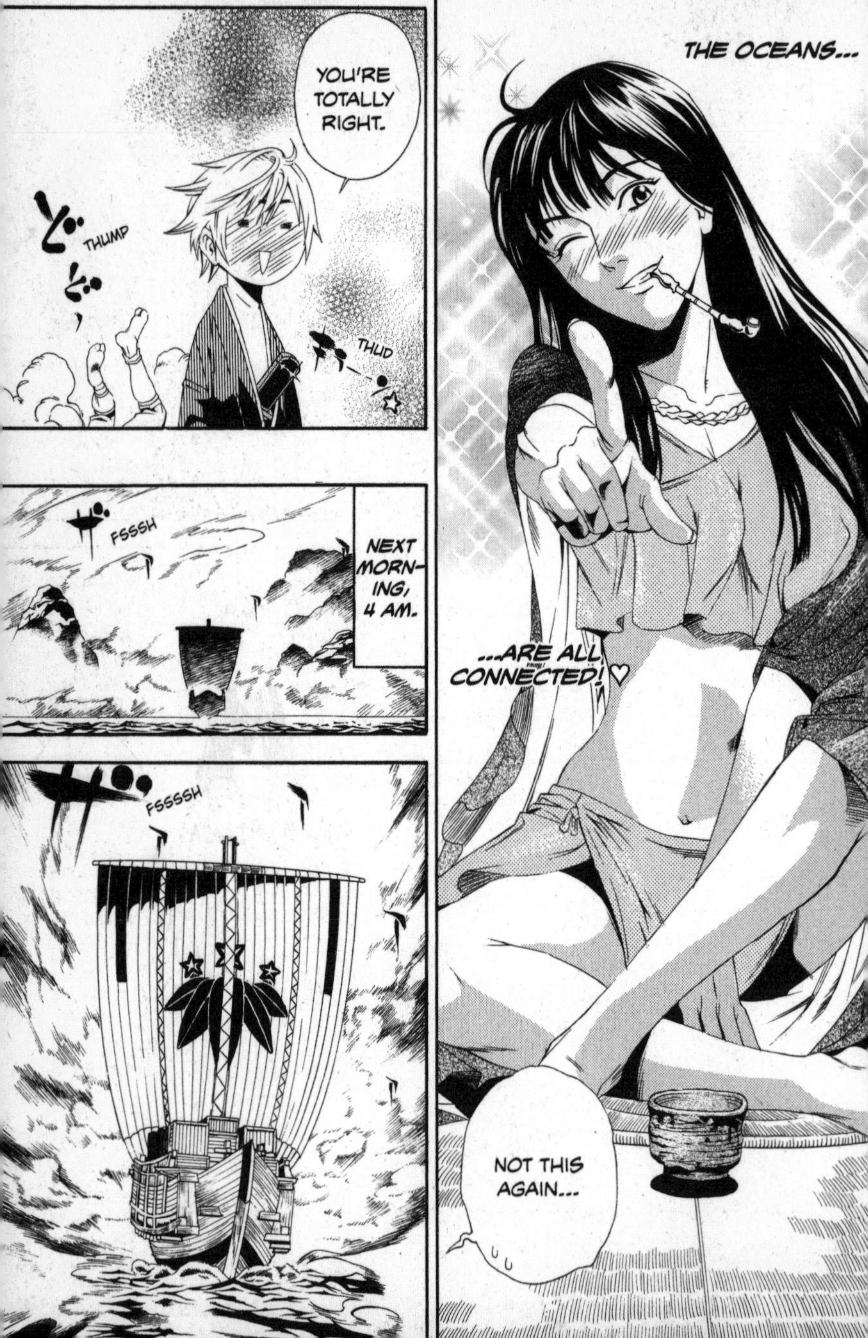
THE OCEANS...
...ARE ALL CONNECTED! ♡
NOT THIS AGAIN...
YOU'RE TOTALLY RIGHT.
THUMP
THUD
NEXT MORNING, 4 AM.
FSSSH
FSSSSH

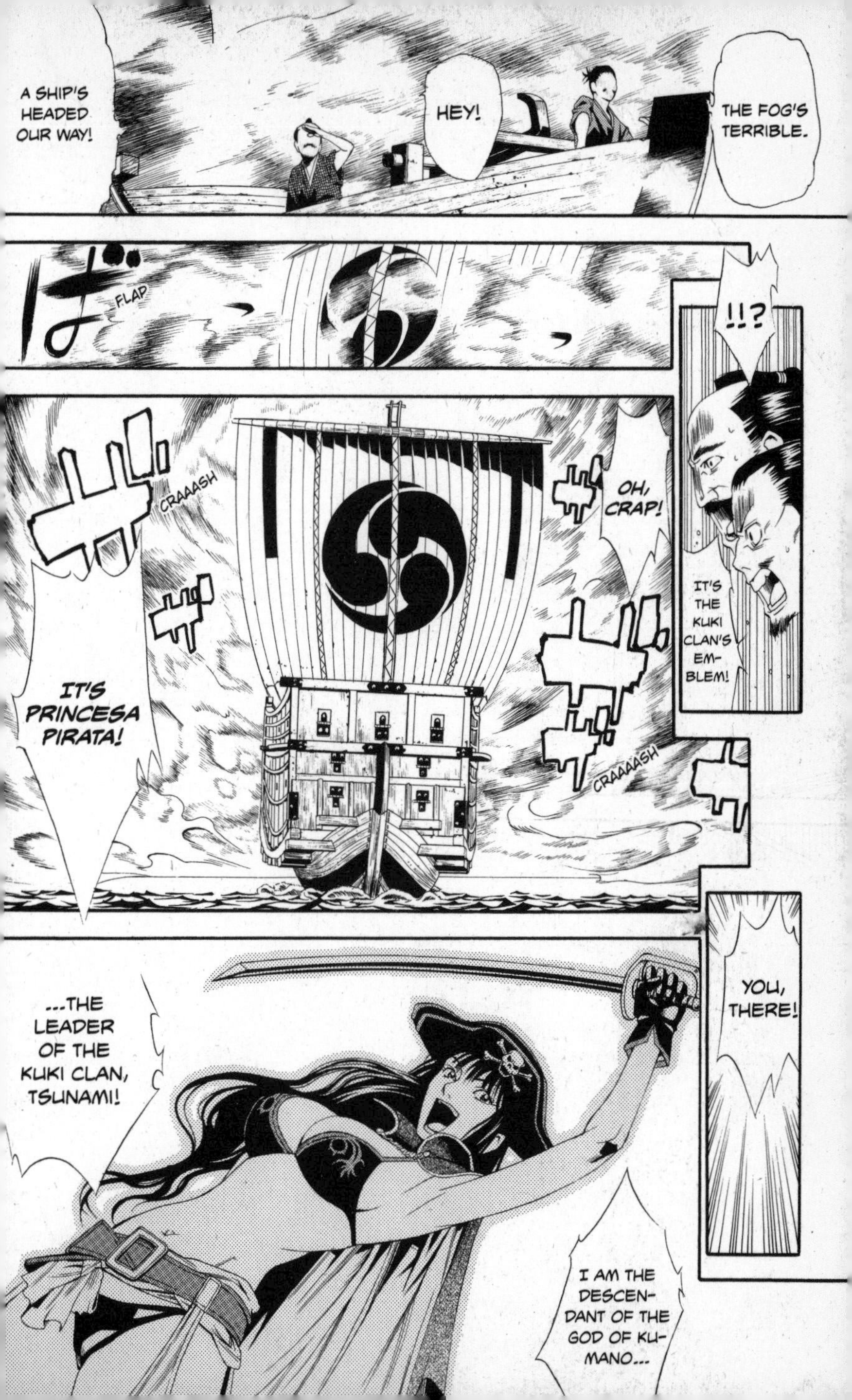
THE FOG'S TERRIBLE.
HEY!
A SHIP'S HEADED OUR WAY!
!!?
IT'S THE KUKI CLAN'S EM-BLEM!
FLAP
OH, CRAP!
CRAAASH
CRAAAASH
IT'S PRINCESA PIRATA!
YOU, THERE!
I AM THE DESCEN-DANT OF THE GOD OF KU-MANO...
...THE LEADER OF THE KUKI CLAN, TSUNAMI!

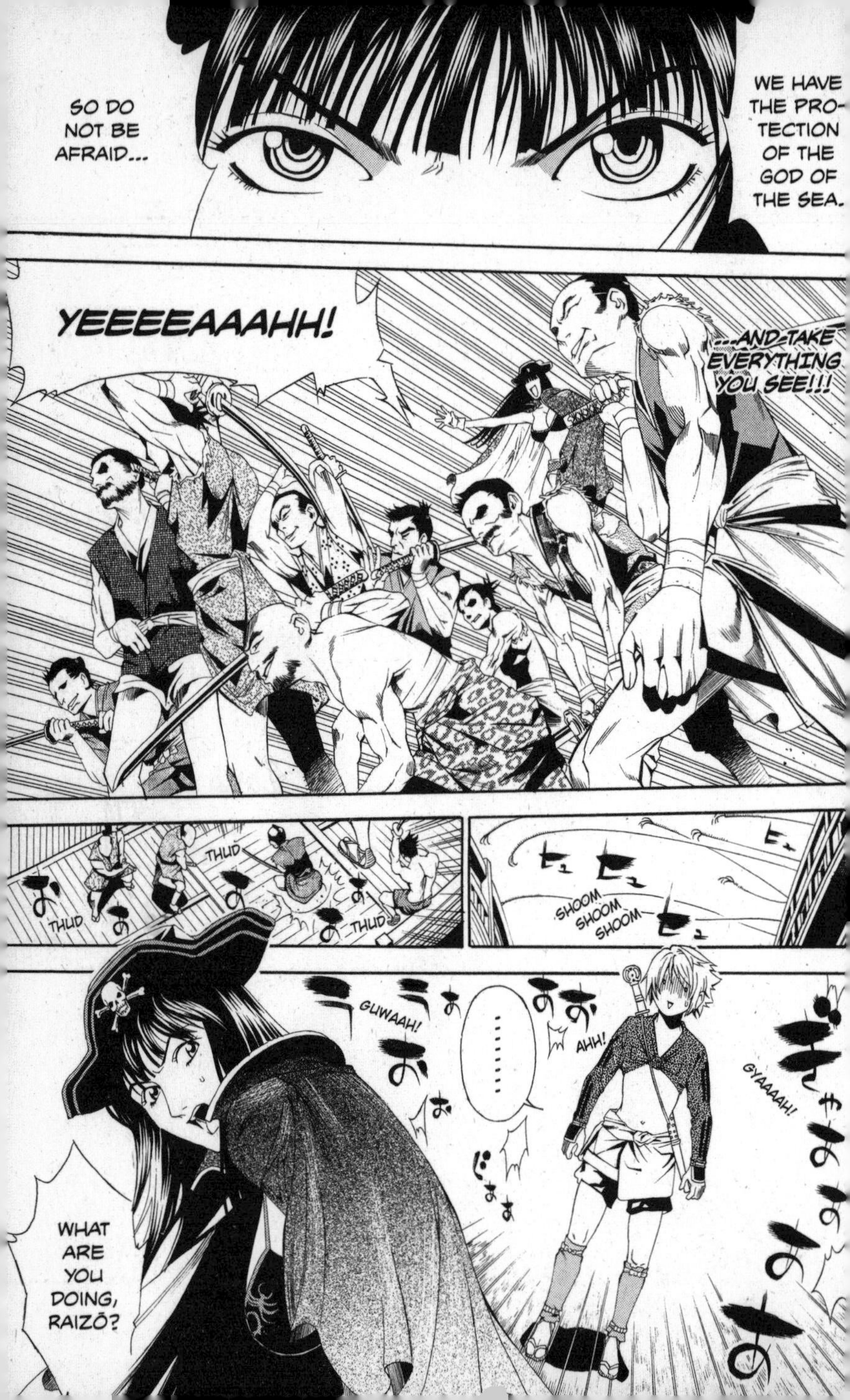
WE HAVE THE PROTECTION OF THE GOD OF THE SEA.
SO DO NOT BE AFRAID...
...AND TAKE EVERYTHING YOU SEE!!!
YEEEEEAAAHH!
SHOOM SHOOM SHOOM
THUD
THUD
THUD
GYAAAAH!
AHH!
......
GUWAAH!
WHAT ARE YOU DOING, RAIZŌ?

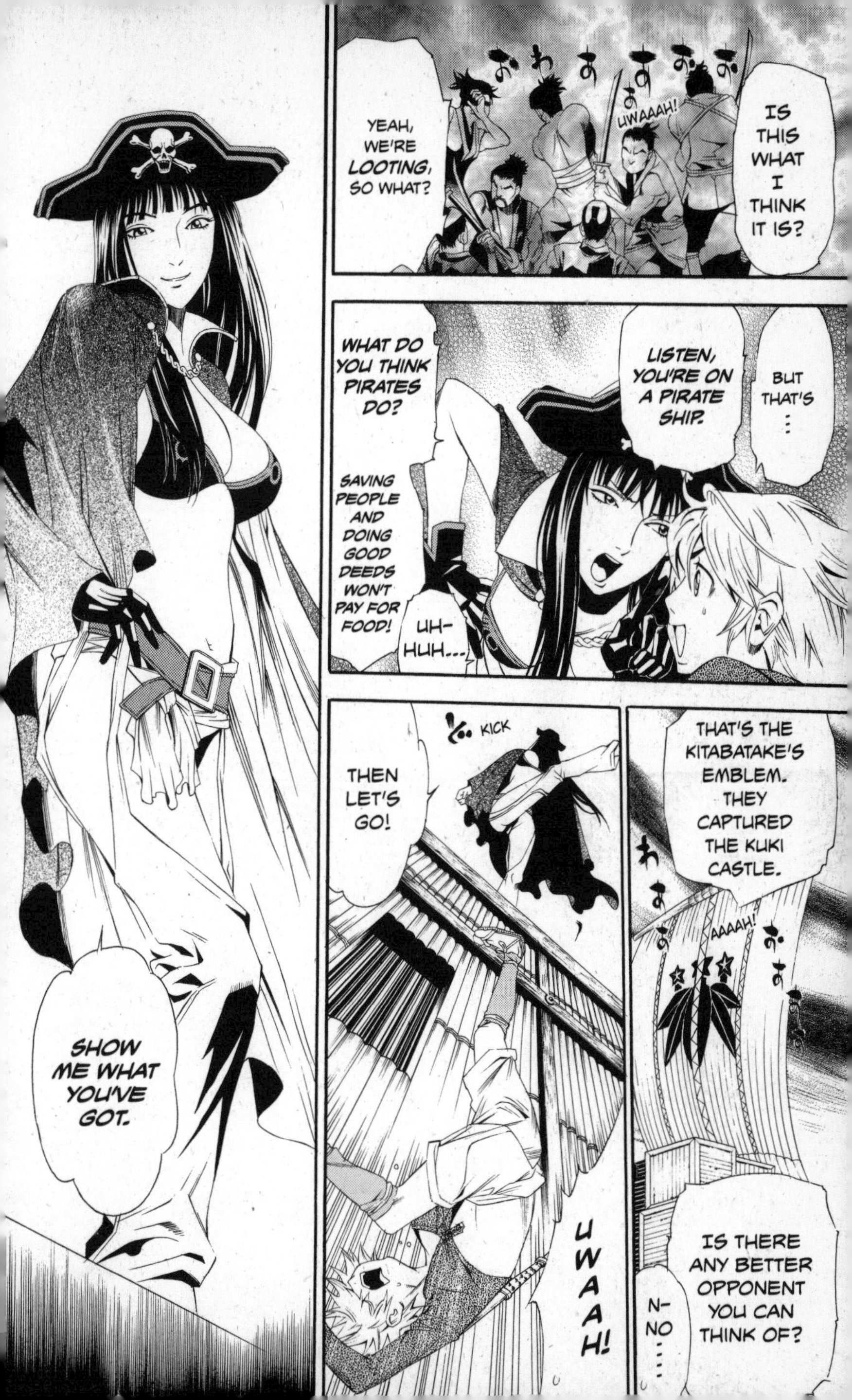
IS THIS WHAT I THINK IT IS?
UWAAAH!
YEAH, WE'RE LOOTING, SO WHAT?
BUT THAT'S ...
LISTEN, YOU'RE ON A PIRATE SHIP.
WHAT DO YOU THINK PIRATES DO?
SAVING PEOPLE AND DOING GOOD DEEDS WON'T PAY FOR FOOD!
UH-HUH...
THAT'S THE KITABATAKE'S EMBLEM. THEY CAPTURED THE KUKI CASTLE.
AAAAH!
IS THERE ANY BETTER OPPONENT YOU CAN THINK OF?
N-NO...
KICK
THEN LET'S GO!
UWAAAH!
SHOW ME WHAT YOU'VE GOT.

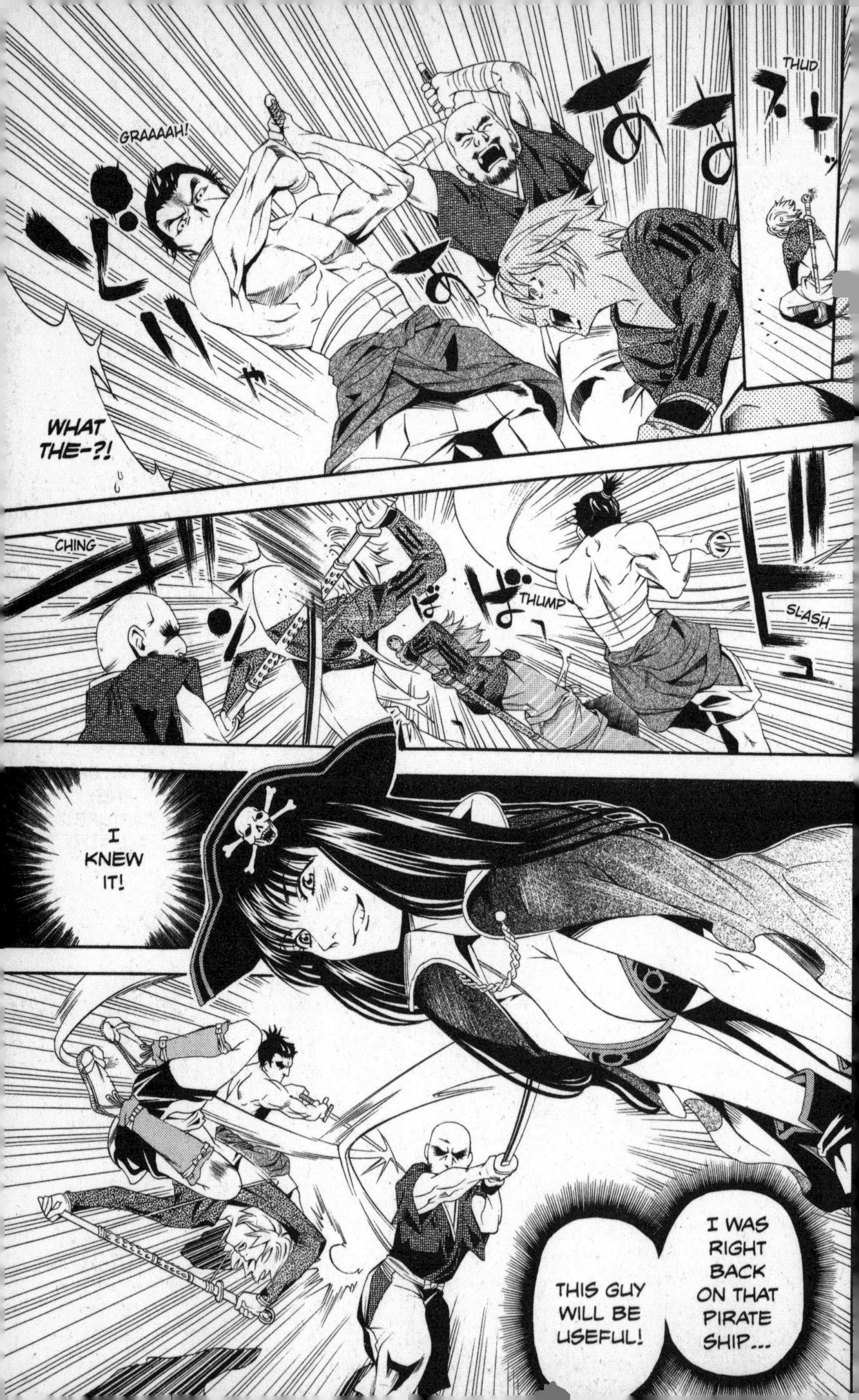
THUD
GRAAAAH!
WHAT THE-?!
SLASH
THUMP
CHING
I KNEW IT!
I WAS RIGHT BACK ON THAT PIRATE SHIP...
THIS GUY WILL BE USEFUL!

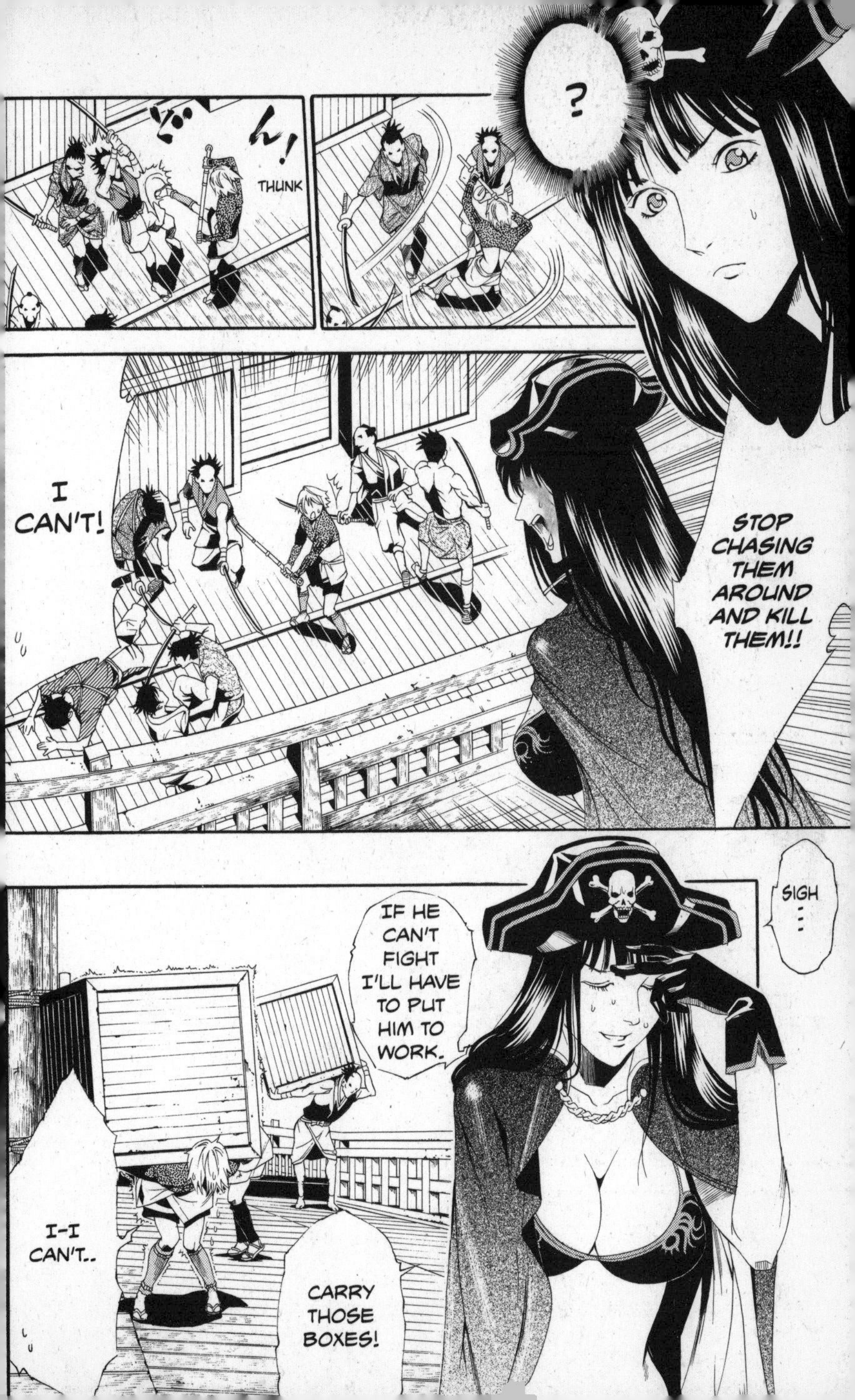
?
THUNK
STOP CHASING THEM AROUND AND KILL THEM!!
I CAN'T!
SIGH...
IF HE CAN'T FIGHT I'LL HAVE TO PUT HIM TO WORK.
CARRY THOSE BOXES!
I-I CAN'T..

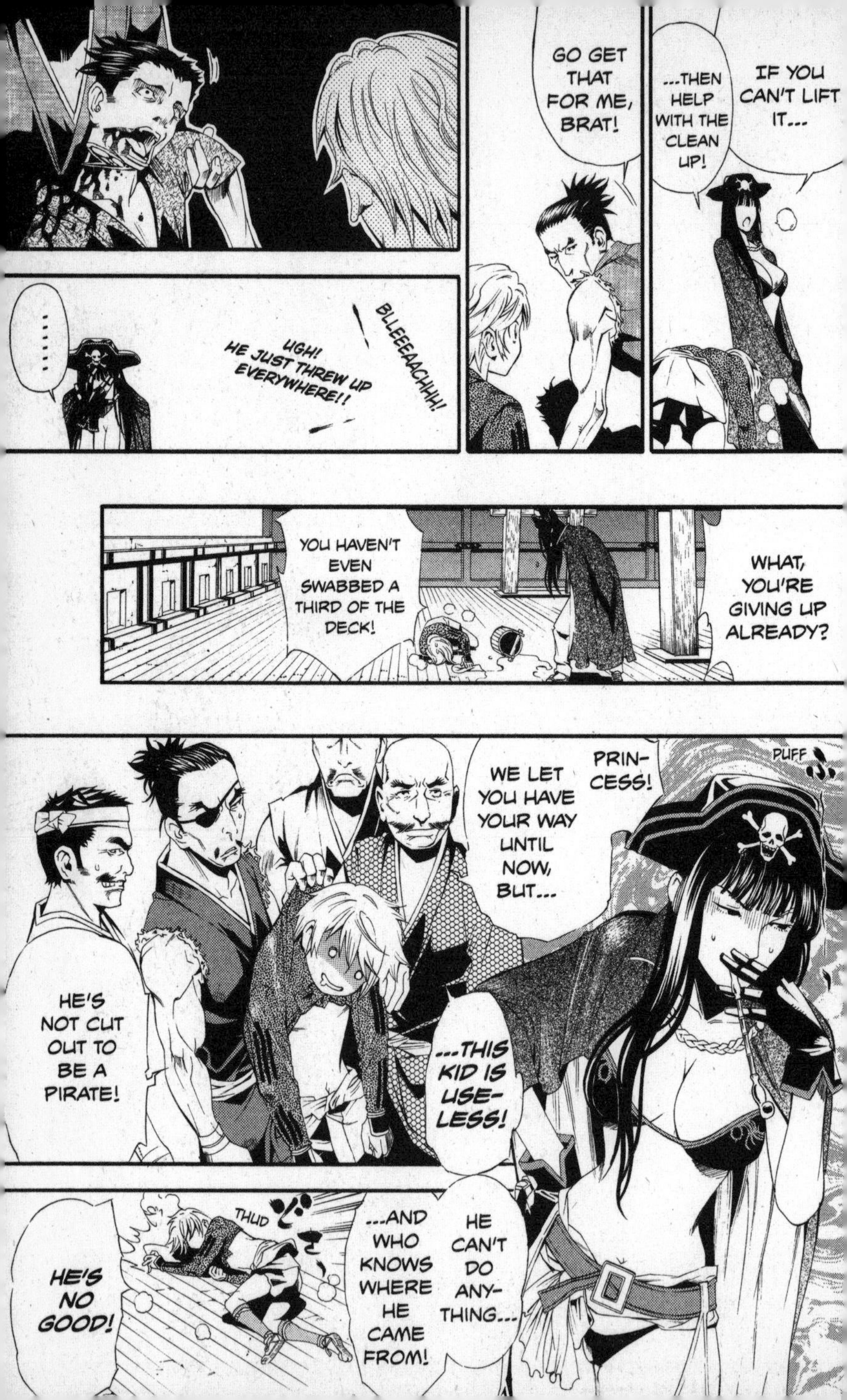
IF YOU CAN'T LIFT IT...
...THEN HELP WITH THE CLEAN UP!
GO GET THAT FOR ME, BRAT!
BLLEEEAACHHH!
UGH! HE JUST THREW UP EVERYWHERE!!
......
WHAT, YOU'RE GIVING UP ALREADY?
YOU HAVEN'T EVEN SWABBED A THIRD OF THE DECK!
PUFF
PRIN-CESS!
WE LET YOU HAVE YOUR WAY UNTIL NOW, BUT...
...THIS KID IS USE-LESS!
HE'S NOT CUT OUT TO BE A PIRATE!
HE CAN'T DO ANY-THING...
...AND WHO KNOWS WHERE HE CAME FROM!
THUD
HE'S NO GOOD!

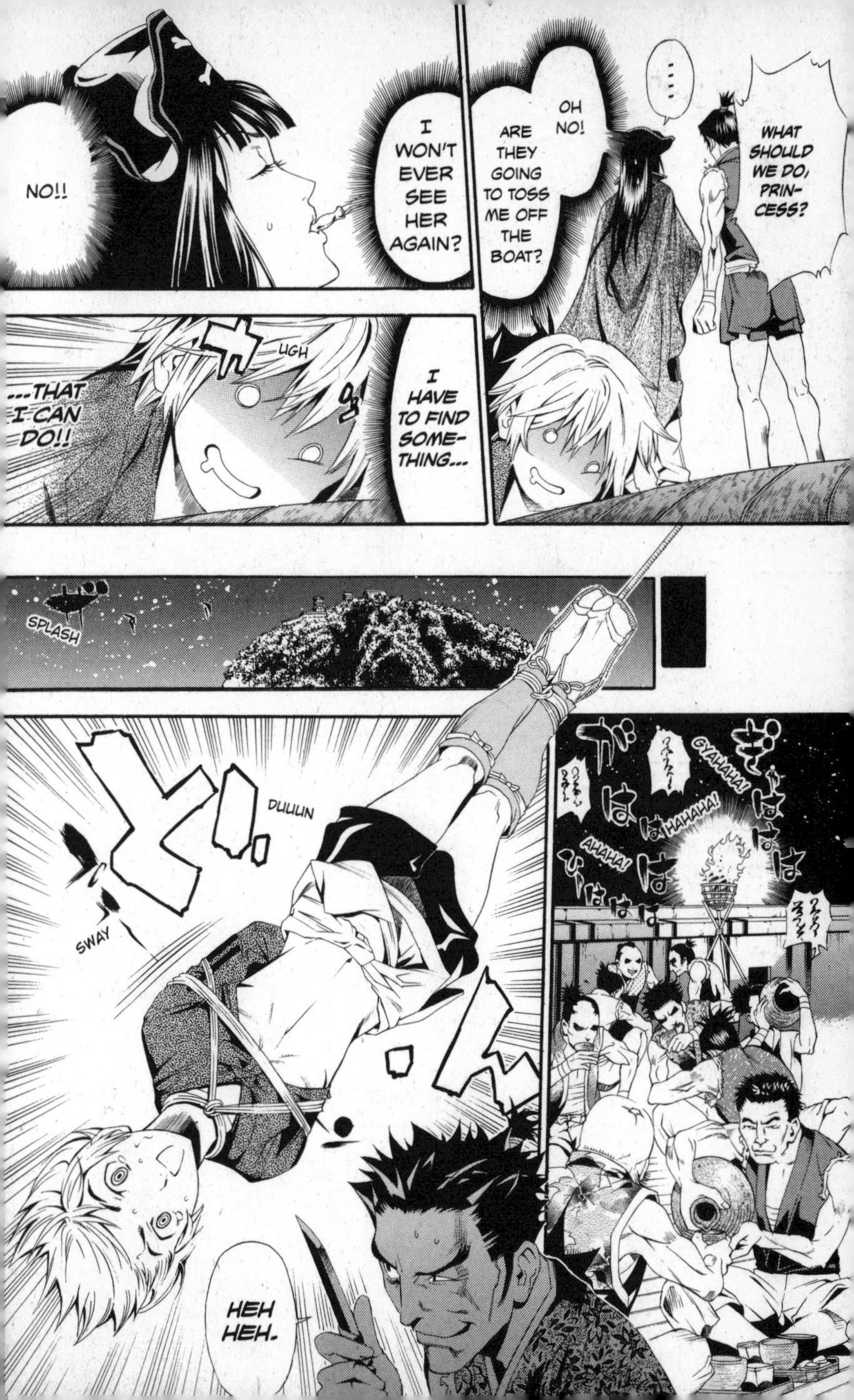

WHAT SHOULD WE DO, PRINCESS?
......
OH NO!
ARE THEY GOING TO TOSS ME OFF THE BOAT?
I WON'T EVER SEE HER AGAIN?
NO!!
I HAVE TO FIND SOMETHING...
UGH
...THAT I CAN DO!!
SPLASH
GYAHAHA!
HAHAHA!
AHAHA!
DUUUN
SWAY
HEH HEH.

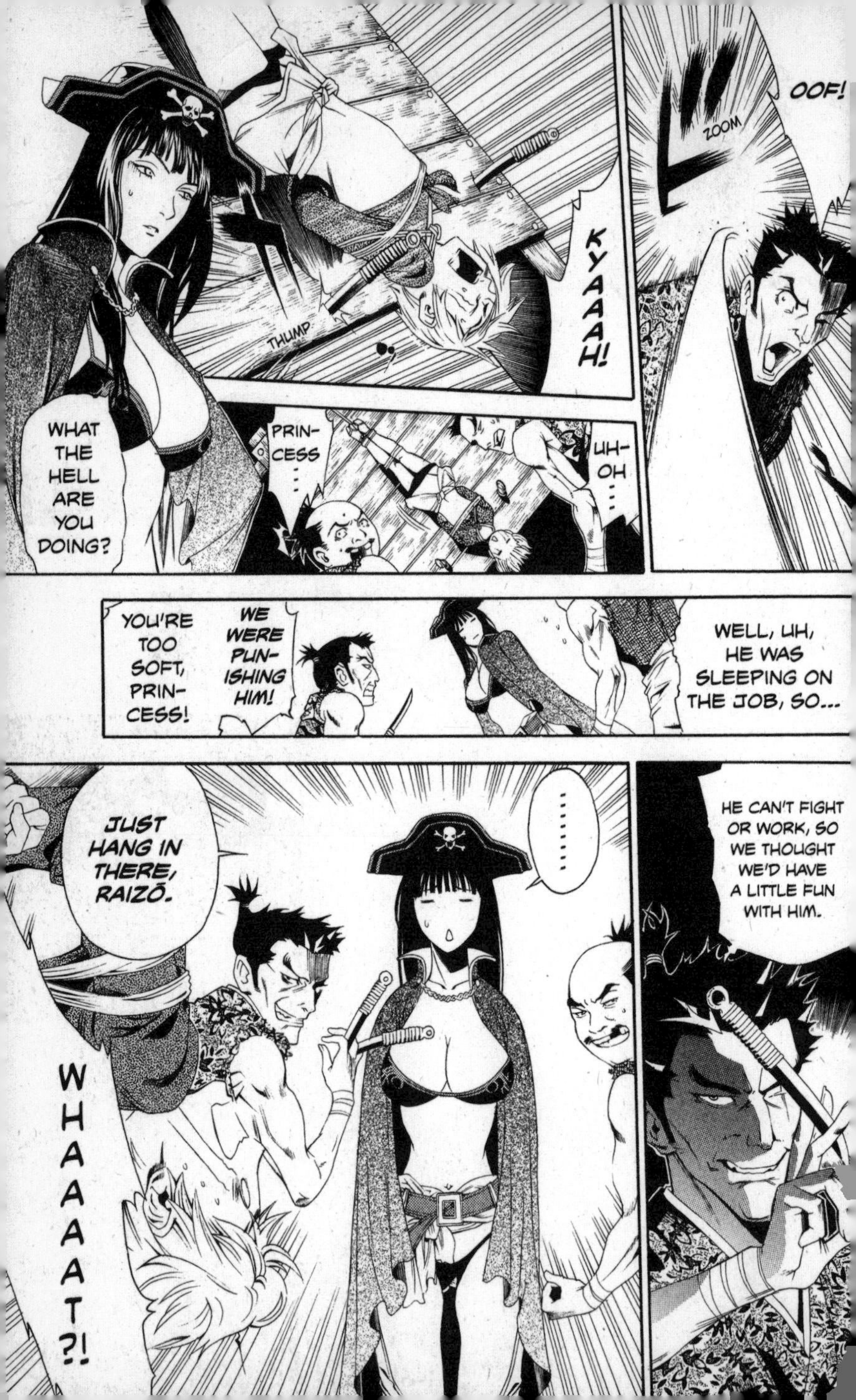
OOF!
ZOOM
KYAAAAH!
THUMP
UH-OH...
PRIN-CESS...
WHAT THE HELL ARE YOU DOING?
WELL, UH, HE WAS SLEEPING ON THE JOB, SO...
WE WERE PUN-ISHING HIM!
YOU'RE TOO SOFT, PRIN-CESS!
HE CAN'T FIGHT OR WORK, SO WE THOUGHT WE'D HAVE A LITTLE FUN WITH HIM.
......
JUST HANG IN THERE, RAIZŌ.
WHAAAAAT?!

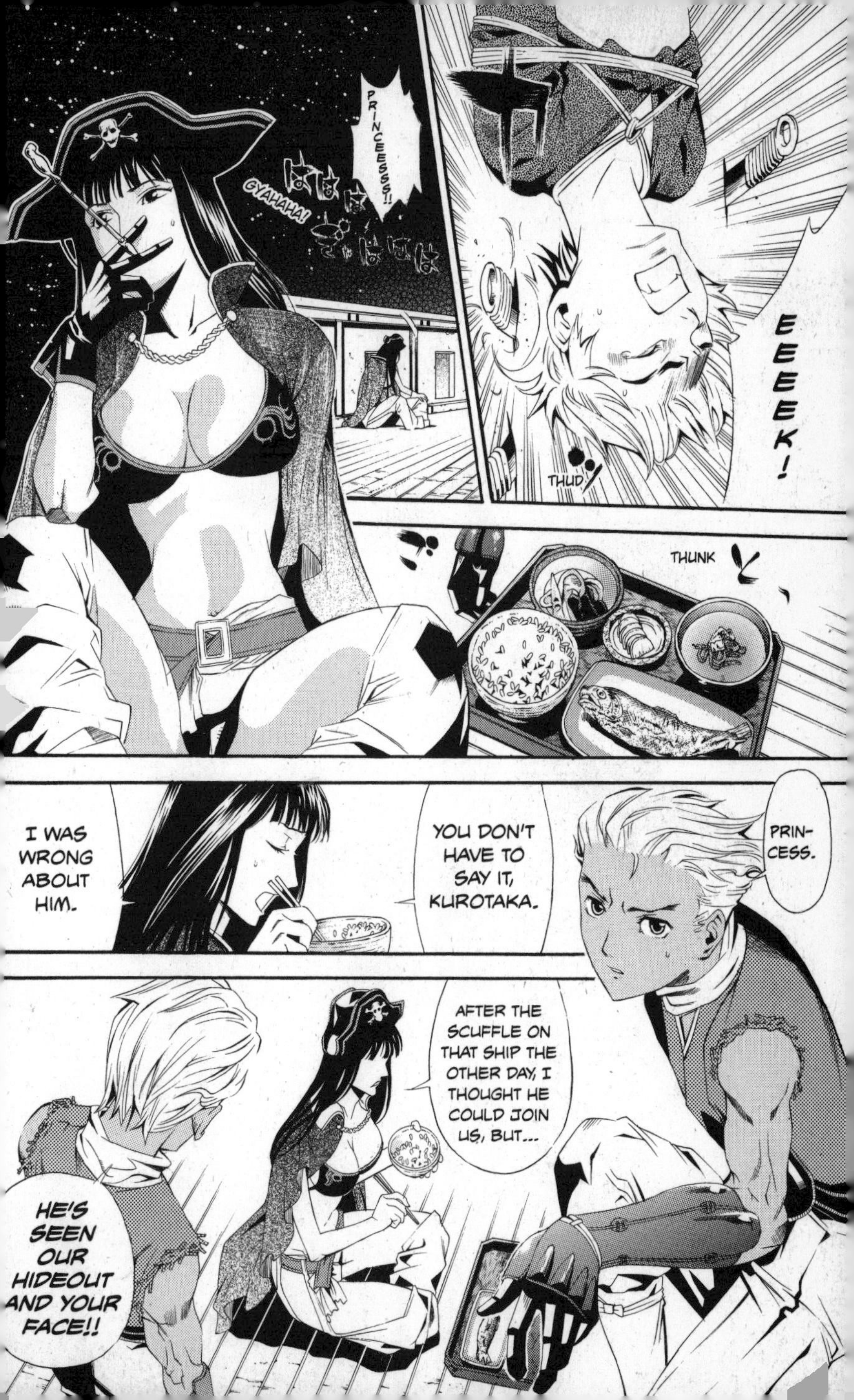
EEEEK!
THUD
THUNK
PRINCESSS!!
GYAHAHA!
PRIN-CESS.
YOU DON'T HAVE TO SAY IT, KUROTAKA.
I WAS WRONG ABOUT HIM.
AFTER THE SCUFFLE ON THAT SHIP THE OTHER DAY, I THOUGHT HE COULD JOIN US, BUT...
HE'S SEEN OUR HIDEOUT AND YOUR FACE!!

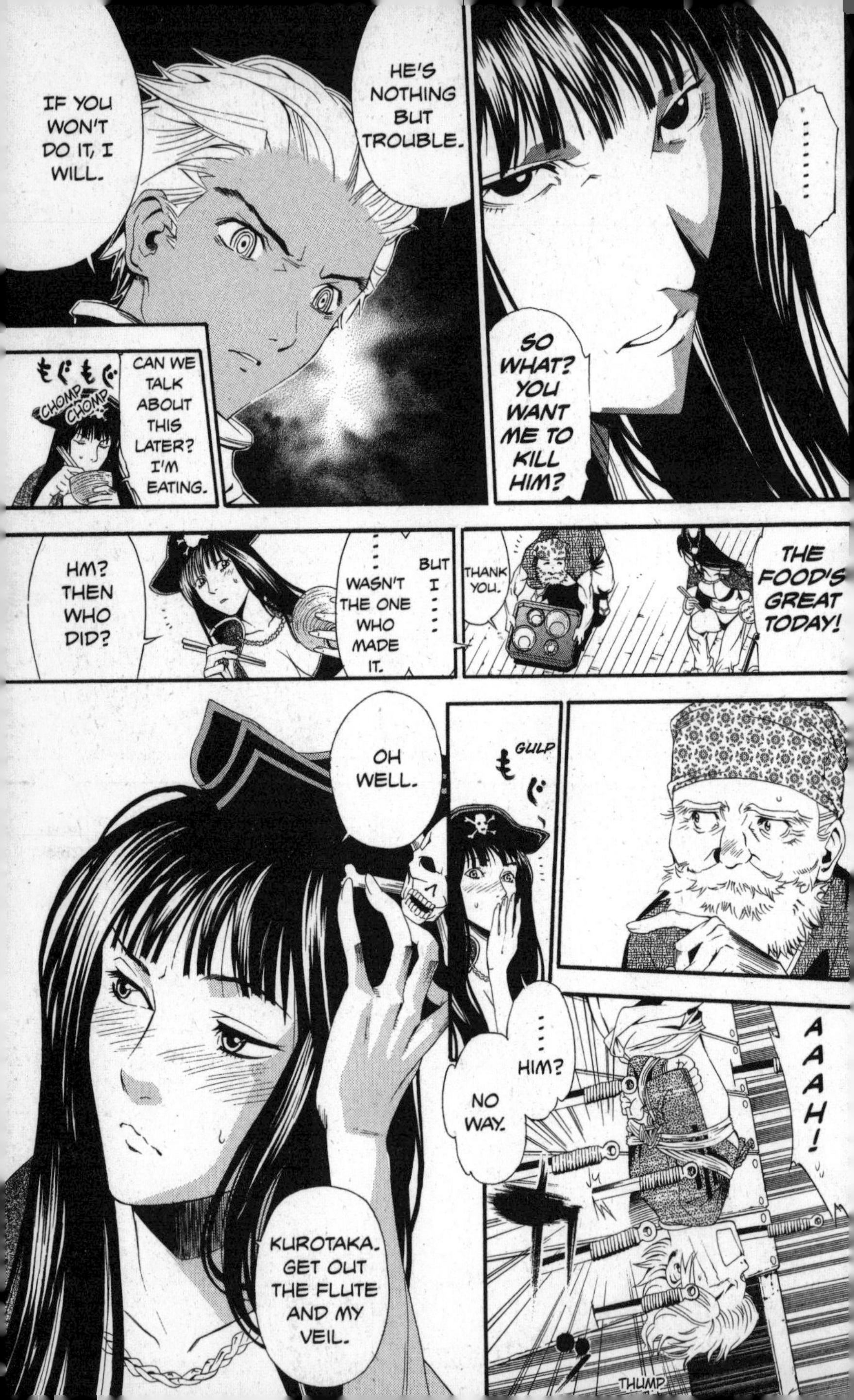
......
SO WHAT? YOU WANT ME TO KILL HIM?
HE'S NOTHING BUT TROUBLE.
IF YOU WON'T DO IT, I WILL.
CAN WE TALK ABOUT THIS LATER? I'M EATING.
もぐもぐ CHOMP CHOMP
THE FOOD'S GREAT TODAY!
THANK YOU.
BUT I ...... WASN'T THE ONE WHO MADE IT.
HM? THEN WHO DID?
もぐ GULP
AAAAH!
... HIM?
NO WAY.
THUMP
OH WELL.
KUROTAKA. GET OUT THE FLUTE AND MY VEIL.

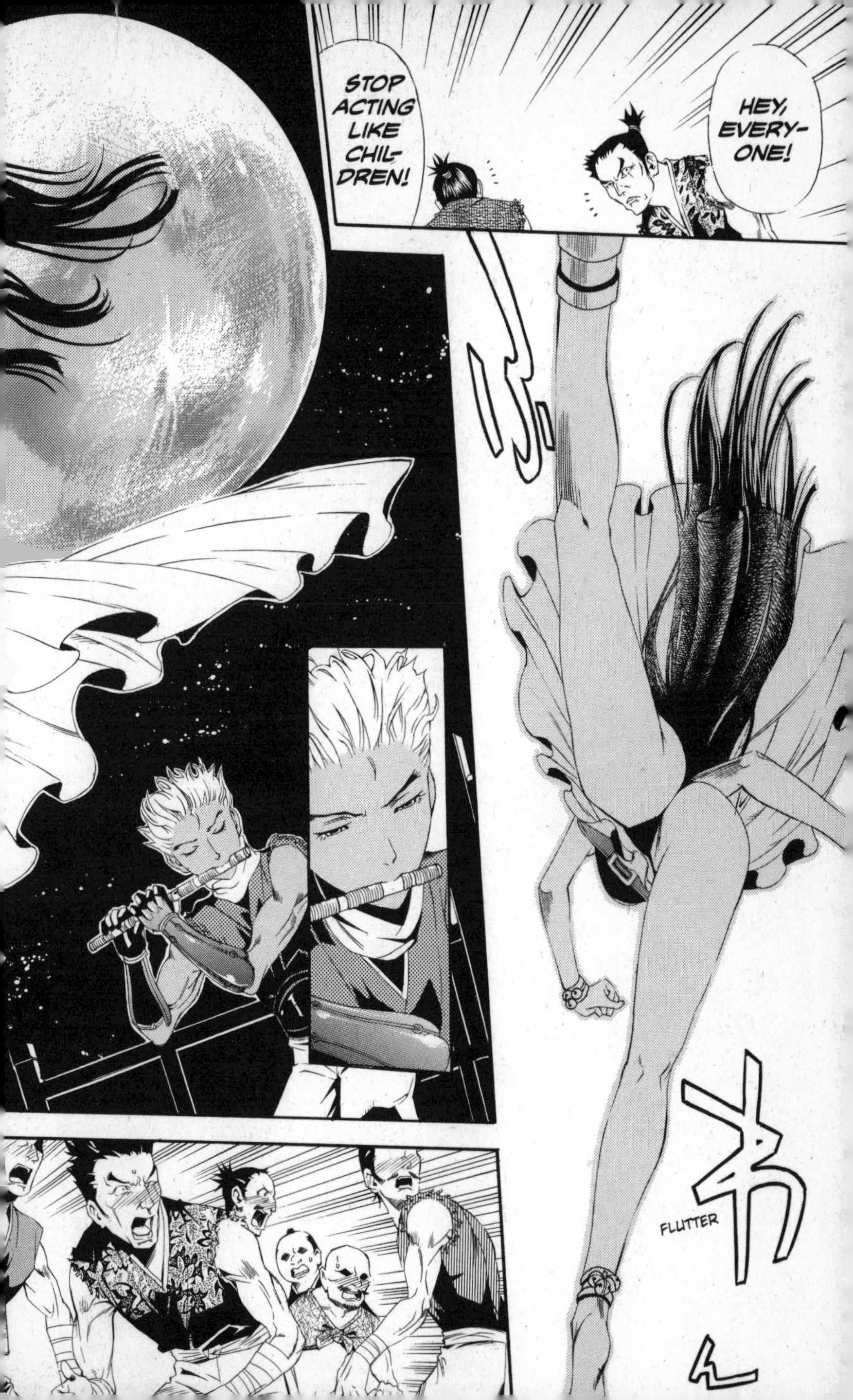
HEY, EVERY-ONE!
STOP ACTING LIKE CHIL-DREN!
FLUTTER

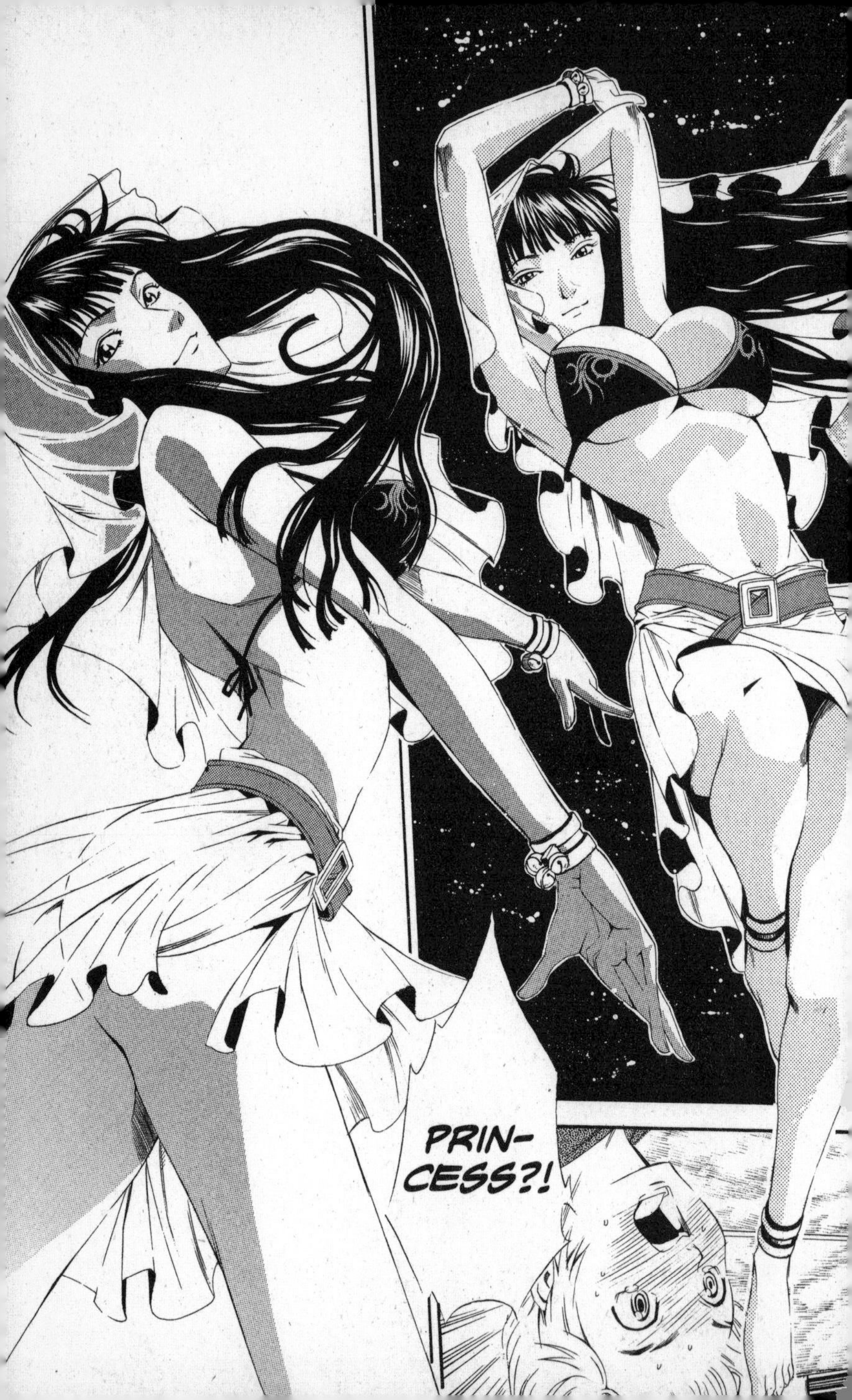
PRIN-
CESS?!

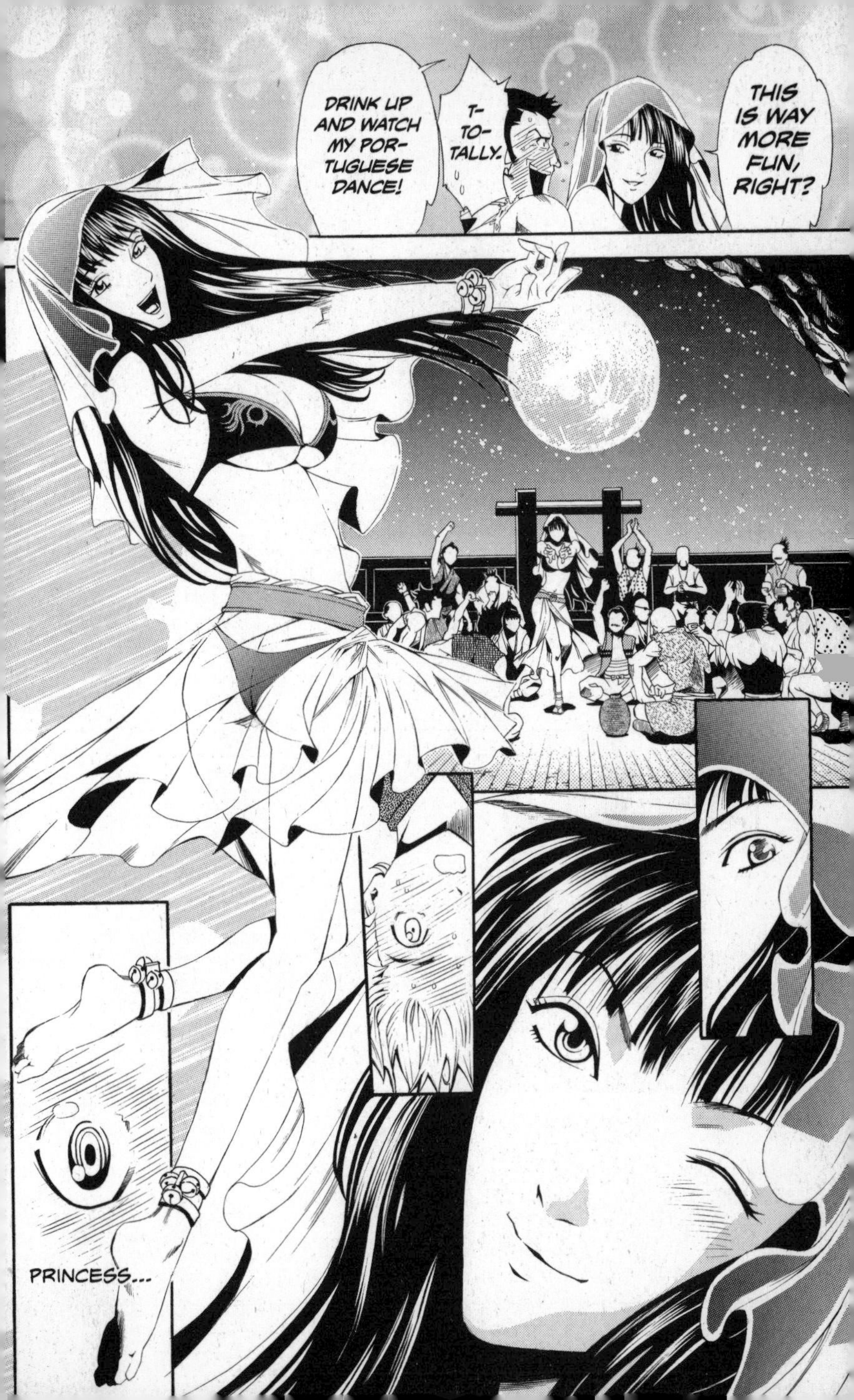
THIS IS WAY MORE FUN, RIGHT?
T-TO-TALLY.
DRINK UP AND WATCH MY POR-TUGUESE DANCE!
PRINCESS...

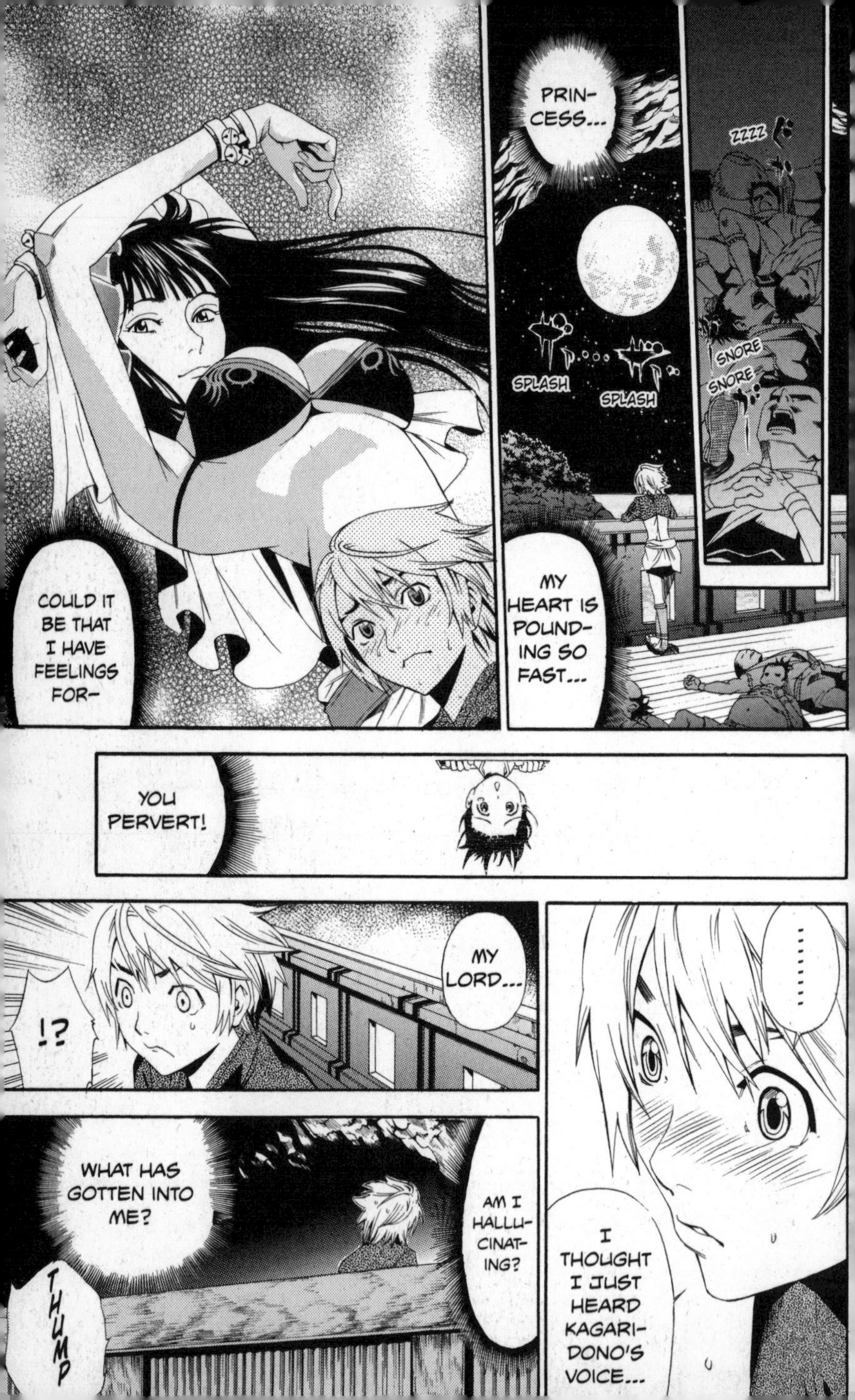
ZZZZ
SNORE
SNORE
PRINCESS...
SPLASH
SPLASH
MY HEART IS POUNDING SO FAST...
COULD IT BE THAT I HAVE FEELINGS FOR-
YOU PERVERT!
......
I THOUGHT I JUST HEARD KAGARI-DONO'S VOICE...
MY LORD...
!?
AM I HALLUCINATING?
WHAT HAS GOTTEN INTO ME?
THUMP

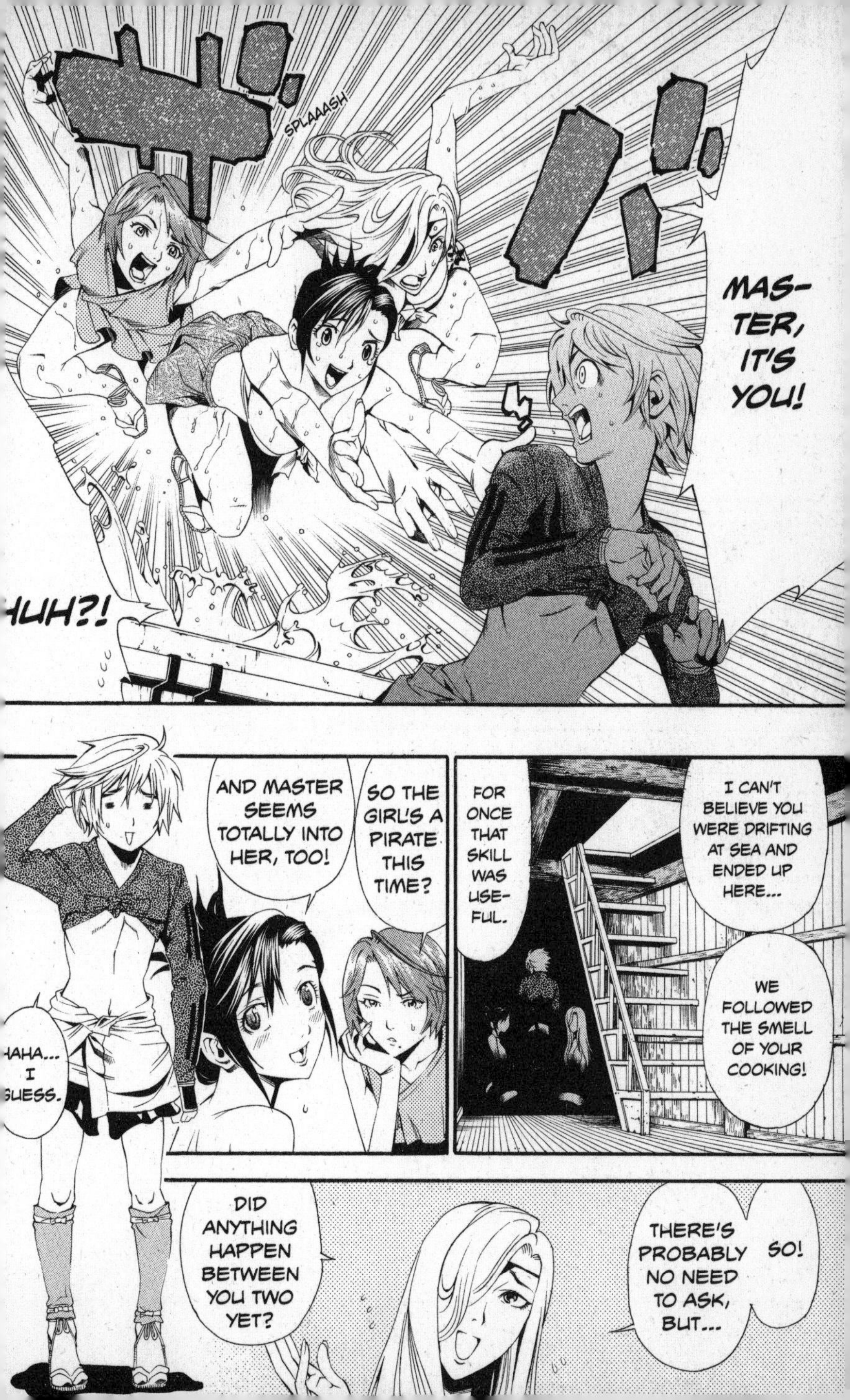
SPLAAASH
MASTER, IT'S YOU!
HUH?!
I CAN'T BELIEVE YOU WERE DRIFTING AT SEA AND ENDED UP HERE...
WE FOLLOWED THE SMELL OF YOUR COOKING!
FOR ONCE THAT SKILL WAS USEFUL.
SO THE GIRL'S A PIRATE THIS TIME?
AND MASTER SEEMS TOTALLY INTO HER, TOO!
HAHA... I GUESS.
SO!
THERE'S PROBABLY NO NEED TO ASK, BUT...
DID ANYTHING HAPPEN BETWEEN YOU TWO YET?

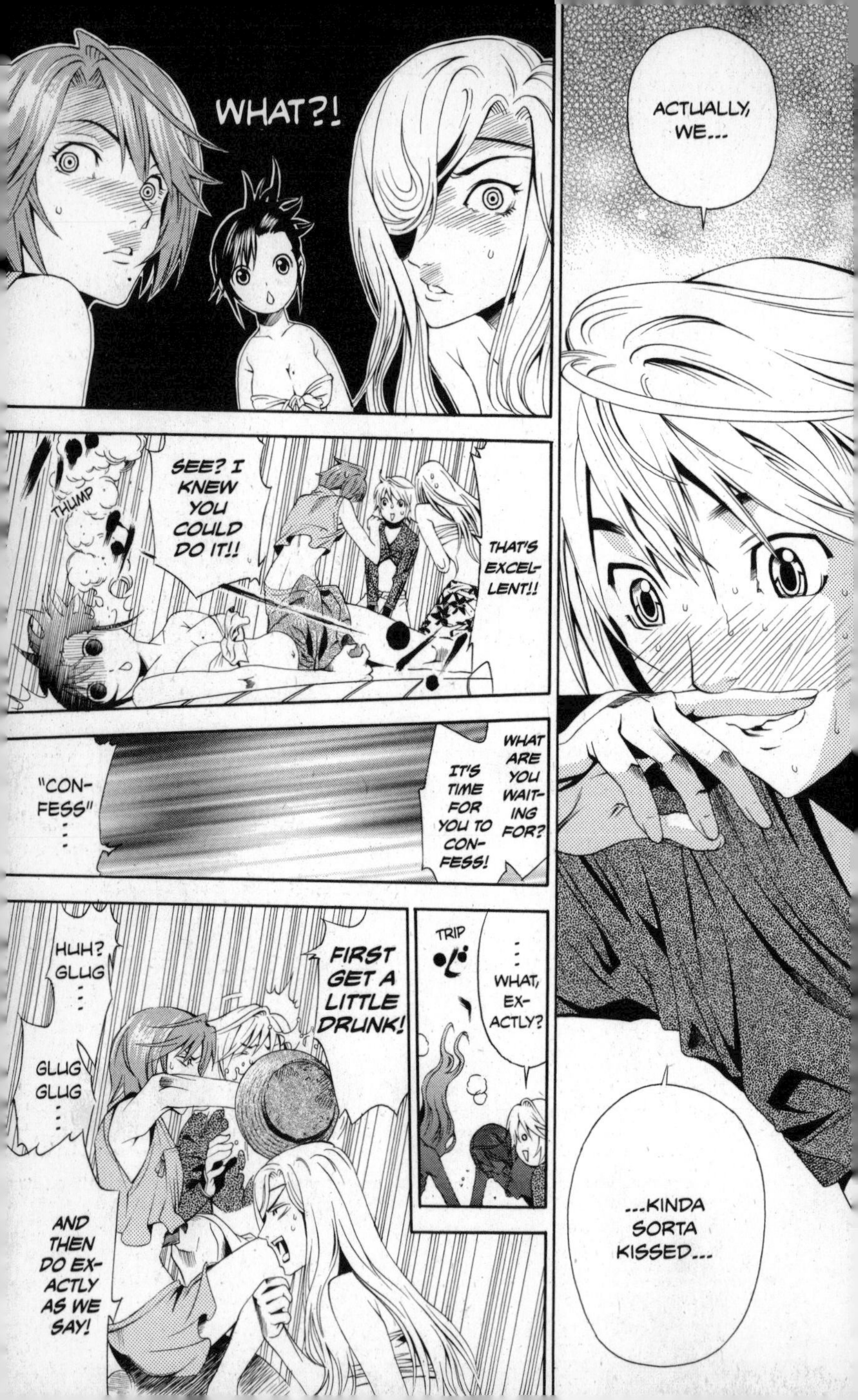
ACTUALLY, WE...
...KINDA SORTA KISSED...
WHAT?!
THAT'S EXCEL-LENT!!
SEE? I KNEW YOU COULD DO IT!!
THUMP
WHAT ARE YOU WAIT-ING FOR?
IT'S TIME FOR YOU TO CON-FESS!
"CON-FESS"...
...WHAT, EX-ACTLY?
TRIP
FIRST GET A LITTLE DRUNK!
HUH? GLUG...
GLUG GLUG...
AND THEN DO EX-ACTLY AS WE SAY!

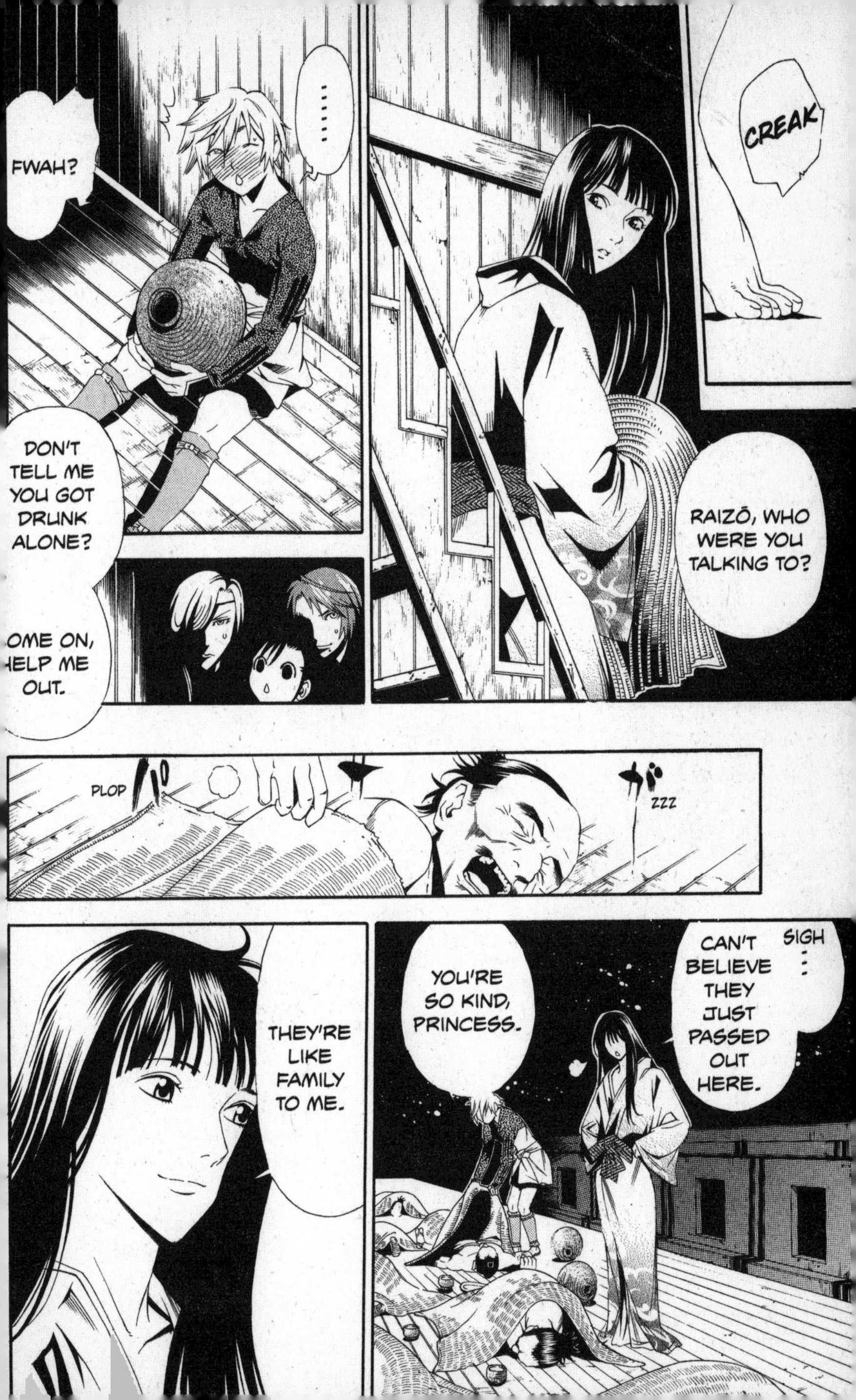
CREAK
RAIZŌ, WHO WERE YOU TALKING TO?
......
FWAH?
DON'T TELL ME YOU GOT DRUNK ALONE?
OME ON, HELP ME OUT.
ZZZ
PLOP
SIGH...
CAN'T BELIEVE THEY JUST PASSED OUT HERE.
YOU'RE SO KIND, PRINCESS.
THEY'RE LIKE FAMILY TO ME.

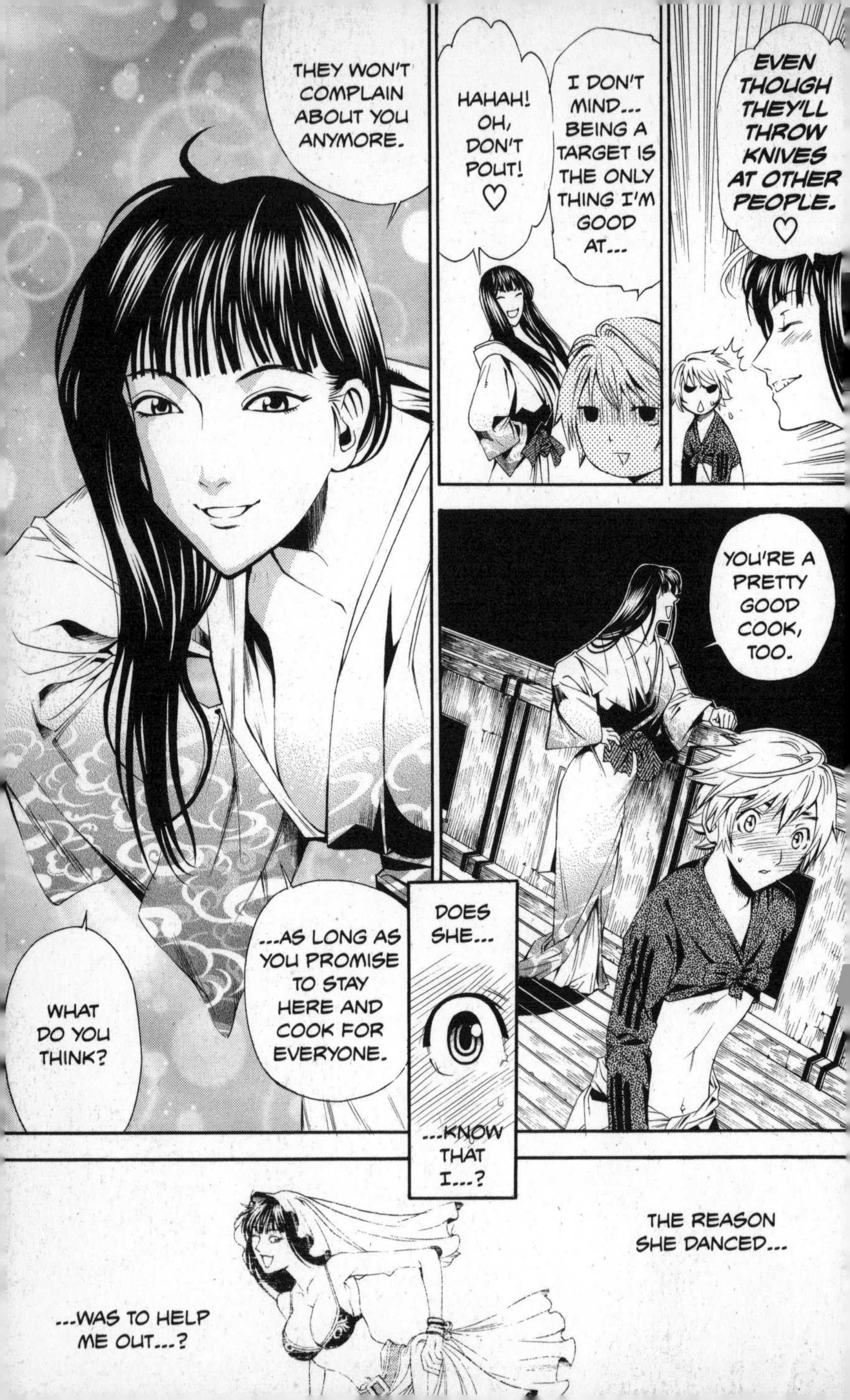
EVEN THOUGH THEY'LL THROW KNIVES AT OTHER PEOPLE. ♡
I DON'T MIND... BEING A TARGET IS THE ONLY THING I'M GOOD AT...
HAHAH! OH, DON'T POUT! ♡
YOU'RE A PRETTY GOOD COOK, TOO.
THEY WON'T COMPLAIN ABOUT YOU ANYMORE.
...AS LONG AS YOU PROMISE TO STAY HERE AND COOK FOR EVERYONE.
WHAT DO YOU THINK?
DOES SHE...
...KNOW THAT I...?
THE REASON SHE DANCED...
...WAS TO HELP ME OUT...?

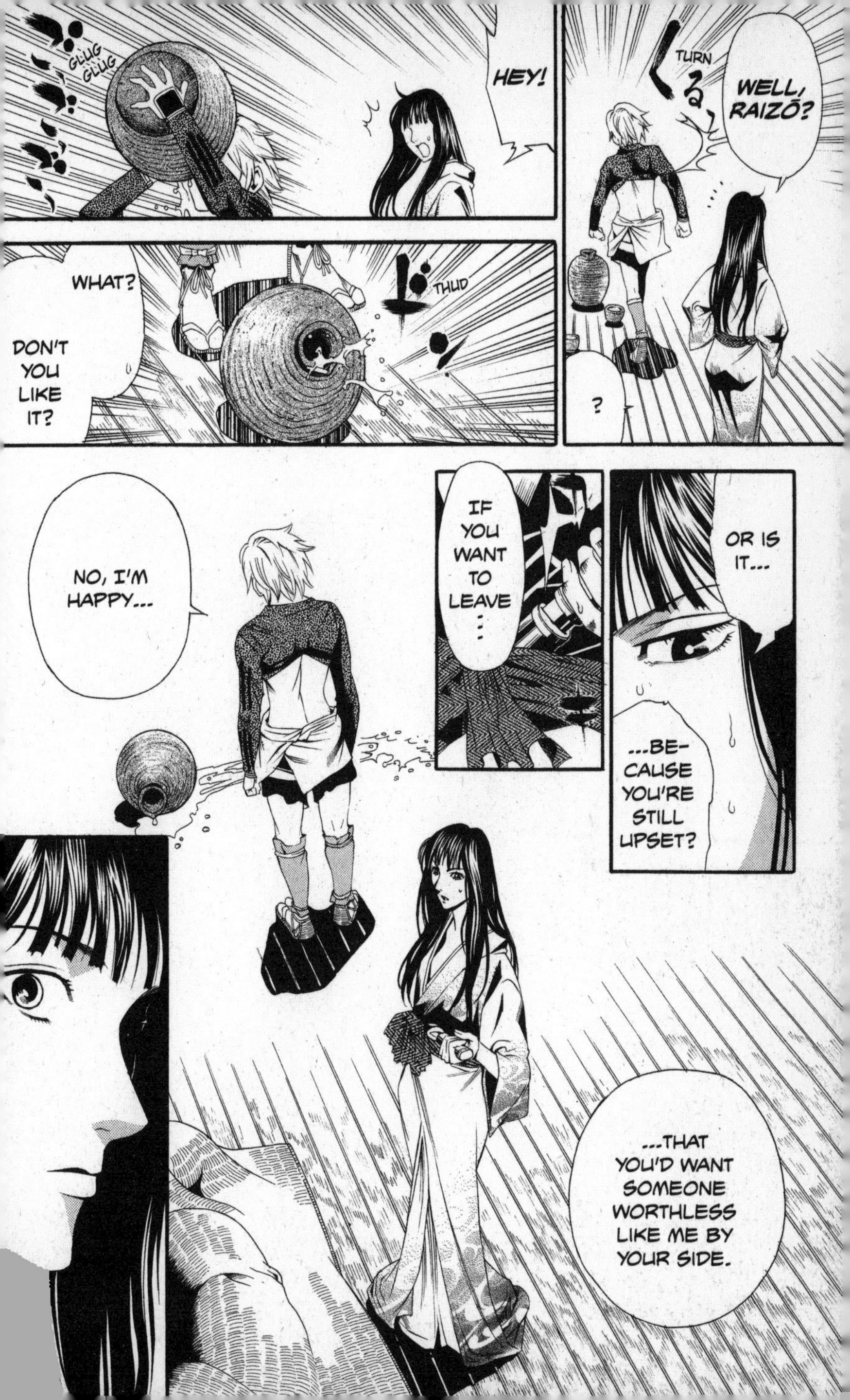
WELL, RAIZŌ?
TURN
...
?
GLUG GLUG
HEY!
THUD
WHAT?
DON'T YOU LIKE IT?
OR IS IT...
...BE-CAUSE YOU'RE STILL UPSET?
IF YOU WANT TO LEAVE...
NO, I'M HAPPY...
...THAT YOU'D WANT SOMEONE WORTHLESS LIKE ME BY YOUR SIDE.

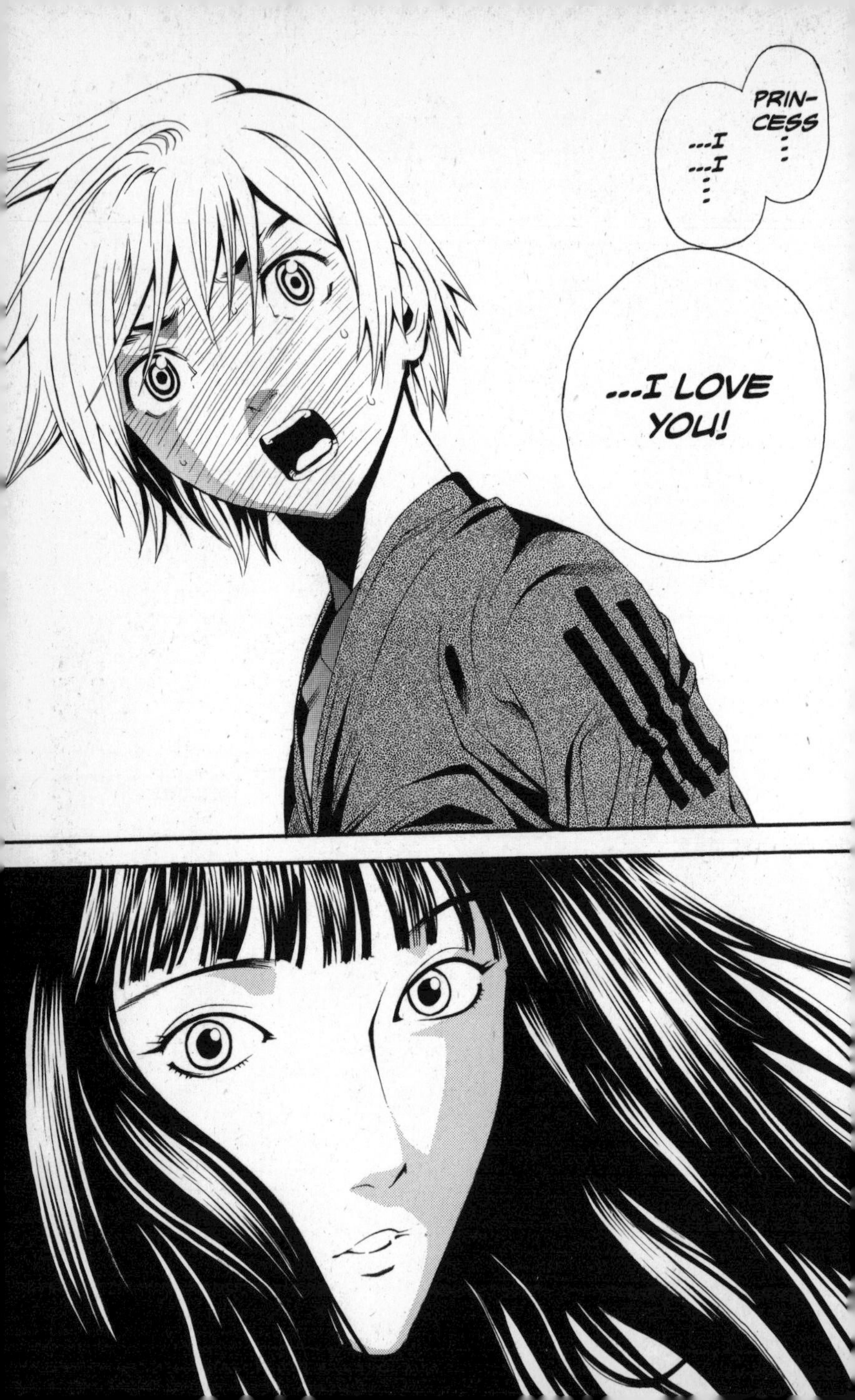
PRIN-CESS...
---I ---I...
---I LOVE YOU!

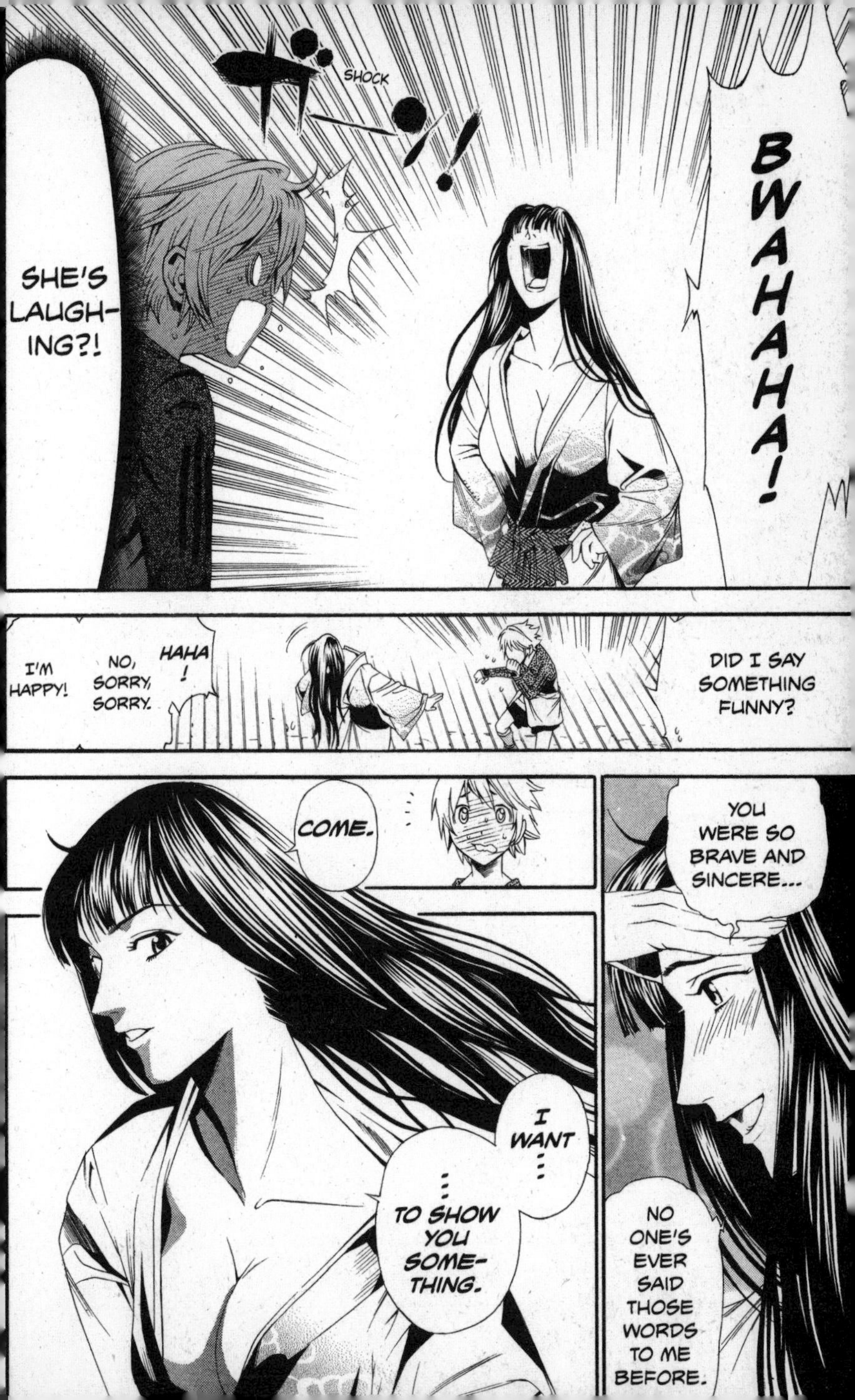
BWAHAHA!
SHOCK
SHE'S LAUGHING?!
DID I SAY SOMETHING FUNNY?
HAHA!
NO, SORRY, SORRY.
I'M HAPPY!
YOU WERE SO BRAVE AND SINCERE...
NO ONE'S EVER SAID THOSE WORDS TO ME BEFORE.
COME.
I WANT...
...TO SHOW YOU SOMETHING.

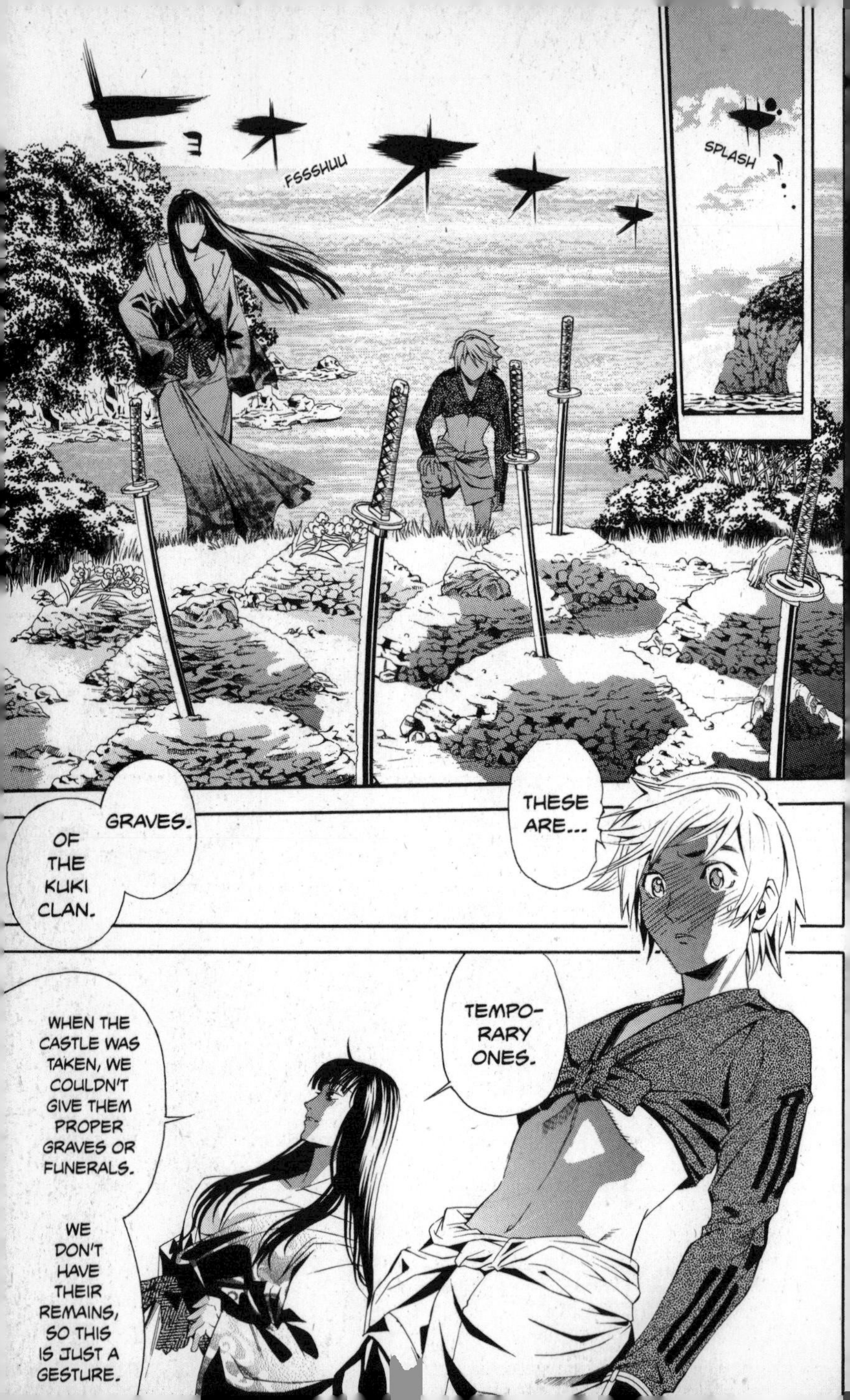
SPLASH
FSSSHUU
THESE ARE...
GRAVES.
OF THE KUKI CLAN.
TEMPORARY ONES.
WHEN THE CASTLE WAS TAKEN, WE COULDN'T GIVE THEM PROPER GRAVES OR FUNERALS.
WE DON'T HAVE THEIR REMAINS, SO THIS IS JUST A GESTURE.

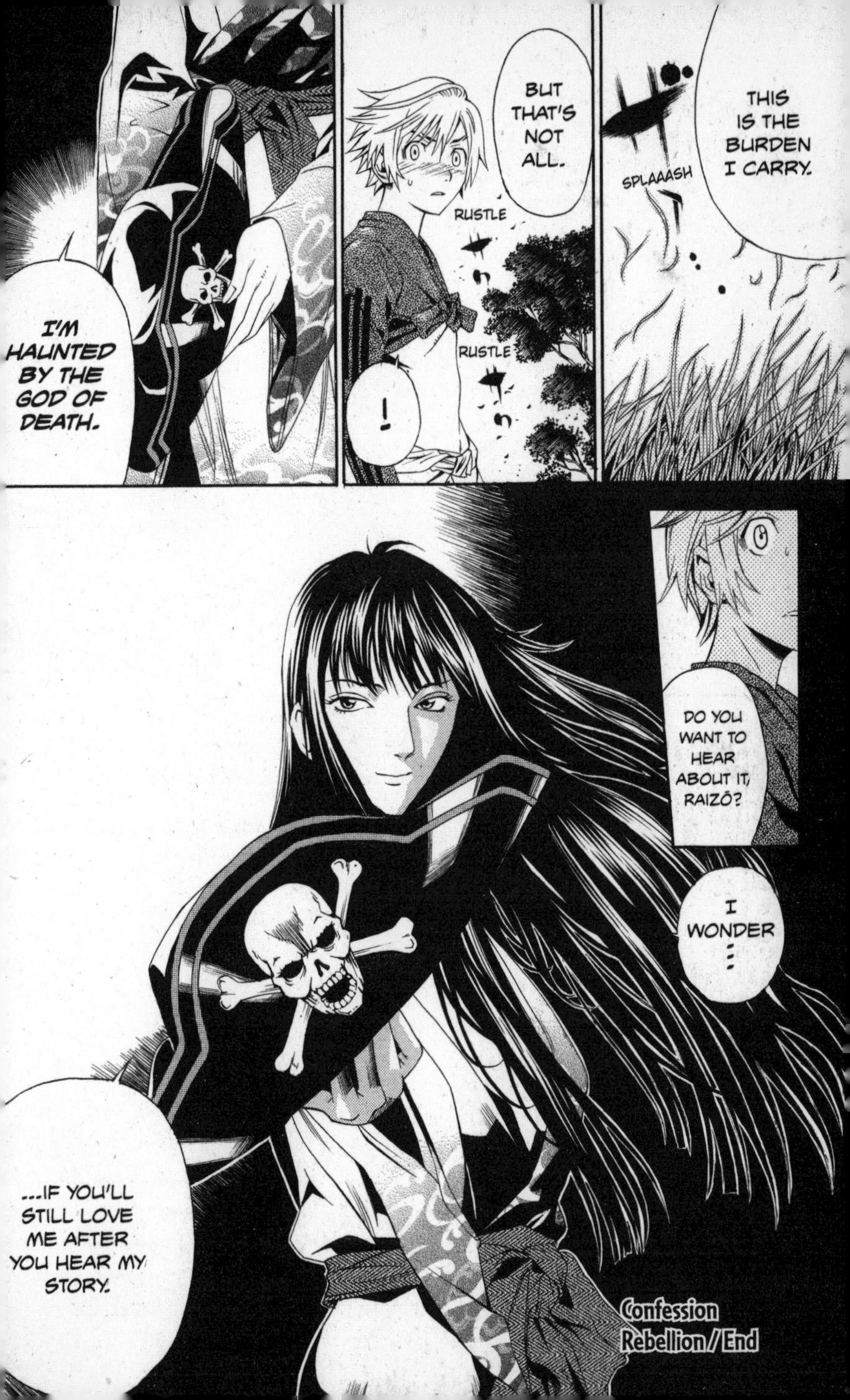
THIS IS THE BURDEN I CARRY.
SPLAAASH
BUT THAT'S NOT ALL.
RUSTLE
RUSTLE
!
I'M HAUNTED BY THE GOD OF DEATH.
DO YOU WANT TO HEAR ABOUT IT, RAIZŌ?
I WONDER...
...IF YOU'LL STILL LOVE ME AFTER YOU HEAR MY STORY.
Confession
Rebellion / End

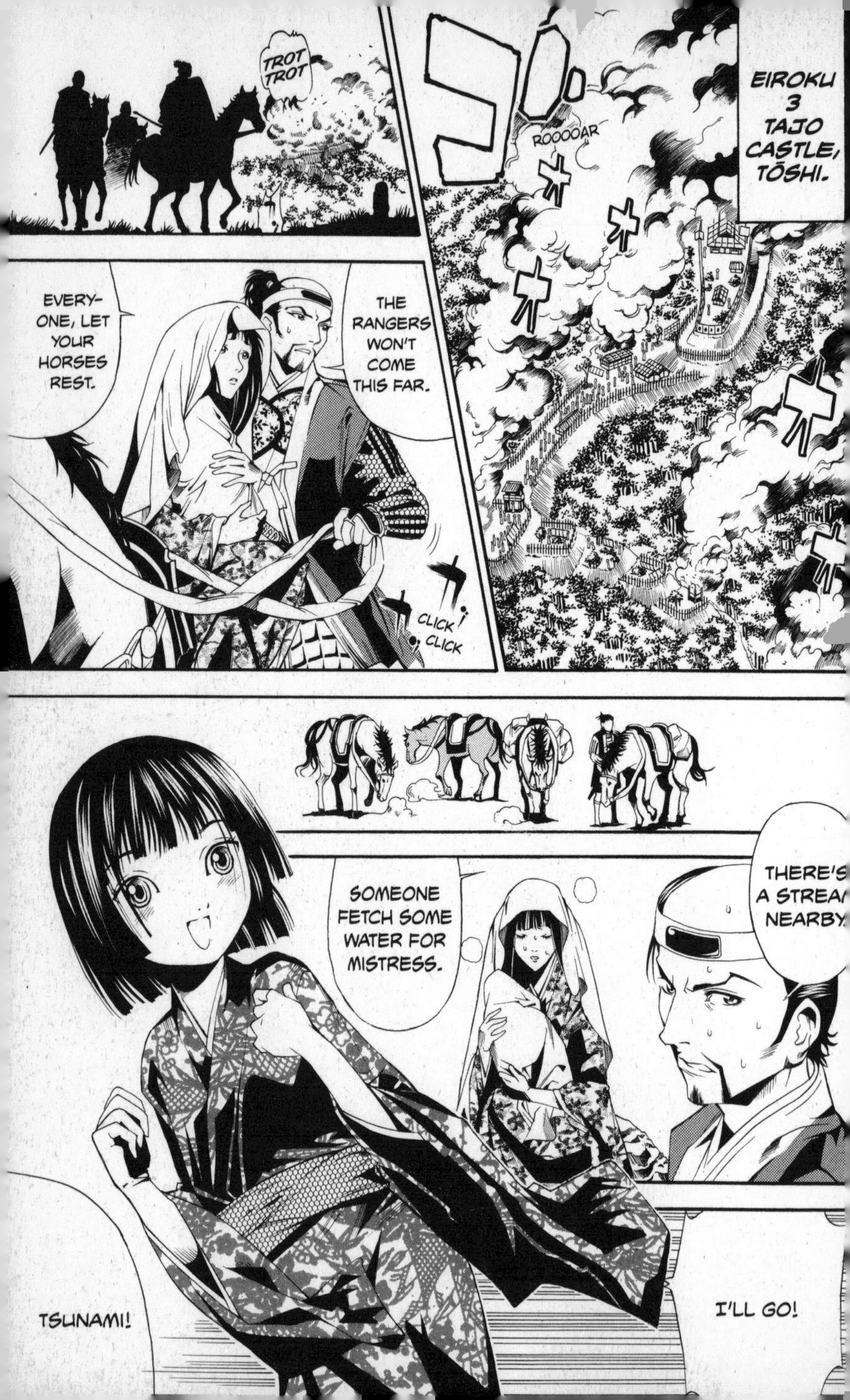

EIROKU 3 TAJO CASTLE, TŌSHI.
ROOOOAR
TROT TROT
THE RANGERS WON'T COME THIS FAR.
EVERY-ONE, LET YOUR HORSES REST.
CLICK CLICK
THERE'S A STREA NEARBY
SOMEONE FETCH SOME WATER FOR MISTRESS.
I'LL GO!
TSUNAMI!

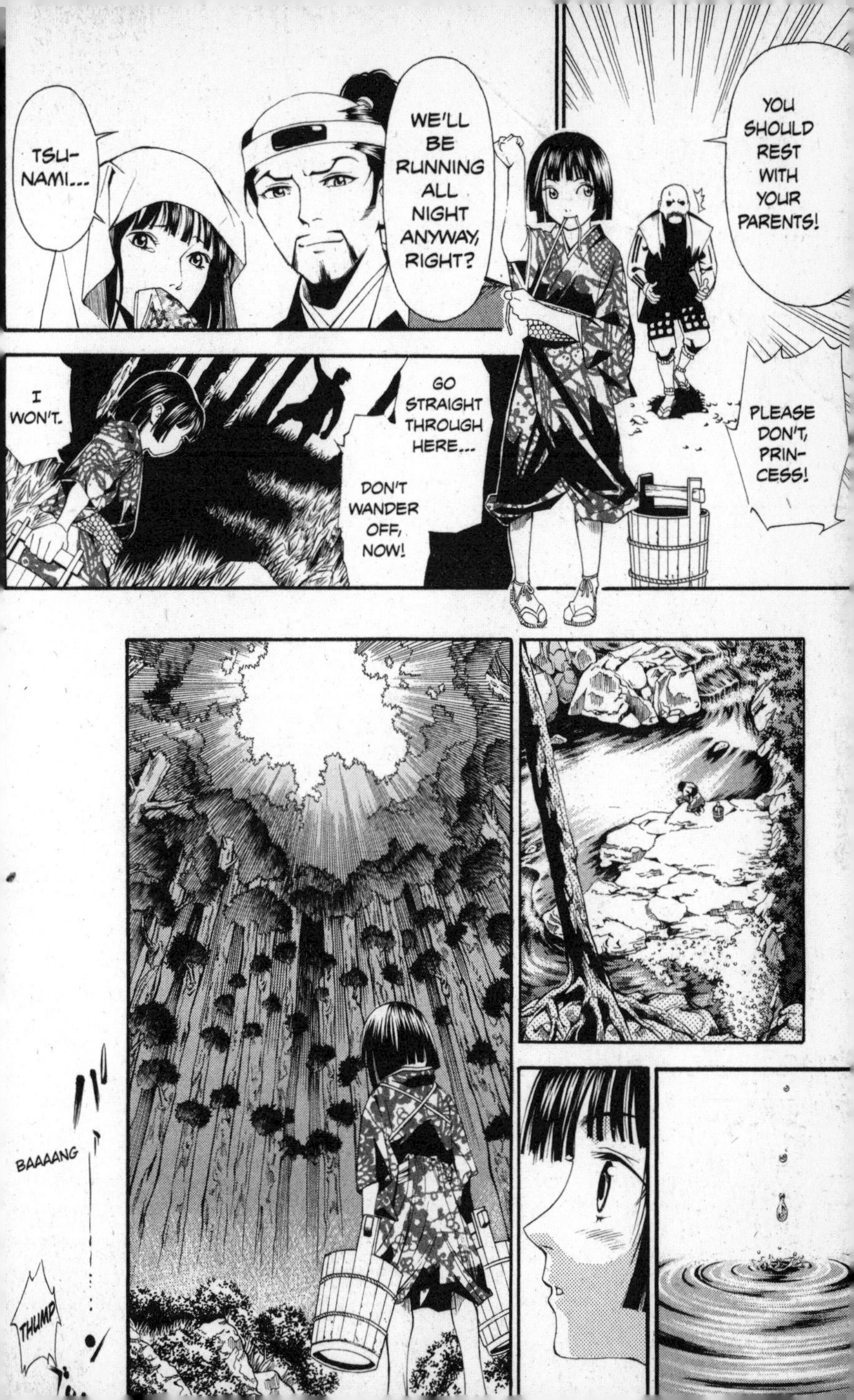
YOU SHOULD REST WITH YOUR PARENTS!
WE'LL BE RUNNING ALL NIGHT ANYWAY, RIGHT?
TSU-NAMI...
PLEASE DON'T, PRINCESS!
GO STRAIGHT THROUGH HERE...
DON'T WANDER OFF, NOW!
I WON'T.
BAAAANG
THUMP

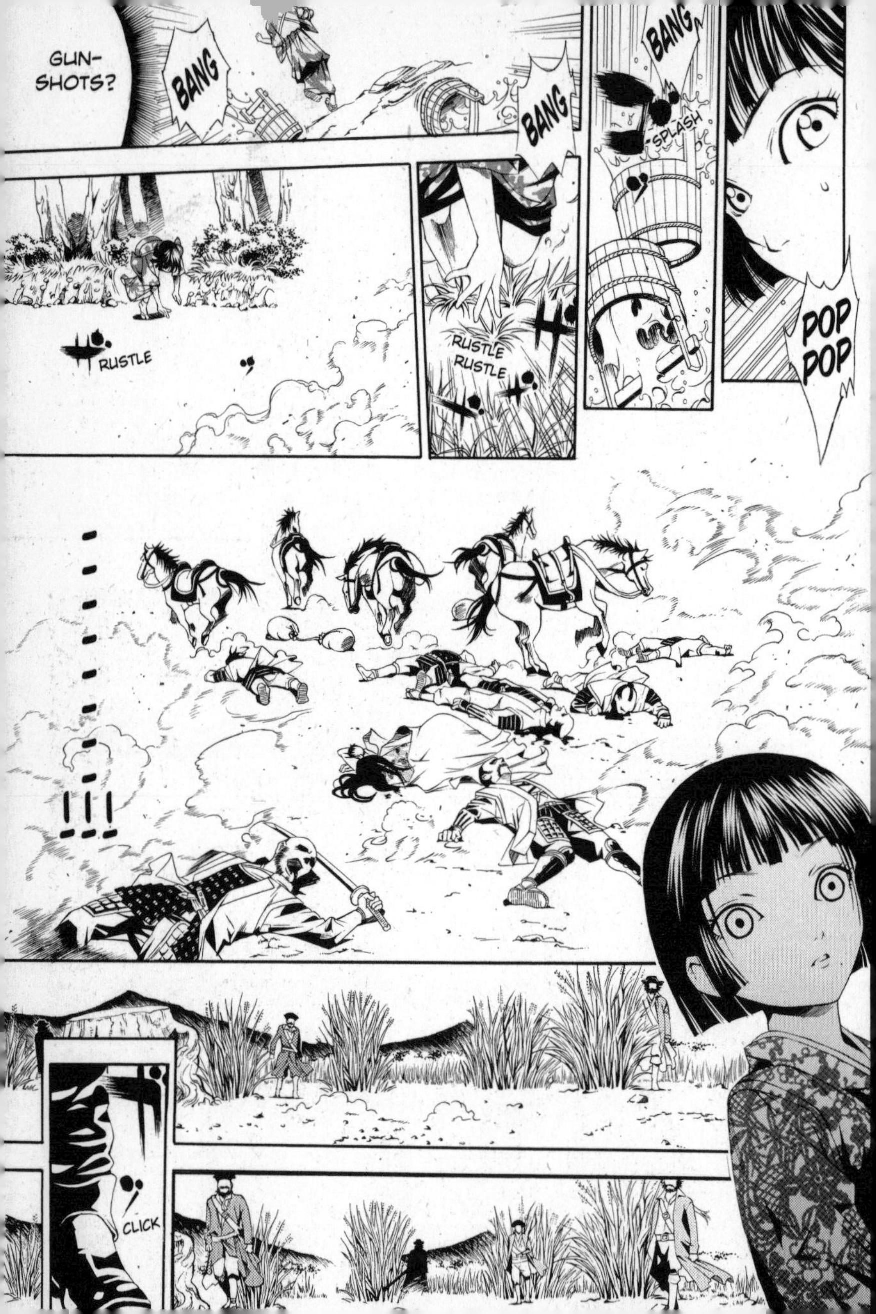

POP POP
BANG
SPLASH
BANG
BANG
GUN-SHOTS?
RUSTLE RUSTLE
RUSTLE
........!!!
CLICK

# 27 Mortal Enemy Rebellion

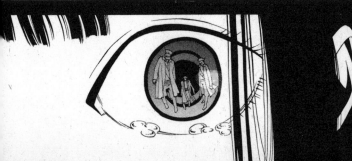

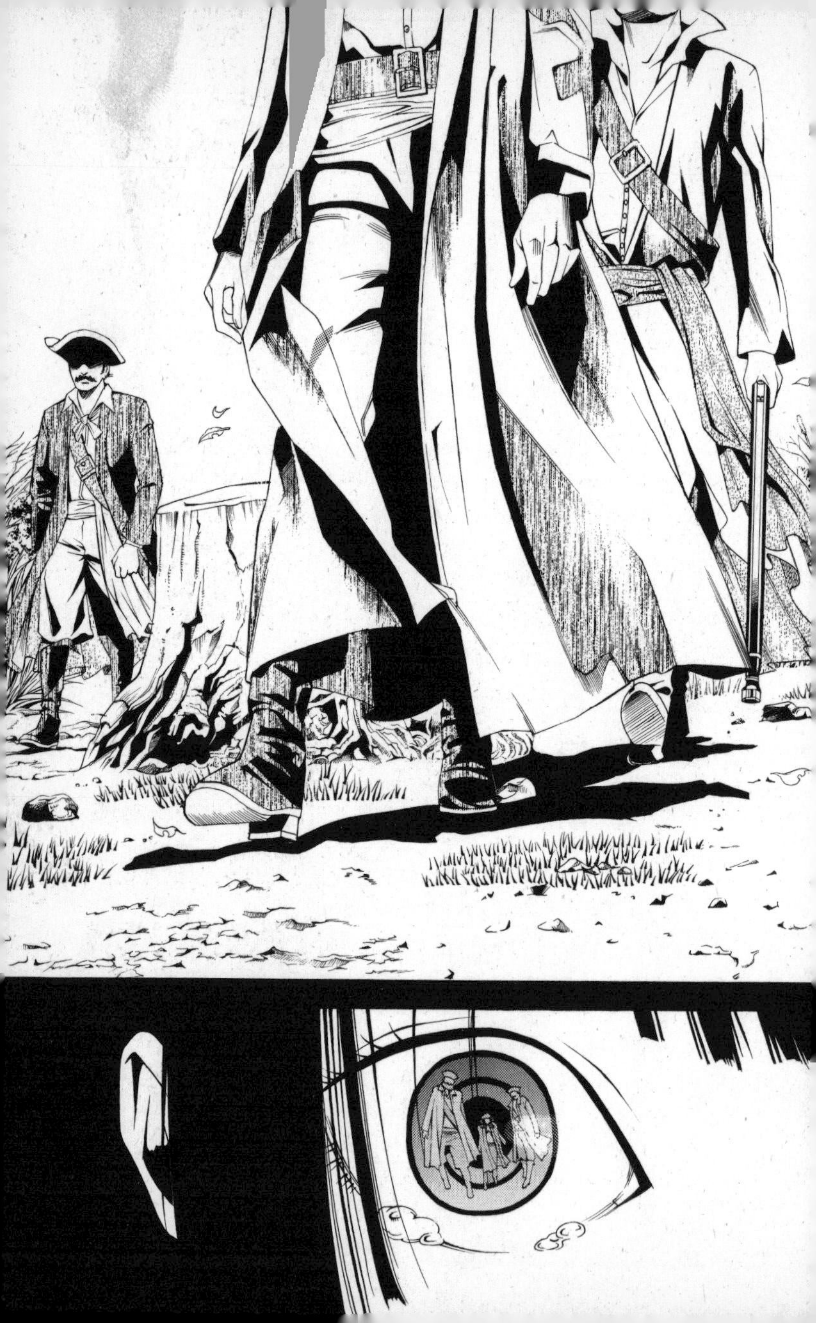

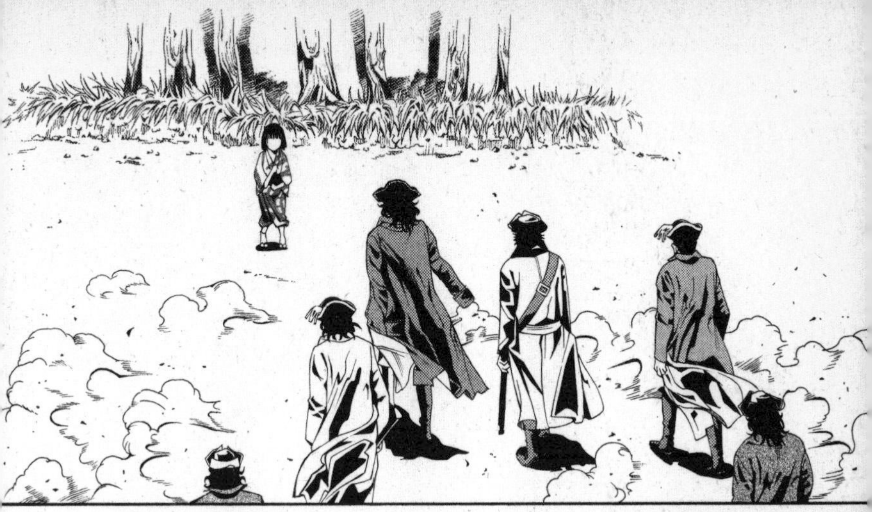
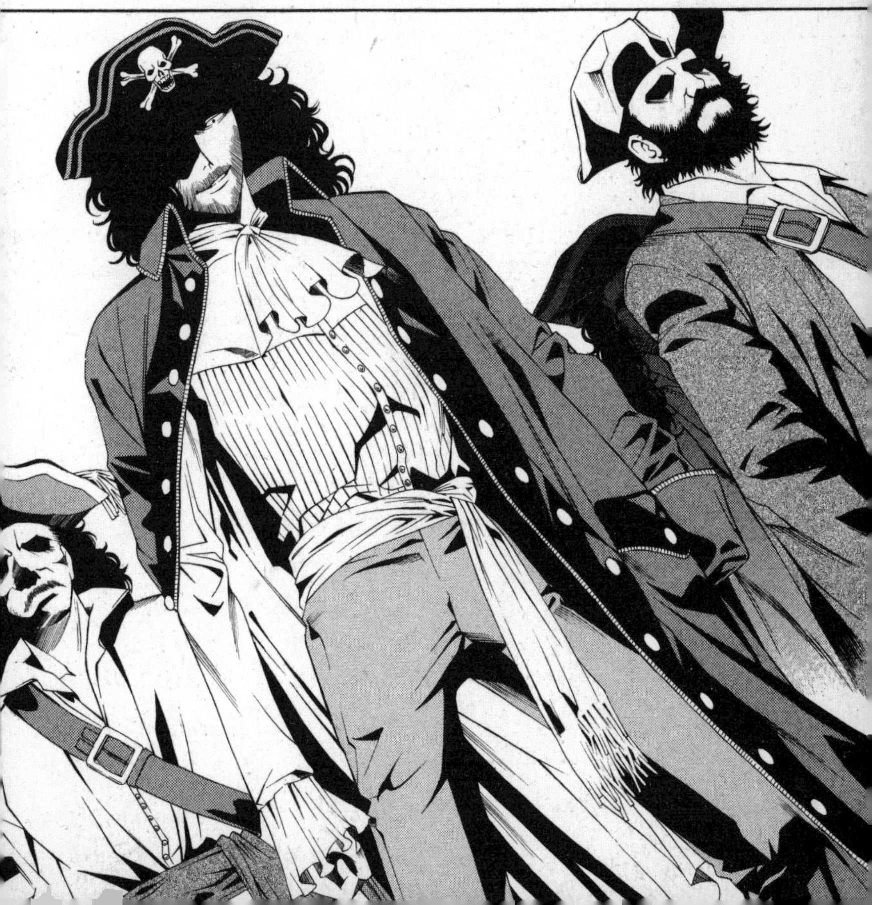

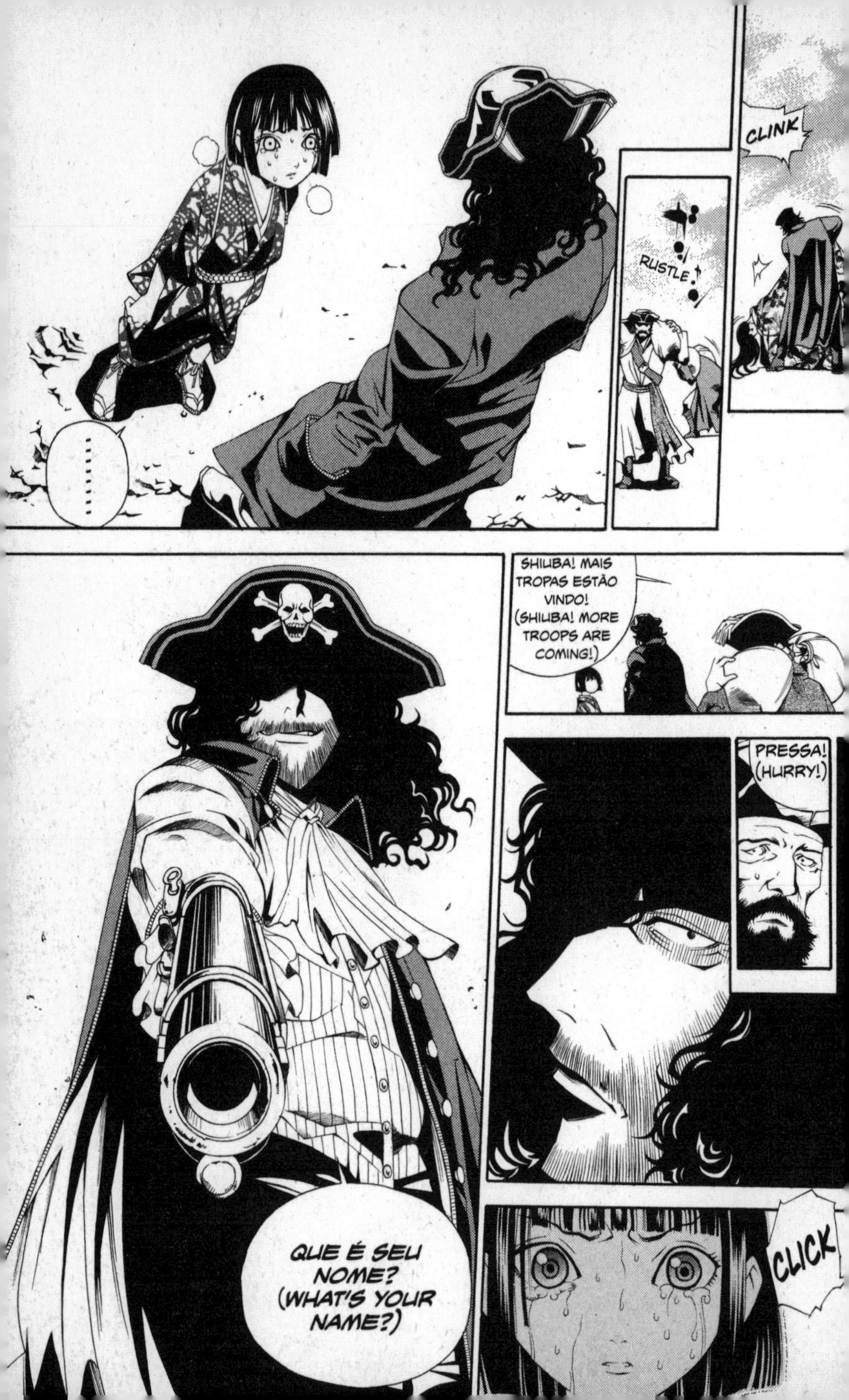
CLINK
RUSTLE
......
SHIUBA! MAIS TROPAS ESTÃO VINDO! (SHIUBA! MORE TROOPS ARE COMING!)
PRESSA! (HURRY!)
CLICK
QUE É SEU NOME? (WHAT'S YOUR NAME?)

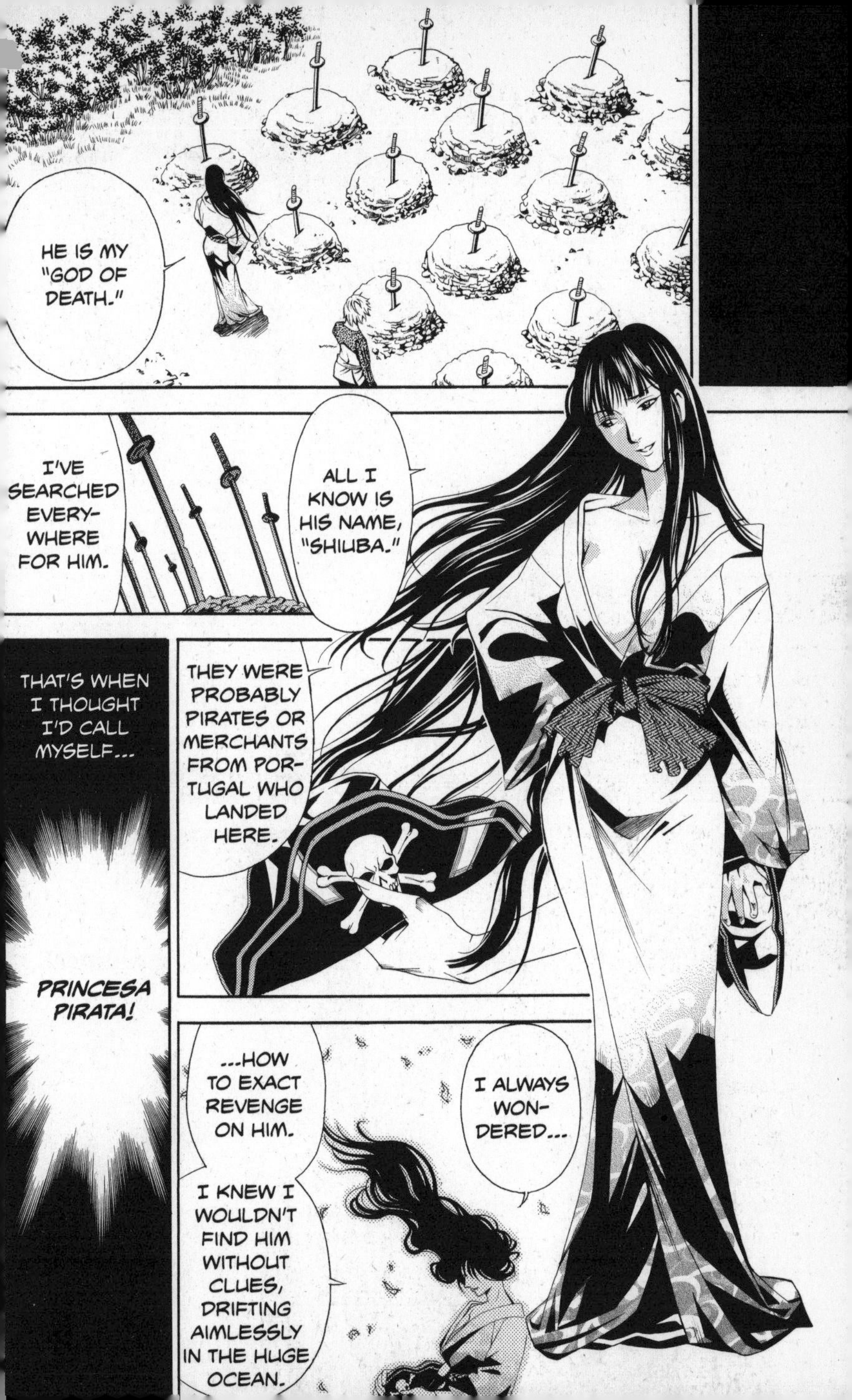
HE IS MY "GOD OF DEATH."
ALL I KNOW IS HIS NAME, "SHIUBA."
I'VE SEARCHED EVERY-WHERE FOR HIM.
THEY WERE PROBABLY PIRATES OR MERCHANTS FROM POR-TUGAL WHO LANDED HERE.
I ALWAYS WON-DERED...
...HOW TO EXACT REVENGE ON HIM.
I KNEW I WOULDN'T FIND HIM WITHOUT CLUES, DRIFTING AIMLESSLY IN THE HUGE OCEAN.
THAT'S WHEN I THOUGHT I'D CALL MYSELF...
PRINCESA PIRATA!

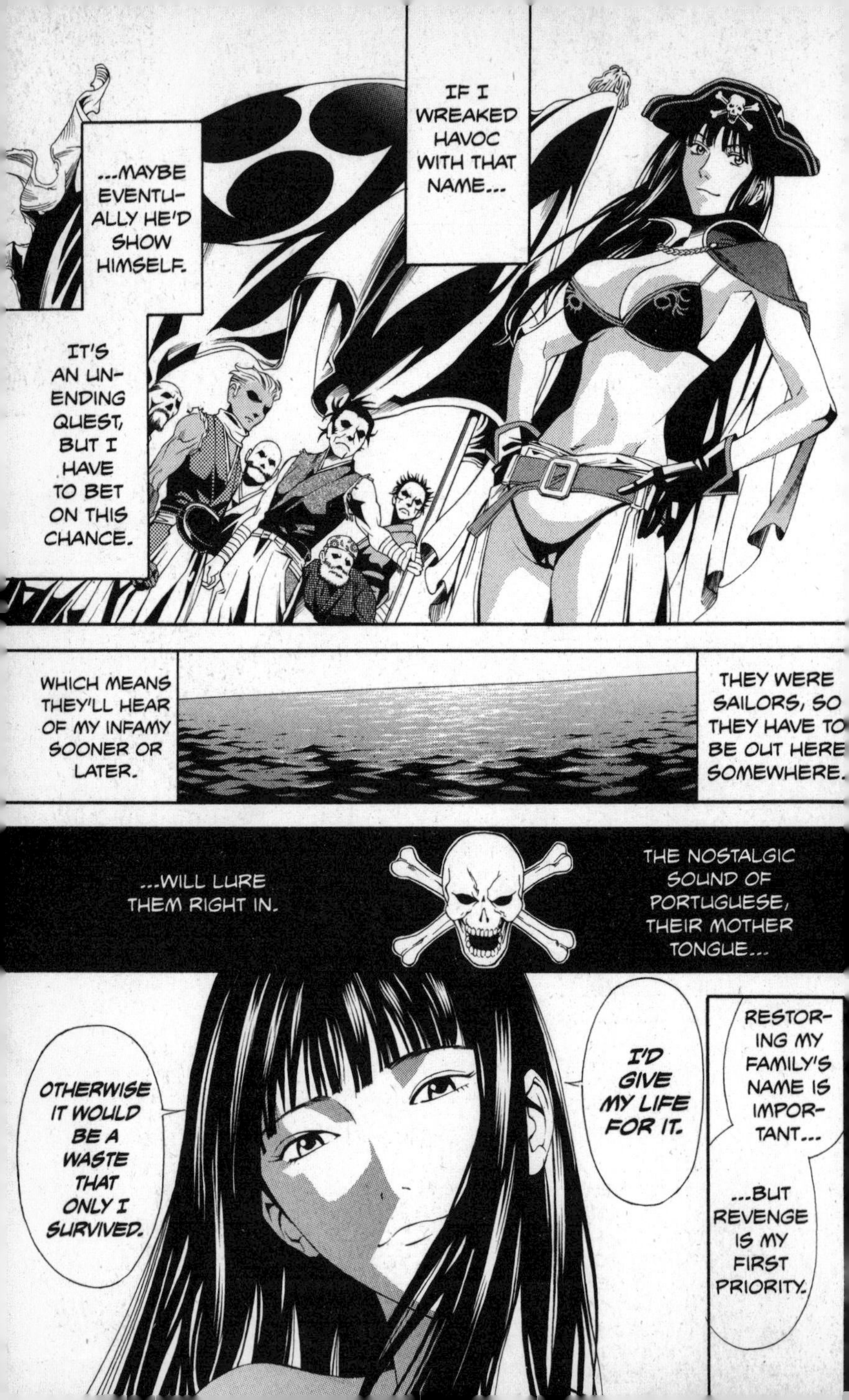

IF I WREAKED HAVOC WITH THAT NAME...
...MAYBE EVENTUALLY HE'D SHOW HIMSELF.
IT'S AN UNENDING QUEST, BUT I HAVE TO BET ON THIS CHANCE.
THEY WERE SAILORS, SO THEY HAVE TO BE OUT HERE SOMEWHERE.
WHICH MEANS THEY'LL HEAR OF MY INFAMY SOONER OR LATER.
THE NOSTALGIC SOUND OF PORTUGUESE, THEIR MOTHER TONGUE...
...WILL LURE THEM RIGHT IN.
RESTORING MY FAMILY'S NAME IS IMPORTANT...
...BUT REVENGE IS MY FIRST PRIORITY.
I'D GIVE MY LIFE FOR IT.
OTHERWISE IT WOULD BE A WASTE THAT ONLY I SURVIVED.

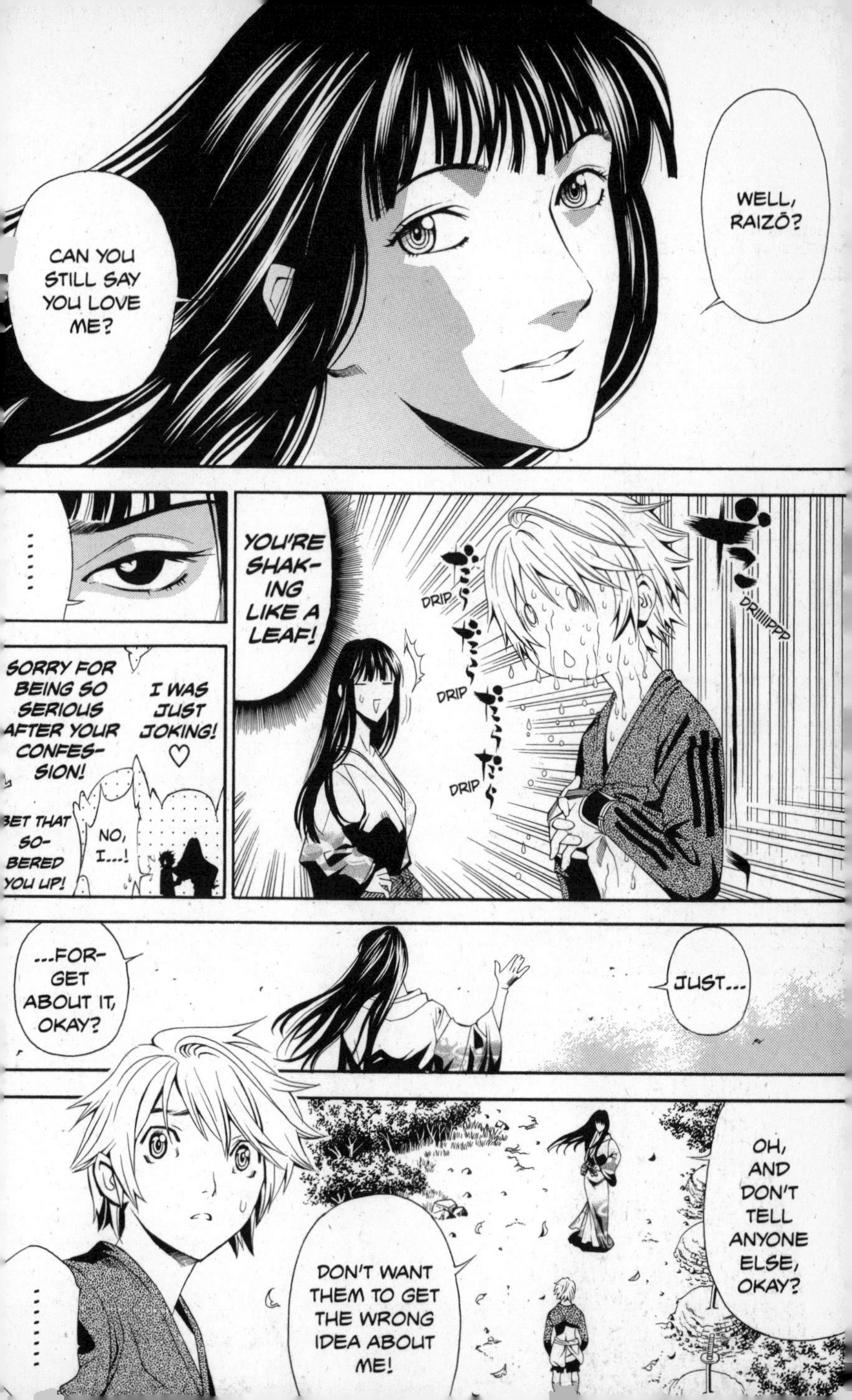
WELL, RAIZŌ?
CAN YOU STILL SAY YOU LOVE ME?
DRIIIIPPP
DRIP
DRIP
DRIP
YOU'RE SHAKING LIKE A LEAF!
......
I WAS JUST JOKING! ♡
SORRY FOR BEING SO SERIOUS AFTER YOUR CONFESSION!
NO, I...!
BET THAT SOBERED YOU UP!
JUST...
...FORGET ABOUT IT, OKAY?
OH, AND DON'T TELL ANYONE ELSE, OKAY?
DON'T WANT THEM TO GET THE WRONG IDEA ABOUT ME!
......

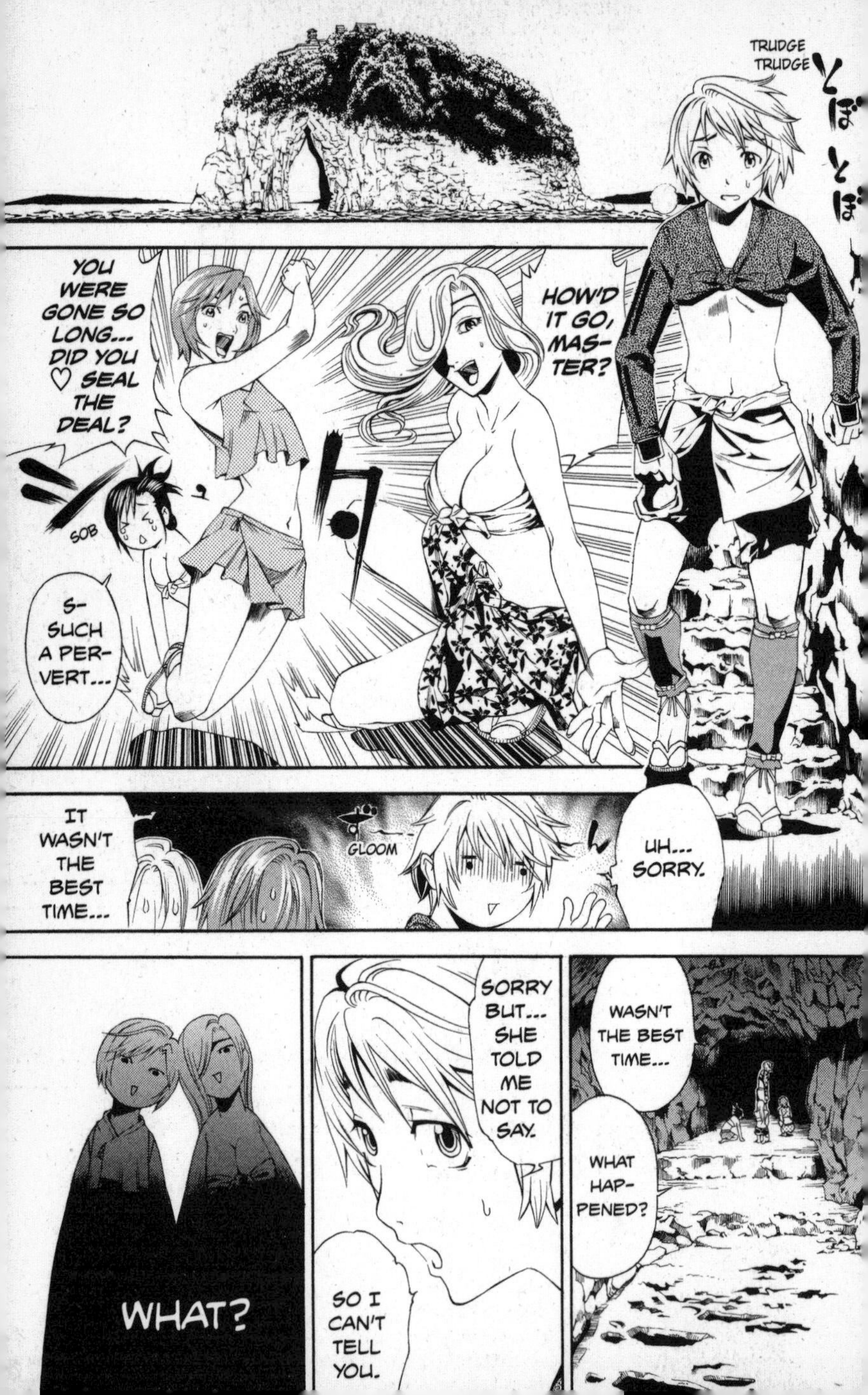

TRUDGE TRUDGE
とぼとぼ
HOW'D IT GO, MAS-TER?
YOU WERE GONE SO LONG... DID YOU ♡ SEAL THE DEAL?
SOB
S-SUCH A PER-VERT...
UH... SORRY.
GLOOM
IT WASN'T THE BEST TIME...
WASN'T THE BEST TIME...
WHAT HAP-PENED?
SORRY BUT... SHE TOLD ME NOT TO SAY.
SO I CAN'T TELL YOU.
WHAT?

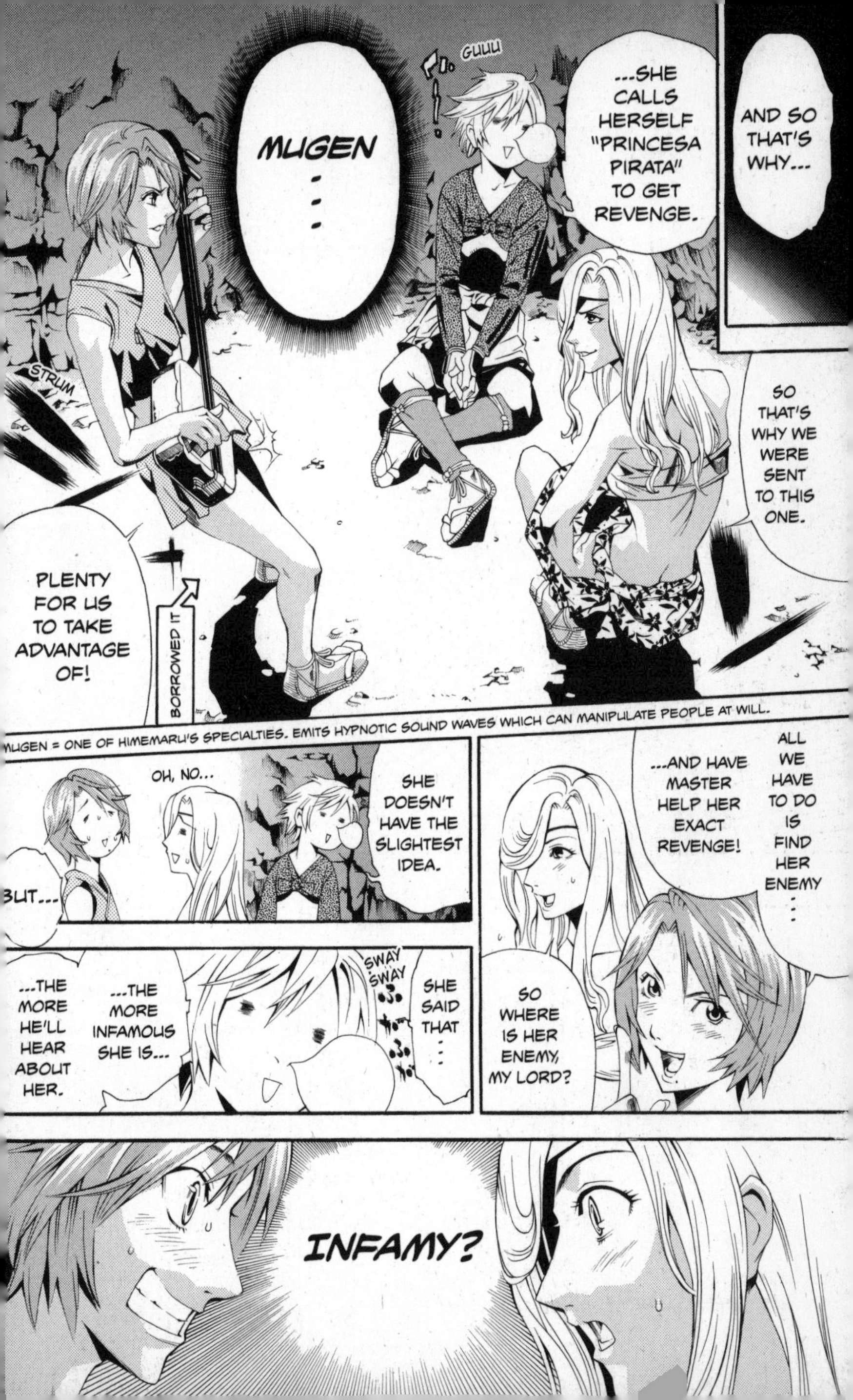
AND SO THAT'S WHY...
...SHE CALLS HERSELF "PRINCESA PIRATA" TO GET REVENGE.
GUUU
MUGEN...
SO THAT'S WHY WE WERE SENT TO THIS ONE.
STRUM
PLENTY FOR US TO TAKE ADVANTAGE OF!
BORROWED IT
MUGEN = ONE OF HIMEMARU'S SPECIALTIES. EMITS HYPNOTIC SOUND WAVES WHICH CAN MANIPULATE PEOPLE AT WILL.
ALL WE HAVE TO DO IS FIND HER ENEMY...
...AND HAVE MASTER HELP HER EXACT REVENGE!
SO WHERE IS HER ENEMY, MY LORD?
SHE DOESN'T HAVE THE SLIGHTEST IDEA.
OH, NO...
BUT...
SHE SAID THAT...
SWAY SWAY
...THE MORE INFAMOUS SHE IS...
...THE MORE HE'LL HEAR ABOUT HER.
INFAMY?

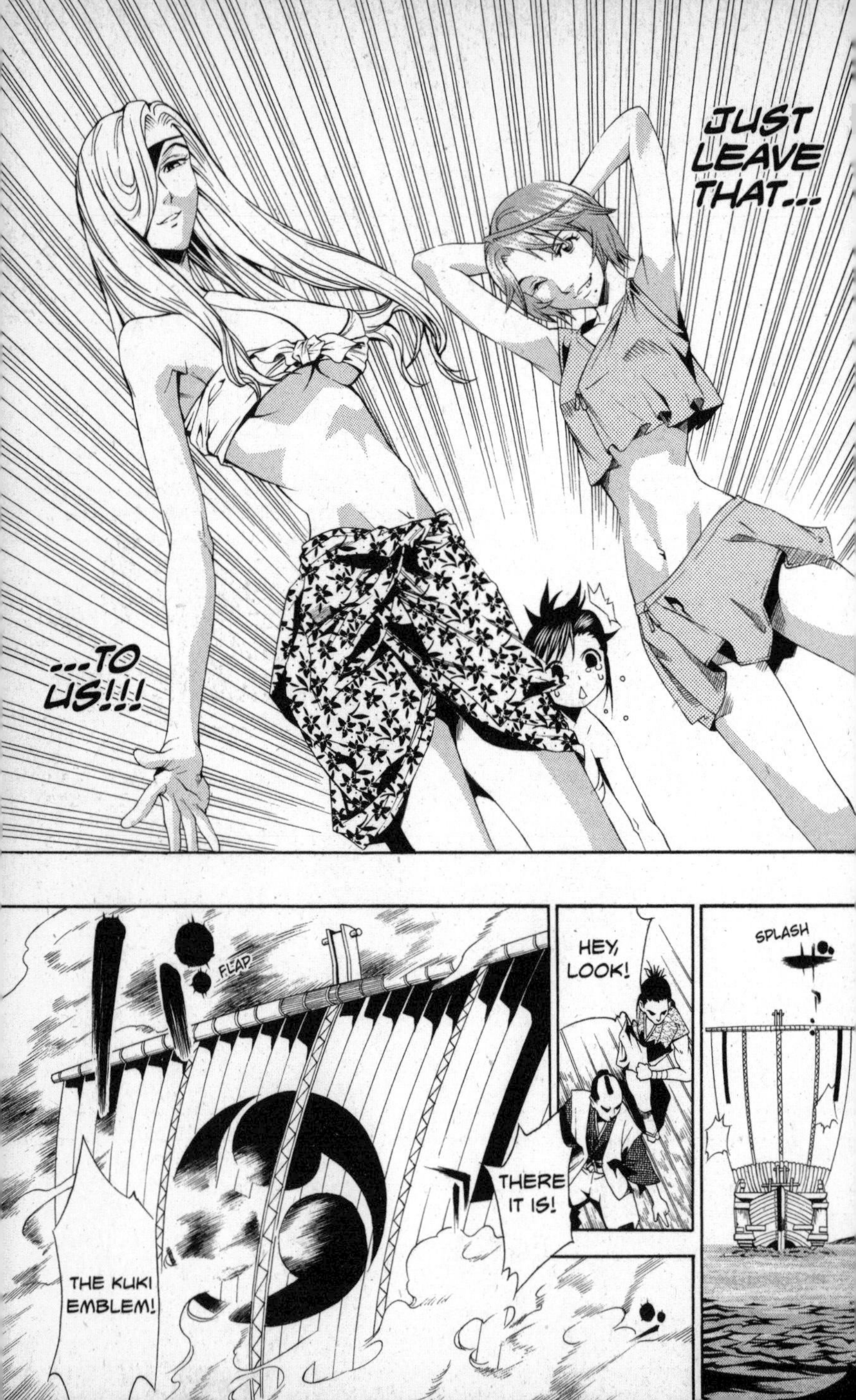
JUST LEAVE THAT...
...TO US!!!
SPLASH
HEY, LOOK!
THERE IT IS!
FLAP
THE KUKI EMBLEM!

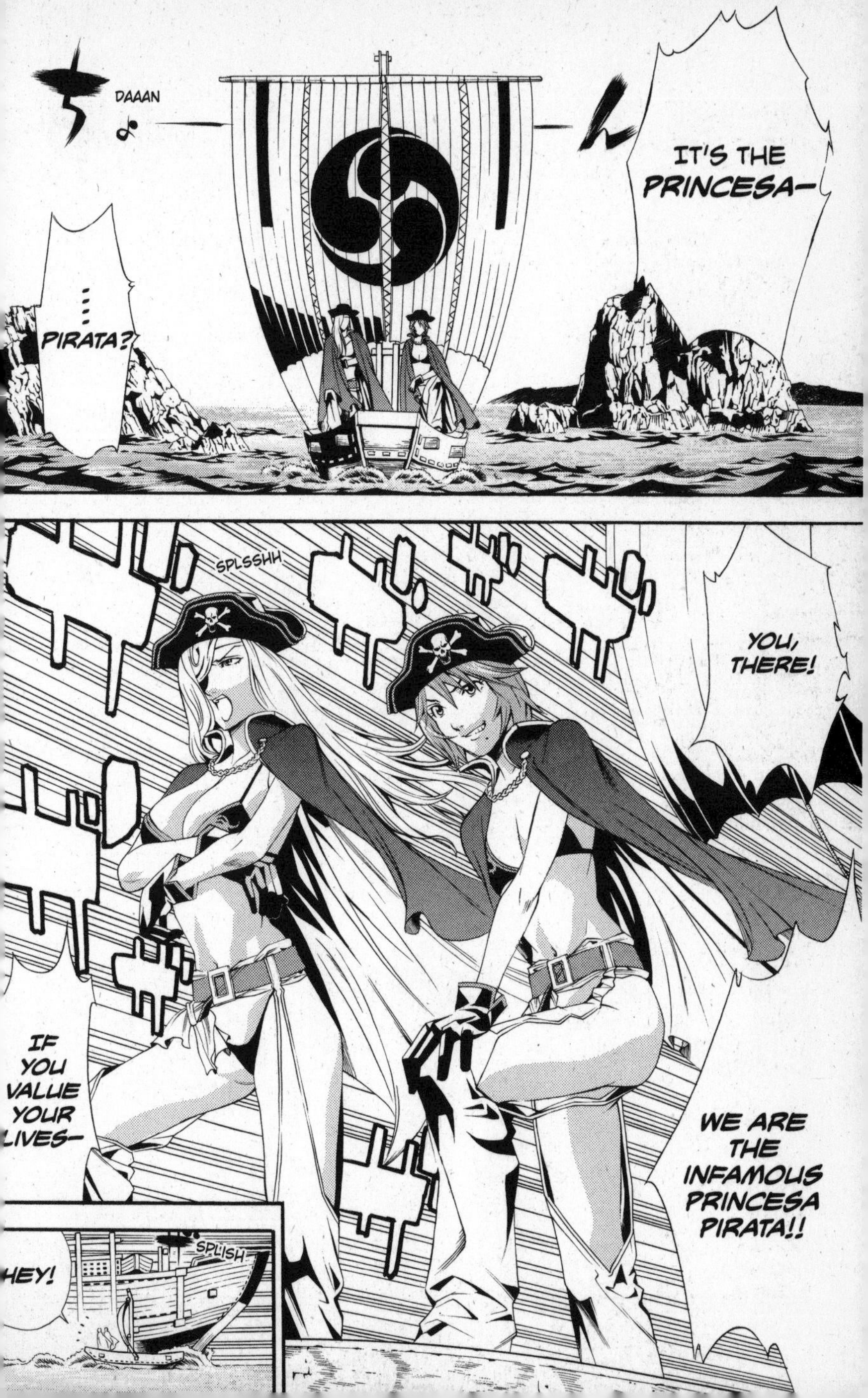
IT'S THE PRINCESA—
DAAAN
...PIRATA?
SPLSSHH
YOU, THERE!
WE ARE THE INFAMOUS PRINCESA PIRATA!!
IF YOU VALUE YOUR LIVES—
SPLISH
HEY!

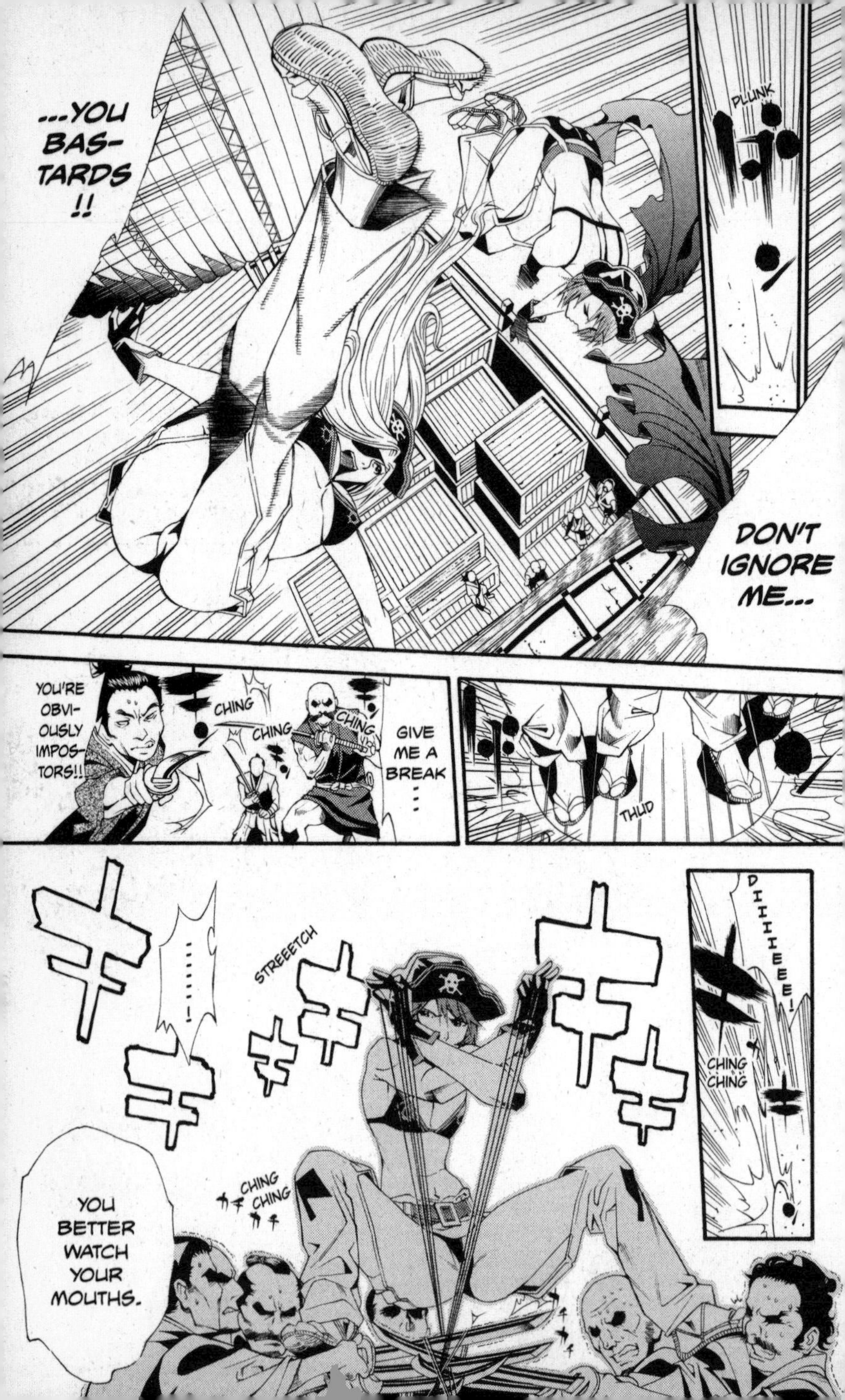
PLUNK
DON'T IGNORE ME...
...YOU BASTARDS!!
THUD
GIVE ME A BREAK...
CHING
CHING
CHING
YOU'RE OBVIOUSLY IMPOSTORS!!
DIIIIEEEE!
CHING CHING
STREEETCH
......!
CHING CHING
YOU BETTER WATCH YOUR MOUTHS.

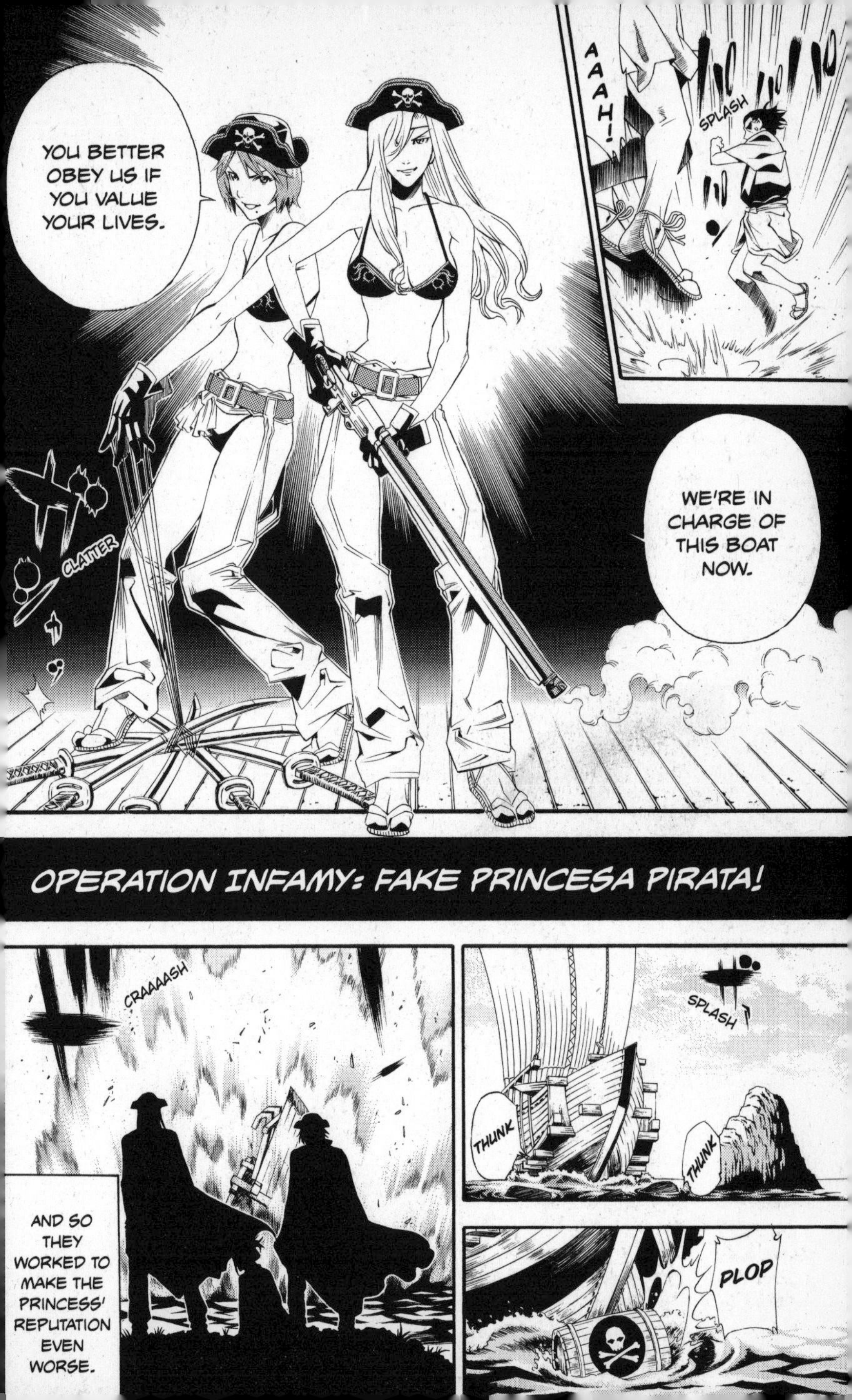
AAAH!
SPLASH
YOU BETTER OBEY US IF YOU VALUE YOUR LIVES.
WE'RE IN CHARGE OF THIS BOAT NOW.
CLATTER
OPERATION INFAMY: FAKE PRINCESA PIRATA!
SPLASH
THUNK
THUNK
PLOP
CRAAAASH
AND SO THEY WORKED TO MAKE THE PRINCESS' REPUTATION EVEN WORSE.

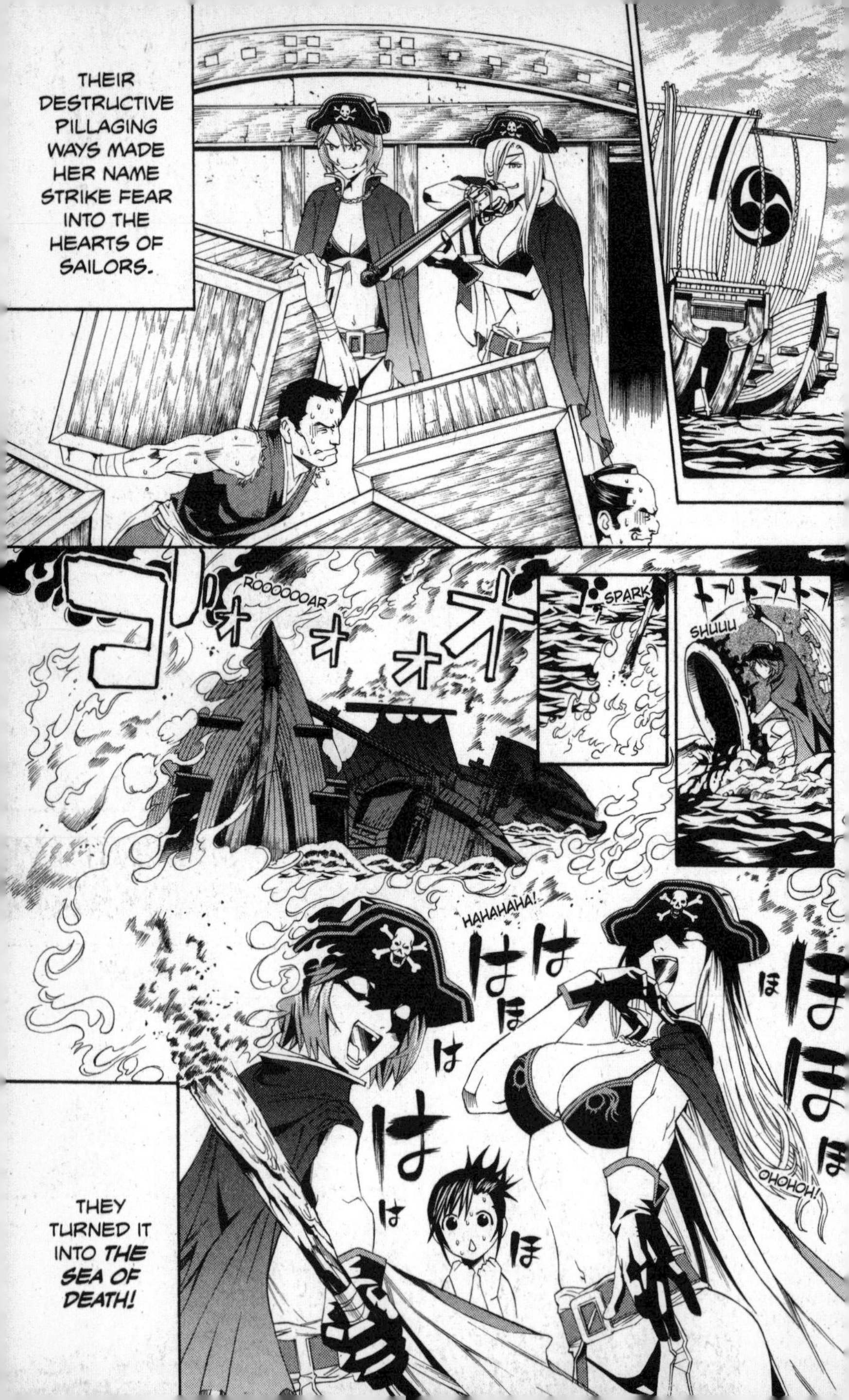
THEIR DESTRUCTIVE PILLAGING WAYS MADE HER NAME STRIKE FEAR INTO THE HEARTS OF SAILORS.
SHUUU
SPARK
ROOOOOOAR
OHOHOH!
HAHAHAHA!
THEY TURNED IT INTO *THE SEA OF DEATH!*

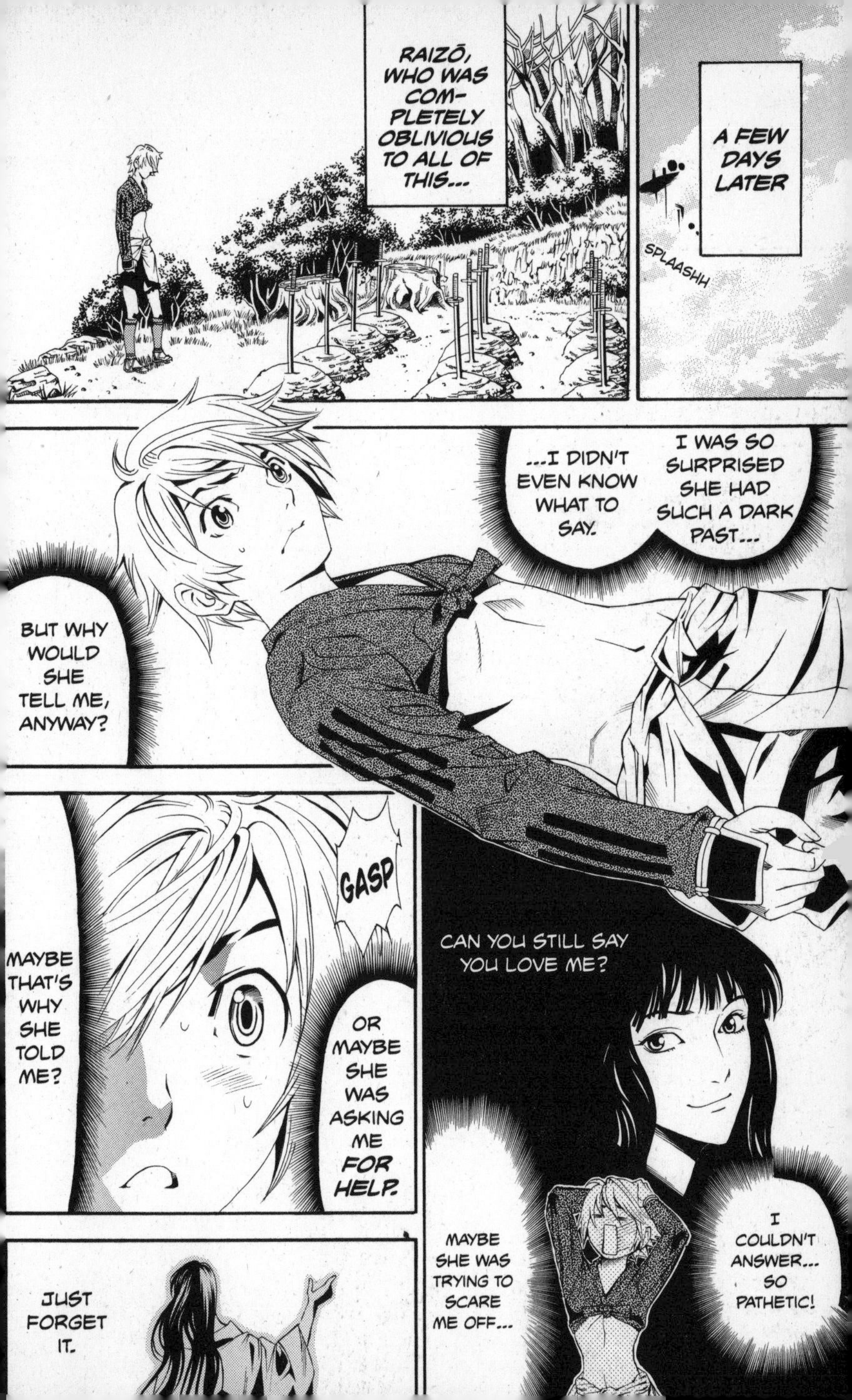
A FEW DAYS LATER
SPLAASHH
RAIZŌ, WHO WAS COMPLETELY OBLIVIOUS TO ALL OF THIS...
I WAS SO SURPRISED SHE HAD SUCH A DARK PAST...
...I DIDN'T EVEN KNOW WHAT TO SAY.
BUT WHY WOULD SHE TELL ME, ANYWAY?
CAN YOU STILL SAY YOU LOVE ME?
GASP
OR MAYBE SHE WAS ASKING ME FOR HELP.
MAYBE THAT'S WHY SHE TOLD ME?
I COULDN'T ANSWER... SO PATHETIC!
MAYBE SHE WAS TRYING TO SCARE ME OFF...
JUST FORGET IT.

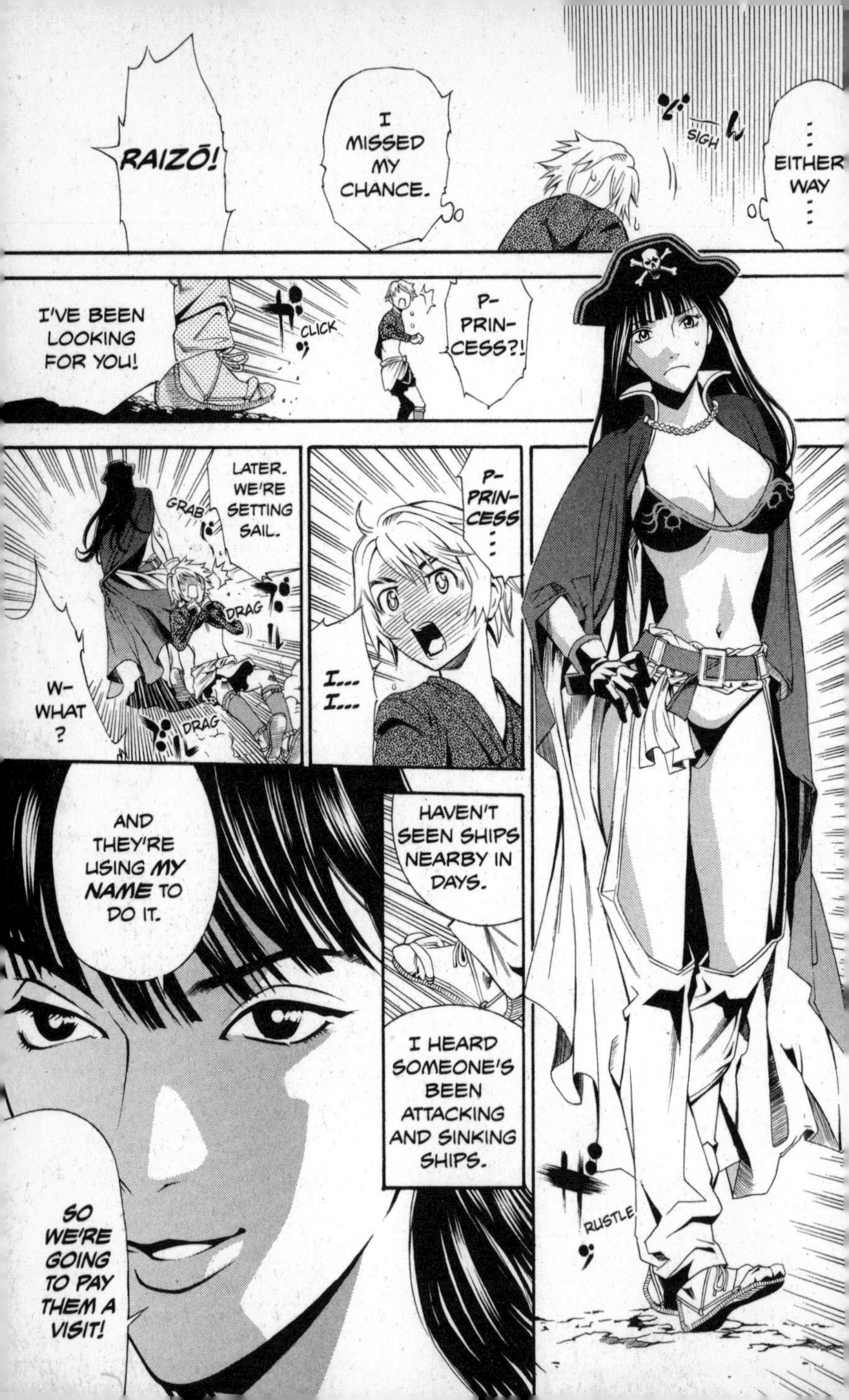
...EITHER WAY...
SIGH
I MISSED MY CHANCE.
RAIZŌ!
RUSTLE
P-PRINCESS?!
CLICK
I'VE BEEN LOOKING FOR YOU!
P-PRINCESS...
I... I...
LATER. WE'RE SETTING SAIL.
GRAB
DRAG
DRAG
W-WHAT?
HAVEN'T SEEN SHIPS NEARBY IN DAYS.
I HEARD SOMEONE'S BEEN ATTACKING AND SINKING SHIPS.
AND THEY'RE USING *MY NAME* TO DO IT.
SO WE'RE GOING TO PAY THEM A VISIT!

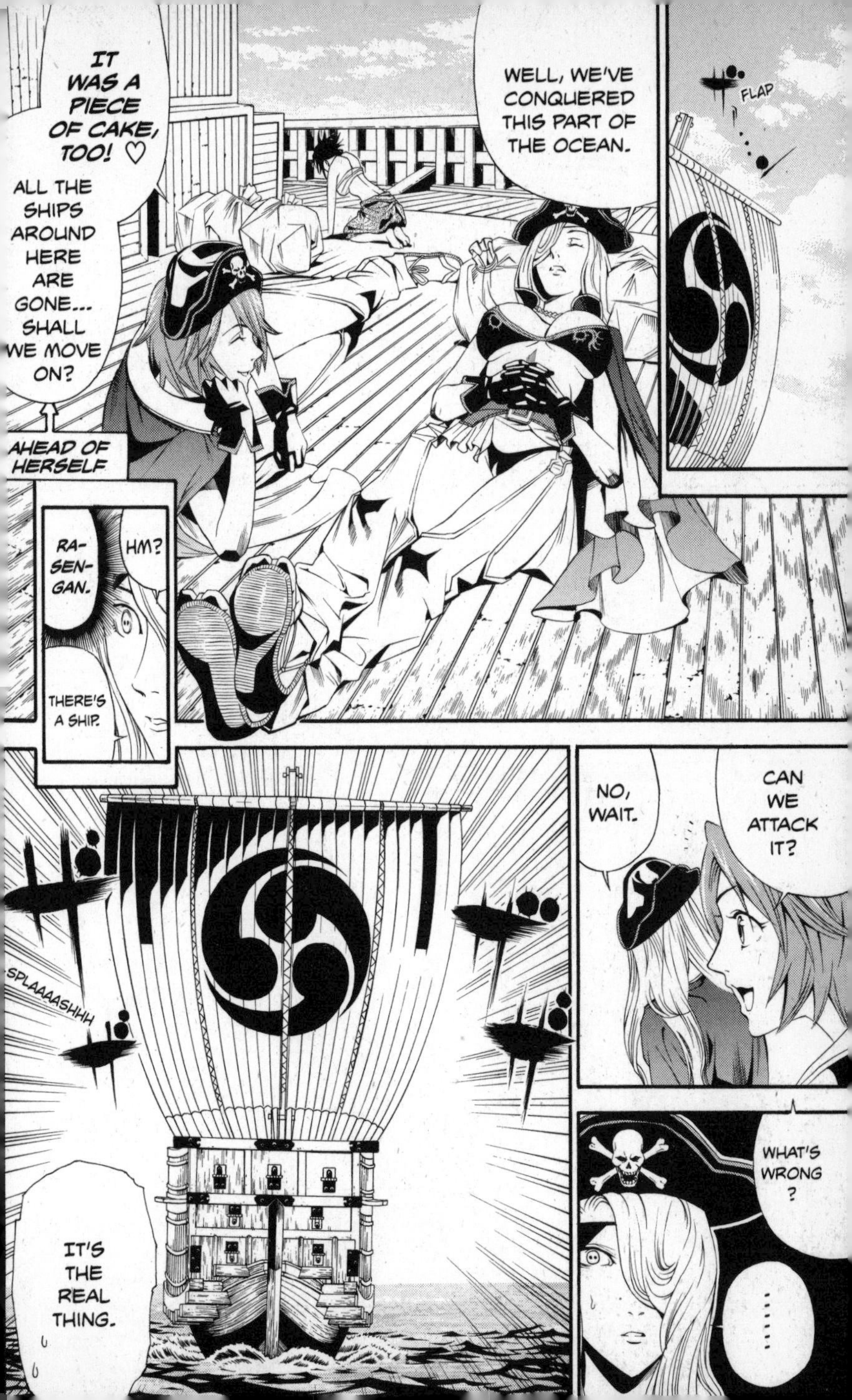
FLAP
WELL, WE'VE CONQUERED THIS PART OF THE OCEAN.
IT WAS A PIECE OF CAKE, TOO! ♡
ALL THE SHIPS AROUND HERE ARE GONE... SHALL WE MOVE ON?
AHEAD OF HERSELF
HM?
RA-SEN-GAN.
THERE'S A SHIP.
CAN WE ATTACK IT?
NO, WAIT.
WHAT'S WRONG?
......
SPLAAAASHHH
IT'S THE REAL THING.

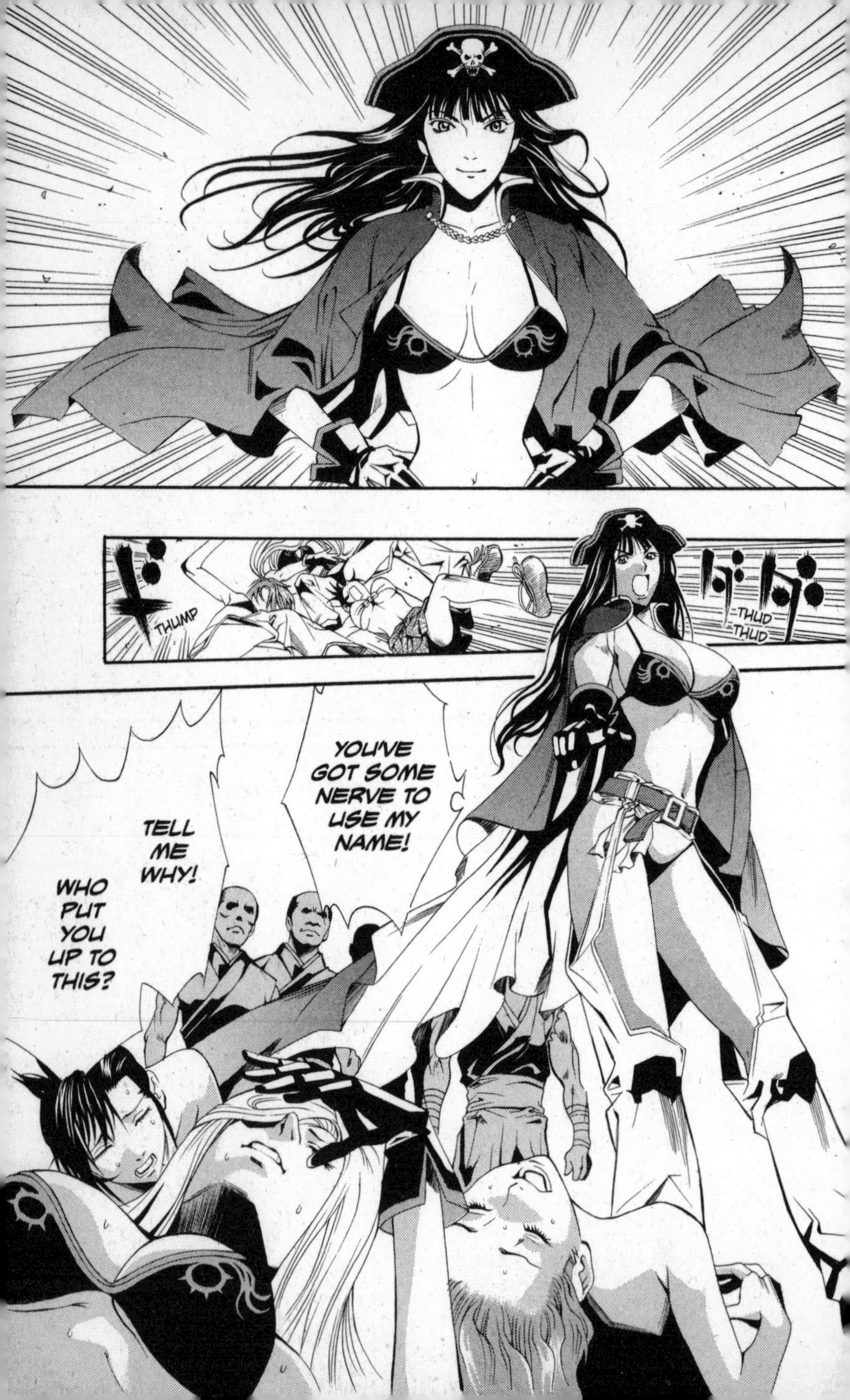
THUD
THUD
THUMP
YOU'VE GOT SOME NERVE TO USE MY NAME!
TELL ME WHY!
WHO PUT YOU UP TO THIS?

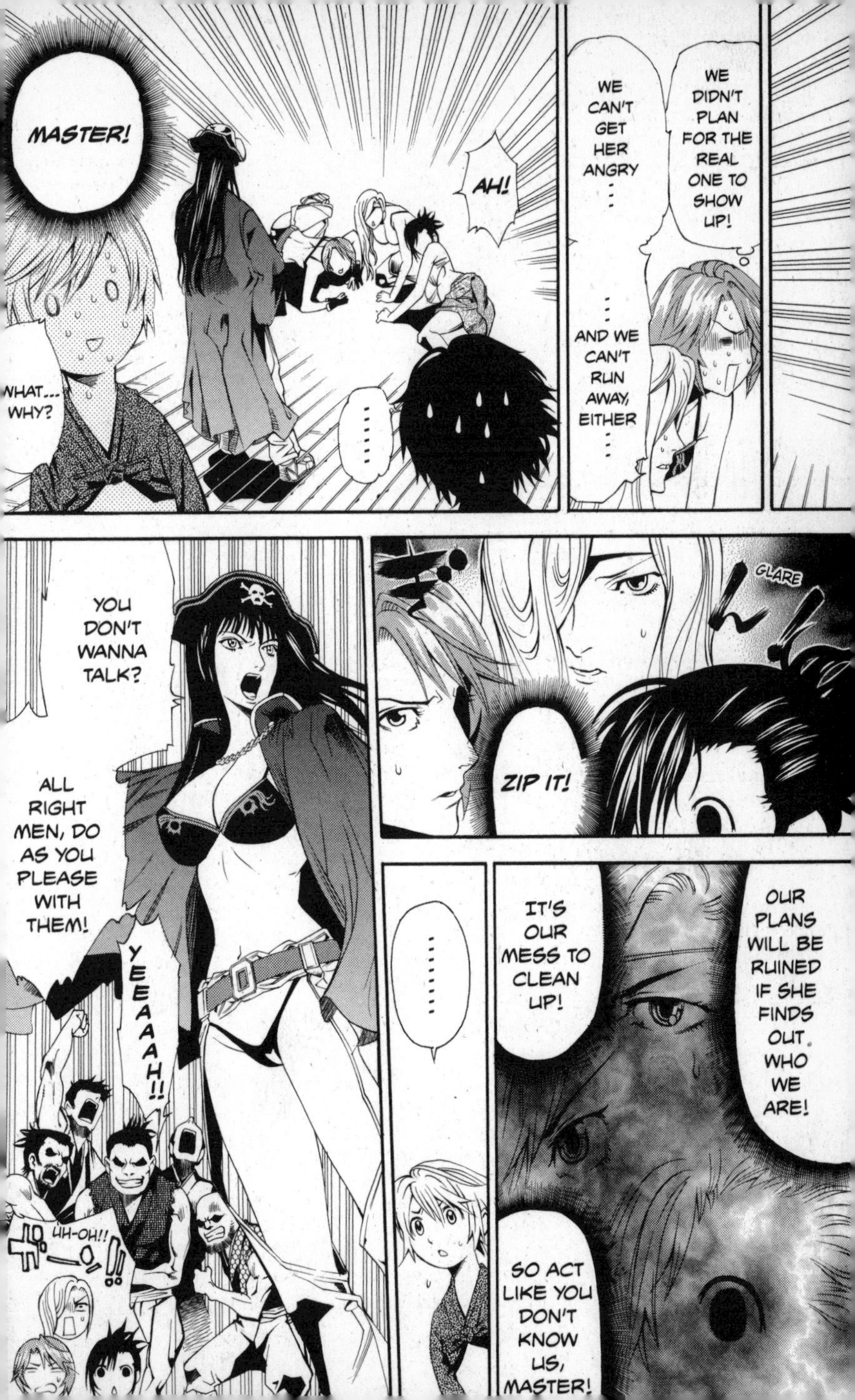

WE DIDN'T PLAN FOR THE REAL ONE TO SHOW UP!
WE CAN'T GET HER ANGRY...
... AND WE CAN'T RUN AWAY, EITHER...
AH!
MASTER!
......
WHAT... WHY?
GLARE
ZIP IT!
OUR PLANS WILL BE RUINED IF SHE FINDS OUT WHO WE ARE!
IT'S OUR MESS TO CLEAN UP!
SO ACT LIKE YOU DON'T KNOW US, MASTER!
......
YOU DON'T WANNA TALK?
ALL RIGHT MEN, DO AS YOU PLEASE WITH THEM!
YEEAAAAH!!
UH-OH!!

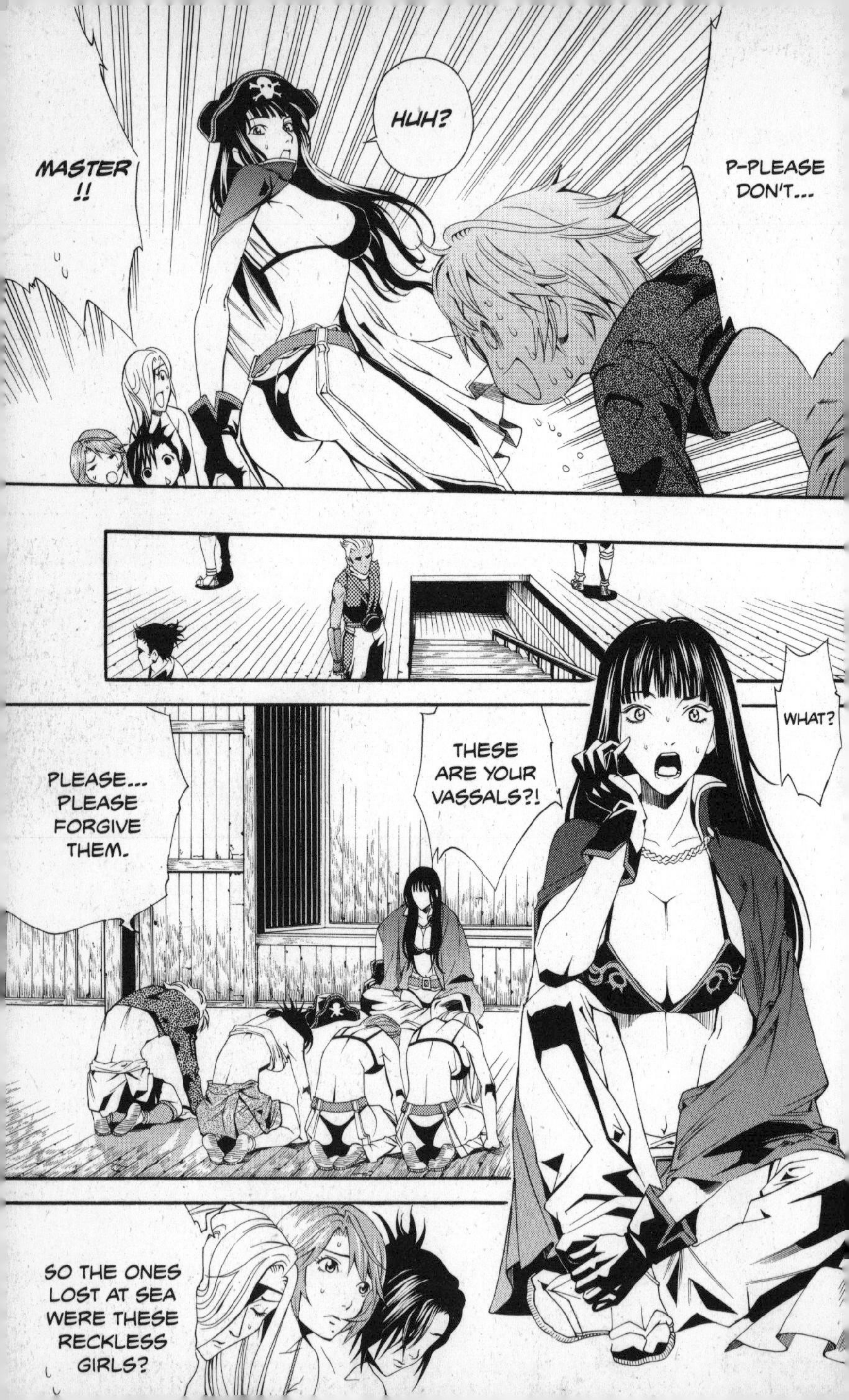
P-PLEASE DON'T...
HUH?
MASTER !!
WHAT?
THESE ARE YOUR VASSALS?!
PLEASE... PLEASE FORGIVE THEM.
SO THE ONES LOST AT SEA WERE THESE RECKLESS GIRLS?

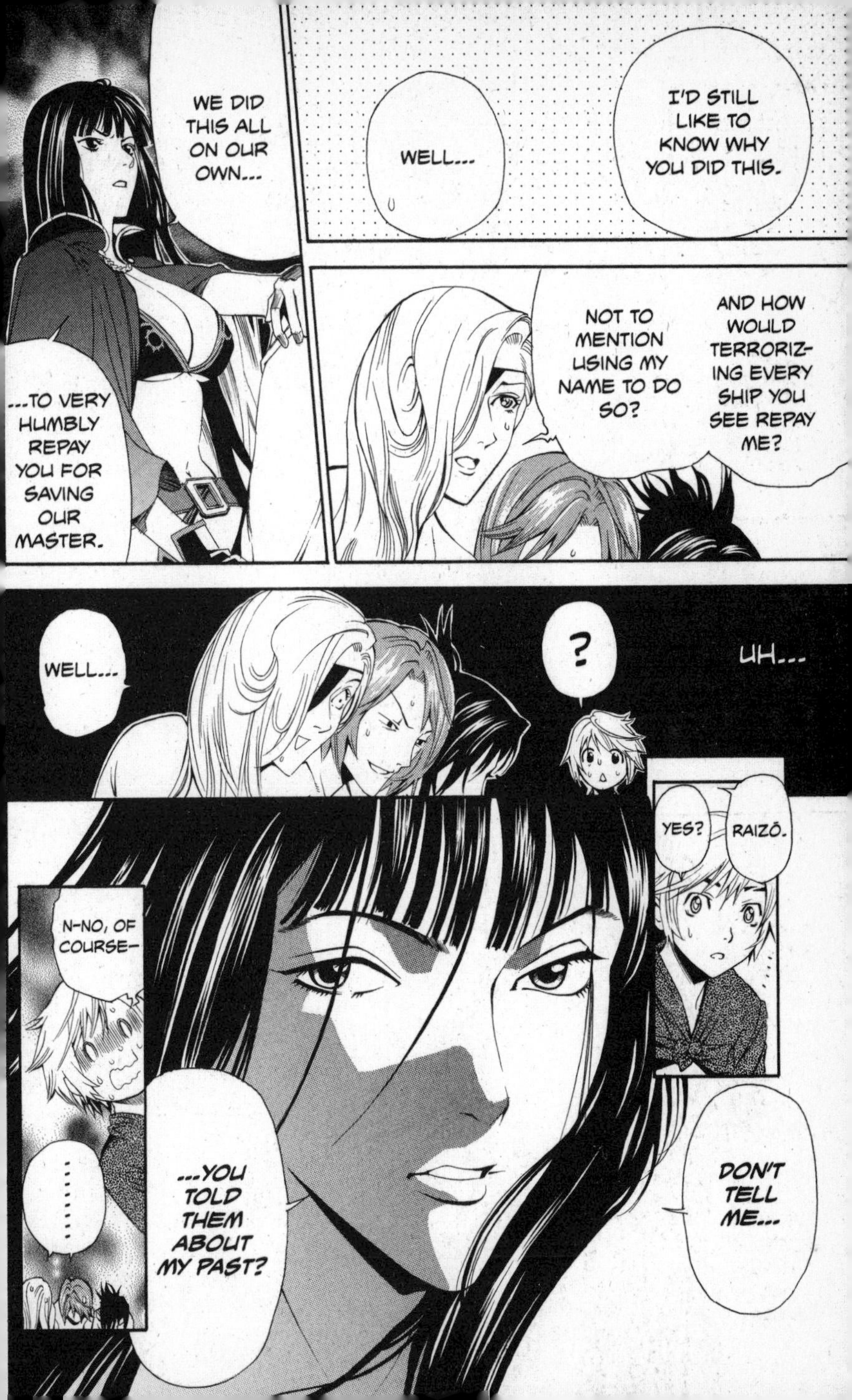
I'D STILL LIKE TO KNOW WHY YOU DID THIS.
WELL...
AND HOW WOULD TERRORIZ-ING EVERY SHIP YOU SEE REPAY ME?
NOT TO MENTION USING MY NAME TO DO SO?
WE DID THIS ALL ON OUR OWN...
...TO VERY HUMBLY REPAY YOU FOR SAVING OUR MASTER.
UH...
?
WELL...
RAIZŌ.
YES?
DON'T TELL ME...
...YOU TOLD THEM ABOUT MY PAST?
N-NO, OF COURSE—
........

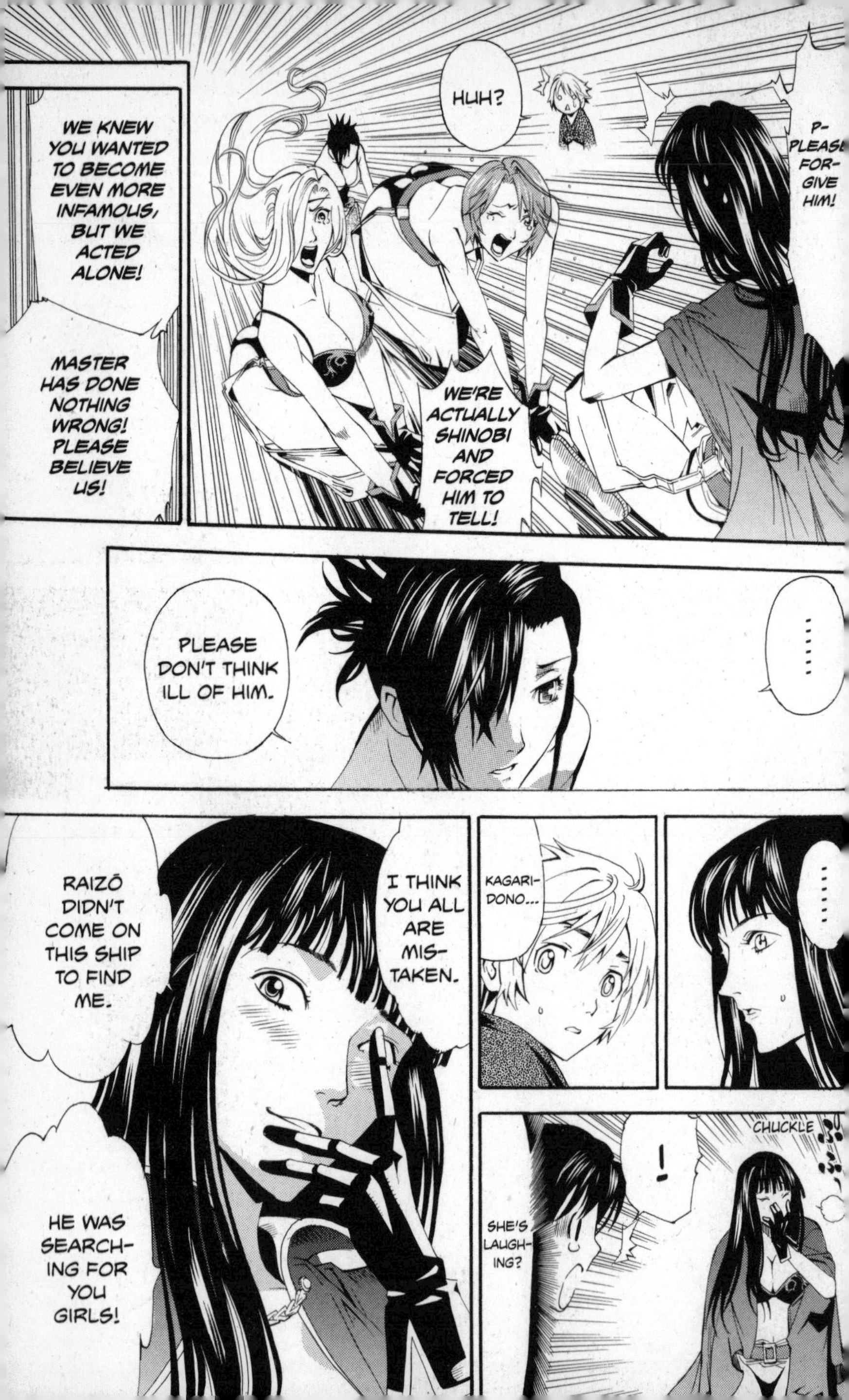
P-PLEASE FORGIVE HIM!
HUH?
WE KNEW YOU WANTED TO BECOME EVEN MORE INFAMOUS, BUT WE ACTED ALONE!
WE'RE ACTUALLY SHINOBI AND FORCED HIM TO TELL!
MASTER HAS DONE NOTHING WRONG! PLEASE BELIEVE US!
......
PLEASE DON'T THINK ILL OF HIM.
......
KAGARI-DONO...
CHUCKLE
!
SHE'S LAUGH-ING?
I THINK YOU ALL ARE MIS-TAKEN.
RAIZŌ DIDN'T COME ON THIS SHIP TO FIND ME.
HE WAS SEARCH-ING FOR YOU GIRLS!

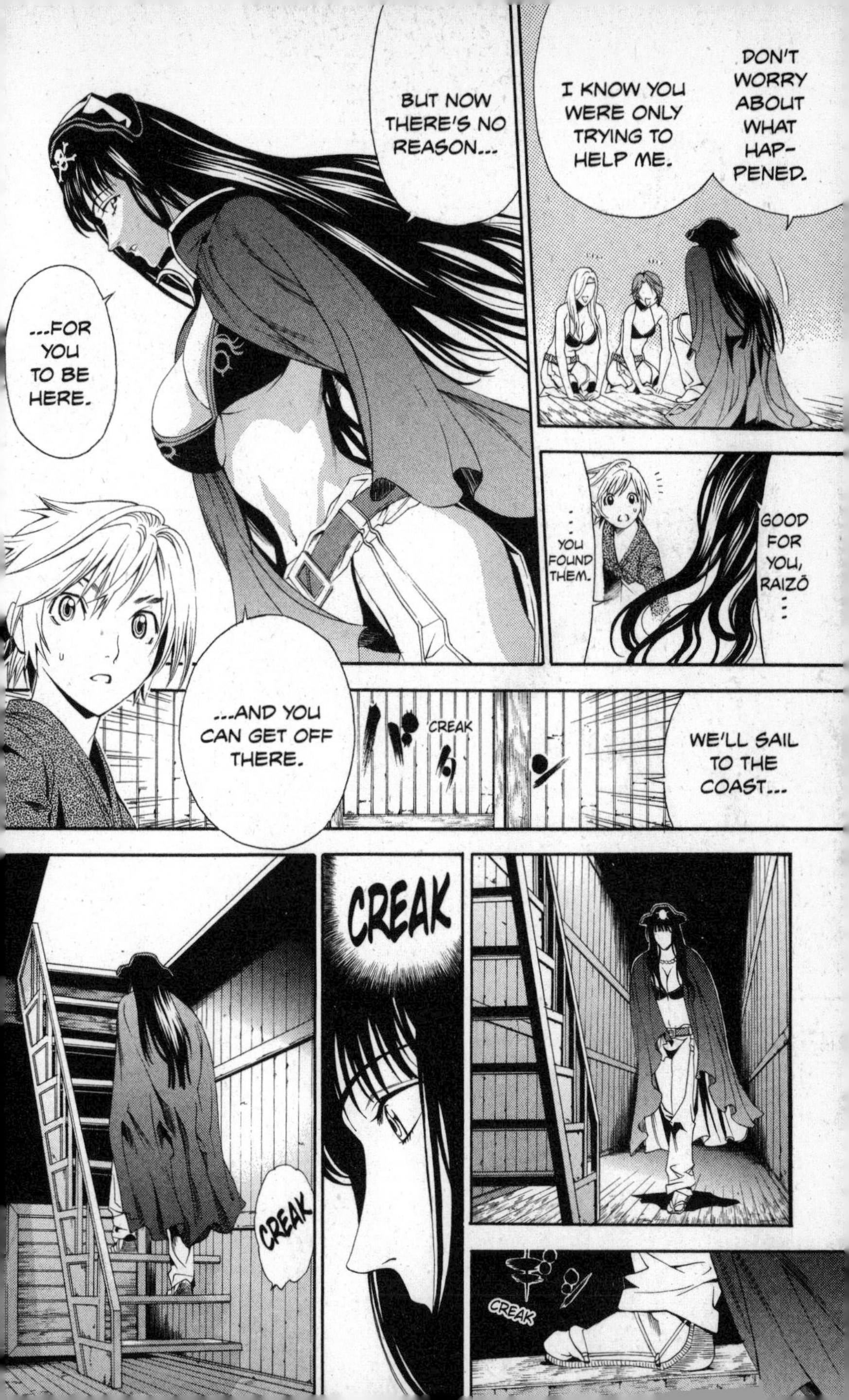
DON'T WORRY ABOUT WHAT HAP-PENED.
I KNOW YOU WERE ONLY TRYING TO HELP ME.
GOOD FOR YOU, RAIZŌ...
...YOU FOUND THEM.
BUT NOW THERE'S NO REASON...
...FOR YOU TO BE HERE.
WE'LL SAIL TO THE COAST...
CREAK
...AND YOU CAN GET OFF THERE.
CREAK
CREAK
CREAK

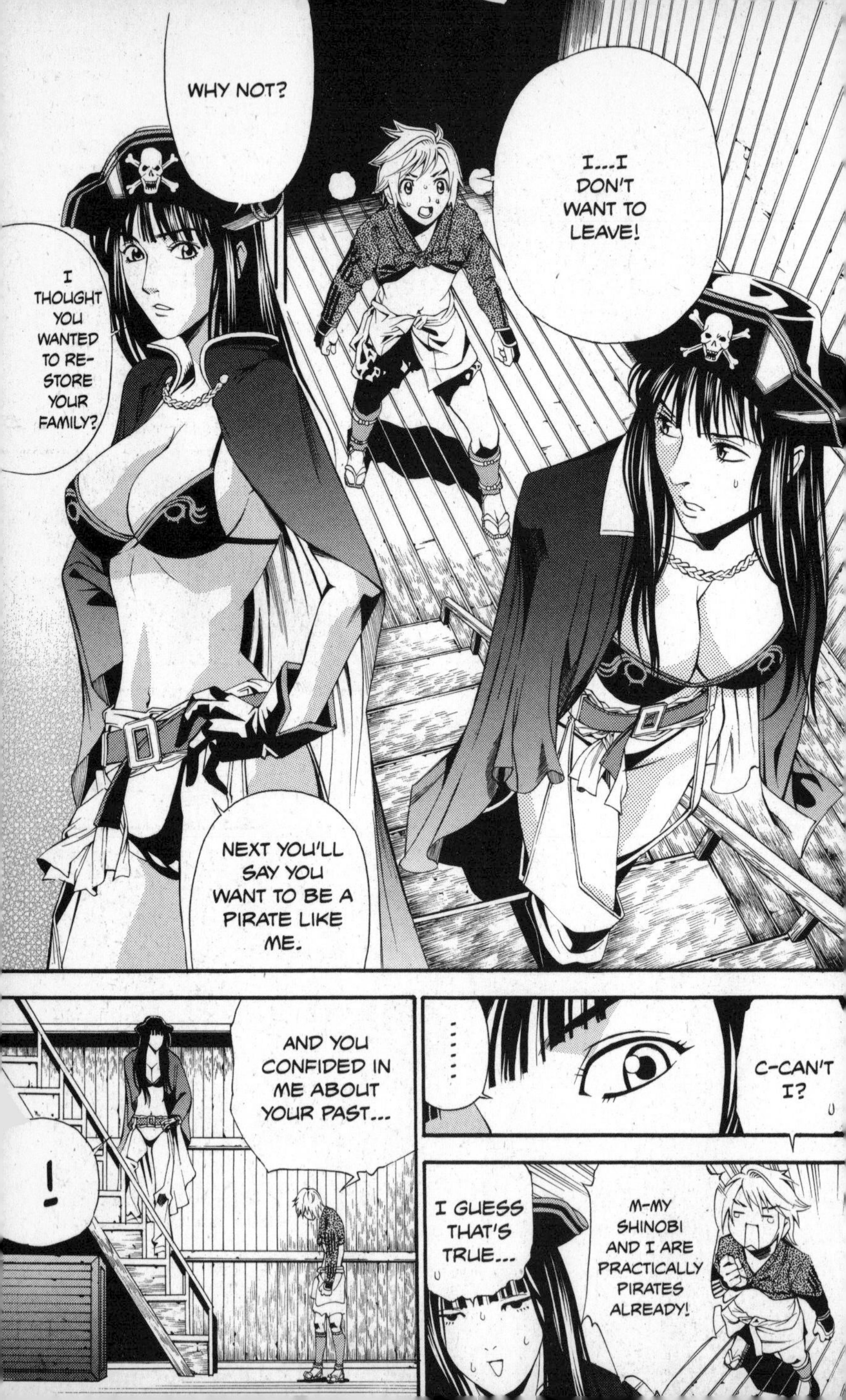
I...I DON'T WANT TO LEAVE!
WHY NOT?
I THOUGHT YOU WANTED TO RE-STORE YOUR FAMILY?
NEXT YOU'LL SAY YOU WANT TO BE A PIRATE LIKE ME.
C-CAN'T I?
......
M-MY SHINOBI AND I ARE PRACTICALLY PIRATES ALREADY!
I GUESS THAT'S TRUE...
AND YOU CONFIDED IN ME ABOUT YOUR PAST...
!

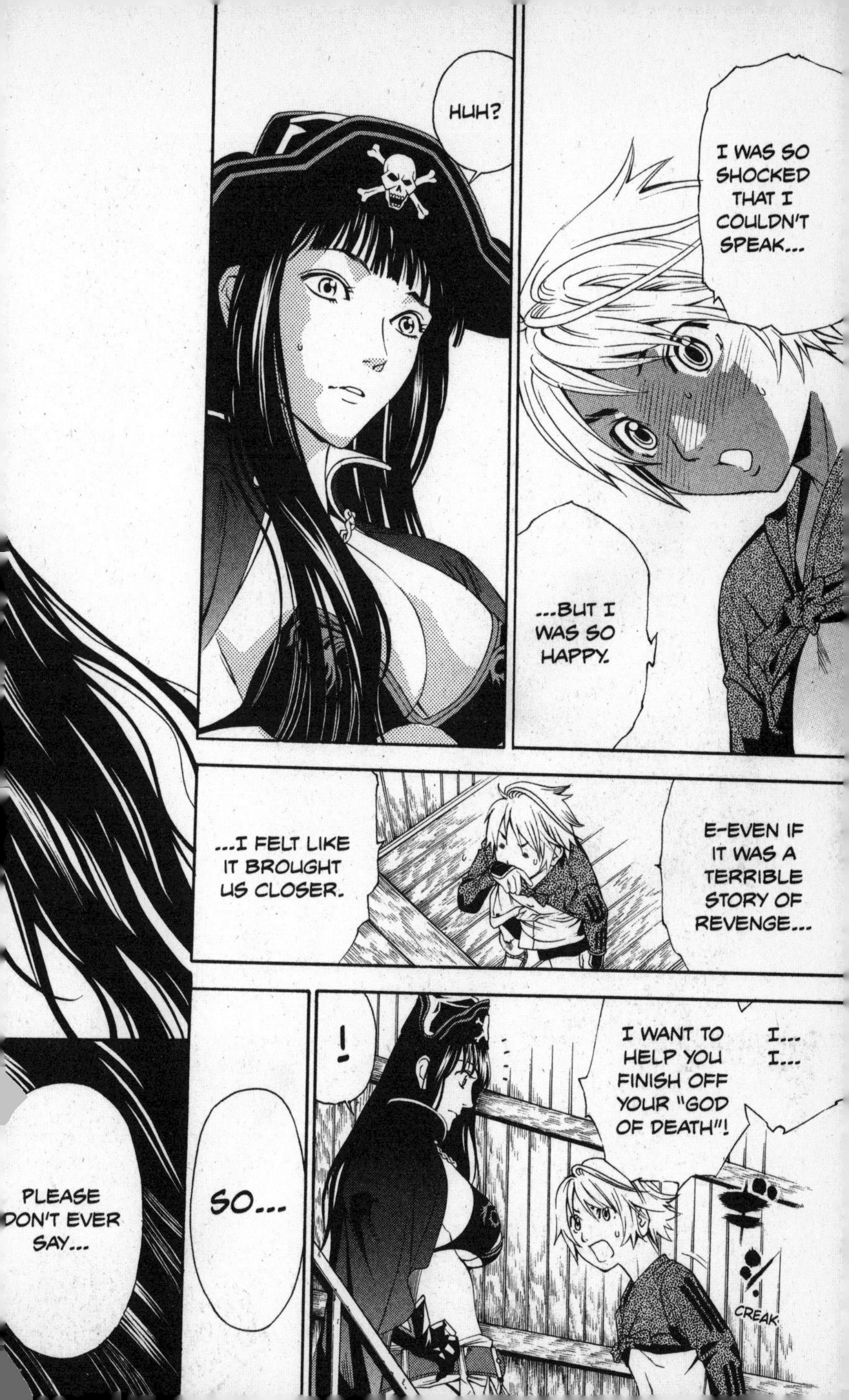
I WAS SO SHOCKED THAT I COULDN'T SPEAK...
...BUT I WAS SO HAPPY.
HUH?
E-EVEN IF IT WAS A TERRIBLE STORY OF REVENGE...
...I FELT LIKE IT BROUGHT US CLOSER.
I... I...
I WANT TO HELP YOU FINISH OFF YOUR "GOD OF DEATH"!
CREAK
!
SO...
PLEASE DON'T EVER SAY...

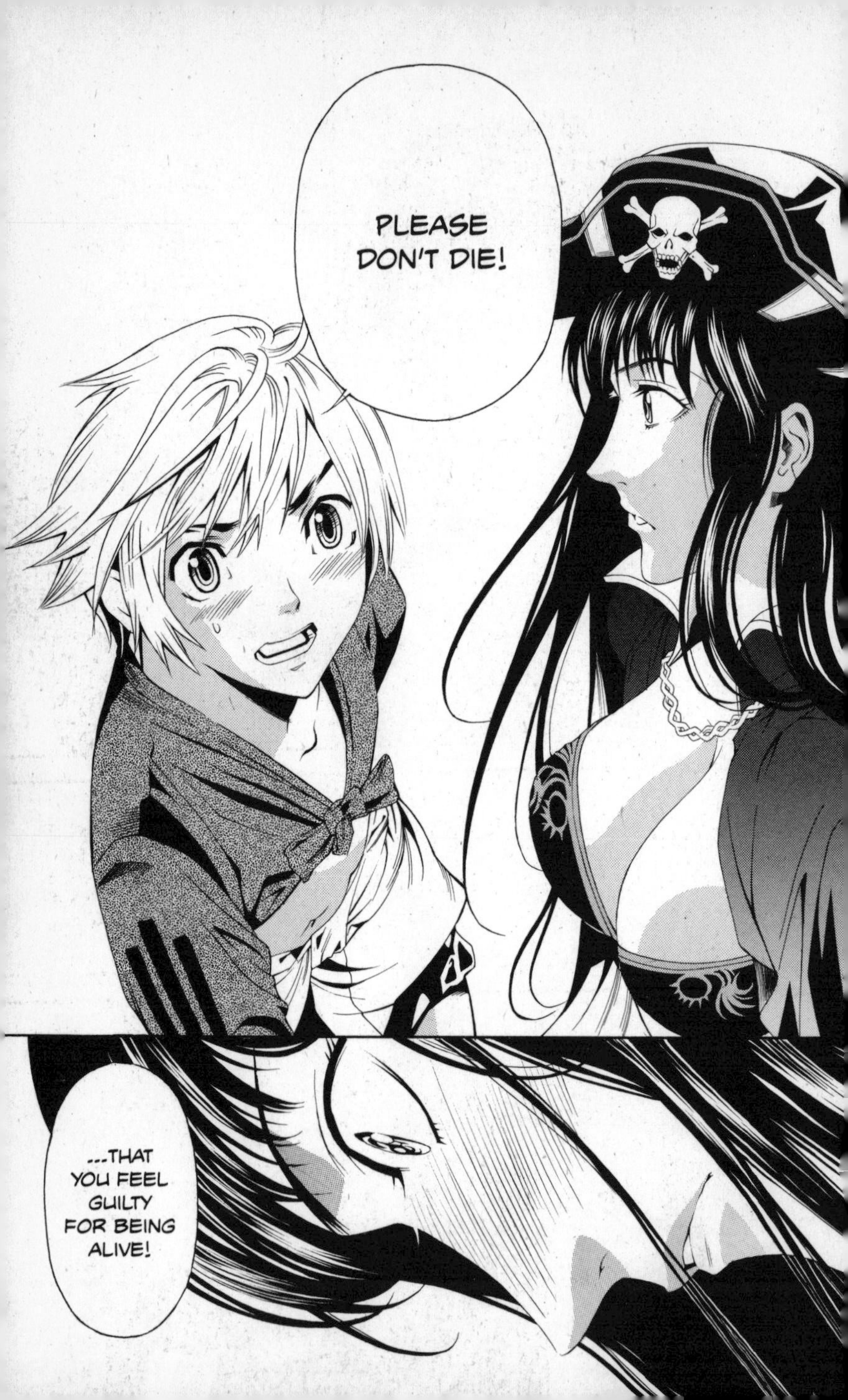
PLEASE DON'T DIE!
...THAT YOU FEEL GUILTY FOR BEING ALIVE!

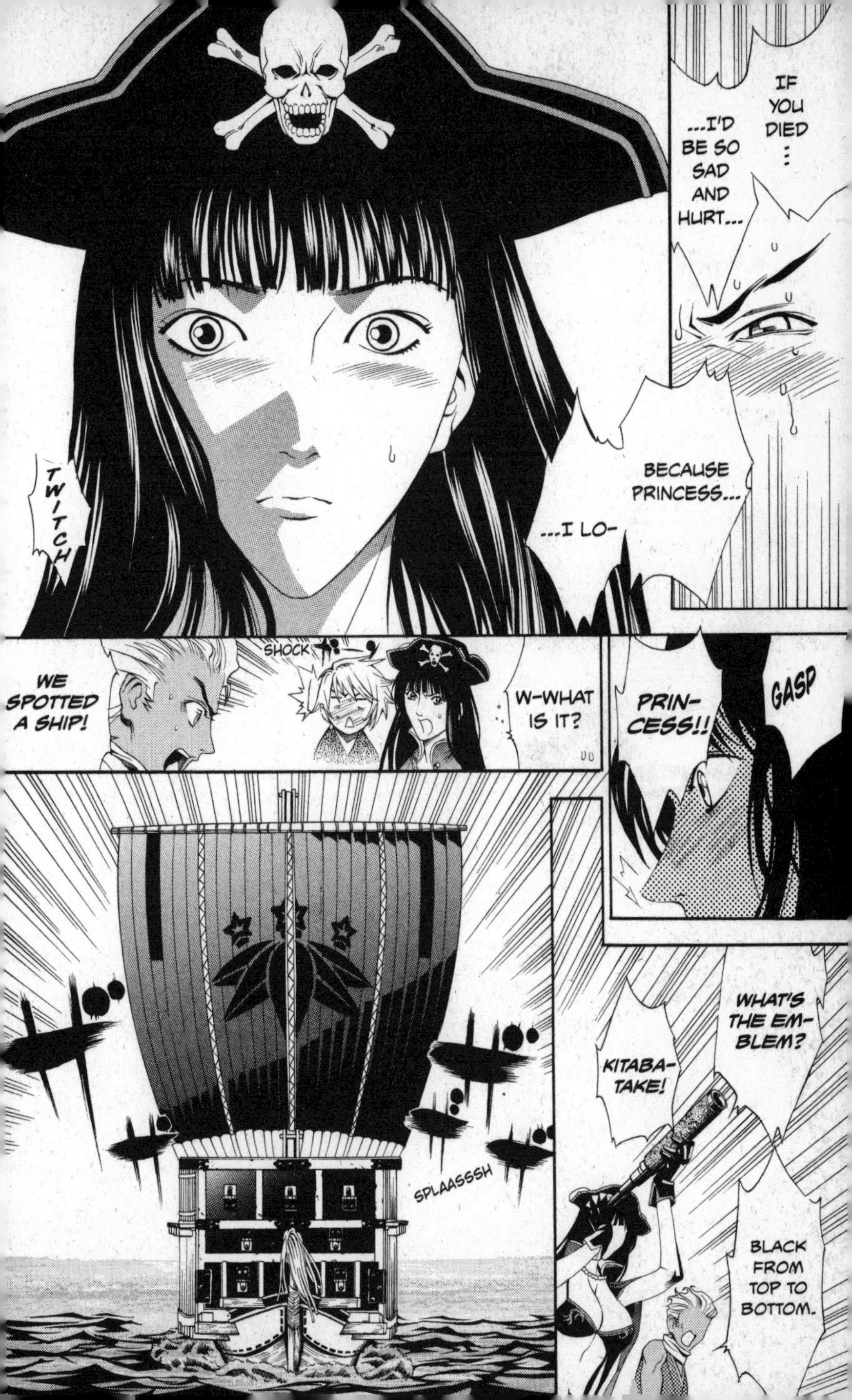
IF YOU DIED...
...I'D BE SO SAD AND HURT...
BECAUSE PRINCESS...
...I LO-
TWITCH
GASP
PRIN-CESS!!
W-WHAT IS IT?
SHOCK
WE SPOTTED A SHIP!
SPLAASSSH
WHAT'S THE EM-BLEM?
KITABA-TAKE!
BLACK FROM TOP TO BOTTOM.

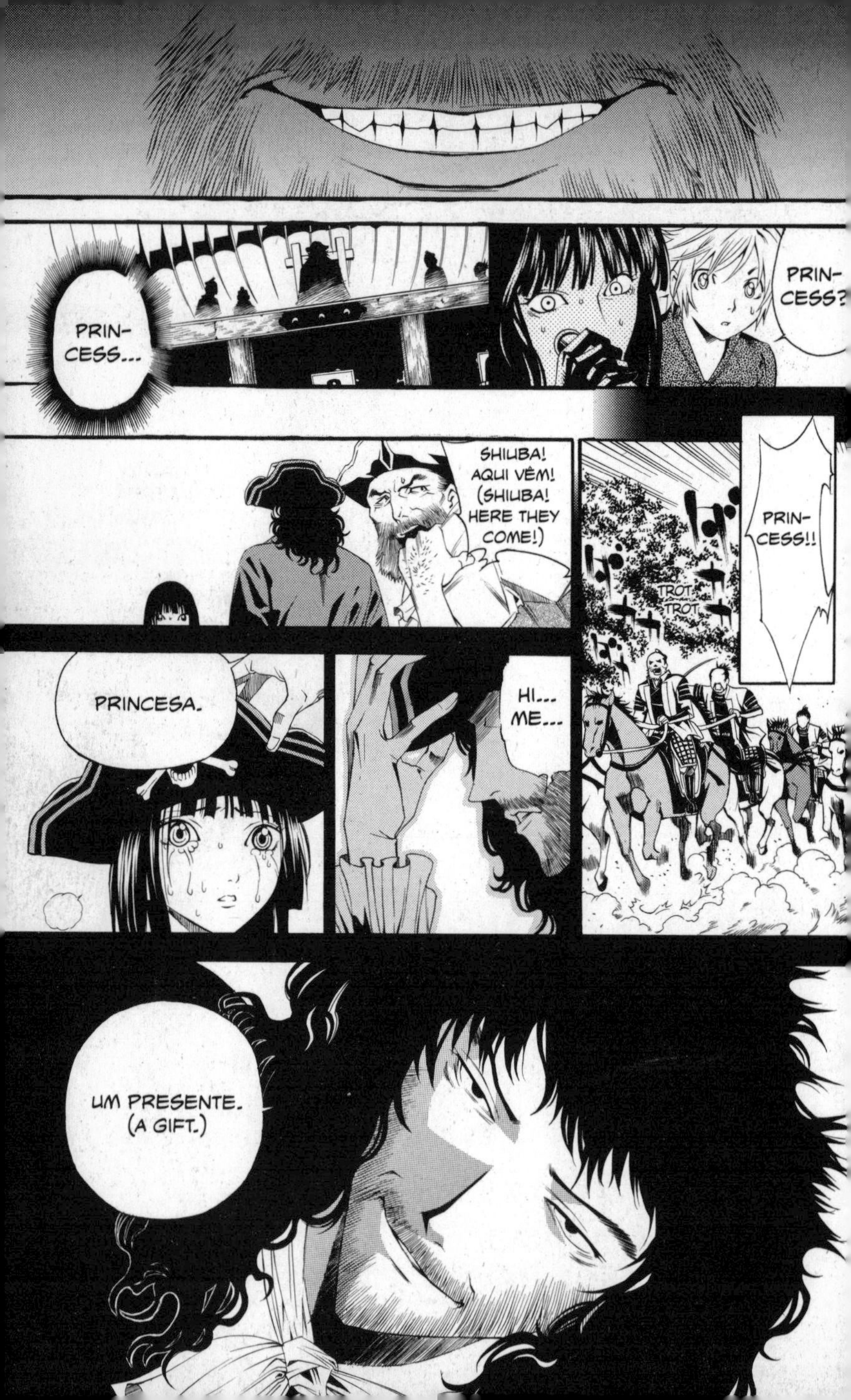
PRIN-CESS?
PRIN-CESS...
PRIN-CESS!!
TROT TROT
SHIUBA! AQUI VÊM! (SHIUBA! HERE THEY COME!)
HI... ME...
PRINCESA.
UM PRESENTE. (A GIFT.)

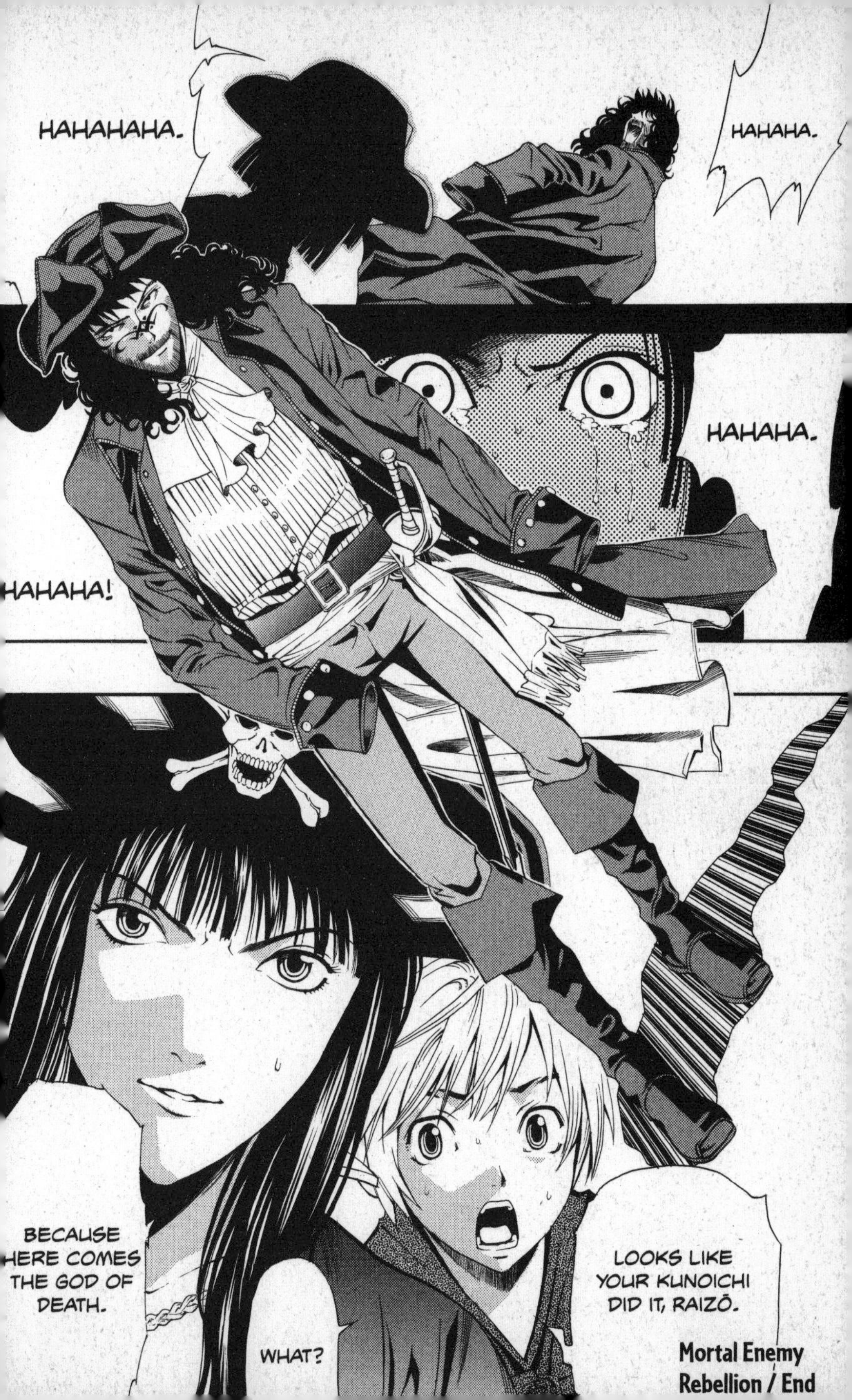
HAHAHA.
HAHAHAHA.
HAHAHA.
HAHAHA!
LOOKS LIKE YOUR KUNOICHI DID IT, RAIZŌ.
BECAUSE HERE COMES THE GOD OF DEATH.
WHAT?
Mortal Enemy Rebellion / End

**Ninja Girls**

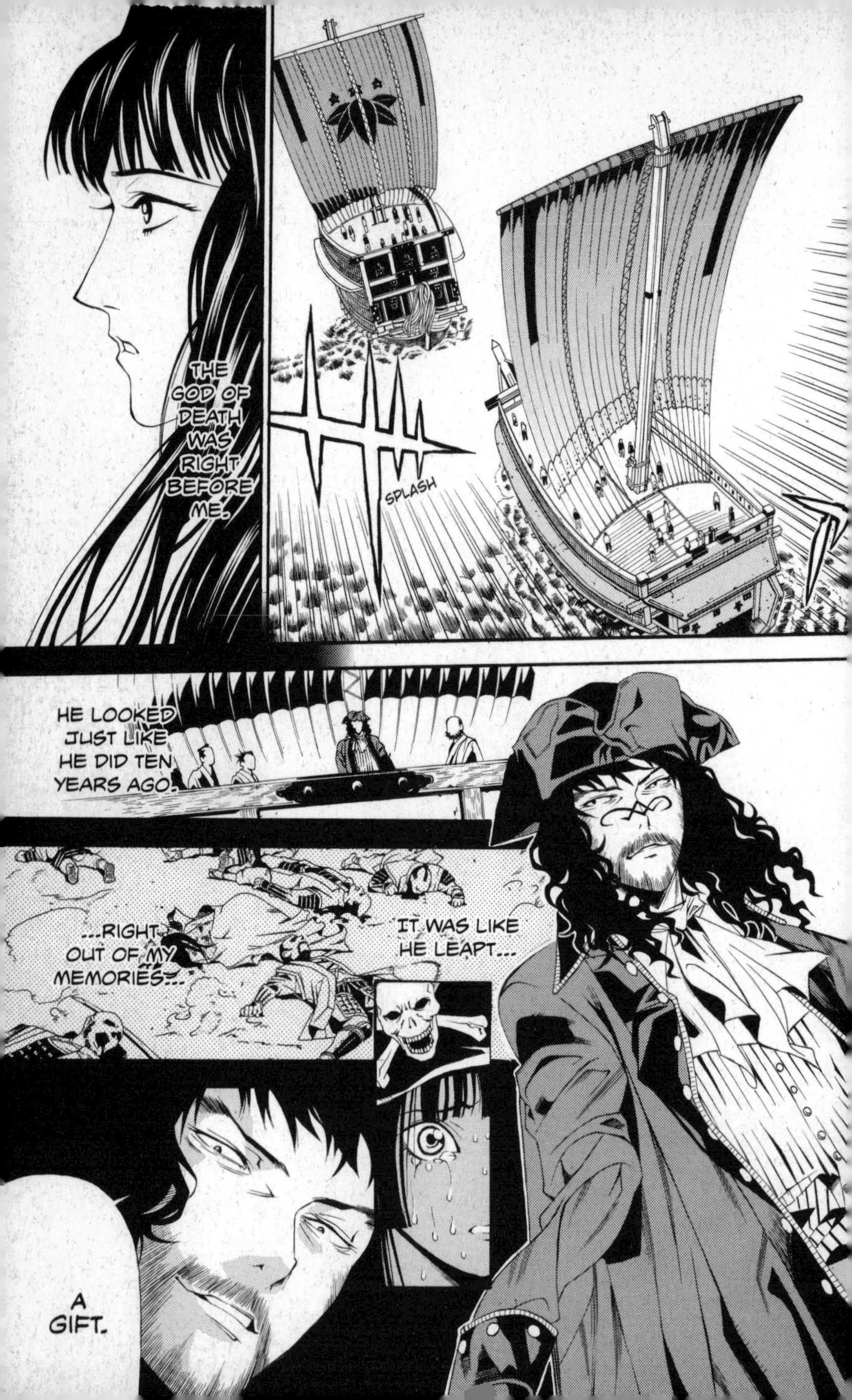
SPLASH
THE GOD OF DEATH WAS RIGHT BEFORE ME.
HE LOOKED JUST LIKE HE DID TEN YEARS AGO.
IT WAS LIKE HE LEAPT...
...RIGHT OUT OF MY MEMORIES...
A GIFT.

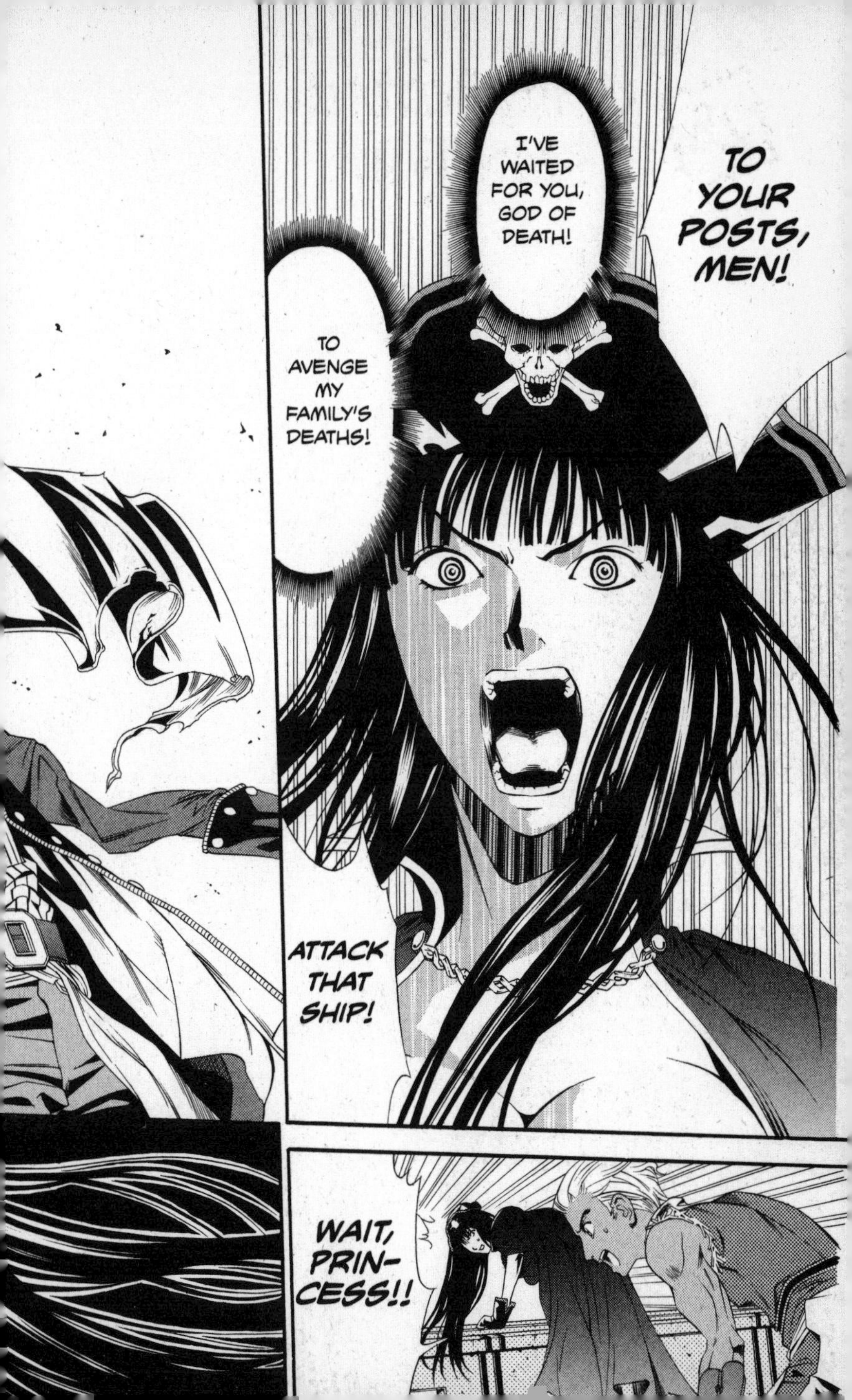
TO YOUR POSTS, MEN!
I'VE WAITED FOR YOU, GOD OF DEATH!
TO AVENGE MY FAMILY'S DEATHS!
ATTACK THAT SHIP!
WAIT, PRIN-CESS!!

# 28 Complicated Rebellion

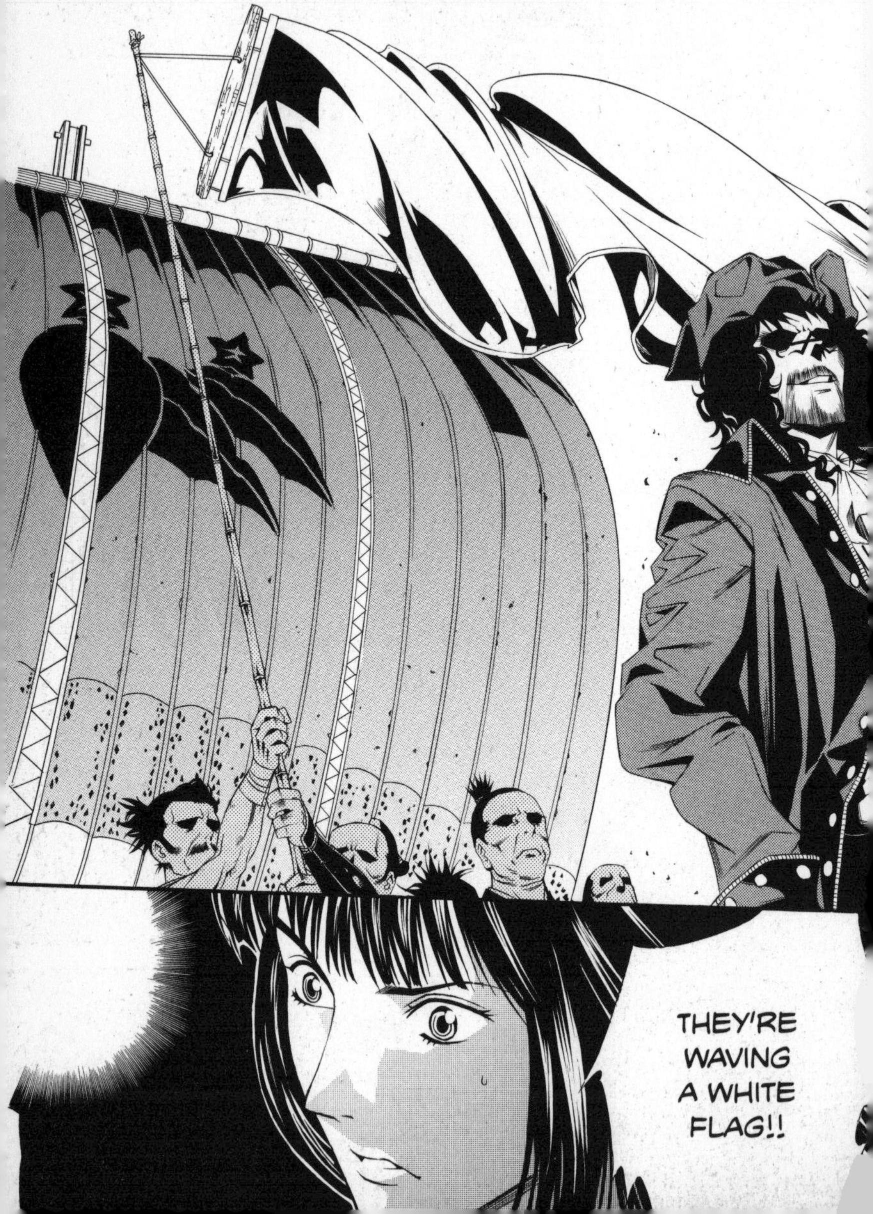
THEY'RE WAVING A WHITE FLAG!!

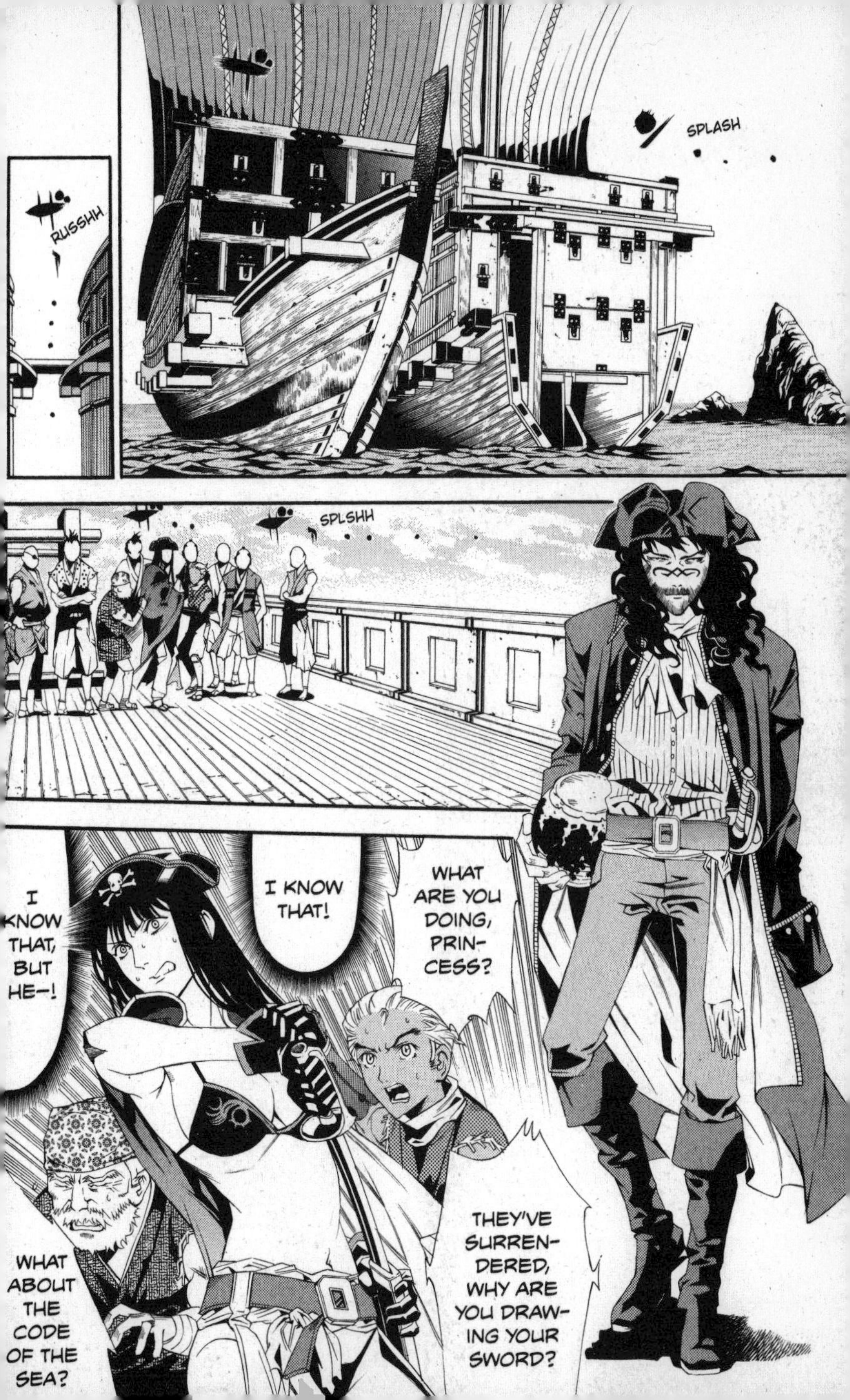
SPLASH
RUSSHH
SPLSHH
WHAT ARE YOU DOING, PRIN- CESS?
I KNOW THAT!
I KNOW THAT, BUT HE—!
THEY'VE SURREN- DERED, WHY ARE YOU DRAW- ING YOUR SWORD?
WHAT ABOUT THE CODE OF THE SEA?

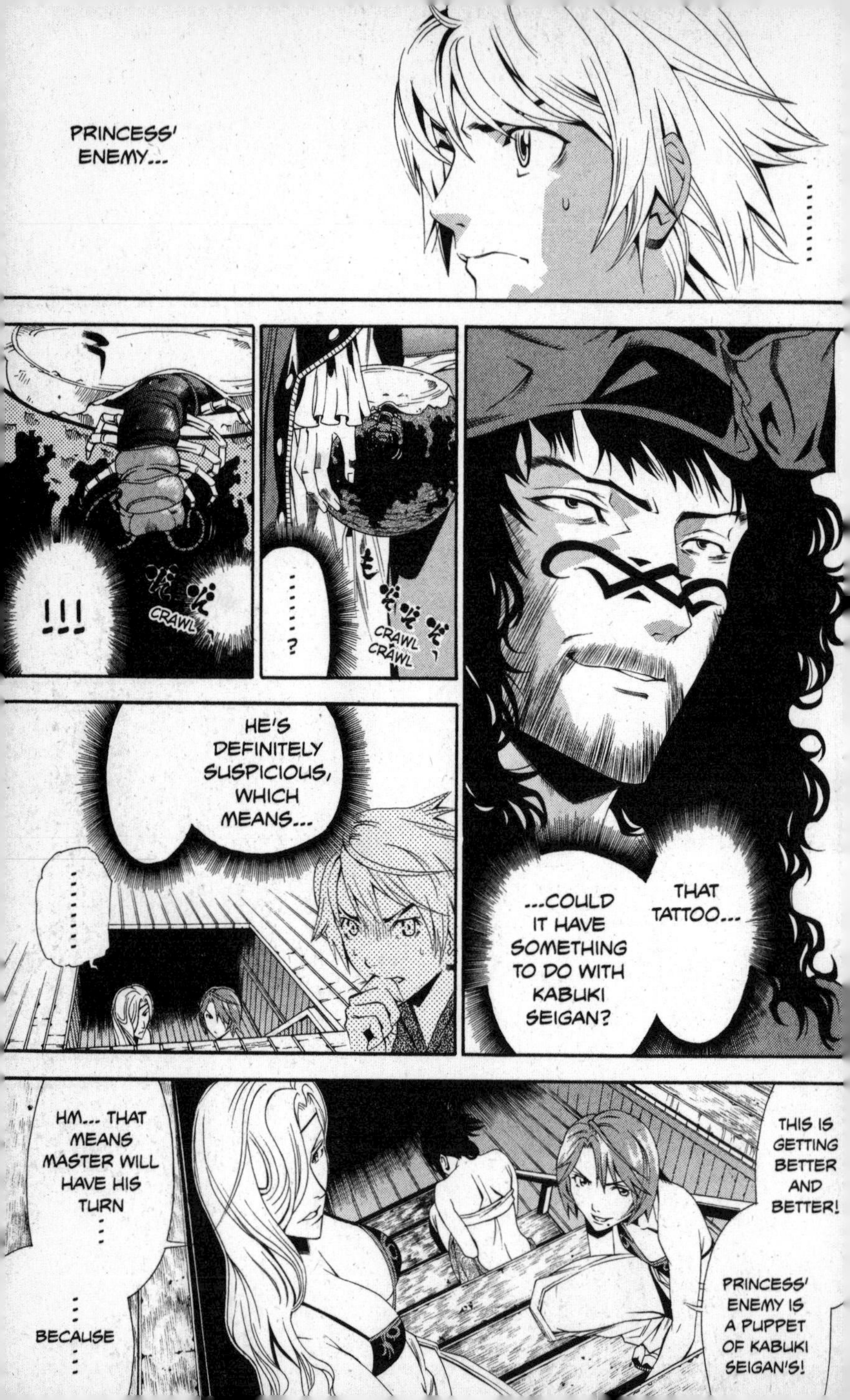
......
PRINCESS' ENEMY...
THAT TATTOO...
...COULD IT HAVE SOMETHING TO DO WITH KABUKI SEIGAN?
......?
CRAWL CRAWL
CRAWL
!!!
HE'S DEFINITELY SUSPICIOUS, WHICH MEANS...
......
THIS IS GETTING BETTER AND BETTER!
PRINCESS' ENEMY IS A PUPPET OF KABUKI SEIGAN'S!
HM... THAT MEANS MASTER WILL HAVE HIS TURN ...
... BECAUSE ...

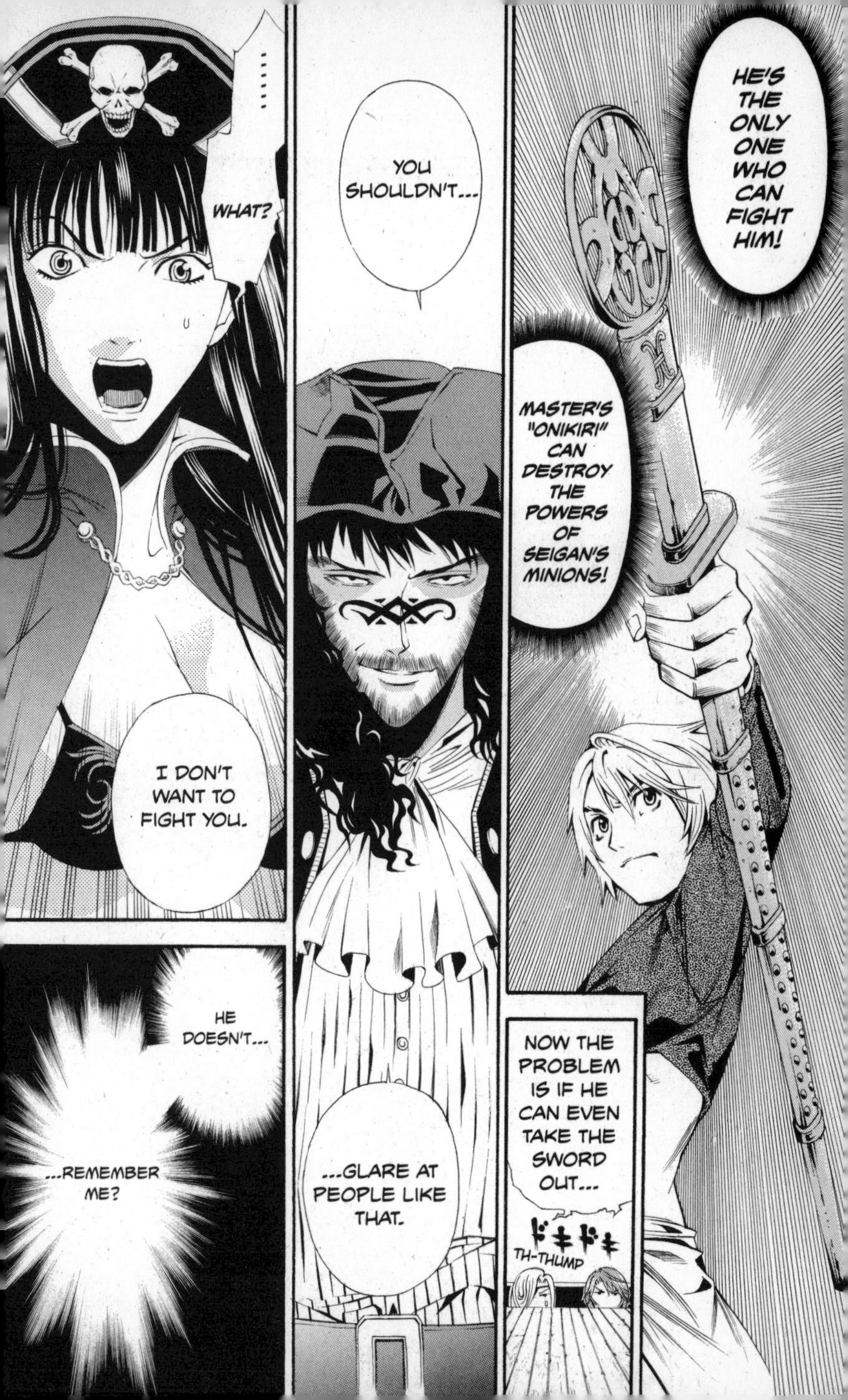
HE'S THE ONLY ONE WHO CAN FIGHT HIM!
MASTER'S "ONIKIRI" CAN DESTROY THE POWERS OF SEIGAN'S MINIONS!
NOW THE PROBLEM IS IF HE CAN EVEN TAKE THE SWORD OUT...
ドキドキ
TH-THUMP
YOU SHOULDN'T...
...GLARE AT PEOPLE LIKE THAT.
WHAT?
I DON'T WANT TO FIGHT YOU.
HE DOESN'T...
...REMEMBER ME?

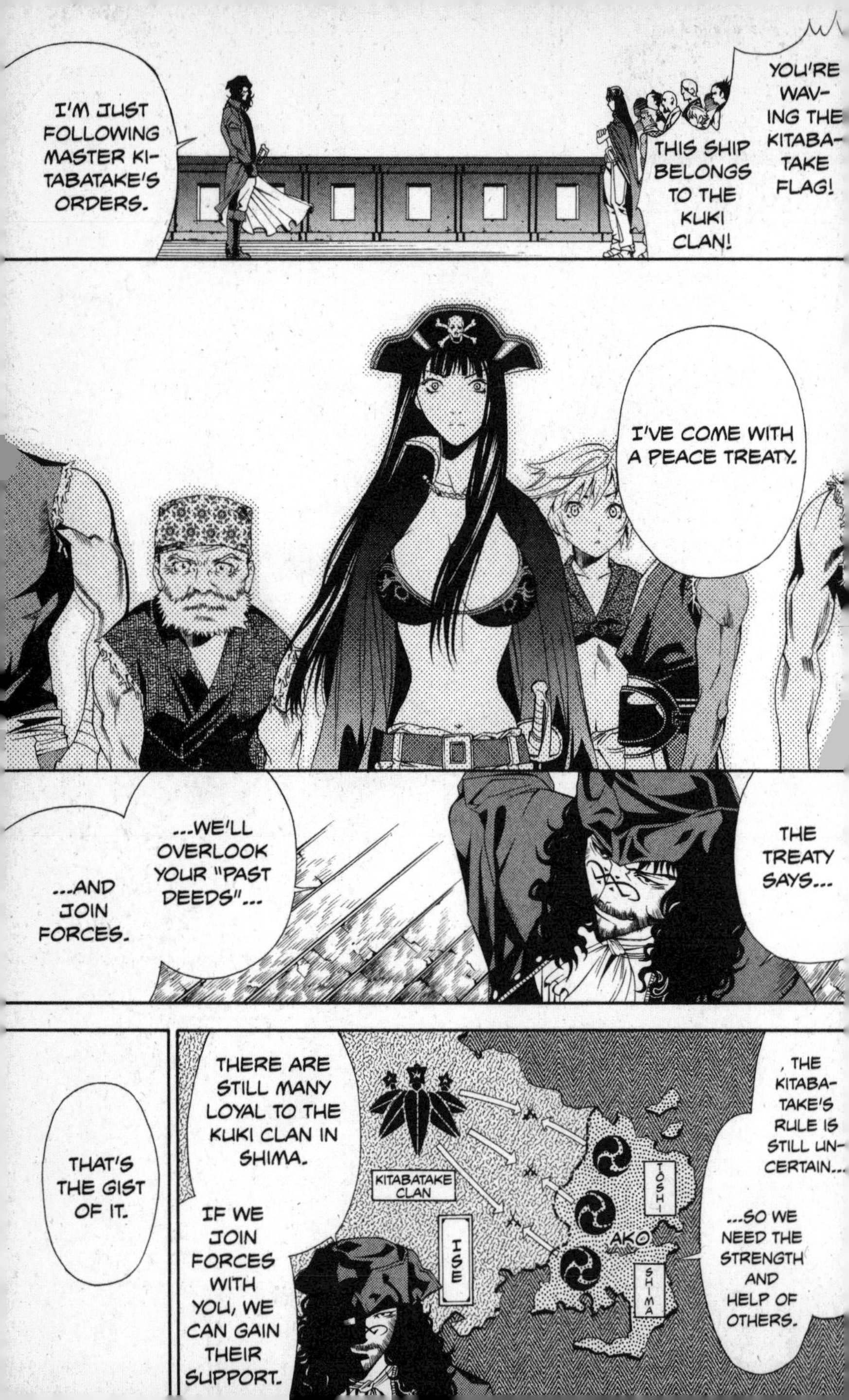
YOU'RE WAVING THE KITABATAKE FLAG!
THIS SHIP BELONGS TO THE KUKI CLAN!
I'M JUST FOLLOWING MASTER KITABATAKE'S ORDERS.
I'VE COME WITH A PEACE TREATY.
THE TREATY SAYS...
...WE'LL OVERLOOK YOUR "PAST DEEDS"...
...AND JOIN FORCES.
, THE KITABATAKE'S RULE IS STILL UNCERTAIN...
...SO WE NEED THE STRENGTH AND HELP OF OTHERS.
TOSHI
AKO
SHIMA
KITABATAKE CLAN
ISE
THERE ARE STILL MANY LOYAL TO THE KUKI CLAN IN SHIMA.
IF WE JOIN FORCES WITH YOU, WE CAN GAIN THEIR SUPPORT.
THAT'S THE GIST OF IT.

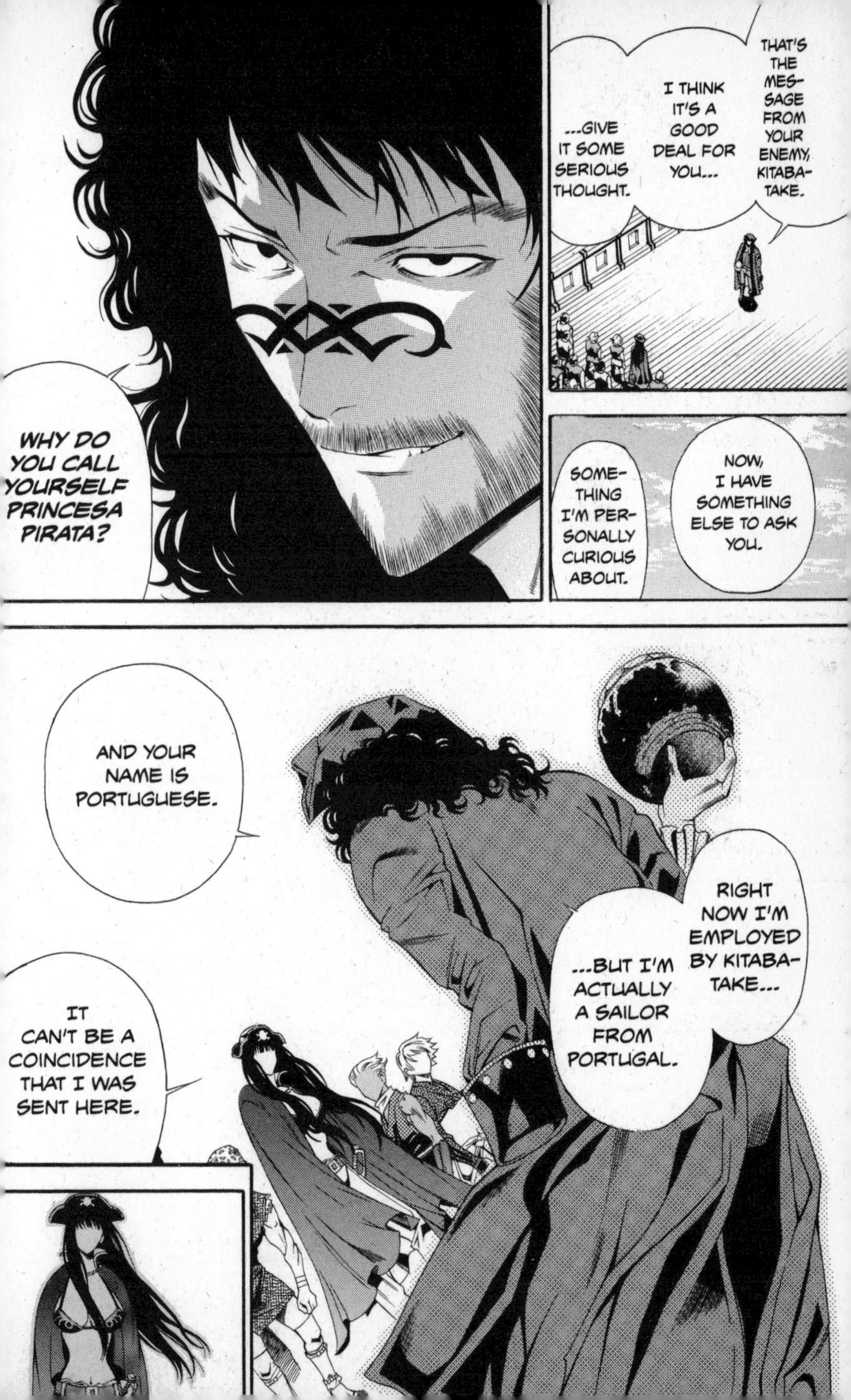

THAT'S THE MES-SAGE FROM YOUR ENEMY, KITABA-TAKE.
I THINK IT'S A GOOD DEAL FOR YOU...
...GIVE IT SOME SERIOUS THOUGHT.
NOW, I HAVE SOMETHING ELSE TO ASK YOU.
SOME-THING I'M PER-SONALLY CURIOUS ABOUT.
WHY DO YOU CALL YOURSELF PRINCESA PIRATA?
AND YOUR NAME IS PORTUGUESE.
RIGHT NOW I'M EMPLOYED BY KITABA-TAKE...
...BUT I'M ACTUALLY A SAILOR FROM PORTUGAL.
IT CAN'T BE A COINCIDENCE THAT I WAS SENT HERE.

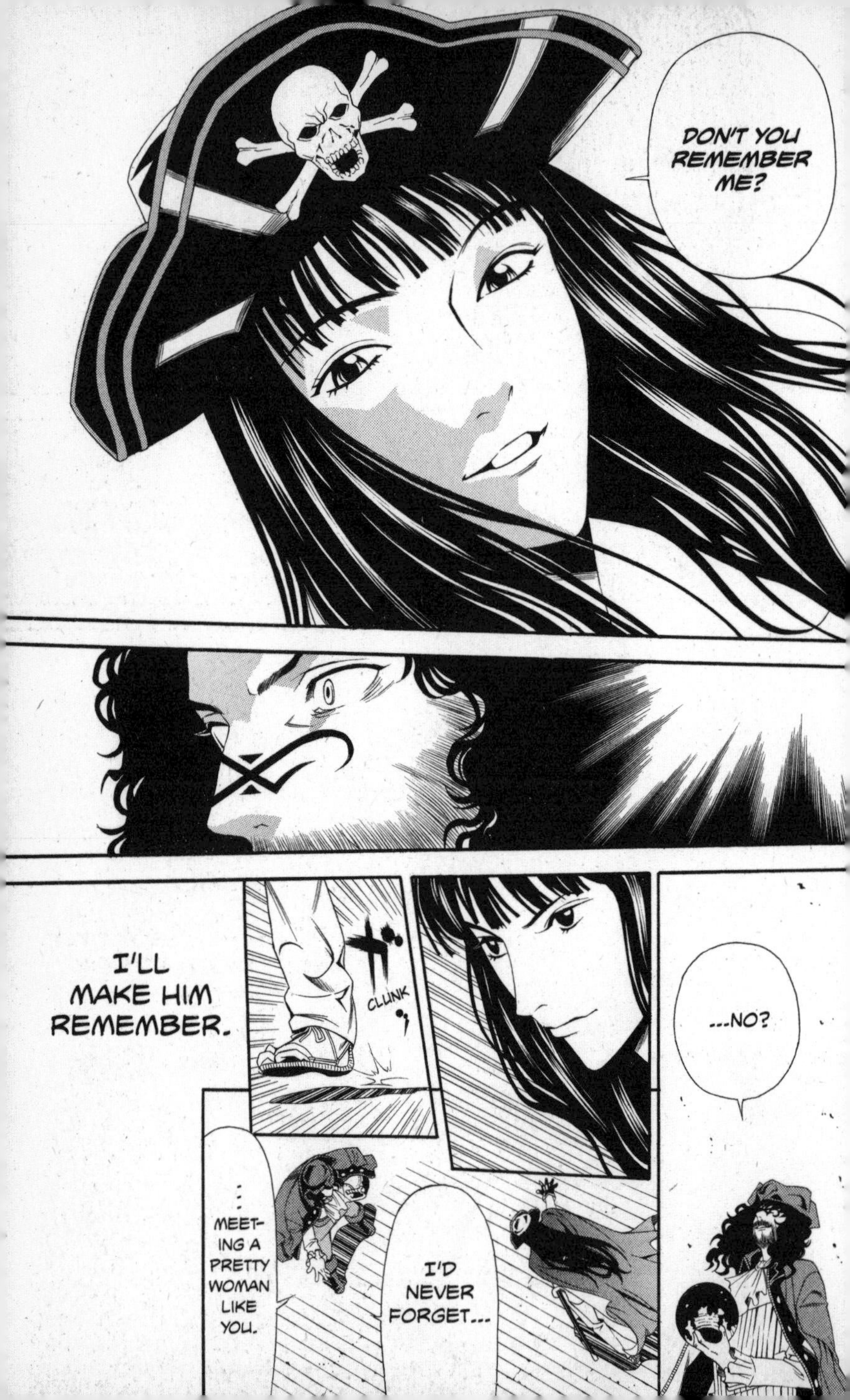
DON'T YOU REMEMBER ME?
...NO?
CLUNK
I'LL MAKE HIM REMEMBER.
I'D NEVER FORGET...
... MEET-ING A PRETTY WOMAN LIKE YOU.

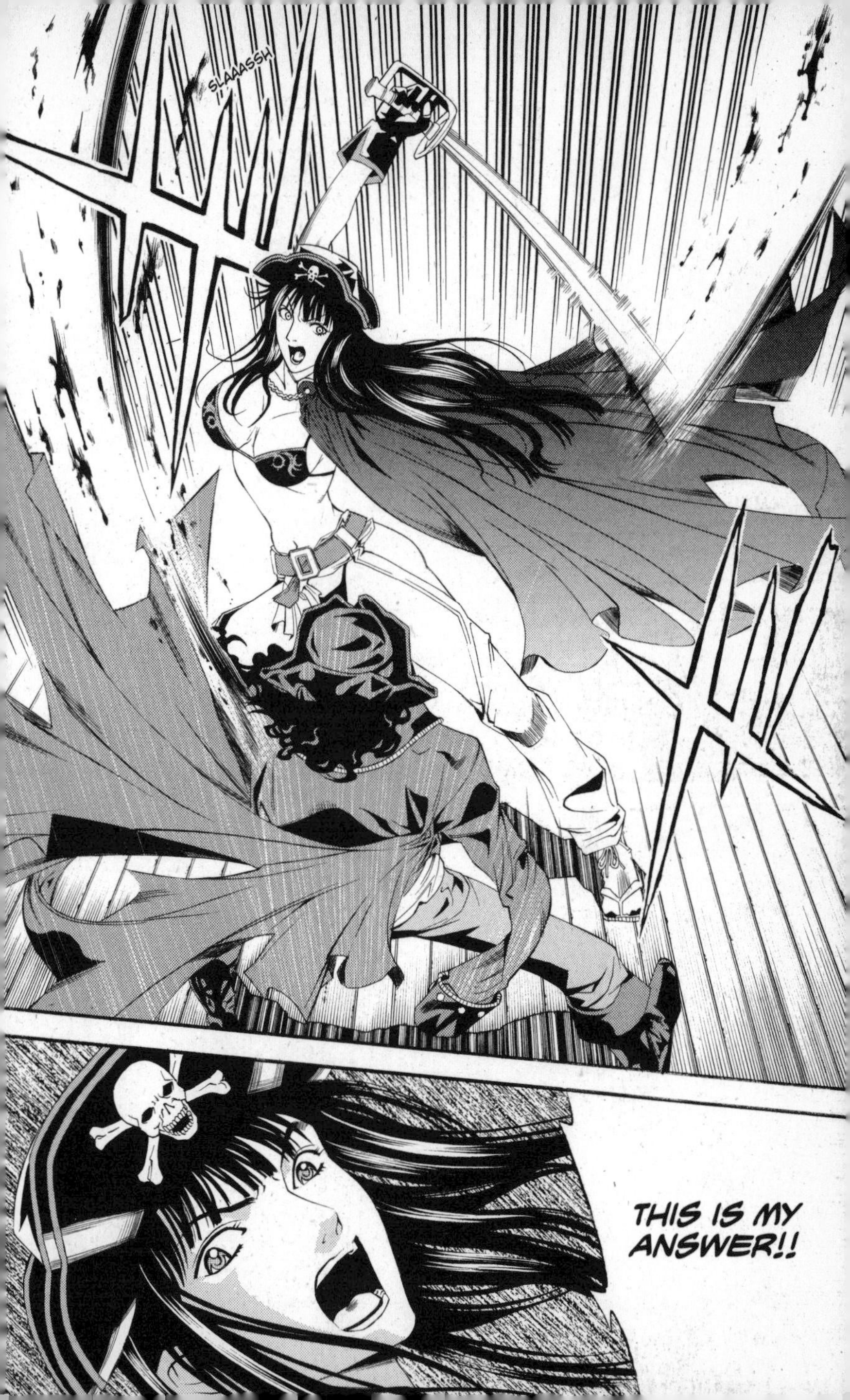
SLAAASSH
THIS IS MY ANSWER!!

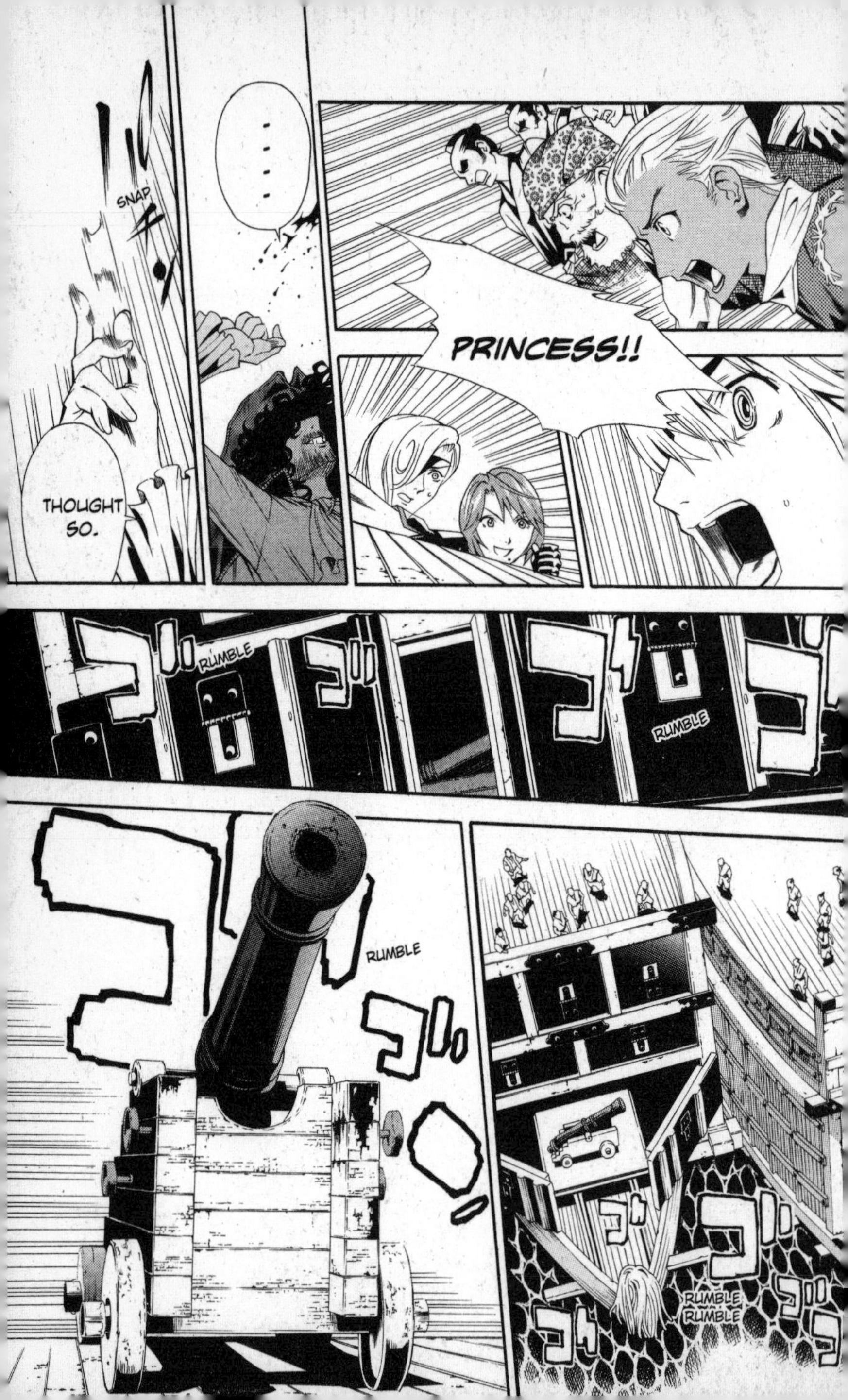
PRINCESS!!
....
SNAP
THOUGHT SO.
RUMBLE
RUMBLE
RUMBLE
RUMBLE
RUMBLE

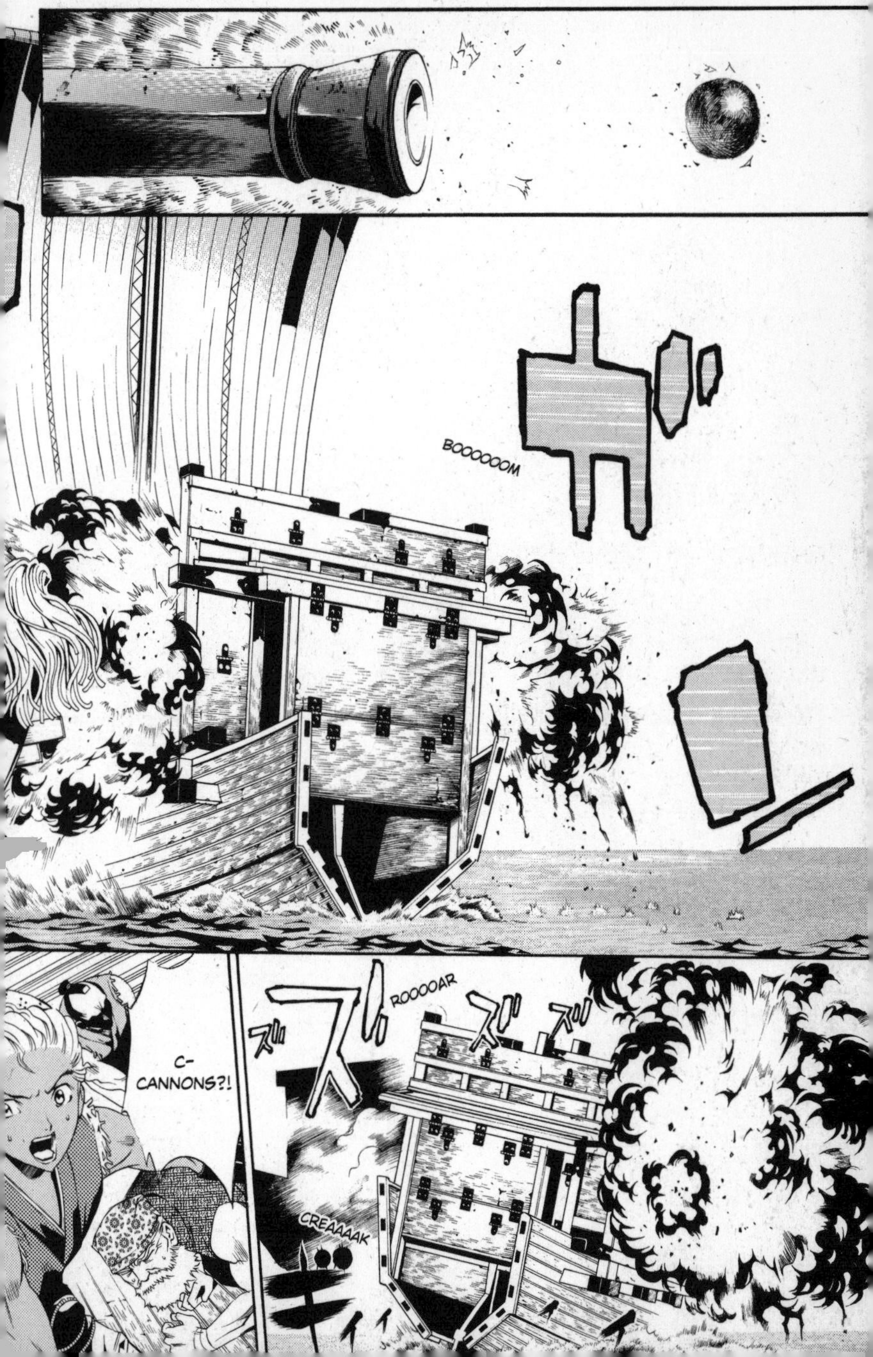
BOOOOOOM
ROOOOAR
CREAAAAK
C-
CANNONS?!

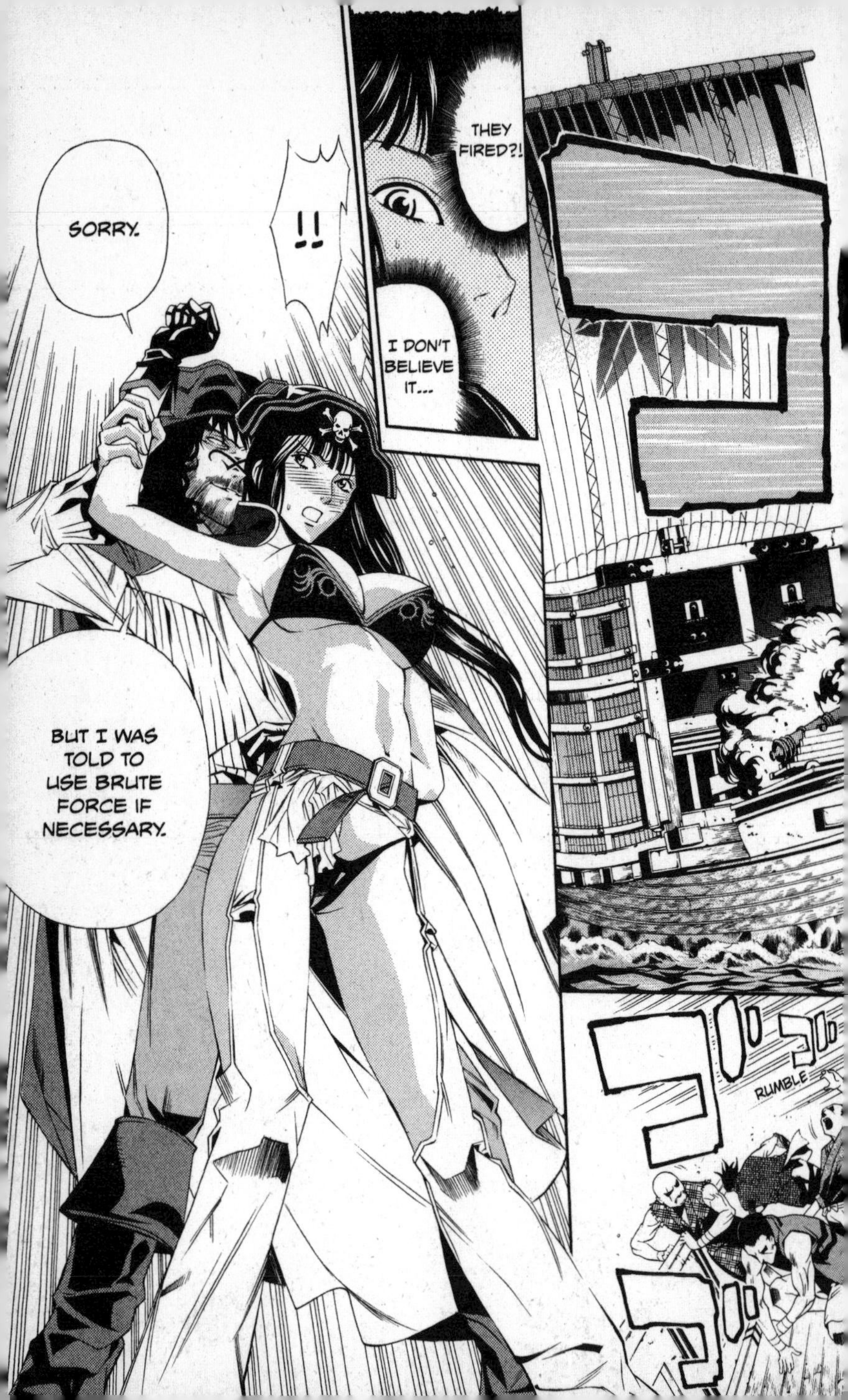
RUMBLE
THEY FIRED?!
I DON'T BELIEVE IT...
!!
SORRY.
BUT I WAS TOLD TO USE BRUTE FORCE IF NECESSARY.

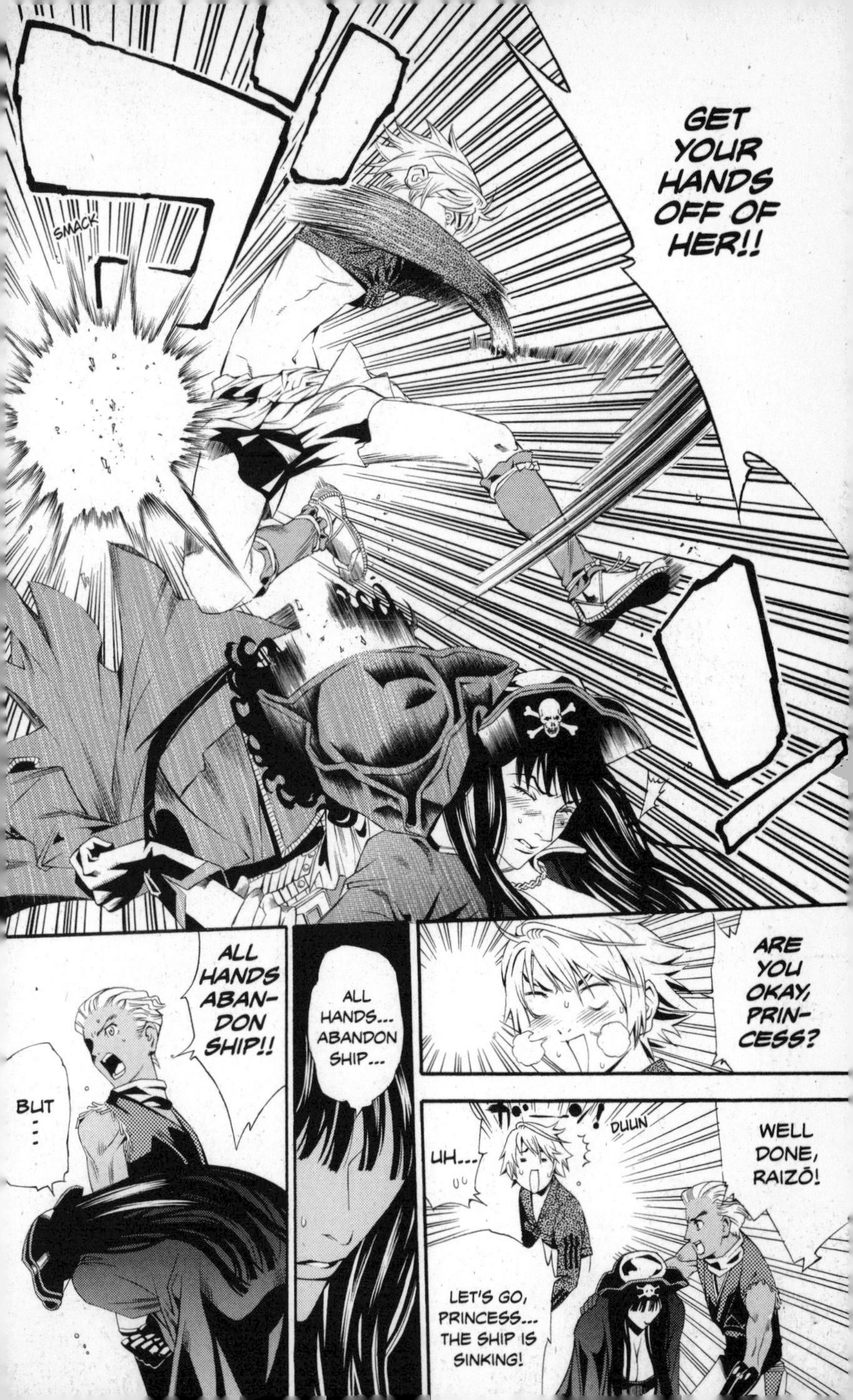
GET YOUR HANDS OFF OF HER!!
SMACK
ARE YOU OKAY, PRINCESS?
WELL DONE, RAIZŌ!
DUUN
UH...
LET'S GO, PRINCESS... THE SHIP IS SINKING!
ALL HANDS... ABANDON SHIP...
ALL HANDS ABANDON SHIP!!
BUT...

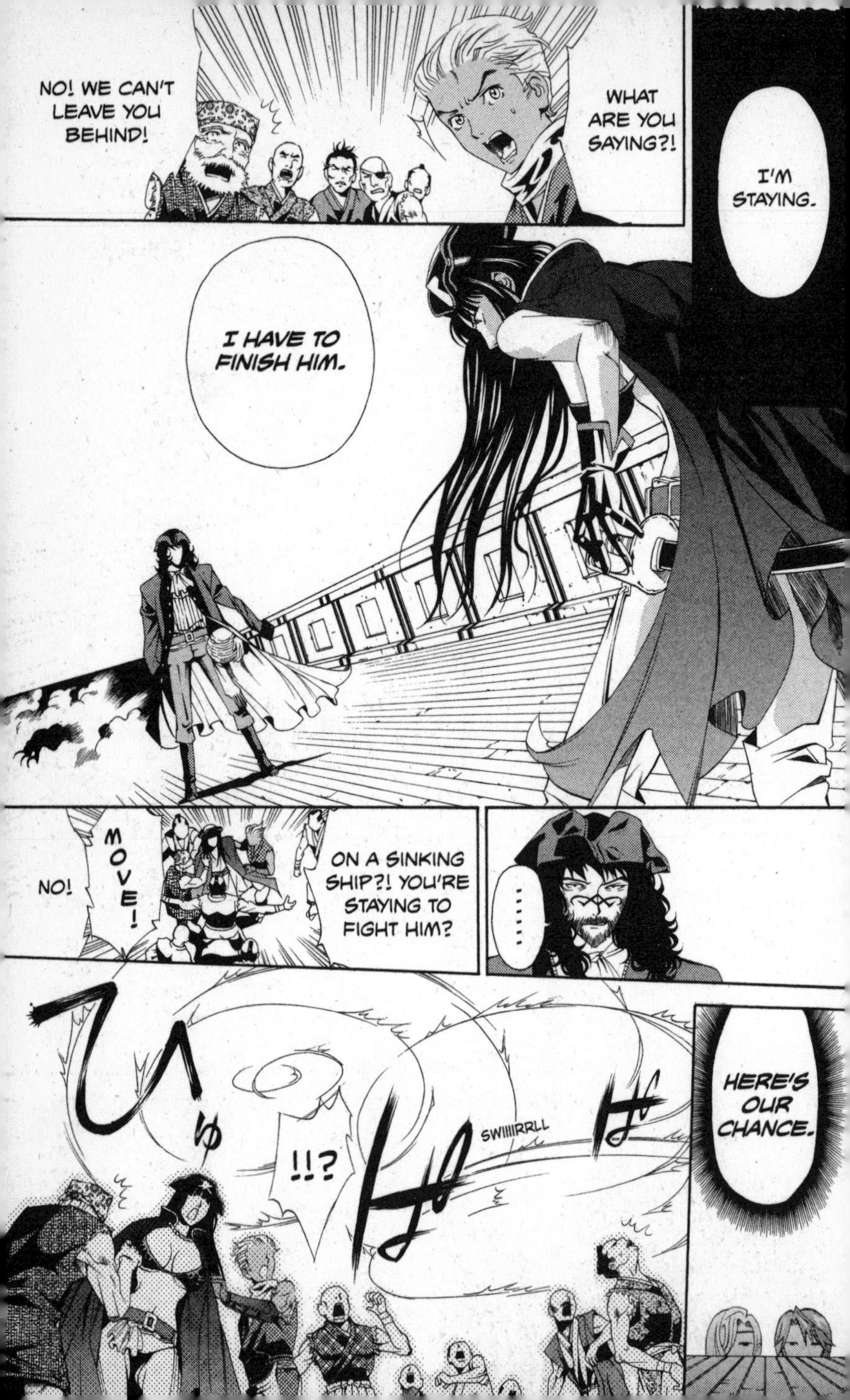
I'M STAYING.
WHAT ARE YOU SAYING?!
NO! WE CAN'T LEAVE YOU BEHIND!
I HAVE TO FINISH HIM.
......
ON A SINKING SHIP?! YOU'RE STAYING TO FIGHT HIM?
MOVE!
NO!
HERE'S OUR CHANCE.
SWIIIIRRLL
!!?

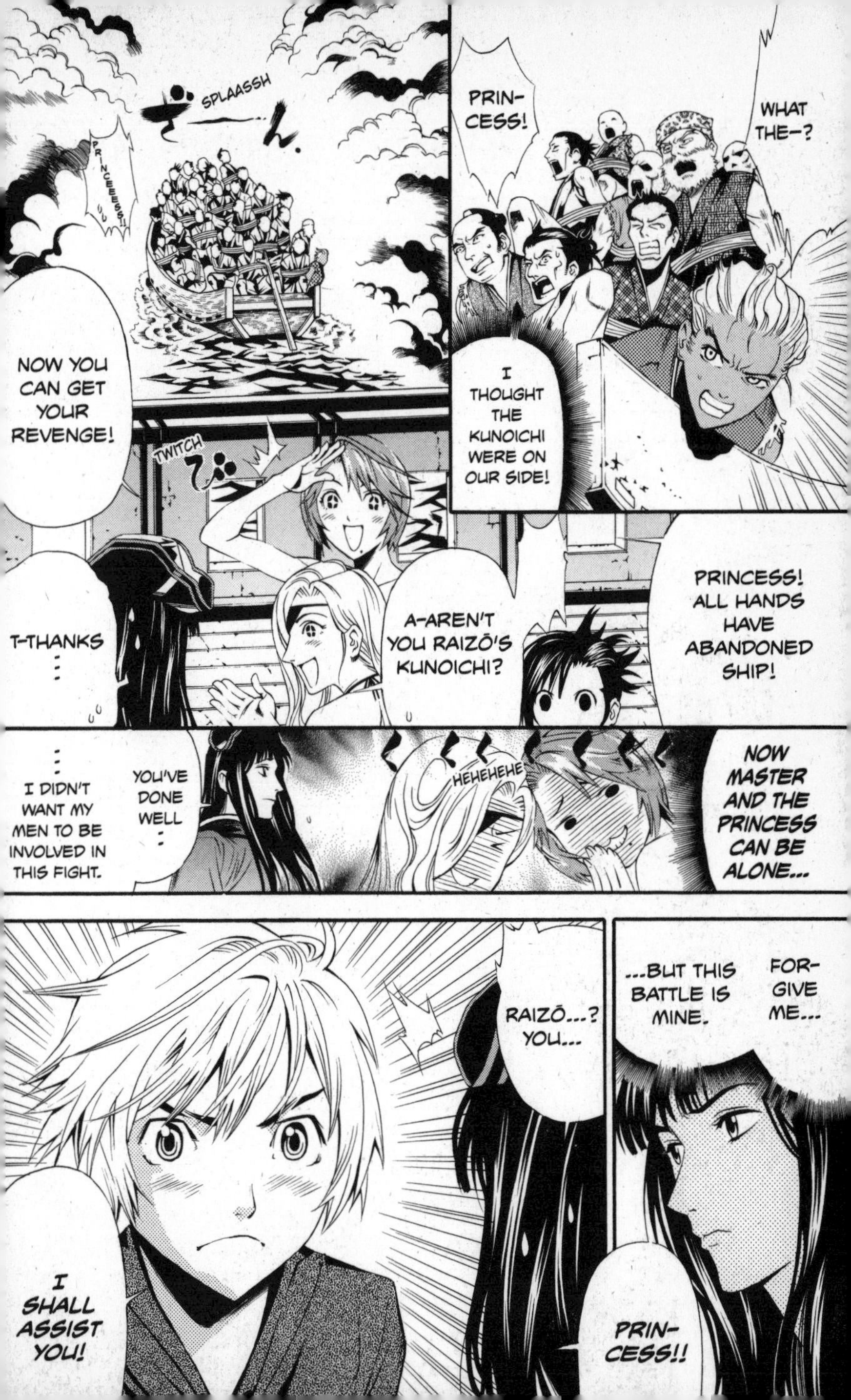
WHAT THE–?
PRIN-CESS!
I THOUGHT THE KUNOICHI WERE ON OUR SIDE!
SPLAASSH
PRINCEEESS!!
PRINCESS! ALL HANDS HAVE ABANDONED SHIP!
A-AREN'T YOU RAIZŌ'S KUNOICHI?
TWITCH
NOW YOU CAN GET YOUR REVENGE!
T-THANKS...
NOW MASTER AND THE PRINCESS CAN BE ALONE...
HEHEHEHE
YOU'VE DONE WELL...
...I DIDN'T WANT MY MEN TO BE INVOLVED IN THIS FIGHT.
FOR-GIVE ME...
...BUT THIS BATTLE IS MINE.
RAIZŌ...? YOU...
PRIN-CESS!!
I SHALL ASSIST YOU!

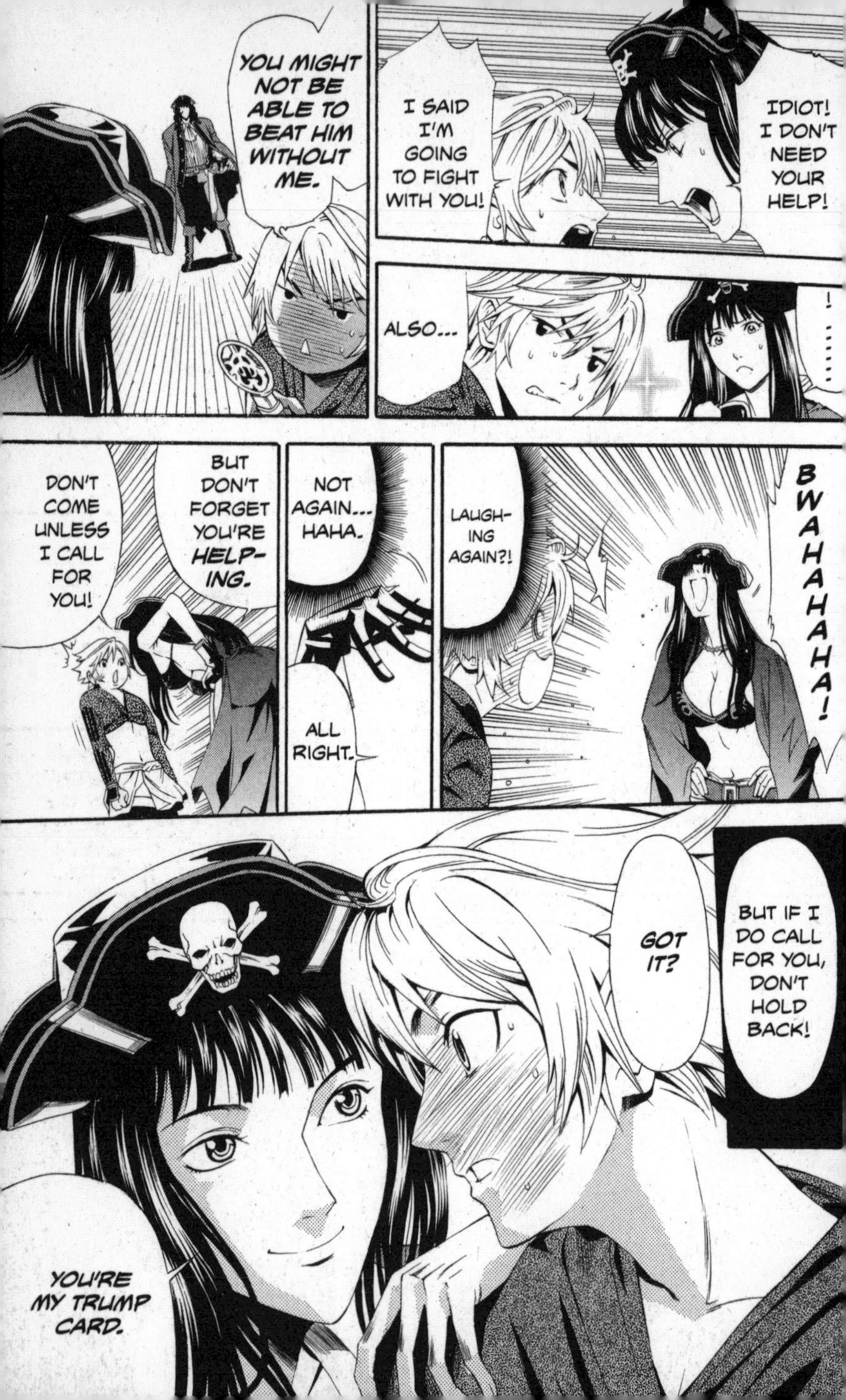

IDIOT! I DON'T NEED YOUR HELP!
I SAID I'M GOING TO FIGHT WITH YOU!
!......
ALSO...
YOU MIGHT NOT BE ABLE TO BEAT HIM WITHOUT ME.
BWAHAHAHAHA!
LAUGHING AGAIN?!
NOT AGAIN... HAHA.
ALL RIGHT.
BUT DON'T FORGET YOU'RE HELPING.
DON'T COME UNLESS I CALL FOR YOU!
BUT IF I DO CALL FOR YOU, DON'T HOLD BACK!
GOT IT?
YOU'RE MY TRUMP CARD.

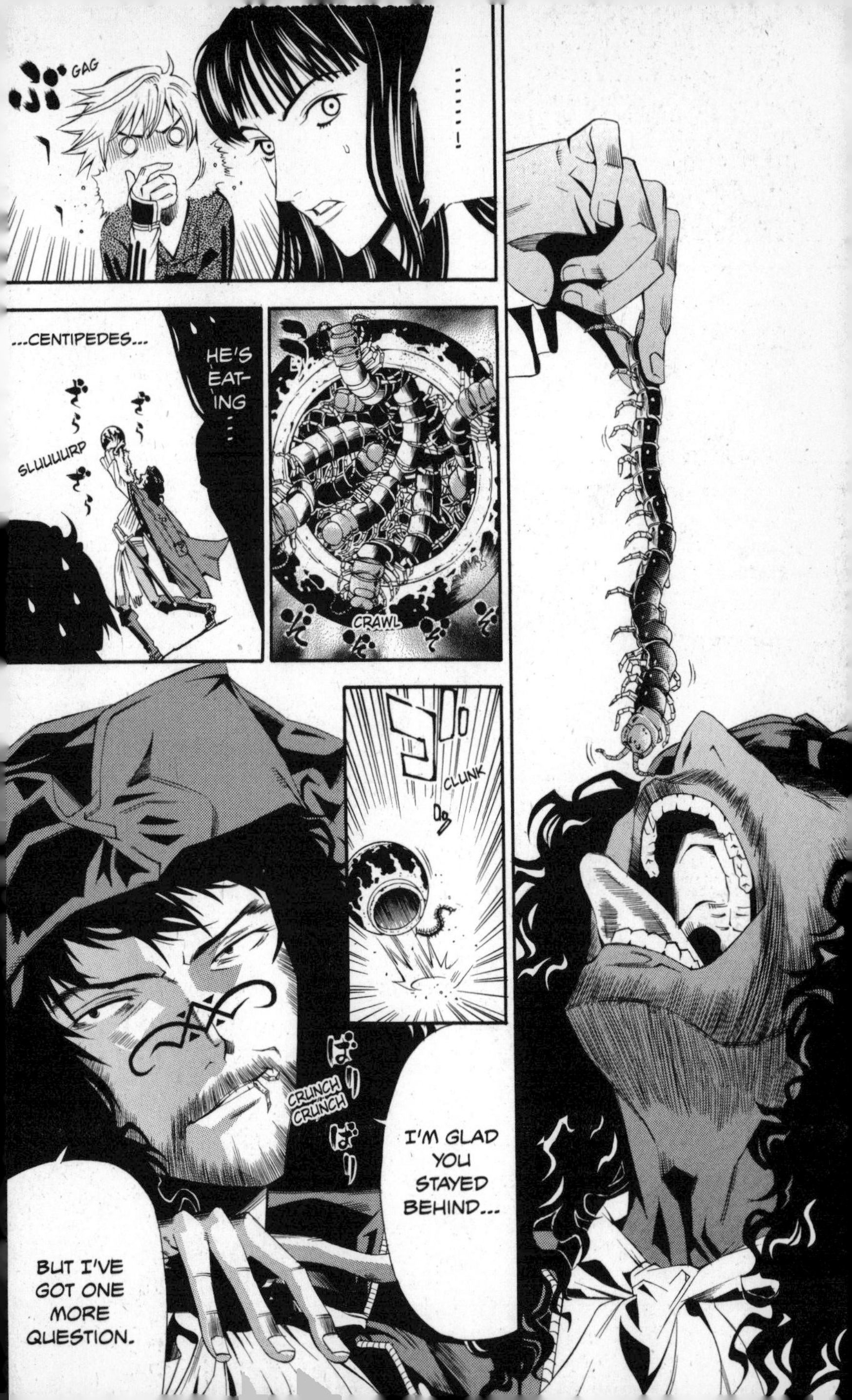
......!
GAG
CRAWL
HE'S EAT-ING...
...CENTIPEDES...
SLUUUURP
CLUNK
CRUNCH CRUNCH
I'M GLAD YOU STAYED BEHIND...
BUT I'VE GOT ONE MORE QUESTION.

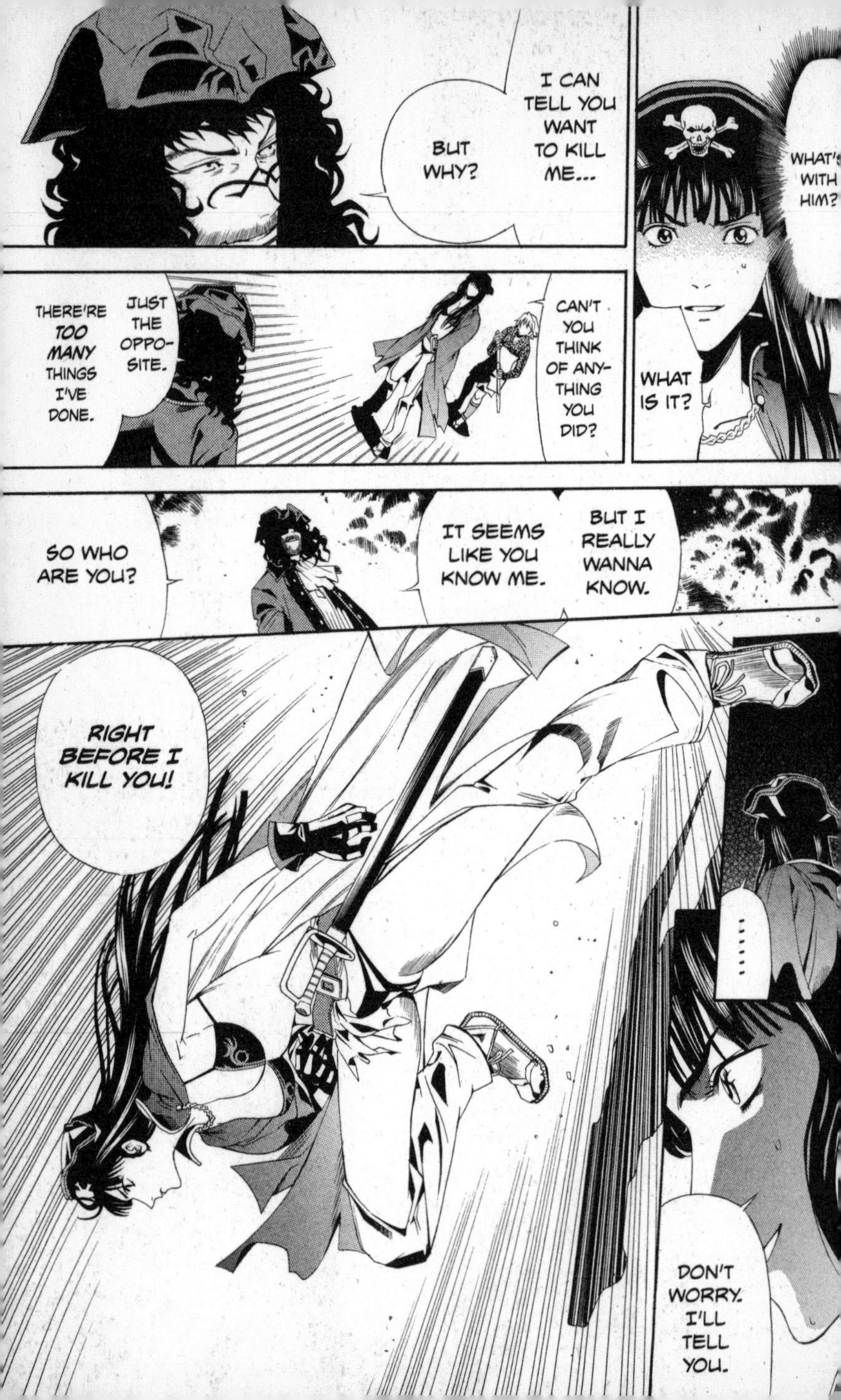
WHAT'S WITH HIM?
I CAN TELL YOU WANT TO KILL ME...
BUT WHY?
WHAT IS IT?
CAN'T YOU THINK OF ANYTHING YOU DID?
JUST THE OPPOSITE.
THERE'RE *TOO MANY* THINGS I'VE DONE.
BUT I REALLY WANNA KNOW.
IT SEEMS LIKE YOU KNOW ME.
SO WHO ARE YOU?
......
DON'T WORRY. I'LL TELL YOU.
RIGHT BEFORE I KILL YOU!

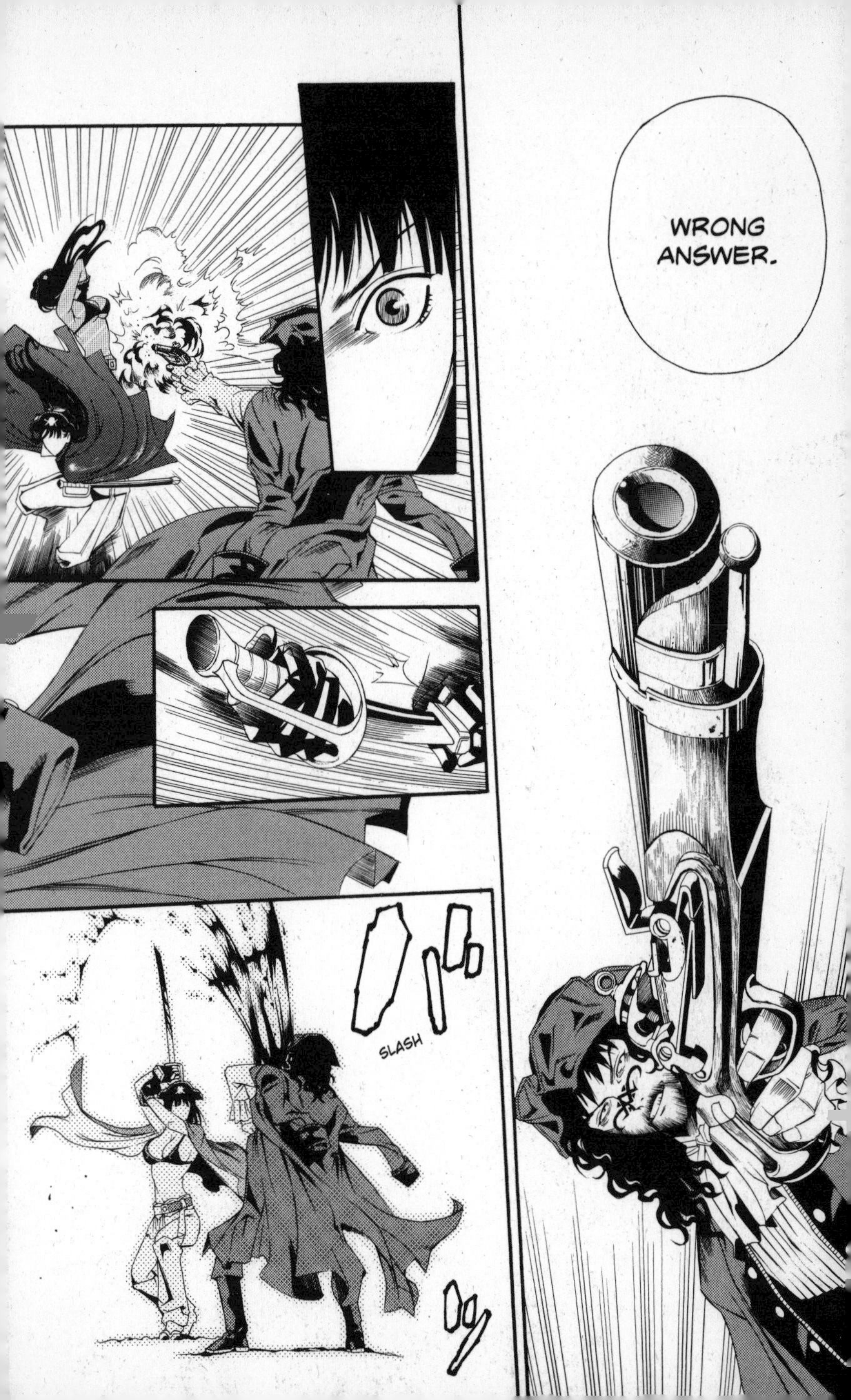
WRONG ANSWER.
SLASH

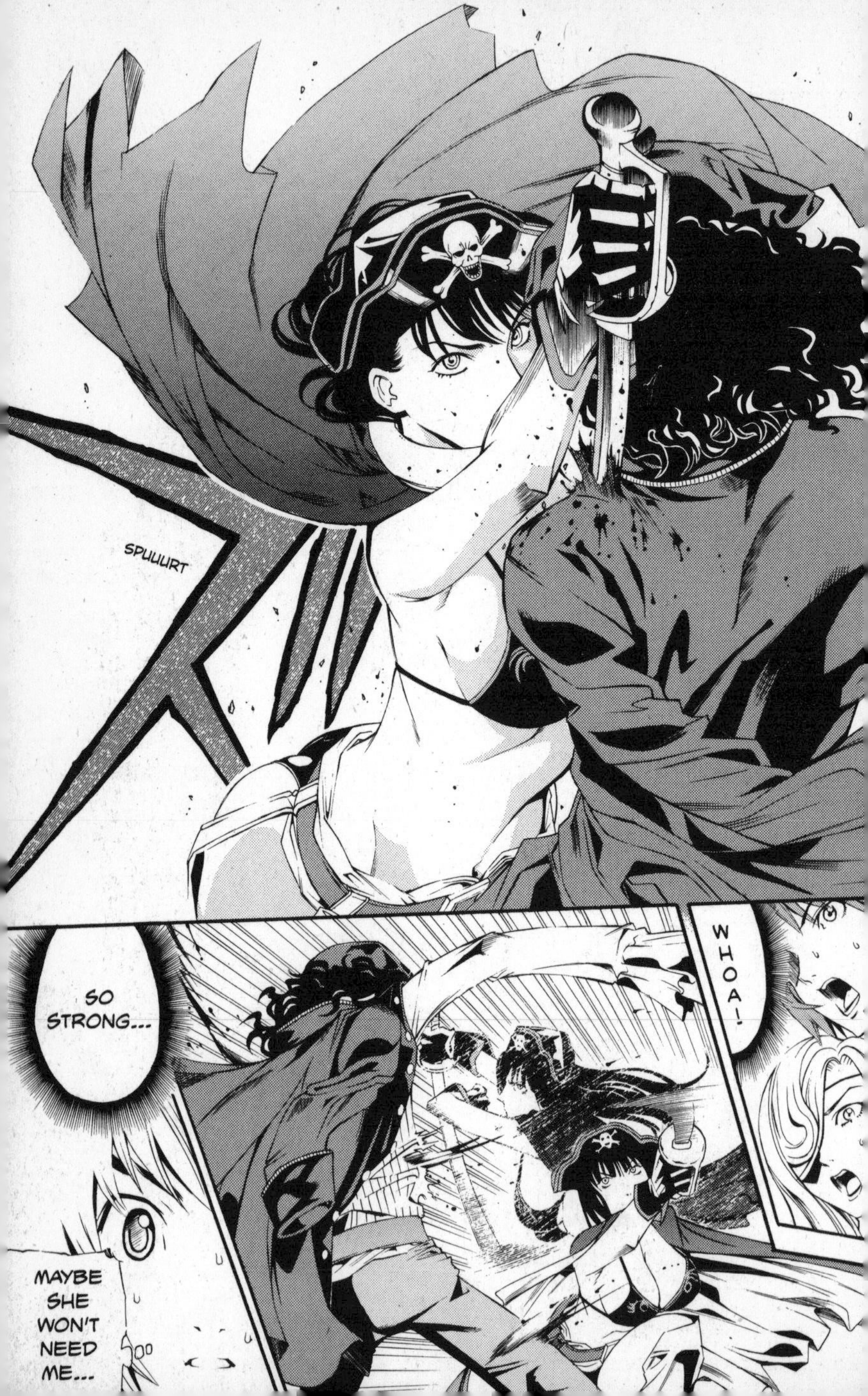
SPUUURT
WHOA!
SO STRONG...
MAYBE SHE WON'T NEED ME...

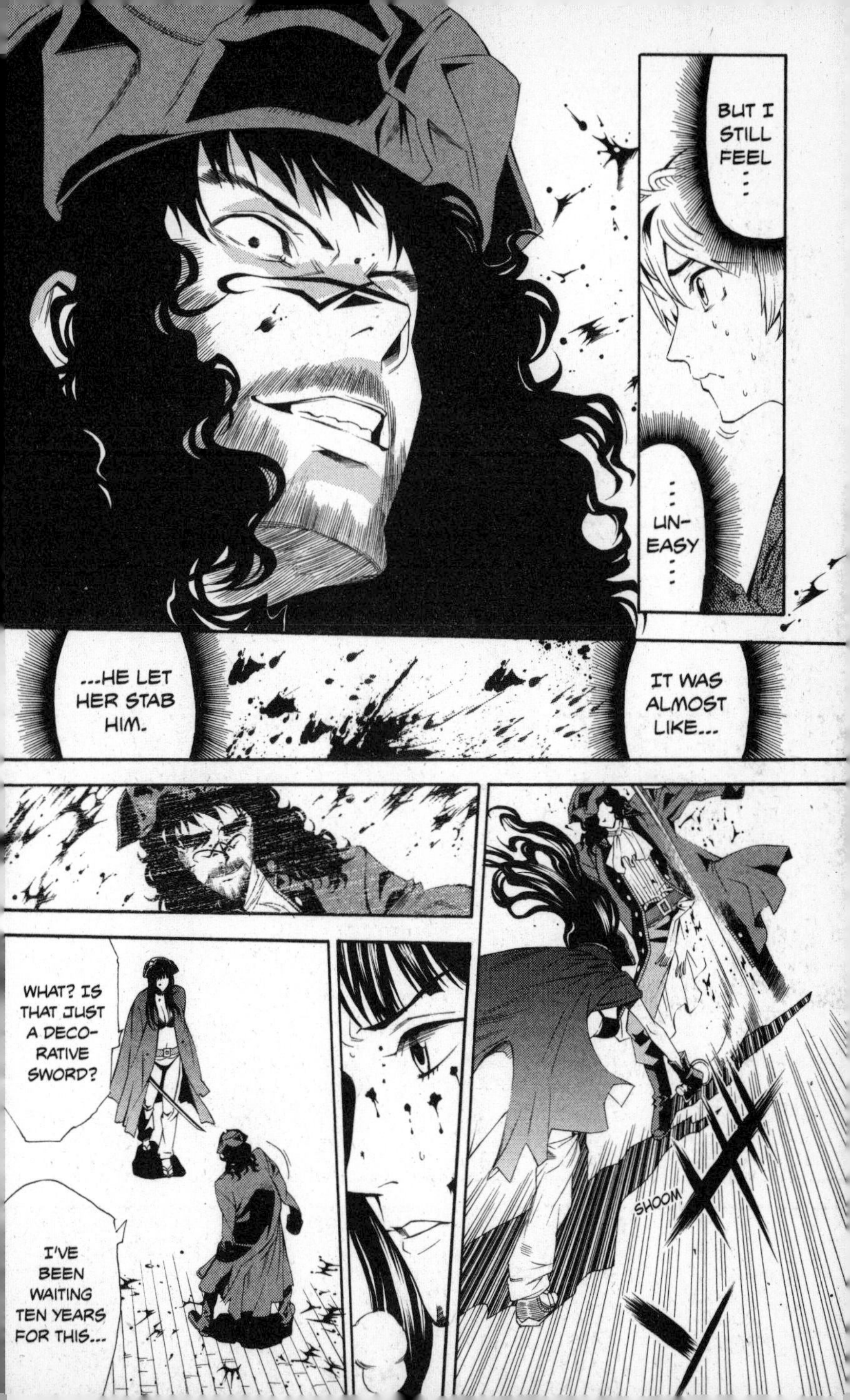

BUT I STILL FEEL...
...UN-EASY...
IT WAS ALMOST LIKE...
...HE LET HER STAB HIM.
SHOOM
WHAT? IS THAT JUST A DECO-RATIVE SWORD?
I'VE BEEN WAITING TEN YEARS FOR THIS...

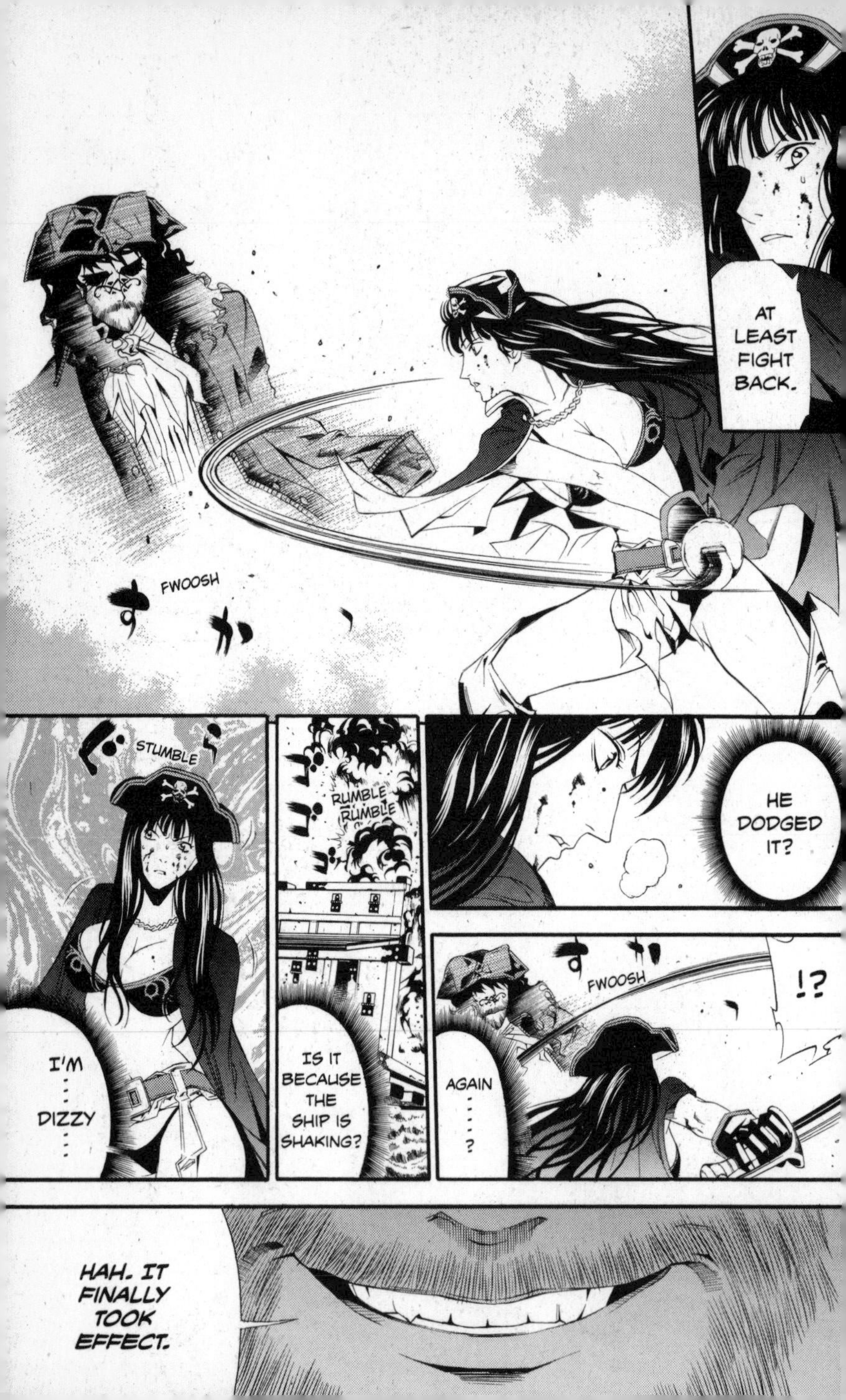
AT LEAST FIGHT BACK.
FWOOSH
HE DODGED IT?
FWOOSH
!?
AGAIN.....?
RUMBLE RUMBLE
IS IT BECAUSE THE SHIP IS SHAKING?
STUMBLE
I'M... DIZZY...
HAH. IT FINALLY TOOK EFFECT.

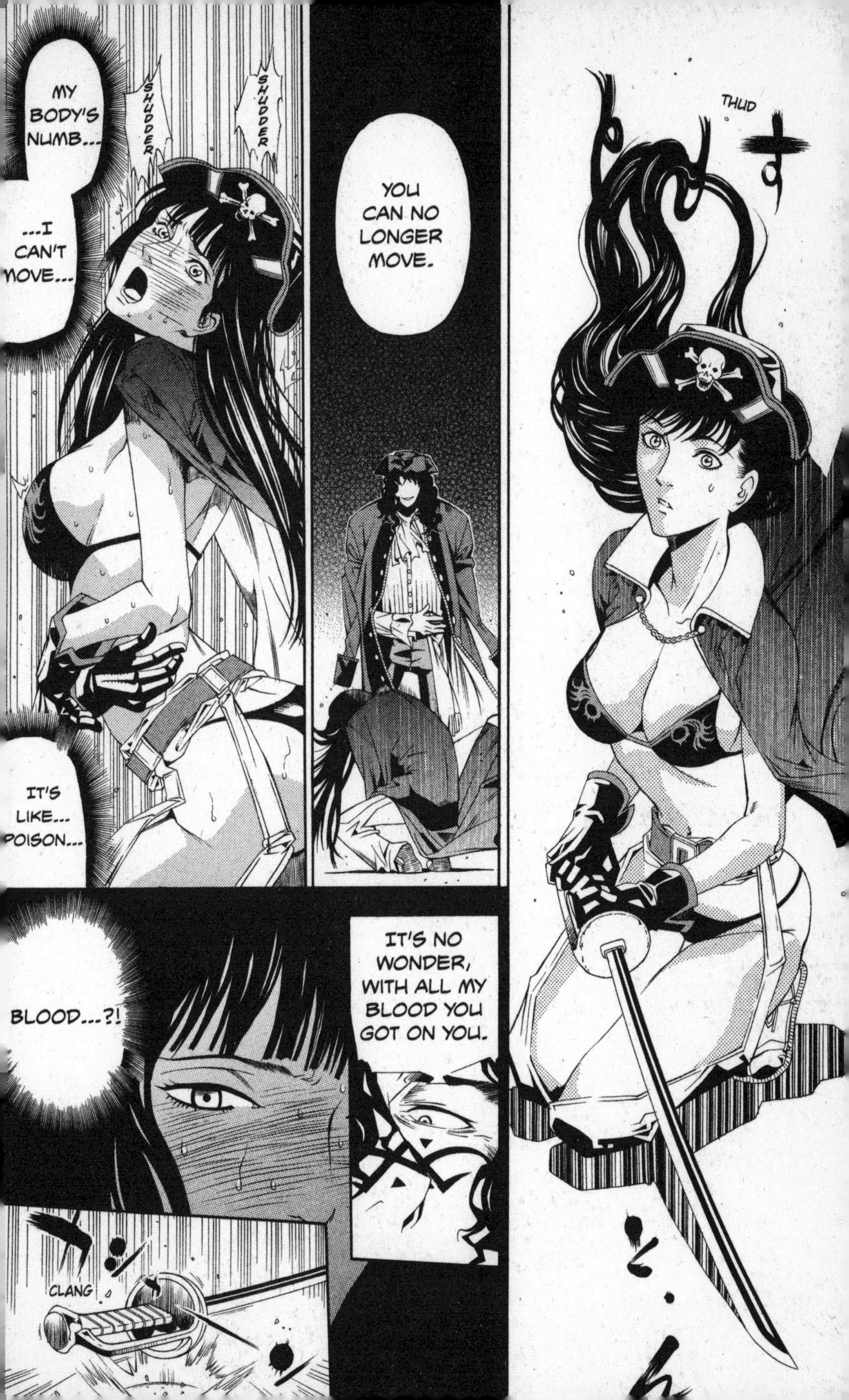
THUD
YOU CAN NO LONGER MOVE.
SHUDDER
SHUDDER
MY BODY'S NUMB...
...I CAN'T MOVE...
IT'S LIKE... POISON...
IT'S NO WONDER, WITH ALL MY BLOOD YOU GOT ON YOU.
BLOOD...?!
CLANG

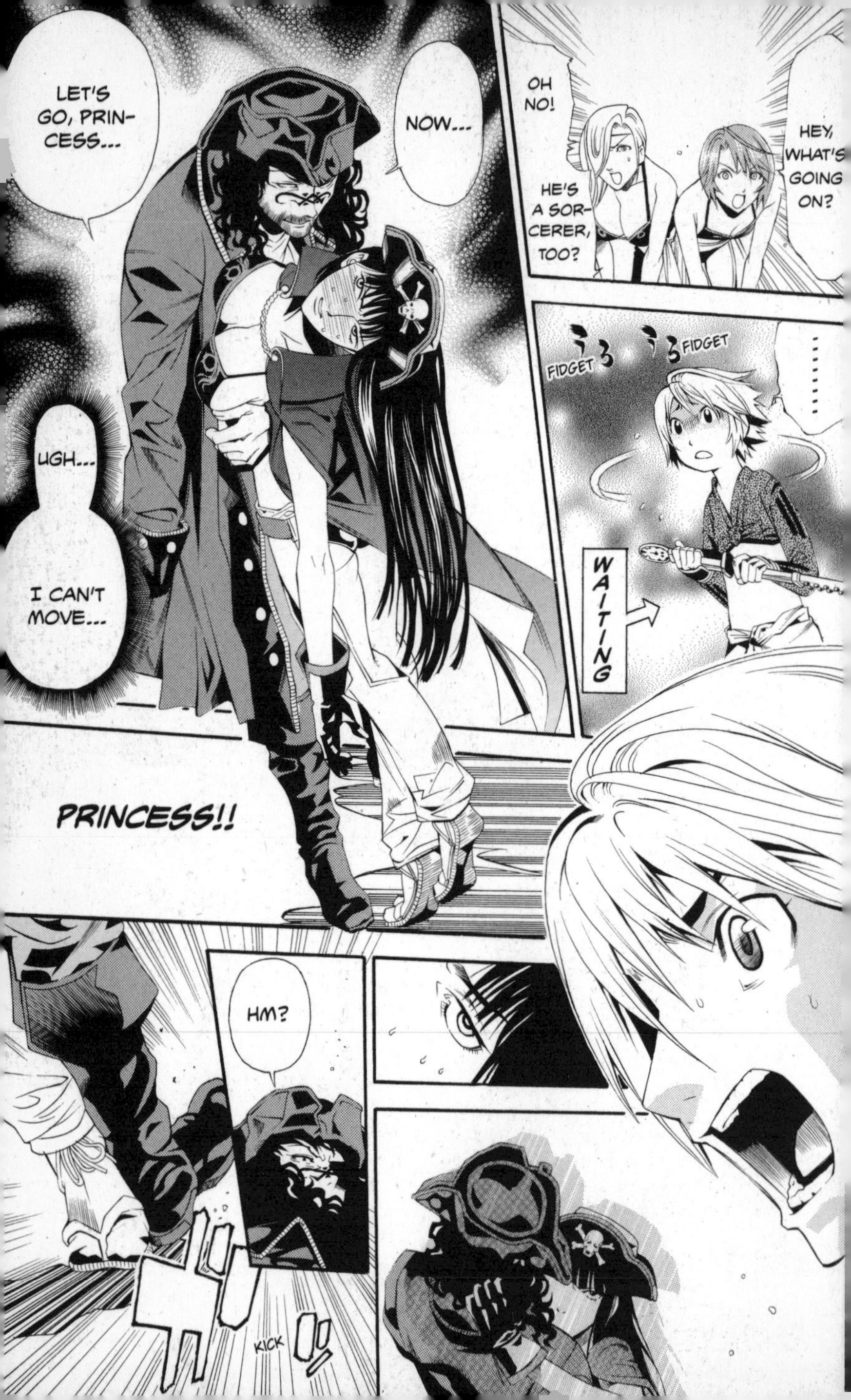
HEY, WHAT'S GOING ON?
OH NO!
HE'S A SORCERER, TOO?
FIDGET
FIDGET
......
WAITING
NOW...
LET'S GO, PRINCESS...
UGH...
I CAN'T MOVE...
PRINCESS!!
HM?
KICK

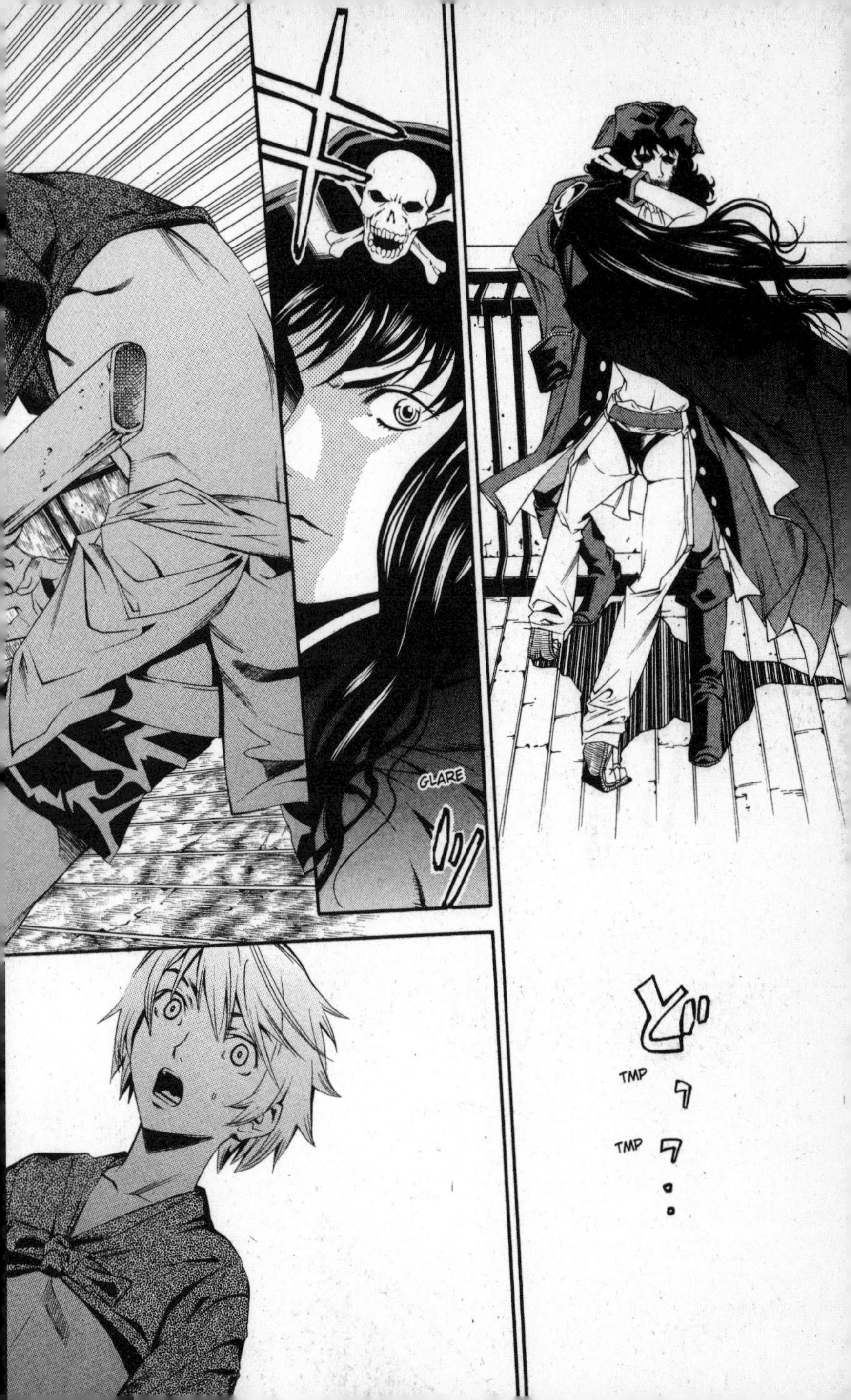

GLARE
TMP
TMP

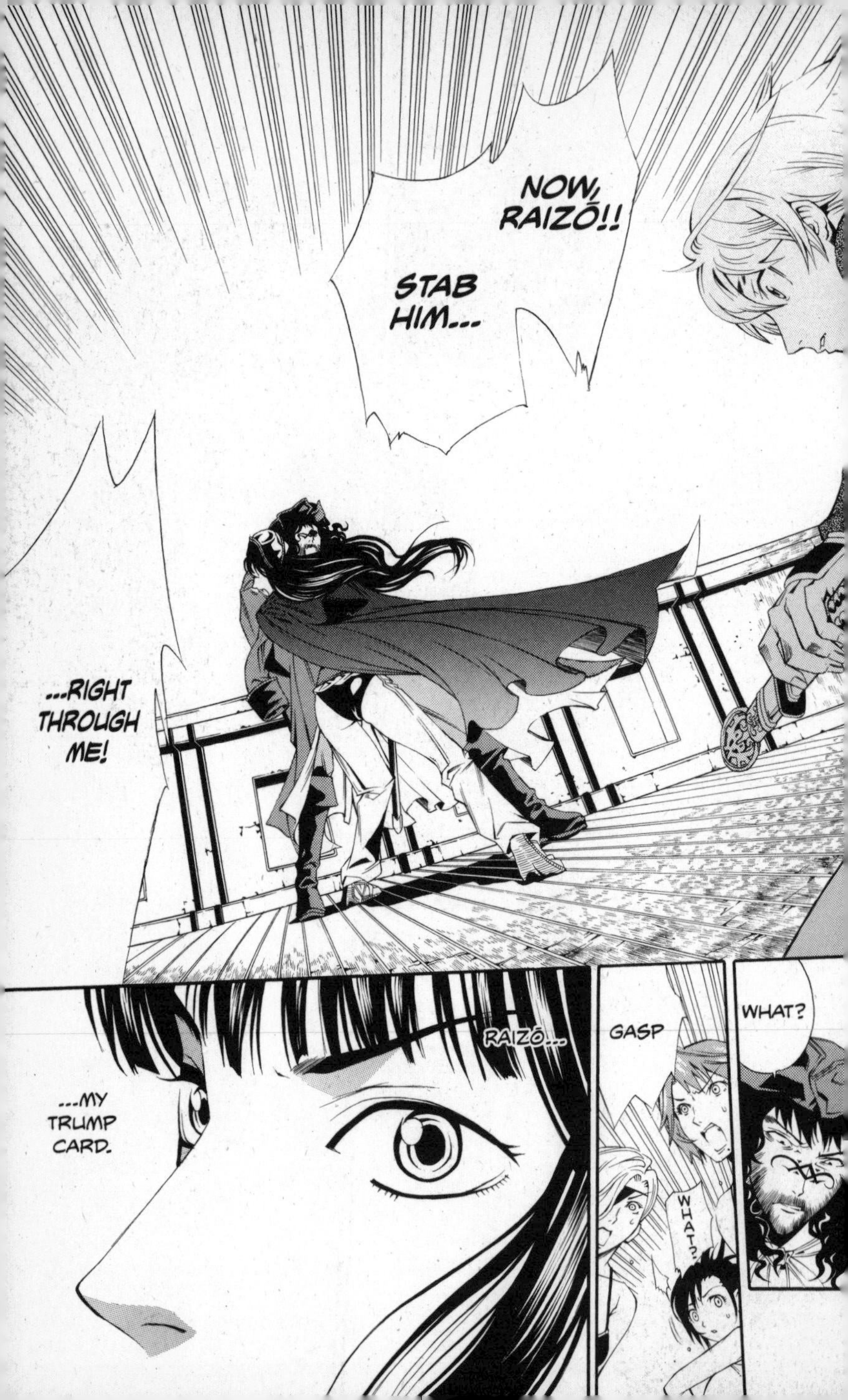
NOW, RAIZŌ!!
STAB HIM...
...RIGHT THROUGH ME!
WHAT?
GASP
WHAT?
RAIZŌ...
...MY TRUMP CARD.

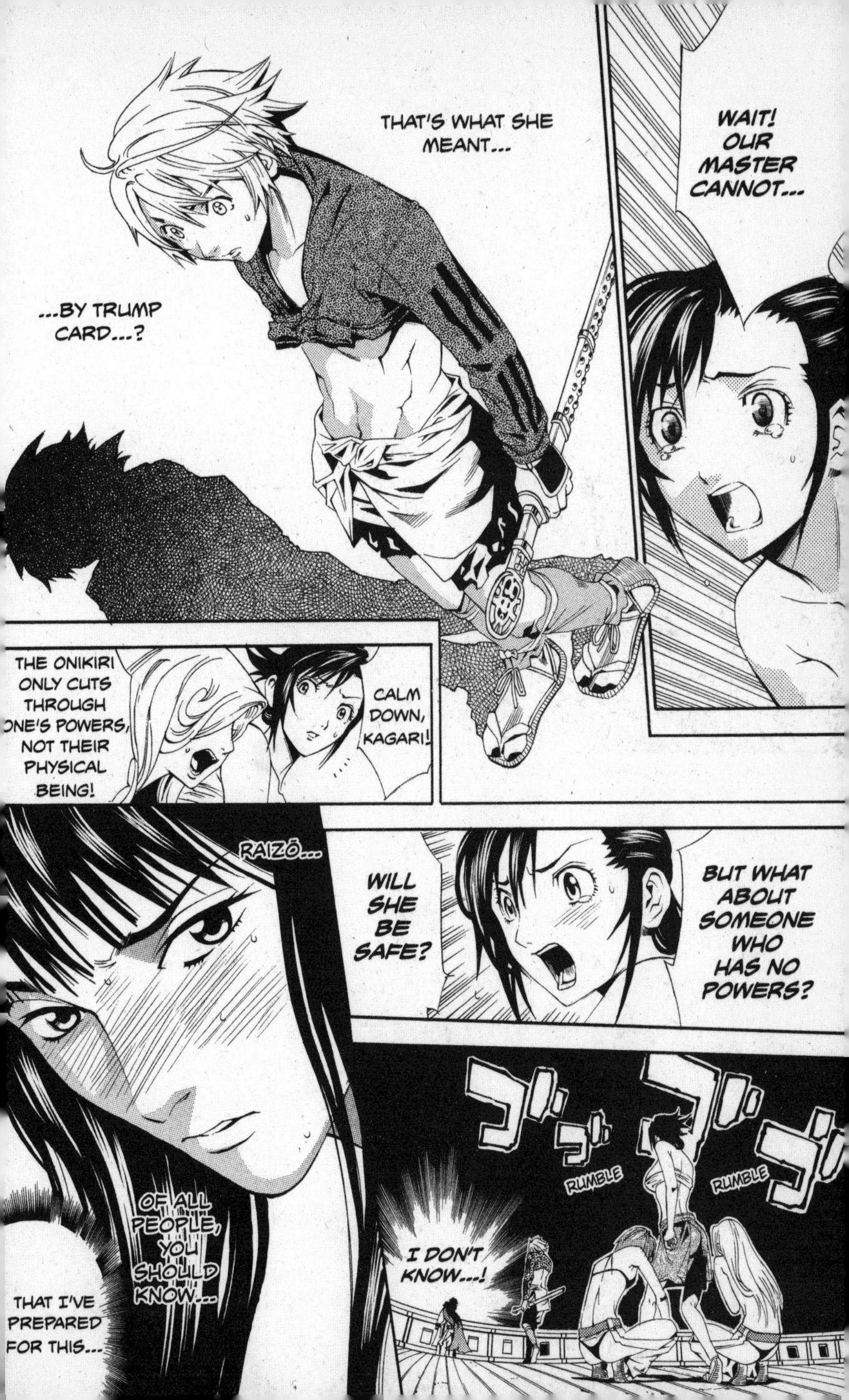
WAIT! OUR MASTER CANNOT...
THAT'S WHAT SHE MEANT...
...BY TRUMP CARD...?
CALM DOWN, KAGARI!
THE ONIKIRI ONLY CUTS THROUGH ONE'S POWERS, NOT THEIR PHYSICAL BEING!
BUT WHAT ABOUT SOMEONE WHO HAS NO POWERS?
WILL SHE BE SAFE?
RUMBLE
RUMBLE
I DON'T KNOW...!
RAIZŌ...
OF ALL PEOPLE, YOU SHOULD KNOW...
THAT I'VE PREPARED FOR THIS...

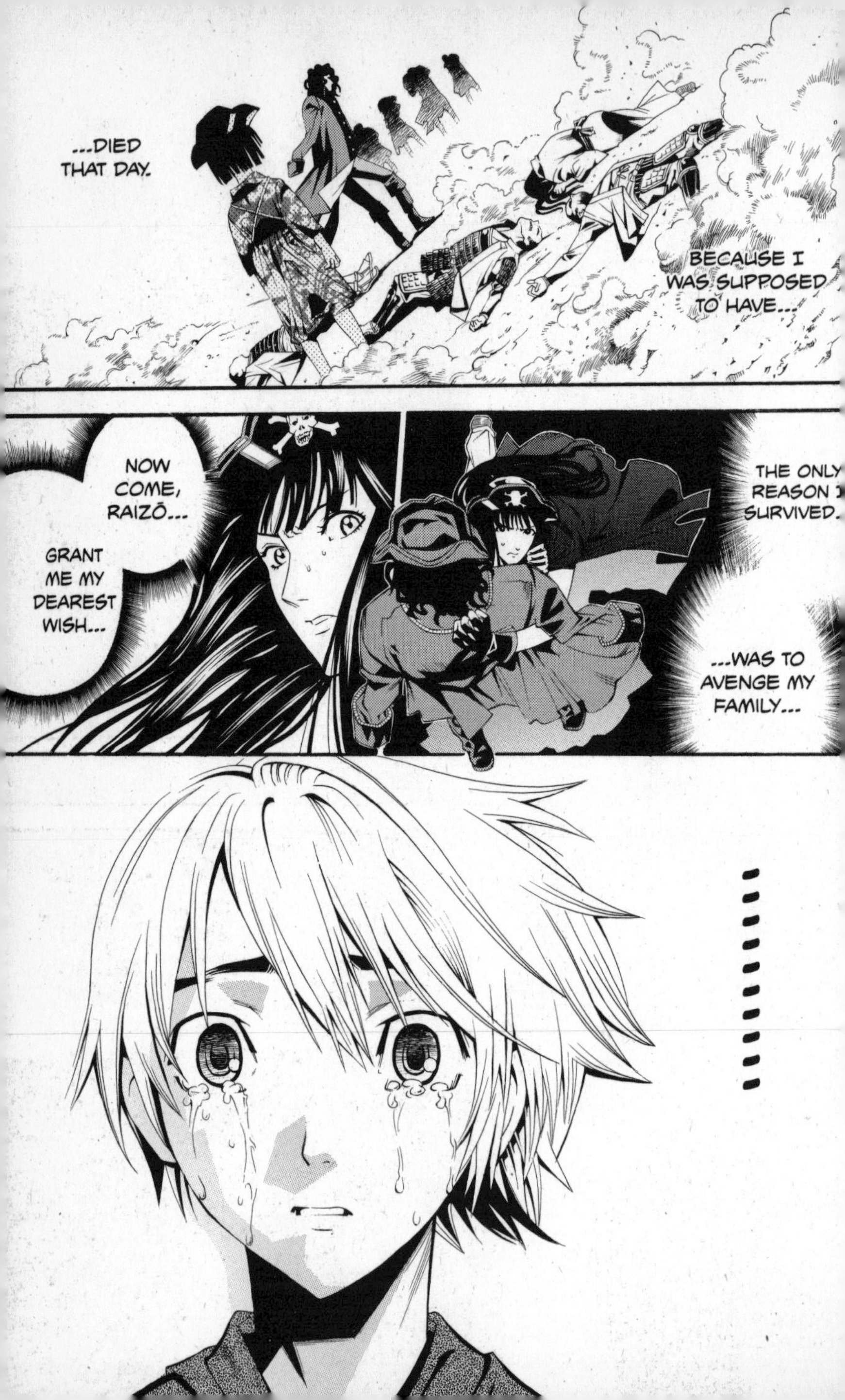
BECAUSE I WAS SUPPOSED TO HAVE...
...DIED THAT DAY.
THE ONLY REASON I SURVIVED...
...WAS TO AVENGE MY FAMILY...
NOW COME, RAIZŌ...
GRANT ME MY DEAREST WISH...
......

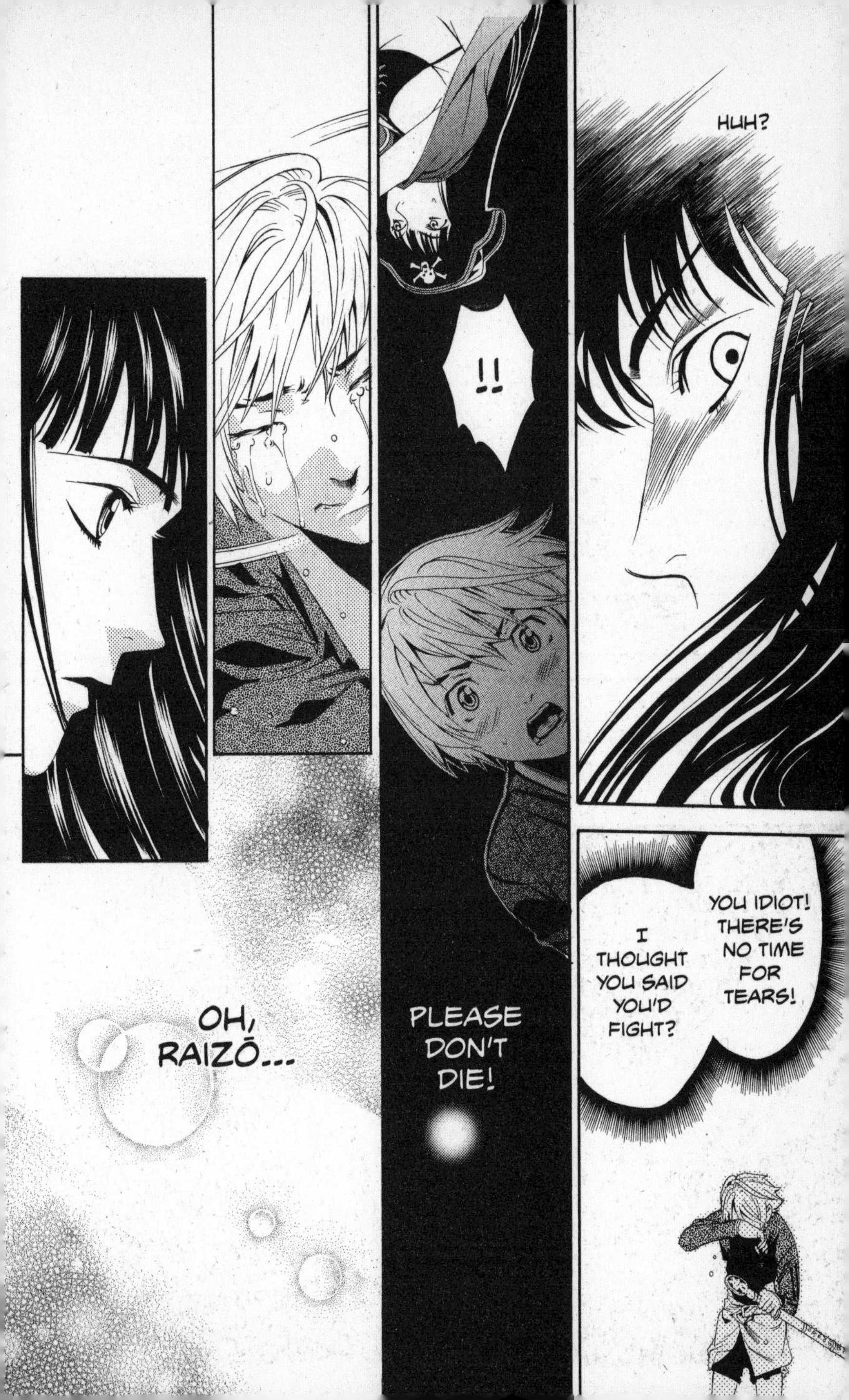
HUH?
YOU IDIOT! THERE'S NO TIME FOR TEARS!
I THOUGHT YOU SAID YOU'D FIGHT?
!!
PLEASE DON'T DIE!
OH, RAIZŌ...

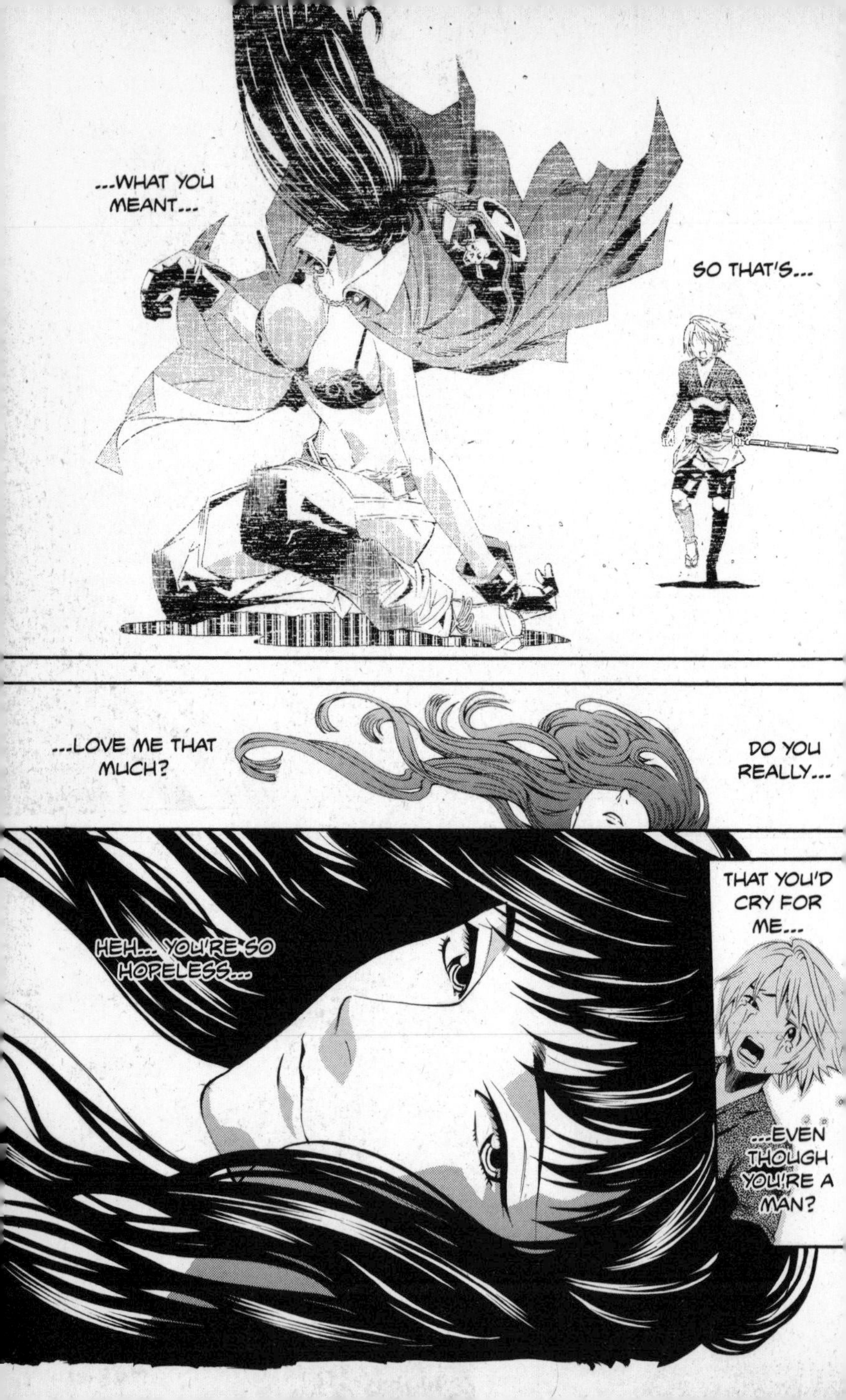
SO THAT'S...
...WHAT YOU MEANT...
DO YOU REALLY...
...LOVE ME THAT MUCH?
THAT YOU'D CRY FOR ME...
...EVEN THOUGH YOU'RE A MAN?
HEH... YOU'RE SO HOPELESS...

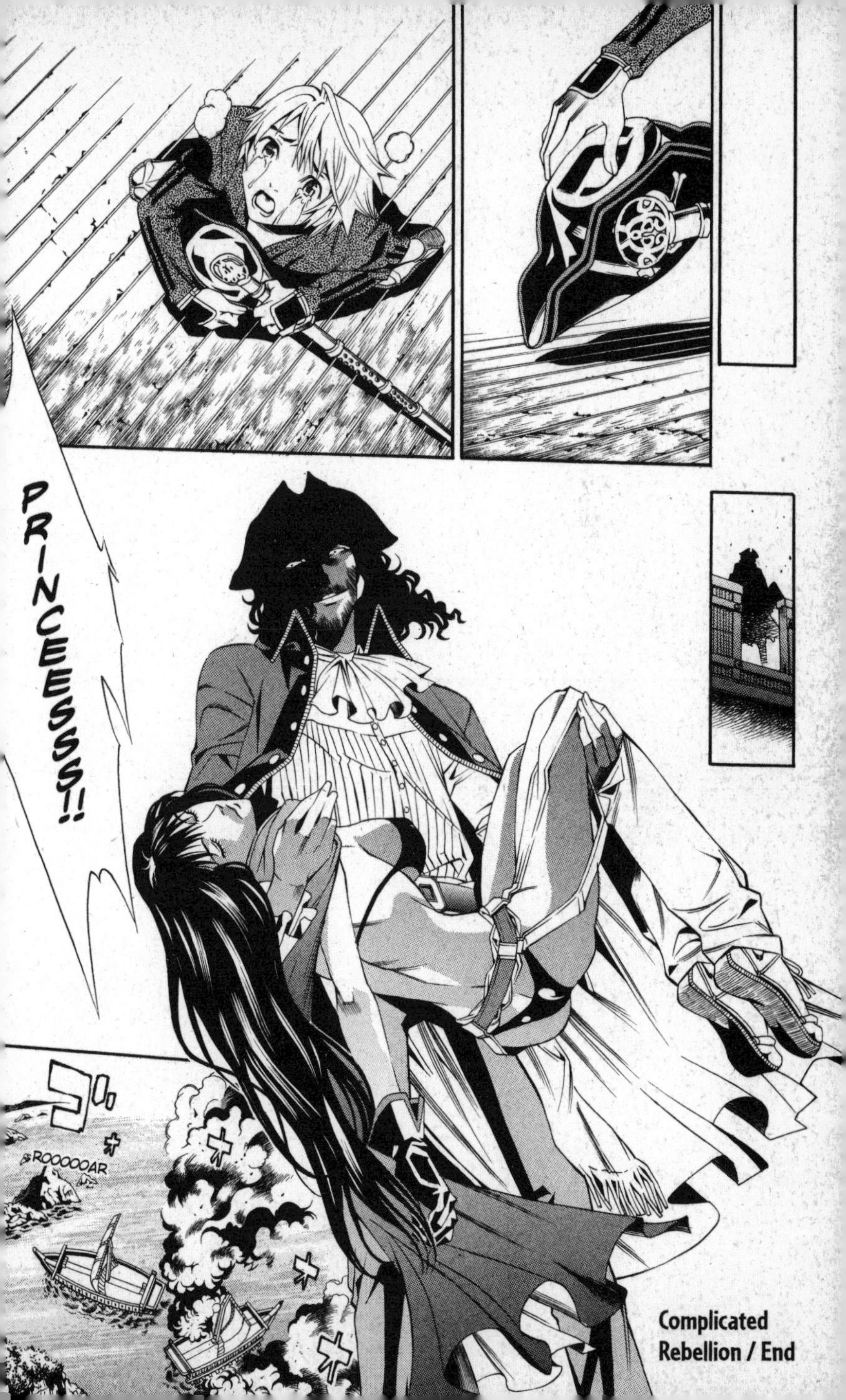
PRINCEESSSS!!
ROOOOOAR

Complicated Rebellion / End

**Ninja Girls**

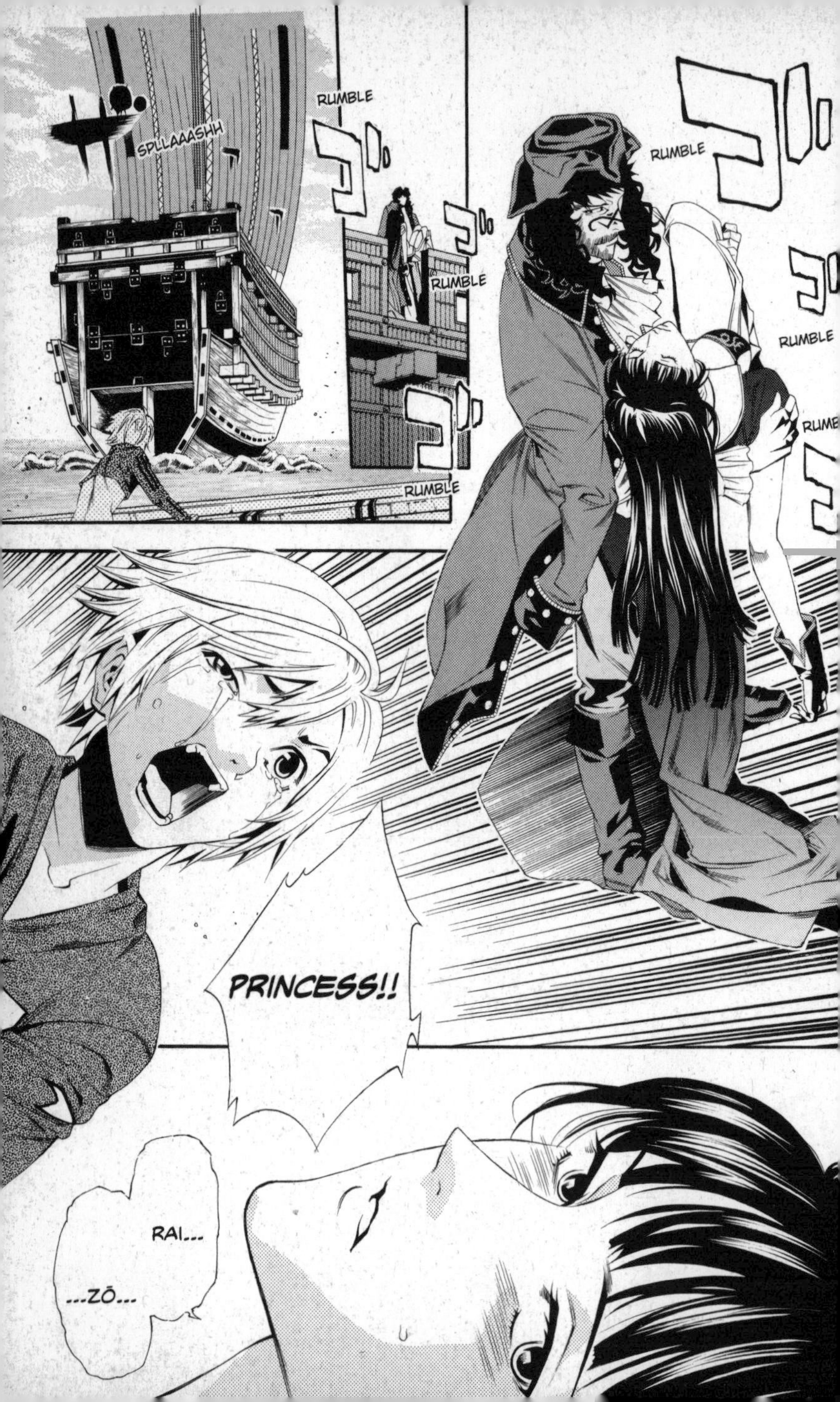

RUMBLE
RUMBLE
RUMBLE
RUMBLE
RUMBLE
SPLLAAASHH
PRINCESS!!
RAI...
...ZŌ...

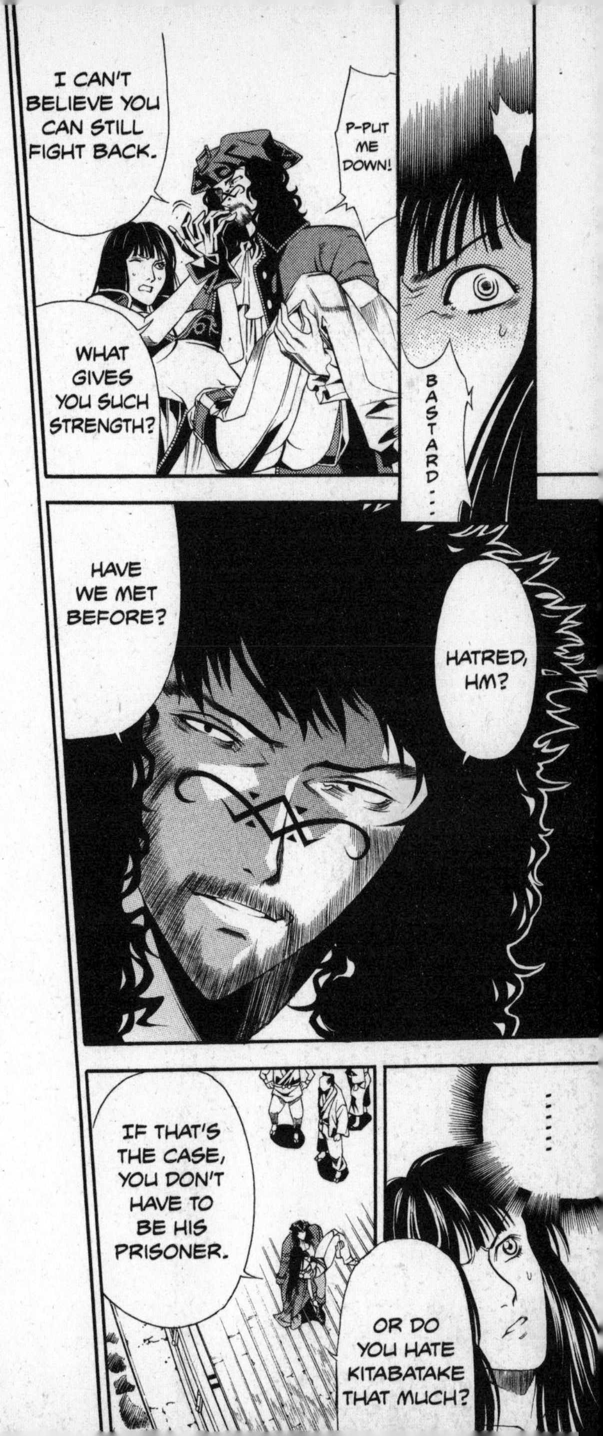
BASTARD...
P-PUT ME DOWN!
I CAN'T BELIEVE YOU CAN STILL FIGHT BACK.
WHAT GIVES YOU SUCH STRENGTH?
HATRED, HM?
HAVE WE MET BEFORE?
......
OR DO YOU HATE KITABATAKE THAT MUCH?
IF THAT'S THE CASE, YOU DON'T HAVE TO BE HIS PRISONER.

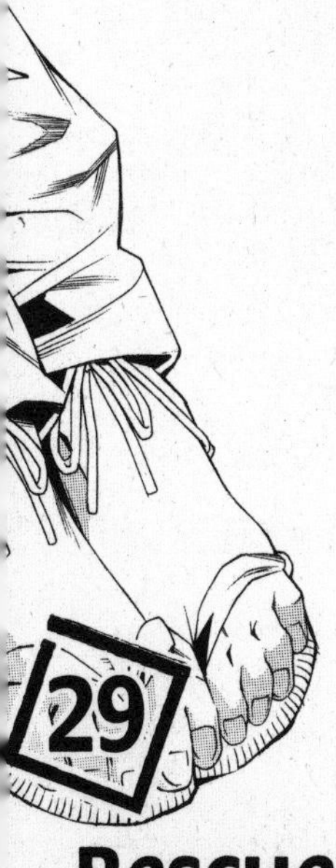
29

# Rescue Rebellion

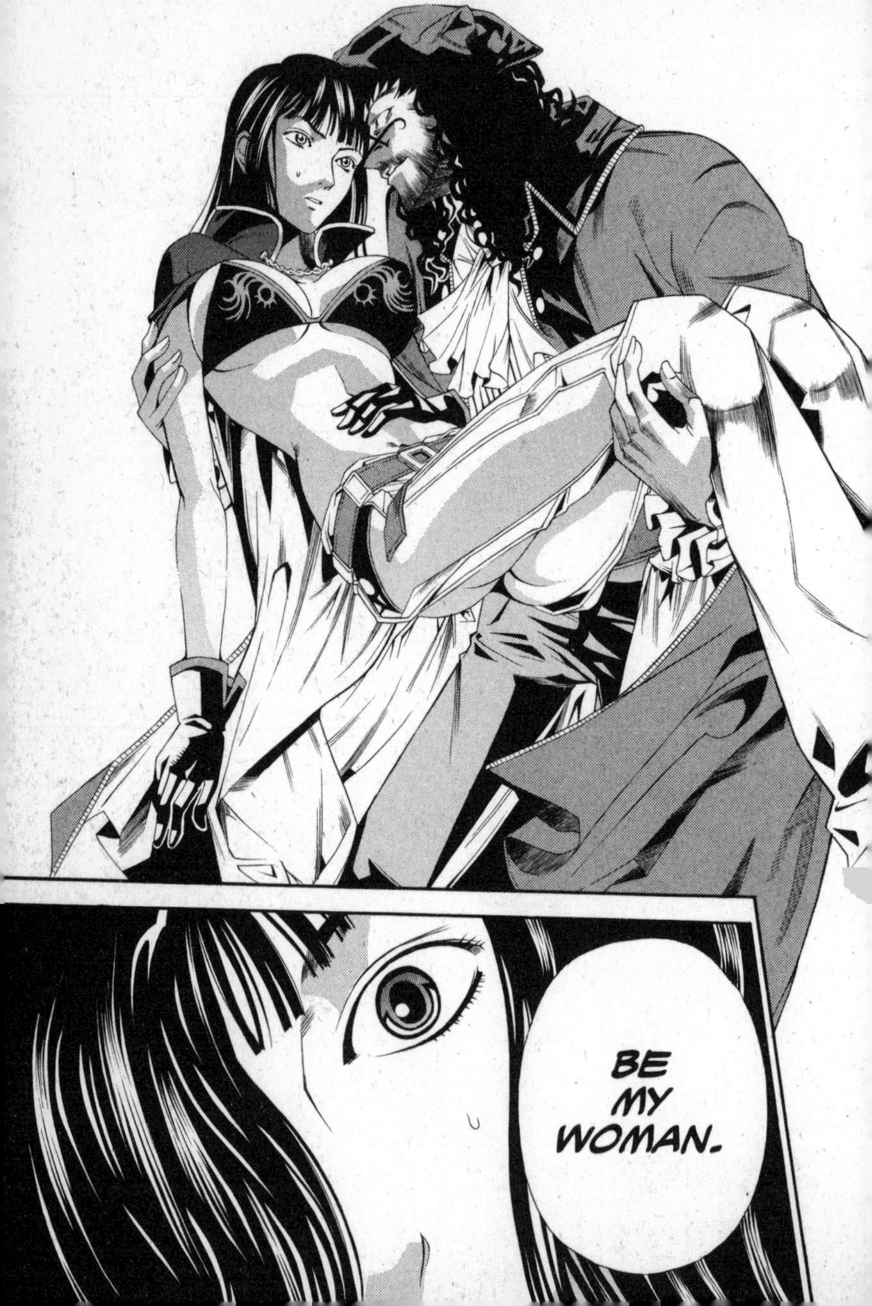
BE MY WOMAN.

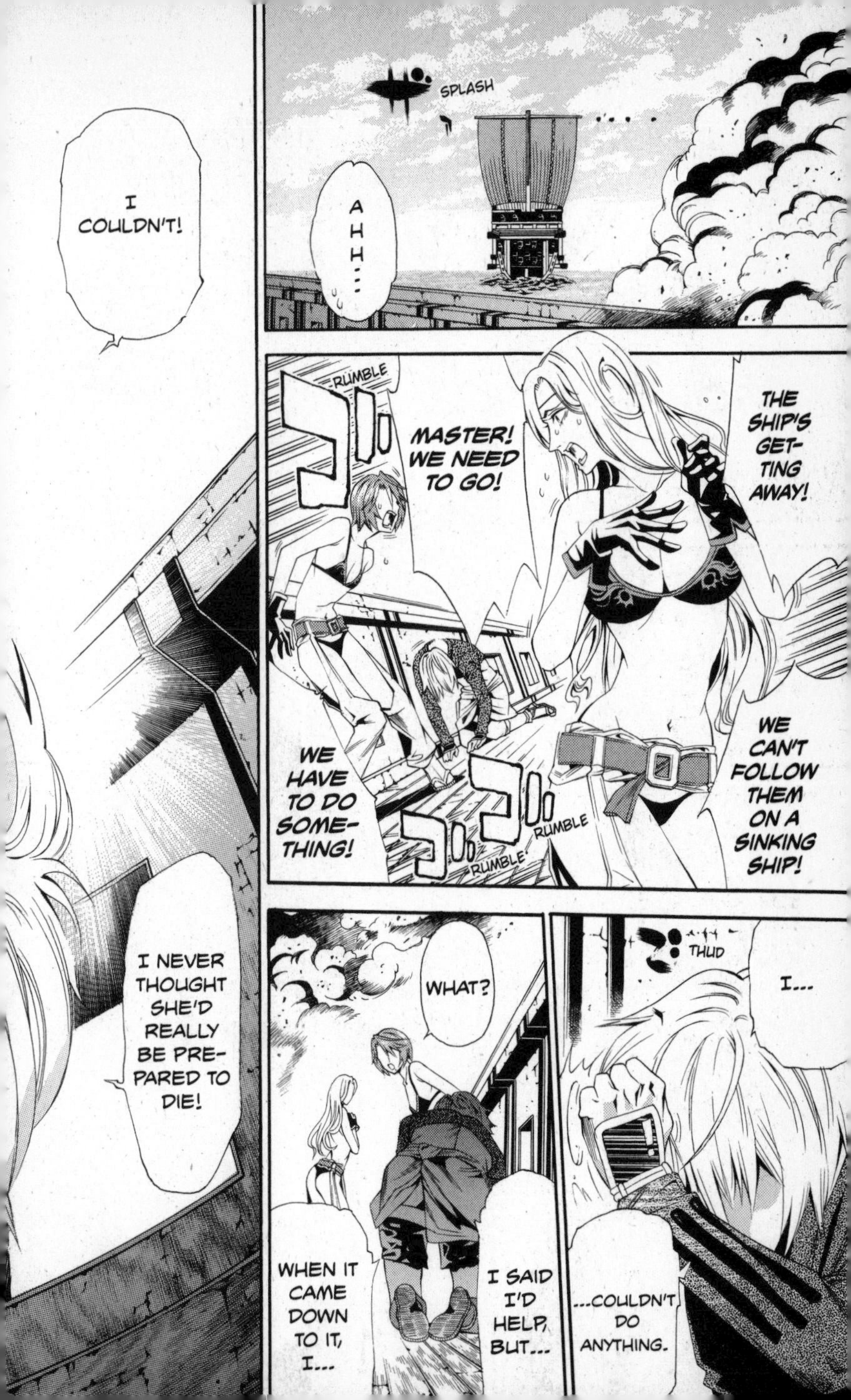
SPLASH
AHH...
THE SHIP'S GET-TING AWAY!
WE CAN'T FOLLOW THEM ON A SINKING SHIP!
MASTER! WE NEED TO GO!
RUMBLE
WE HAVE TO DO SOME-THING!
RUMBLE
RUMBLE
THUD
I...
...COULDN'T DO ANYTHING.
WHAT?
I SAID I'D HELP, BUT...
WHEN IT CAME DOWN TO IT, I...
I COULDN'T!
I NEVER THOUGHT SHE'D REALLY BE PRE-PARED TO DIE!

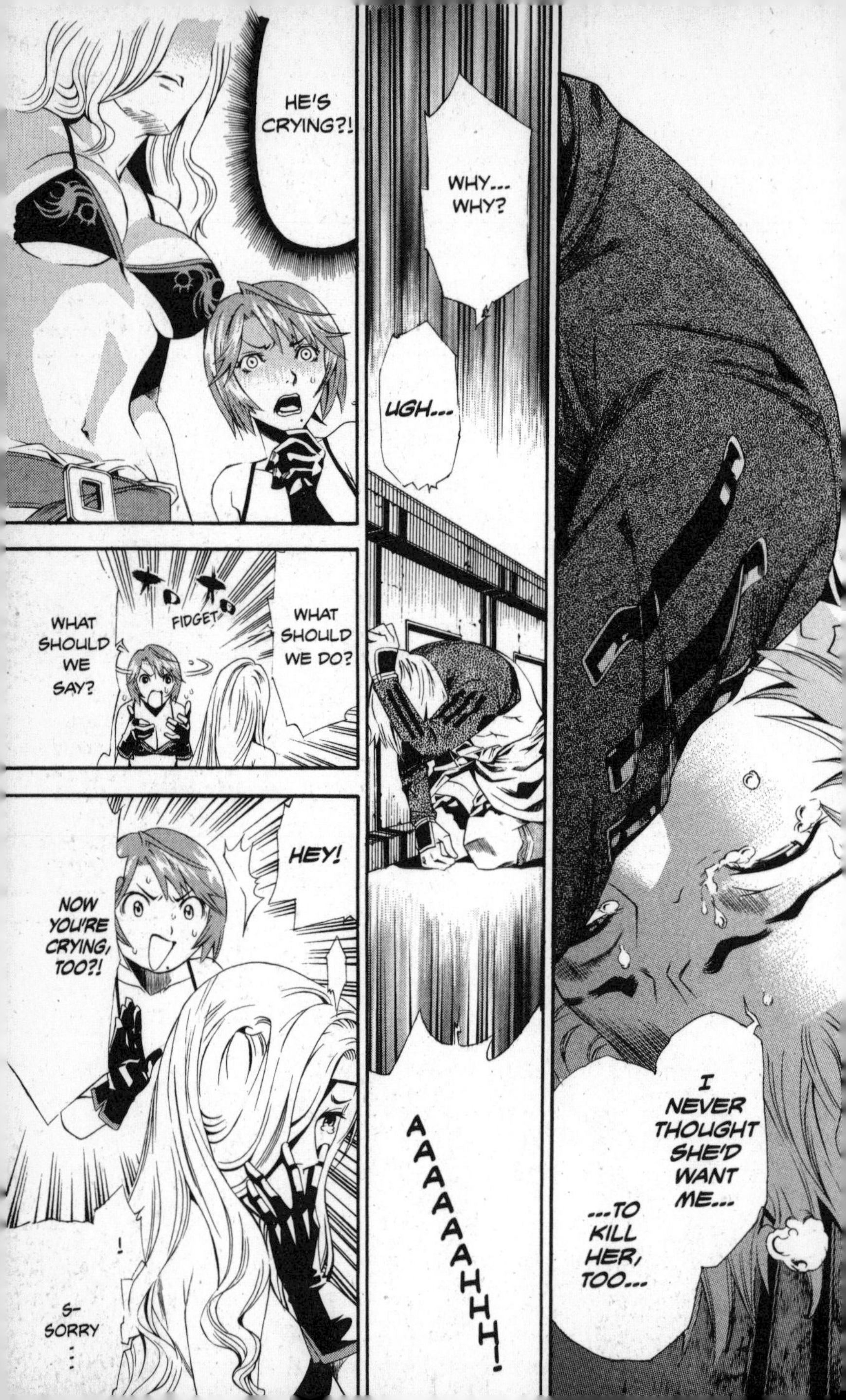
I NEVER THOUGHT SHE'D WANT ME...
...TO KILL HER, TOO...
WHY... WHY?
UGH...
AAAAAAAHHH!
HE'S CRYING?!
WHAT SHOULD WE DO?
FIDGET
WHAT SHOULD WE SAY?
HEY!
NOW YOU'RE CRYING, TOO?!
!
S-SORRY...

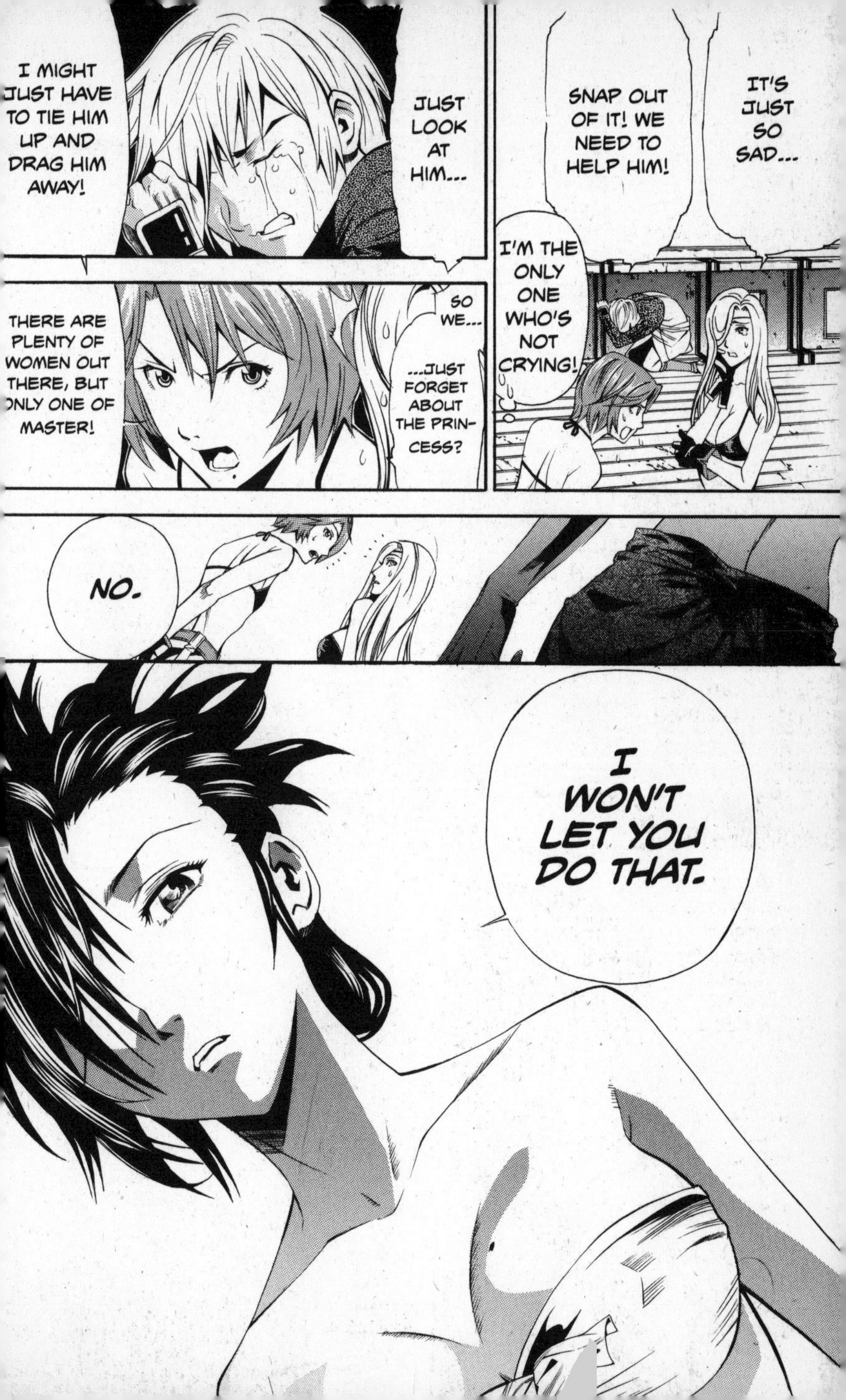

IT'S JUST SO SAD...
SNAP OUT OF IT! WE NEED TO HELP HIM!
I'M THE ONLY ONE WHO'S NOT CRYING!
JUST LOOK AT HIM...
I MIGHT JUST HAVE TO TIE HIM UP AND DRAG HIM AWAY!
SO WE...
...JUST FORGET ABOUT THE PRINCESS?
THERE ARE PLENTY OF WOMEN OUT THERE, BUT ONLY ONE OF MASTER!
NO.
I WON'T LET YOU DO THAT.

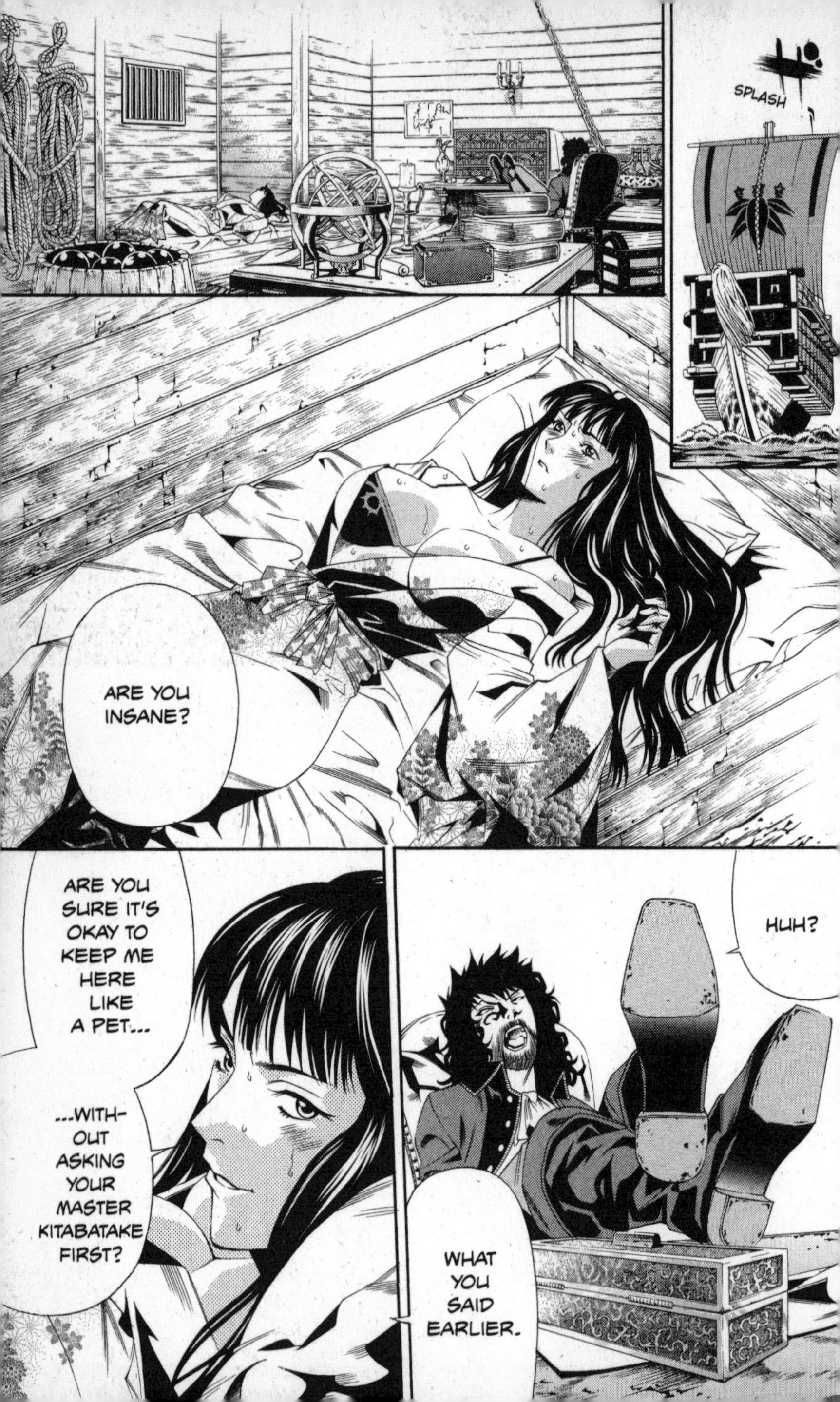
SPLASH
ARE YOU INSANE?
HUH?
WHAT YOU SAID EARLIER.
ARE YOU SURE IT'S OKAY TO KEEP ME HERE LIKE A PET...
...WITHOUT ASKING YOUR MASTER KITABATAKE FIRST?

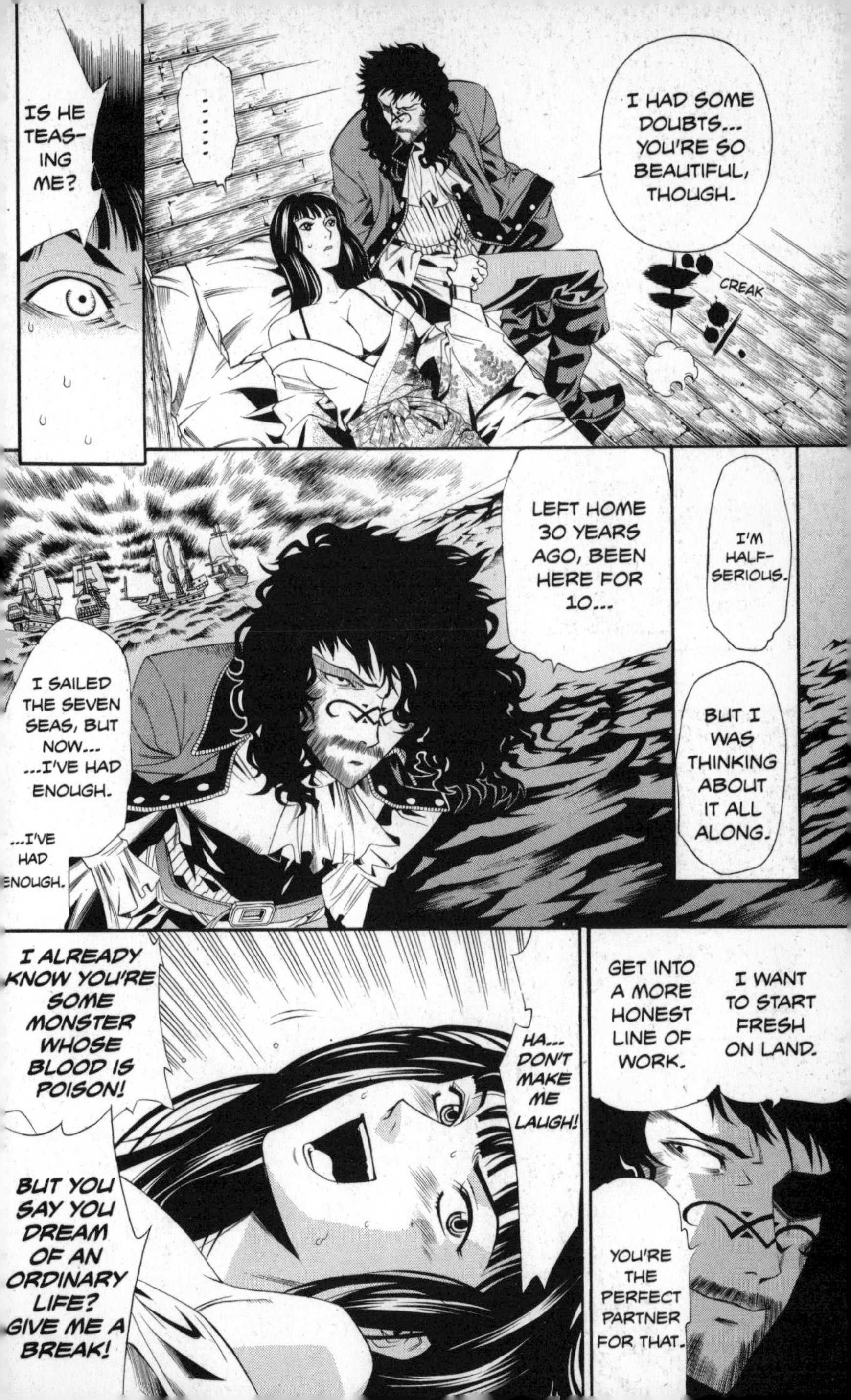
I HAD SOME DOUBTS... YOU'RE SO BEAUTIFUL, THOUGH.
......
CREAK
IS HE TEASING ME?
I'M HALF-SERIOUS.
BUT I WAS THINKING ABOUT IT ALL ALONG.
LEFT HOME 30 YEARS AGO, BEEN HERE FOR 10...
I SAILED THE SEVEN SEAS, BUT NOW... ...I'VE HAD ENOUGH.
...I'VE HAD ENOUGH.
I WANT TO START FRESH ON LAND.
GET INTO A MORE HONEST LINE OF WORK.
YOU'RE THE PERFECT PARTNER FOR THAT.
HA... DON'T MAKE ME LAUGH!
I ALREADY KNOW YOU'RE SOME MONSTER WHOSE BLOOD IS POISON!
BUT YOU SAY YOU DREAM OF AN ORDINARY LIFE? GIVE ME A BREAK!

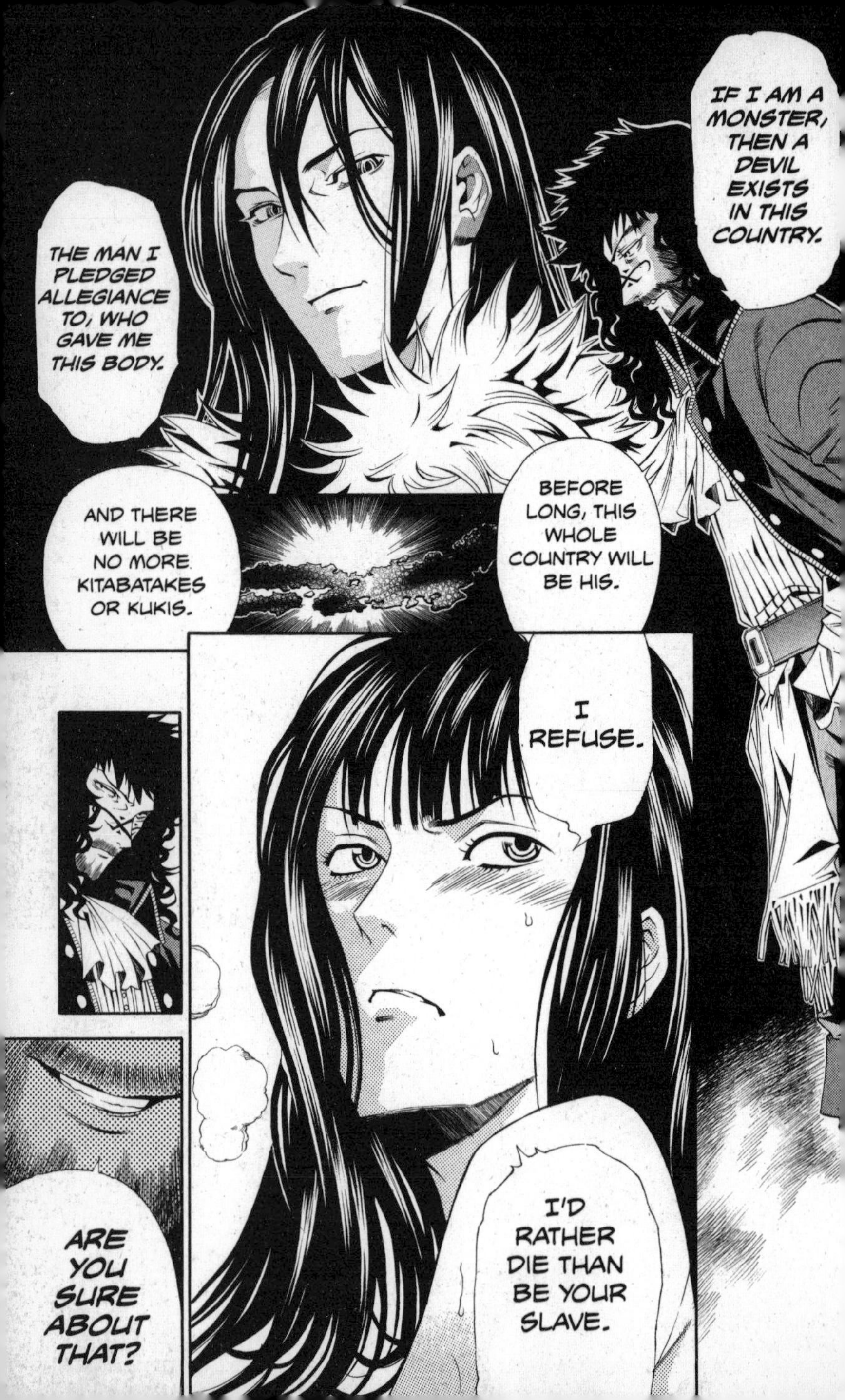
IF I AM A MONSTER, THEN A DEVIL EXISTS IN THIS COUNTRY.
THE MAN I PLEDGED ALLEGIANCE TO, WHO GAVE ME THIS BODY.
BEFORE LONG, THIS WHOLE COUNTRY WILL BE HIS.
AND THERE WILL BE NO MORE KITABATAKES OR KUKIS.
I REFUSE.
I'D RATHER DIE THAN BE YOUR SLAVE.
ARE YOU SURE ABOUT THAT?

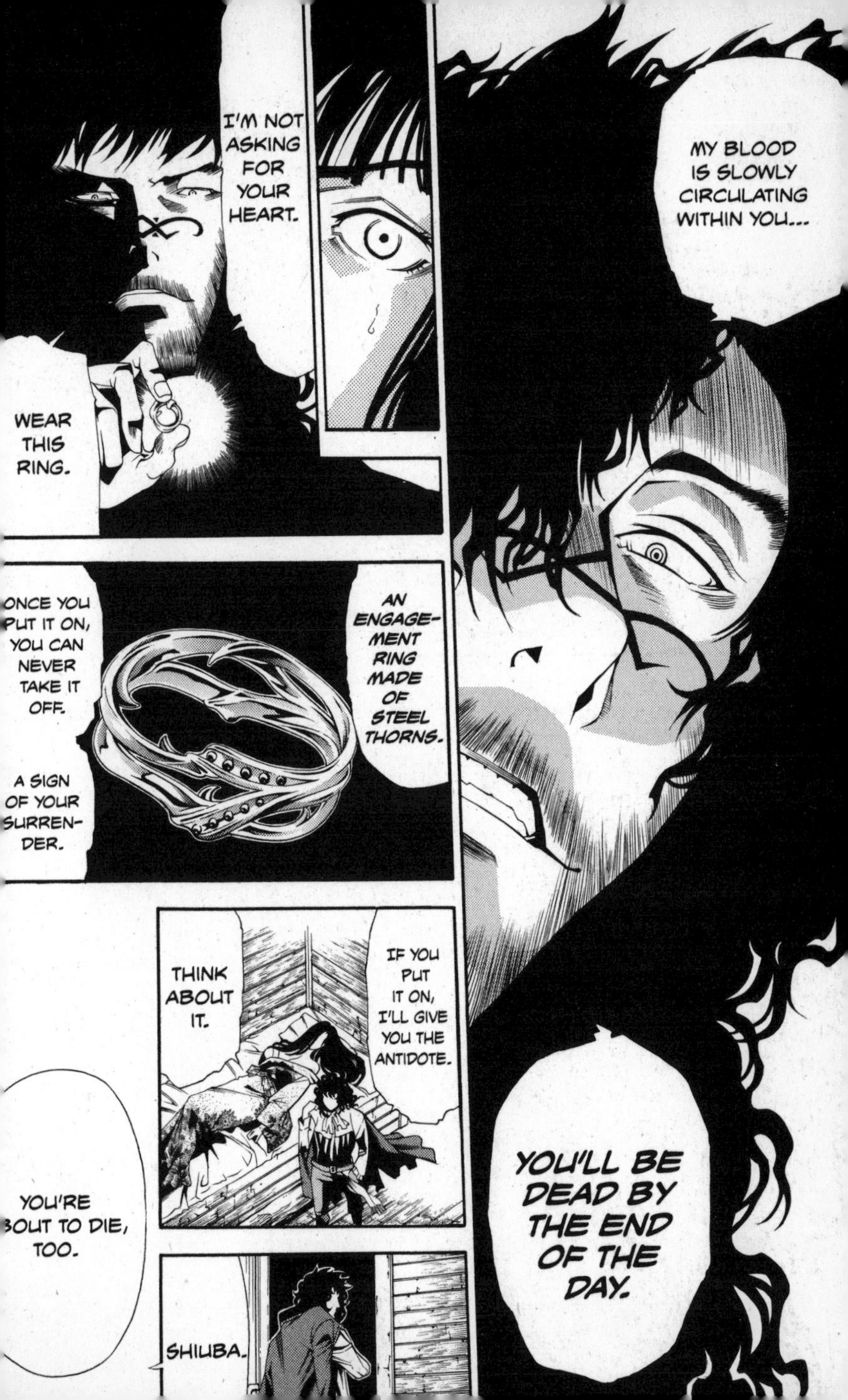
MY BLOOD IS SLOWLY CIRCULATING WITHIN YOU...
YOU'LL BE DEAD BY THE END OF THE DAY.
I'M NOT ASKING FOR YOUR HEART.
WEAR THIS RING.
AN ENGAGEMENT RING MADE OF STEEL THORNS.
ONCE YOU PUT IT ON, YOU CAN NEVER TAKE IT OFF.
A SIGN OF YOUR SURRENDER.
IF YOU PUT IT ON, I'LL GIVE YOU THE ANTIDOTE.
THINK ABOUT IT.
YOU'RE BOUT TO DIE, TOO.
SHIUBA.

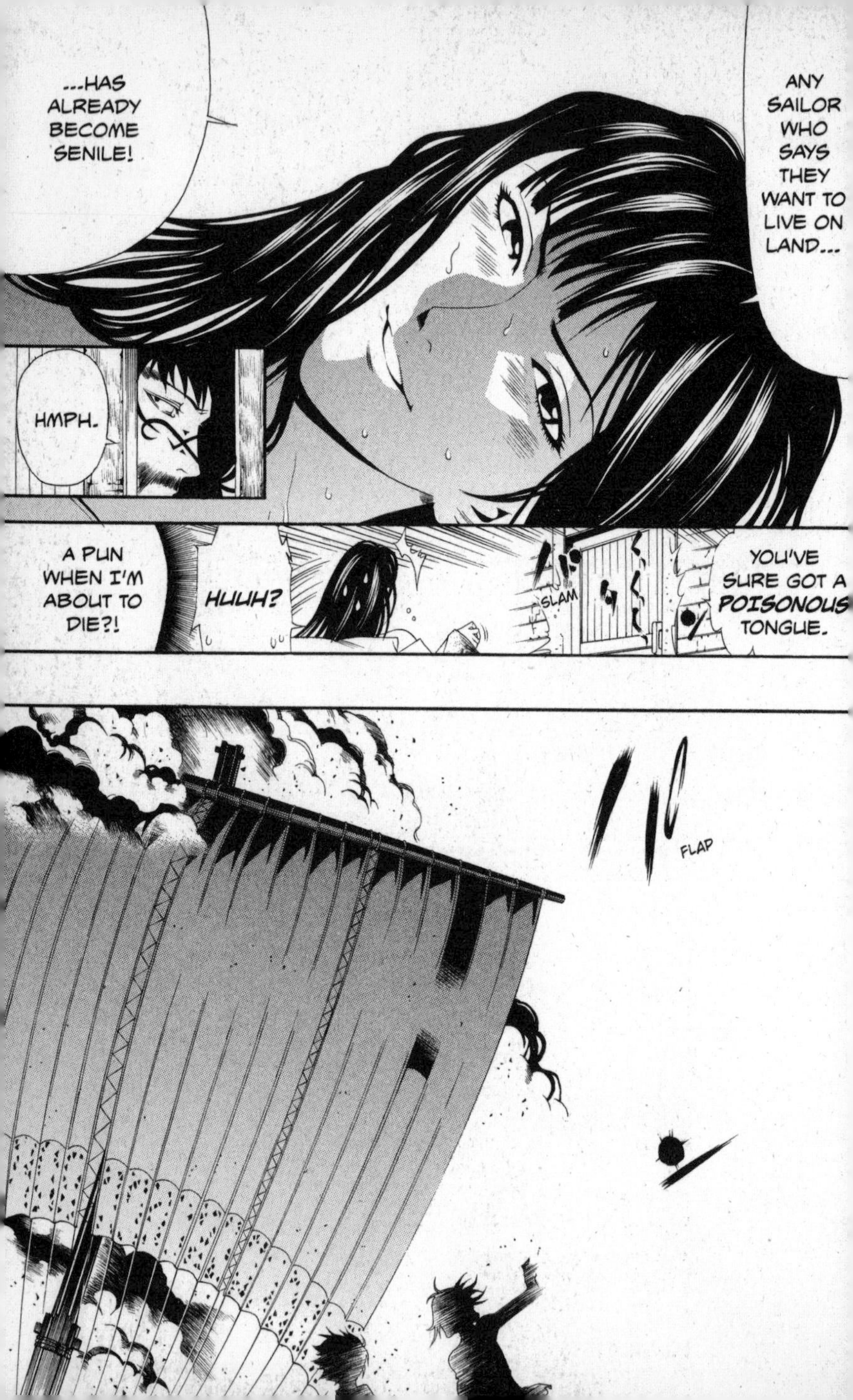
ANY SAILOR WHO SAYS THEY WANT TO LIVE ON LAND...
...HAS ALREADY BECOME SENILE!
HMPH.
YOU'VE SURE GOT A POISONOUS TONGUE.
SLAM
HUUH?
A PUN WHEN I'M ABOUT TO DIE?!
FLAP

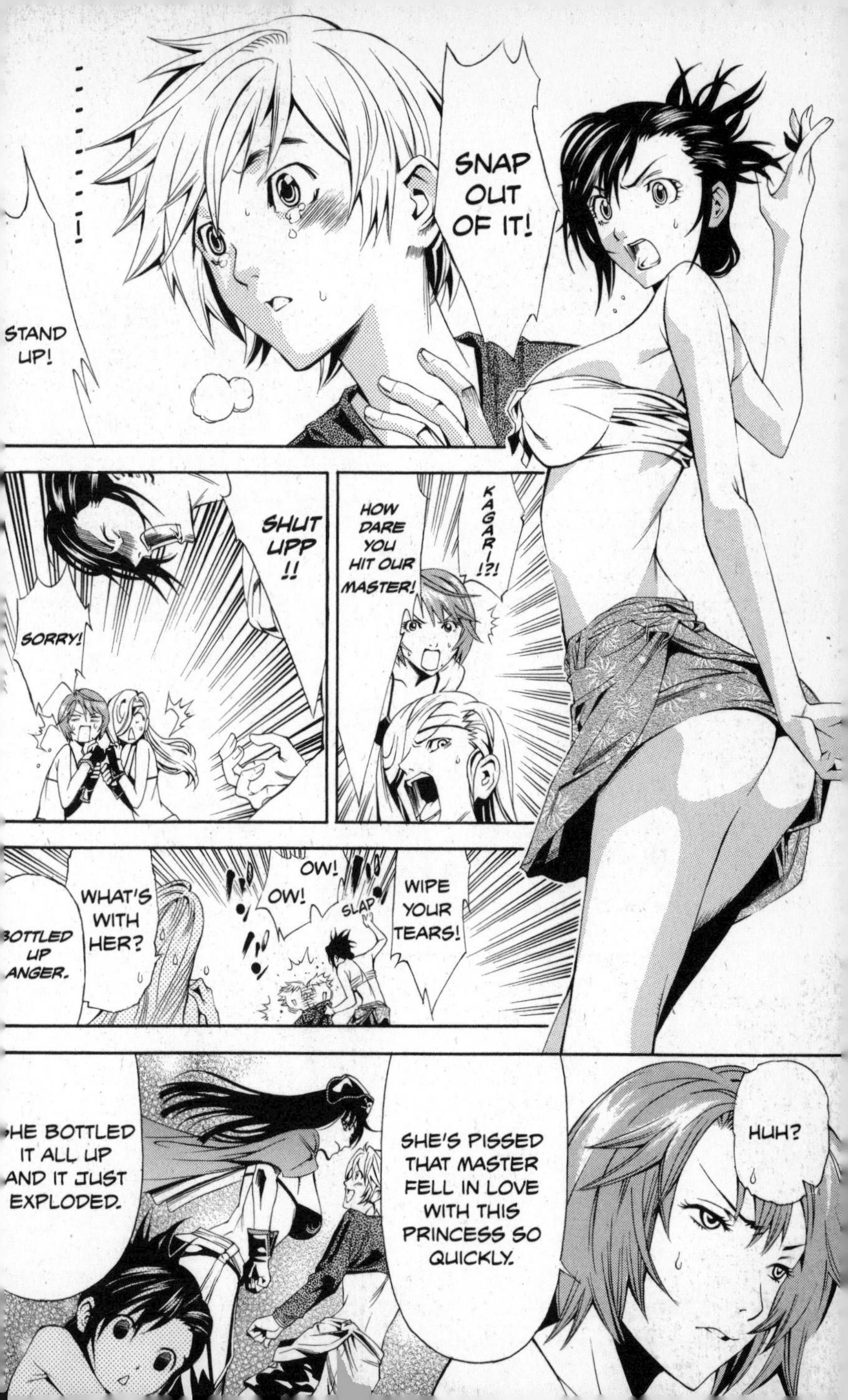
SNAP OUT OF IT!
..........!
STAND UP!
KAGARI !?!
HOW DARE YOU HIT OUR MASTER!
SHUT UPP !!
SORRY!
WIPE YOUR TEARS!
OW!
OW!
SLAP
WHAT'S WITH HER?
OTTLED UP ANGER.
HUH?
SHE'S PISSED THAT MASTER FELL IN LOVE WITH THIS PRINCESS SO QUICKLY.
HE BOTTLED IT ALL UP AND IT JUST EXPLODED.

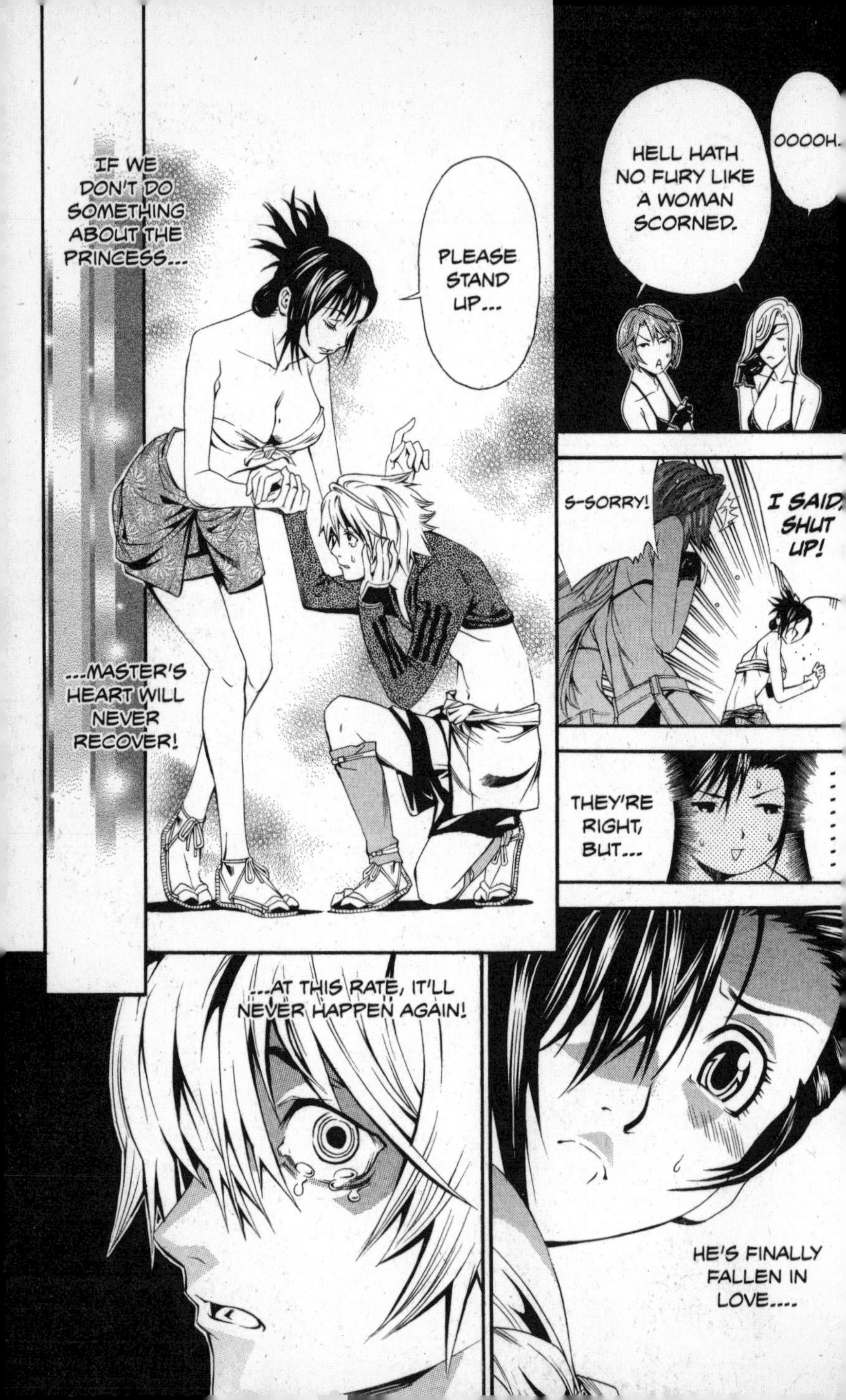
OOOOH.
HELL HATH NO FURY LIKE A WOMAN SCORNED.
I SAID, SHUT UP!
S-SORRY!
THEY'RE RIGHT, BUT...
PLEASE STAND UP...
IF WE DON'T DO SOMETHING ABOUT THE PRINCESS...
...MASTER'S HEART WILL NEVER RECOVER!
HE'S FINALLY FALLEN IN LOVE....
...AT THIS RATE, IT'LL NEVER HAPPEN AGAIN!

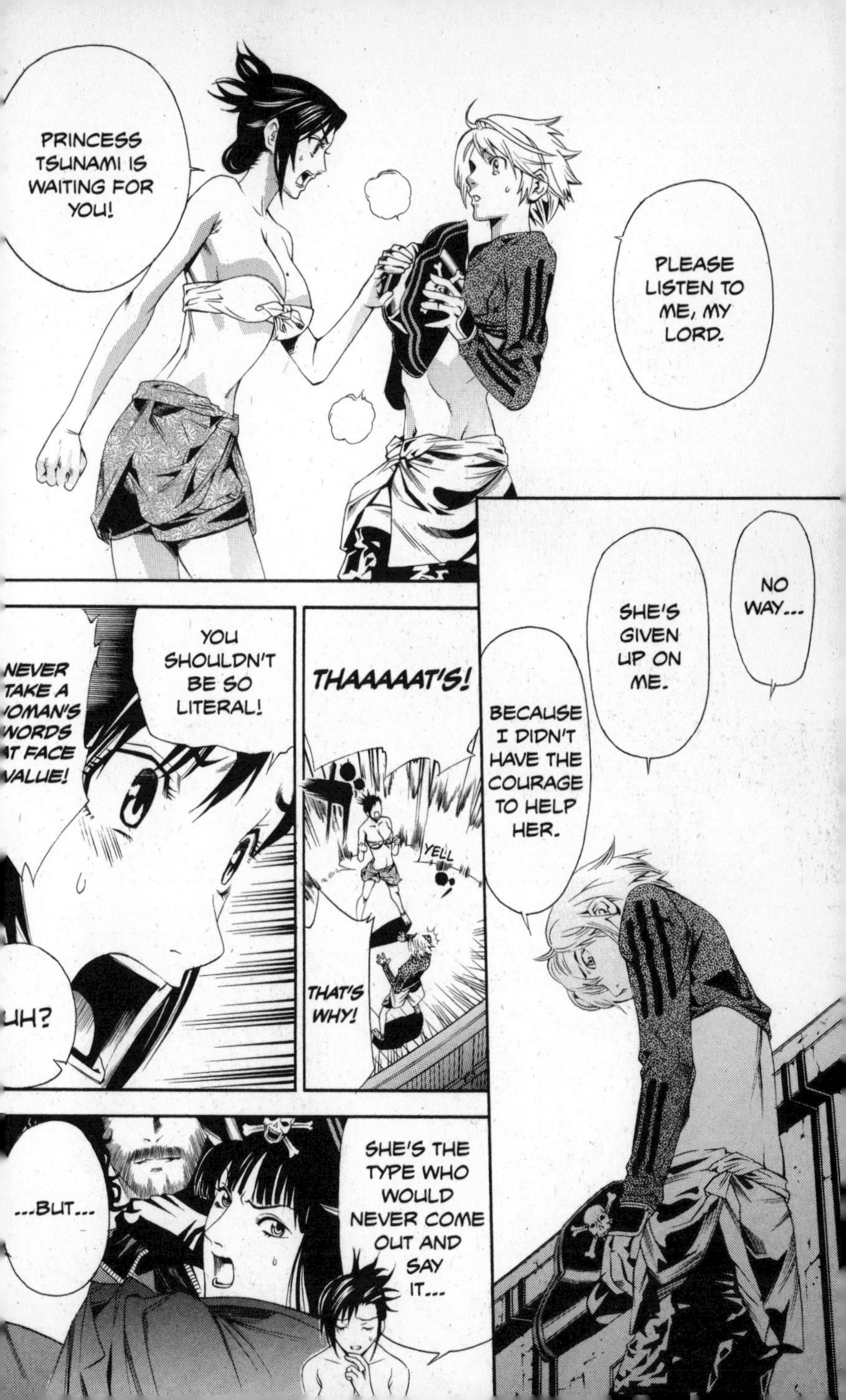
PLEASE LISTEN TO ME, MY LORD.
PRINCESS TSUNAMI IS WAITING FOR YOU!
NO WAY...
SHE'S GIVEN UP ON ME.
BECAUSE I DIDN'T HAVE THE COURAGE TO HELP HER.
THAAAAAT'S!
YELL
THAT'S WHY!
YOU SHOULDN'T BE SO LITERAL!
NEVER TAKE A OMAN'S ORDS T FACE ALUE!
UH?
SHE'S THE TYPE WHO WOULD NEVER COME OUT AND SAY IT...
...BUT...

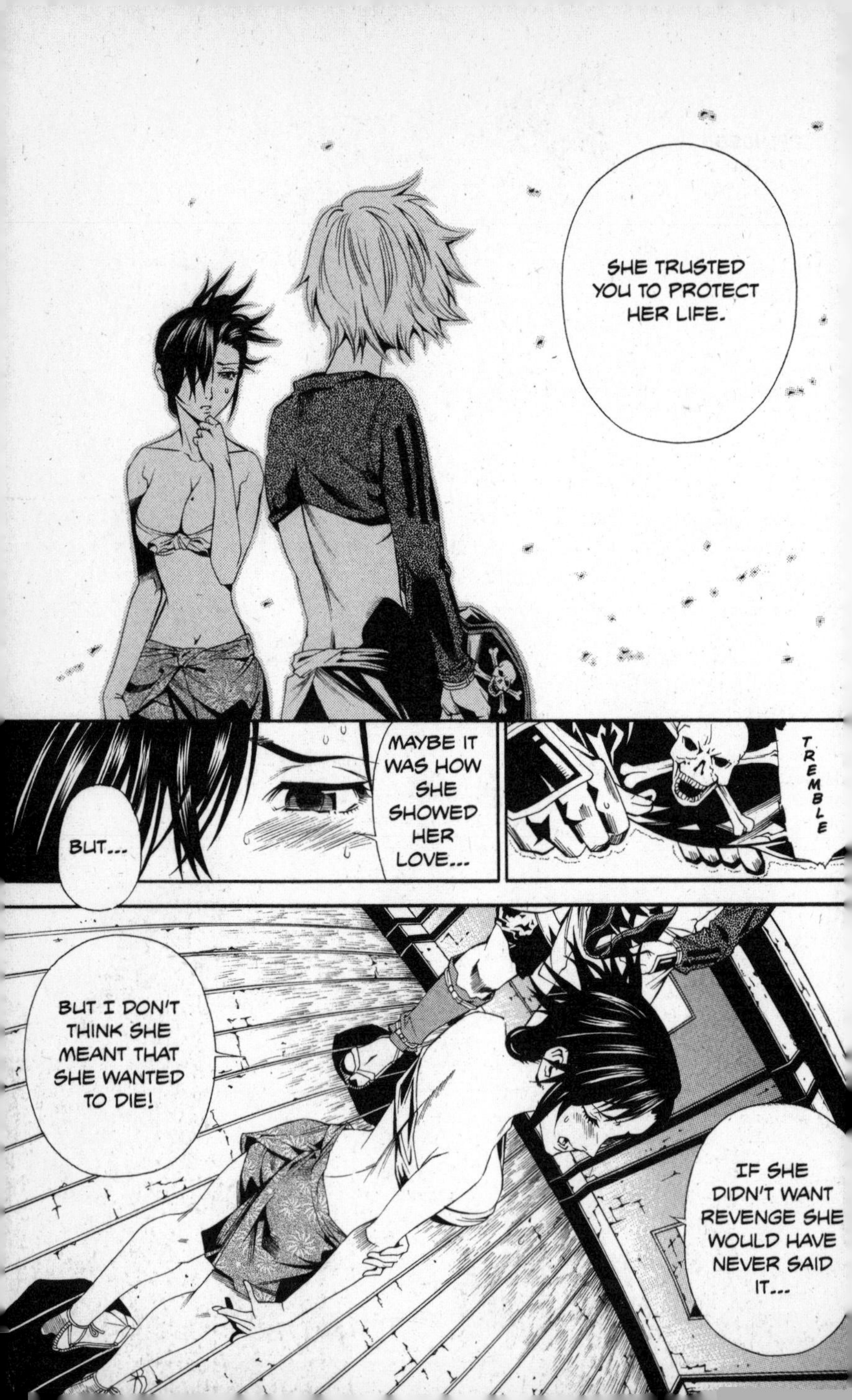
SHE TRUSTED YOU TO PROTECT HER LIFE.
TREMBLE
MAYBE IT WAS HOW SHE SHOWED HER LOVE...
BUT...
IF SHE DIDN'T WANT REVENGE SHE WOULD HAVE NEVER SAID IT...
BUT I DON'T THINK SHE MEANT THAT SHE WANTED TO DIE!

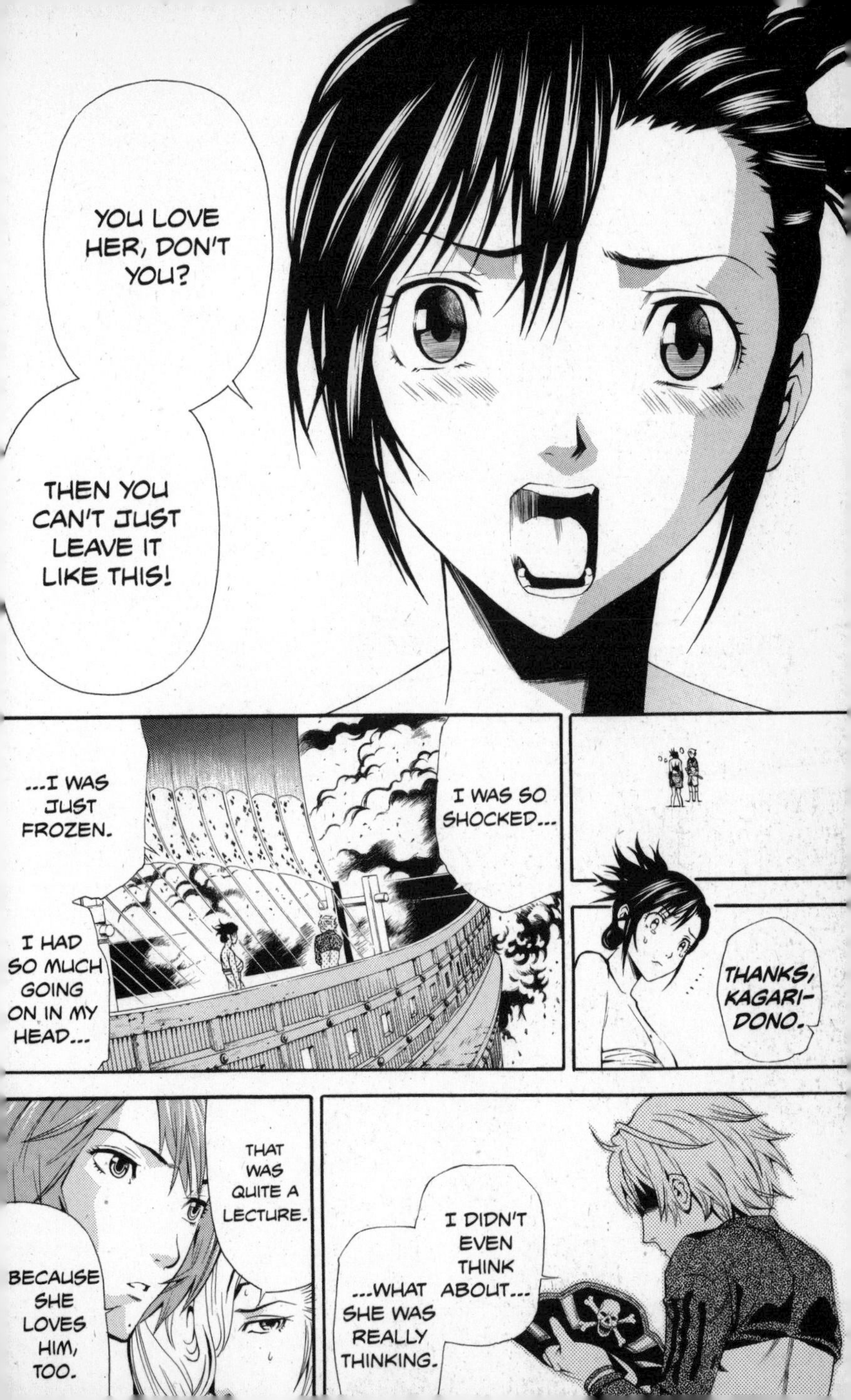
YOU LOVE HER, DON'T YOU?
THEN YOU CAN'T JUST LEAVE IT LIKE THIS!
THANKS, KAGARI-DONO.
I WAS SO SHOCKED...
...I WAS JUST FROZEN.
I HAD SO MUCH GOING ON IN MY HEAD...
I DIDN'T EVEN THINK ABOUT...
...WHAT SHE WAS REALLY THINKING.
THAT WAS QUITE A LECTURE.
BECAUSE SHE LOVES HIM, TOO.

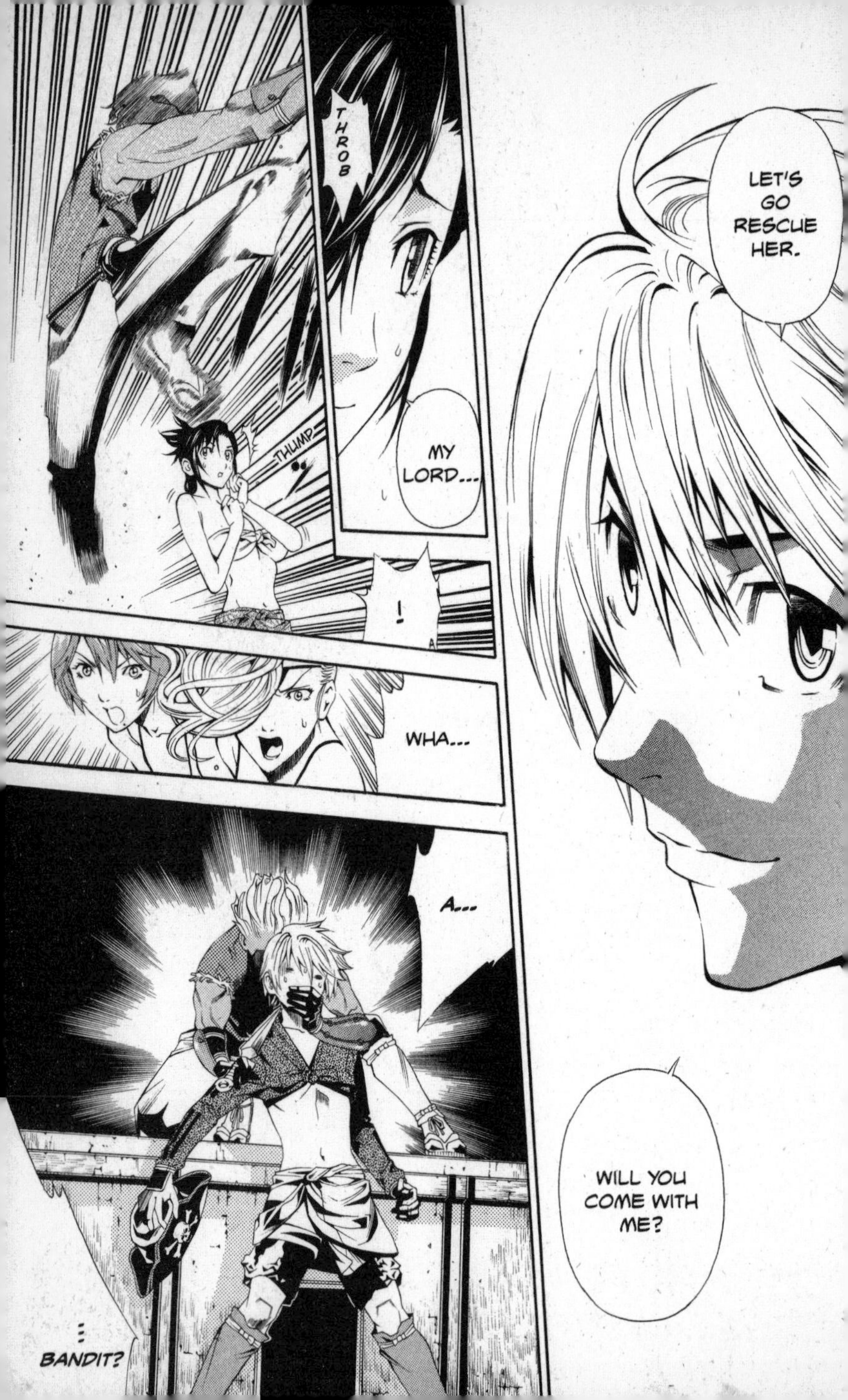
LET'S GO RESCUE HER.
WILL YOU COME WITH ME?
THROB
MY LORD...
THUMP
!
WHA...
A...
...BANDIT?

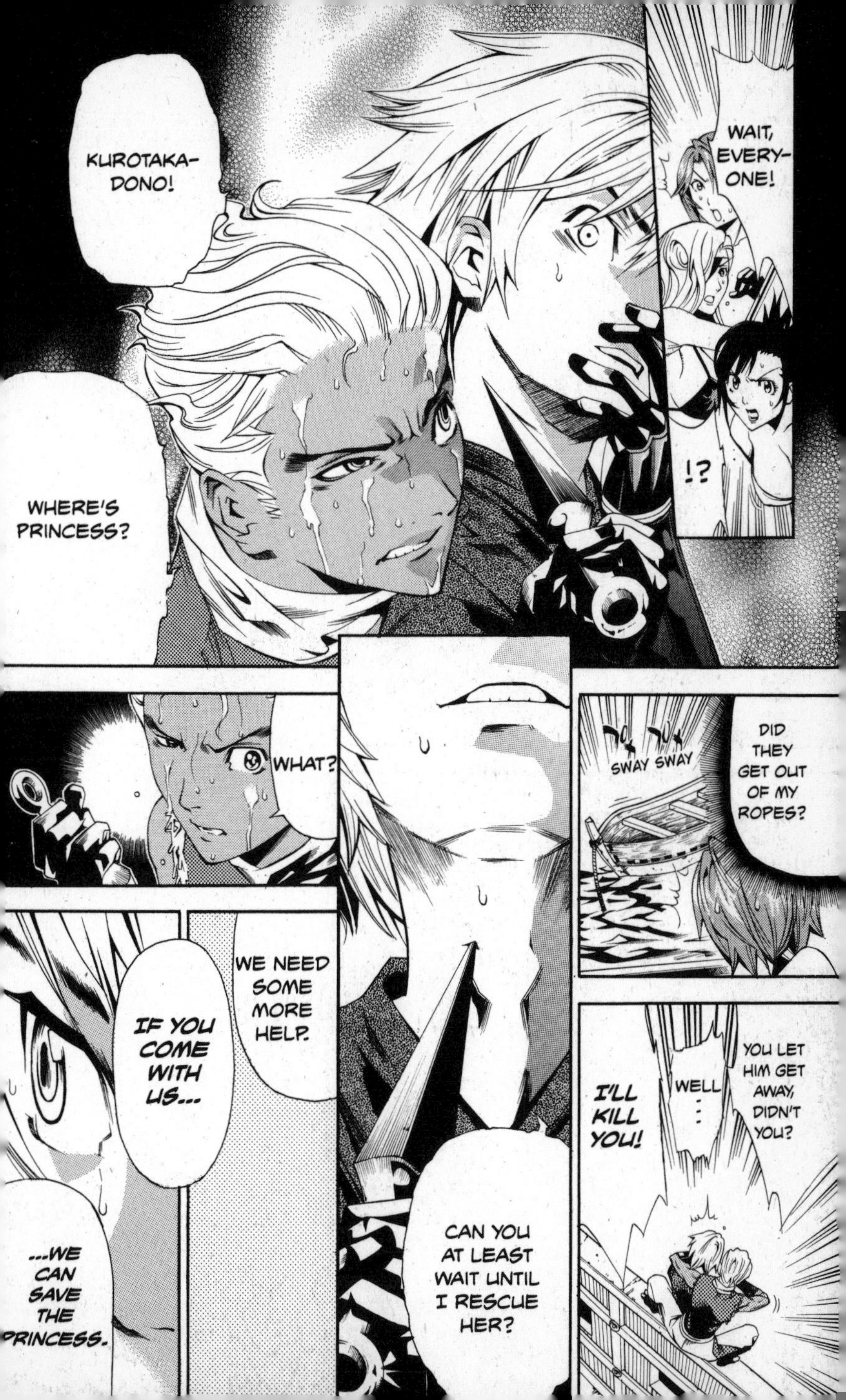
WAIT, EVERY-ONE!
!?
KUROTAKA-DONO!
WHERE'S PRINCESS?
DID THEY GET OUT OF MY ROPES?
SWAY SWAY
YOU LET HIM GET AWAY, DIDN'T YOU?
WELL...
I'LL KILL YOU!
CAN YOU AT LEAST WAIT UNTIL I RESCUE HER?
WHAT?
WE NEED SOME MORE HELP.
IF YOU COME WITH US...
...WE CAN SAVE THE PRINCESS.

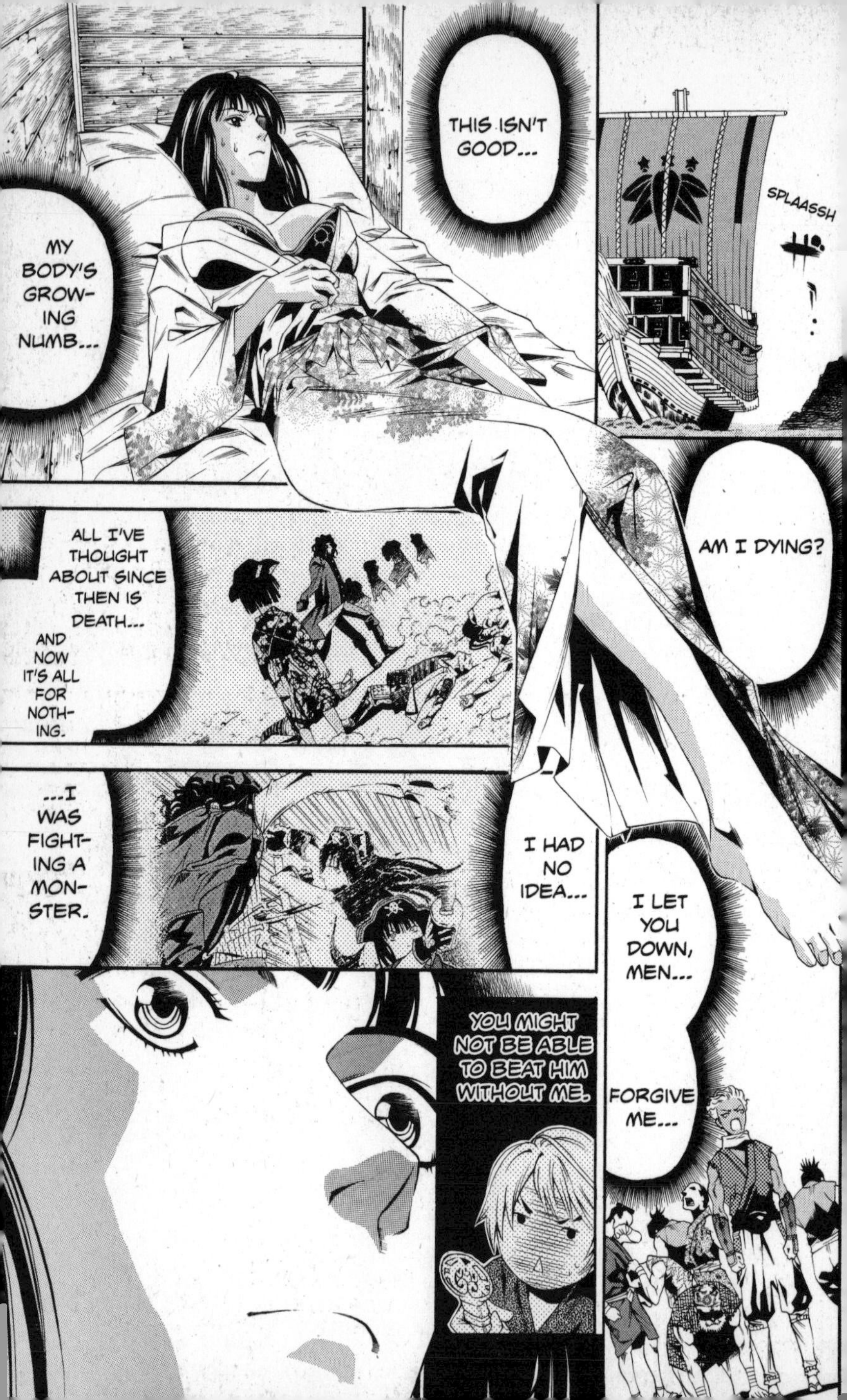
SPLAASSH
THIS ISN'T GOOD...
MY BODY'S GROWING NUMB...
AM I DYING?
ALL I'VE THOUGHT ABOUT SINCE THEN IS DEATH...
AND NOW IT'S ALL FOR NOTHING.
I HAD NO IDEA...
...I WAS FIGHTING A MONSTER.
I LET YOU DOWN, MEN...
FORGIVE ME...
YOU MIGHT NOT BE ABLE TO BEAT HIM WITHOUT ME.

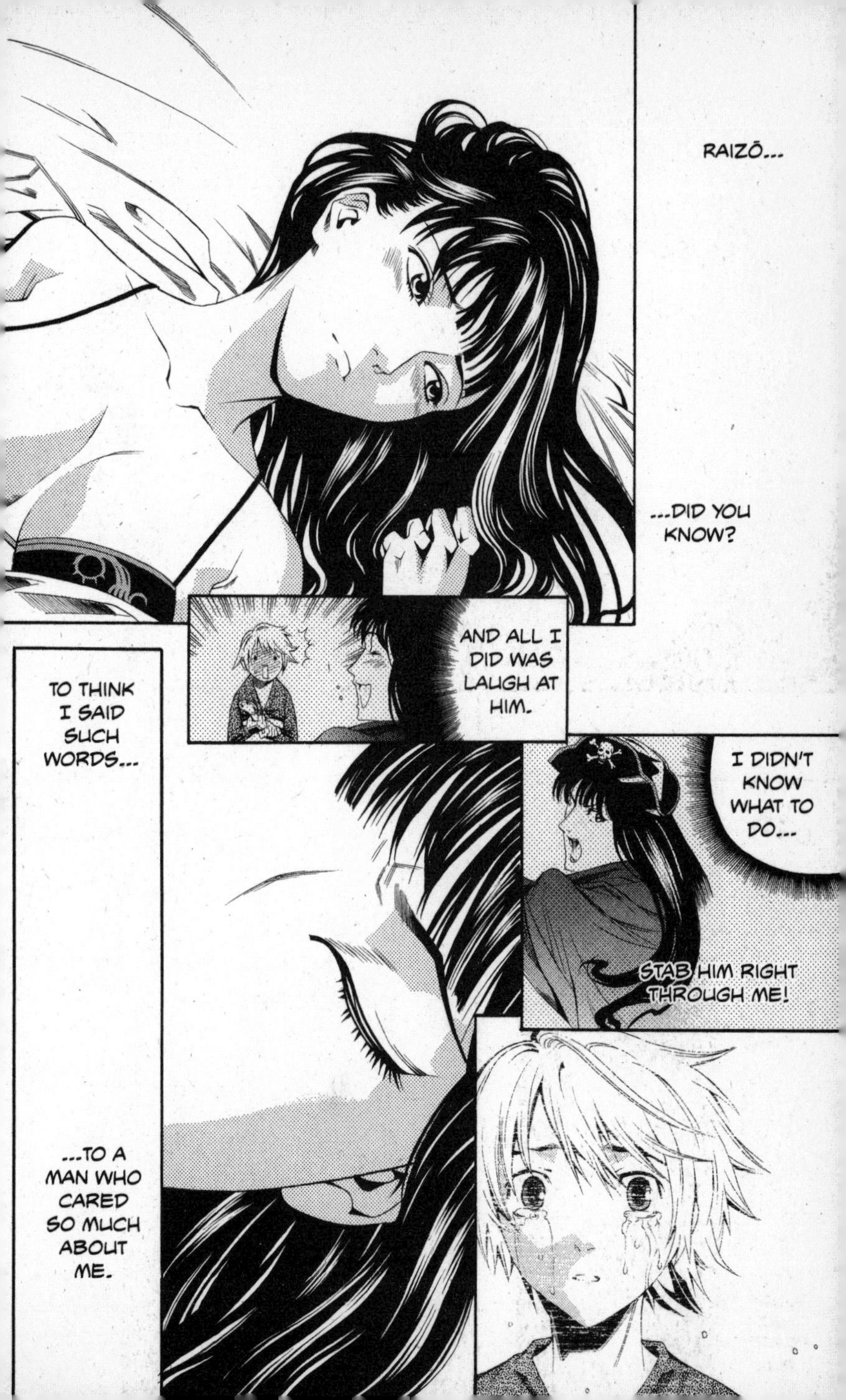
RAIZŌ...
...DID YOU KNOW?
AND ALL I DID WAS LAUGH AT HIM.
I DIDN'T KNOW WHAT TO DO...
STAB HIM RIGHT THROUGH ME!
TO THINK I SAID SUCH WORDS...
...TO A MAN WHO CARED SO MUCH ABOUT ME.

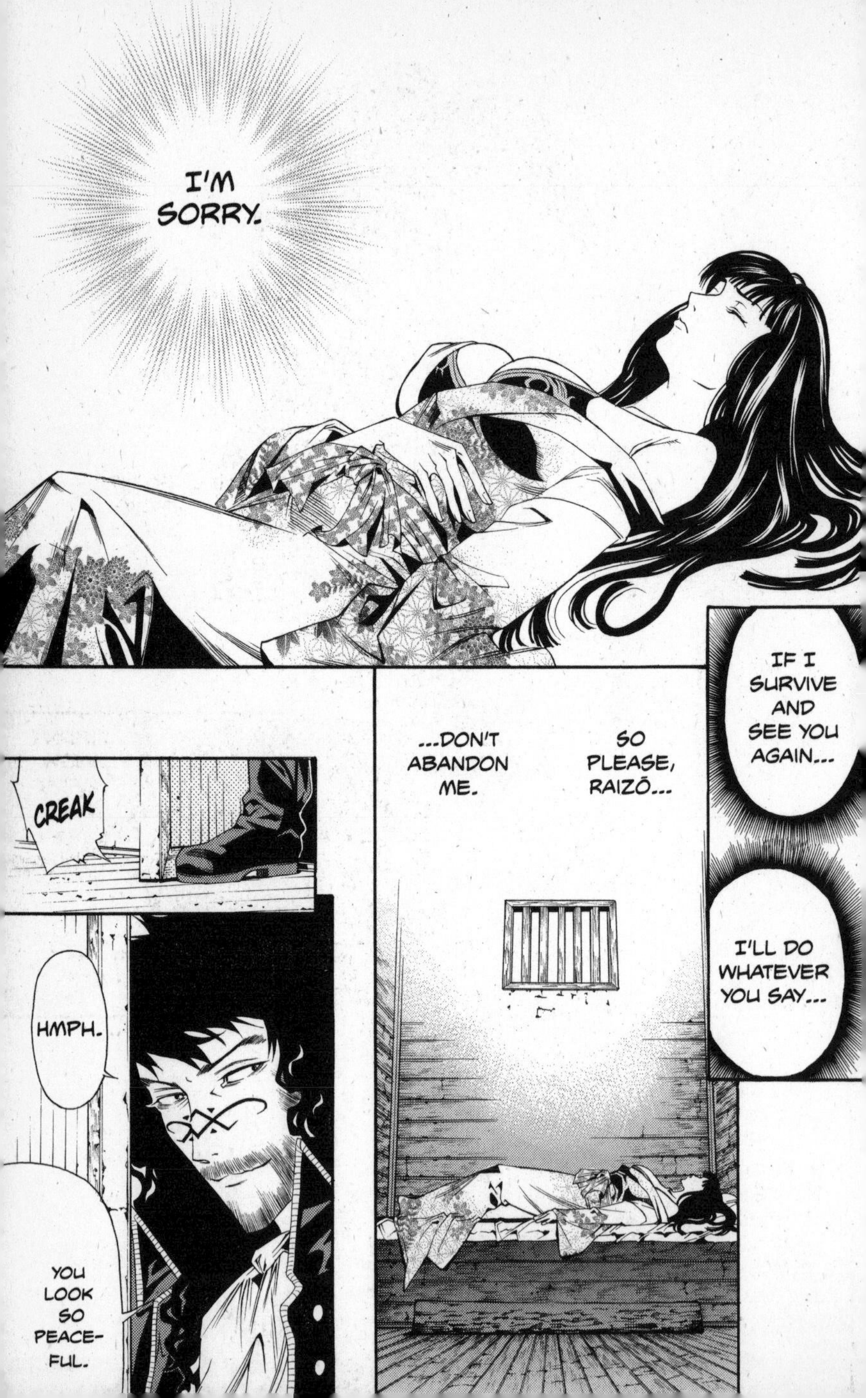
I'M SORRY.
IF I SURVIVE AND SEE YOU AGAIN...
I'LL DO WHATEVER YOU SAY...
SO PLEASE, RAIZŌ...
...DON'T ABANDON ME.
CREAK
HMPH.
YOU LOOK SO PEACE-FUL.

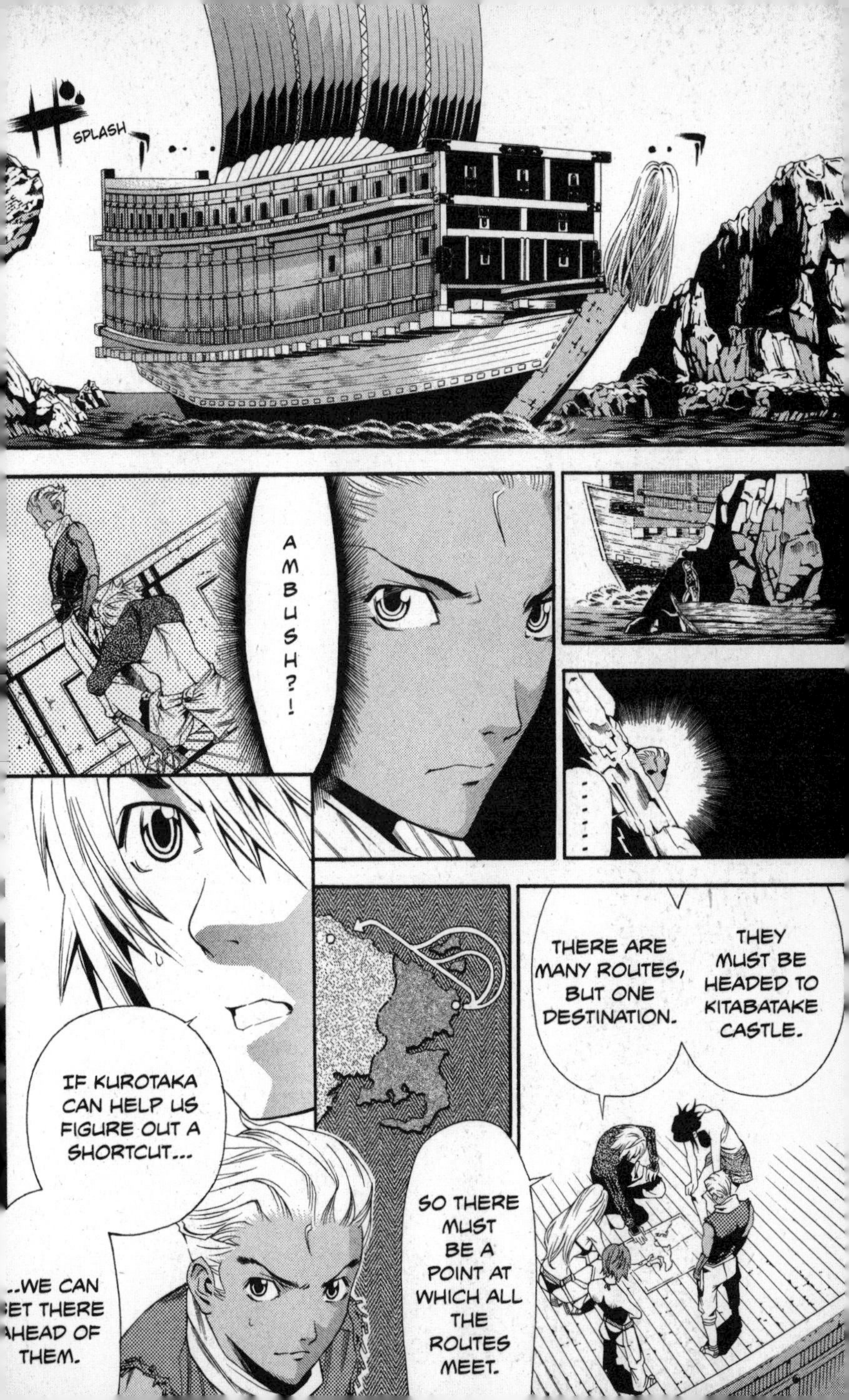
SPLASH
AMBUSH?!
THEY MUST BE HEADED TO KITABATAKE CASTLE.
THERE ARE MANY ROUTES, BUT ONE DESTINATION.
SO THERE MUST BE A POINT AT WHICH ALL THE ROUTES MEET.
IF KUROTAKA CAN HELP US FIGURE OUT A SHORTCUT...
...WE CAN ET THERE HEAD OF THEM.

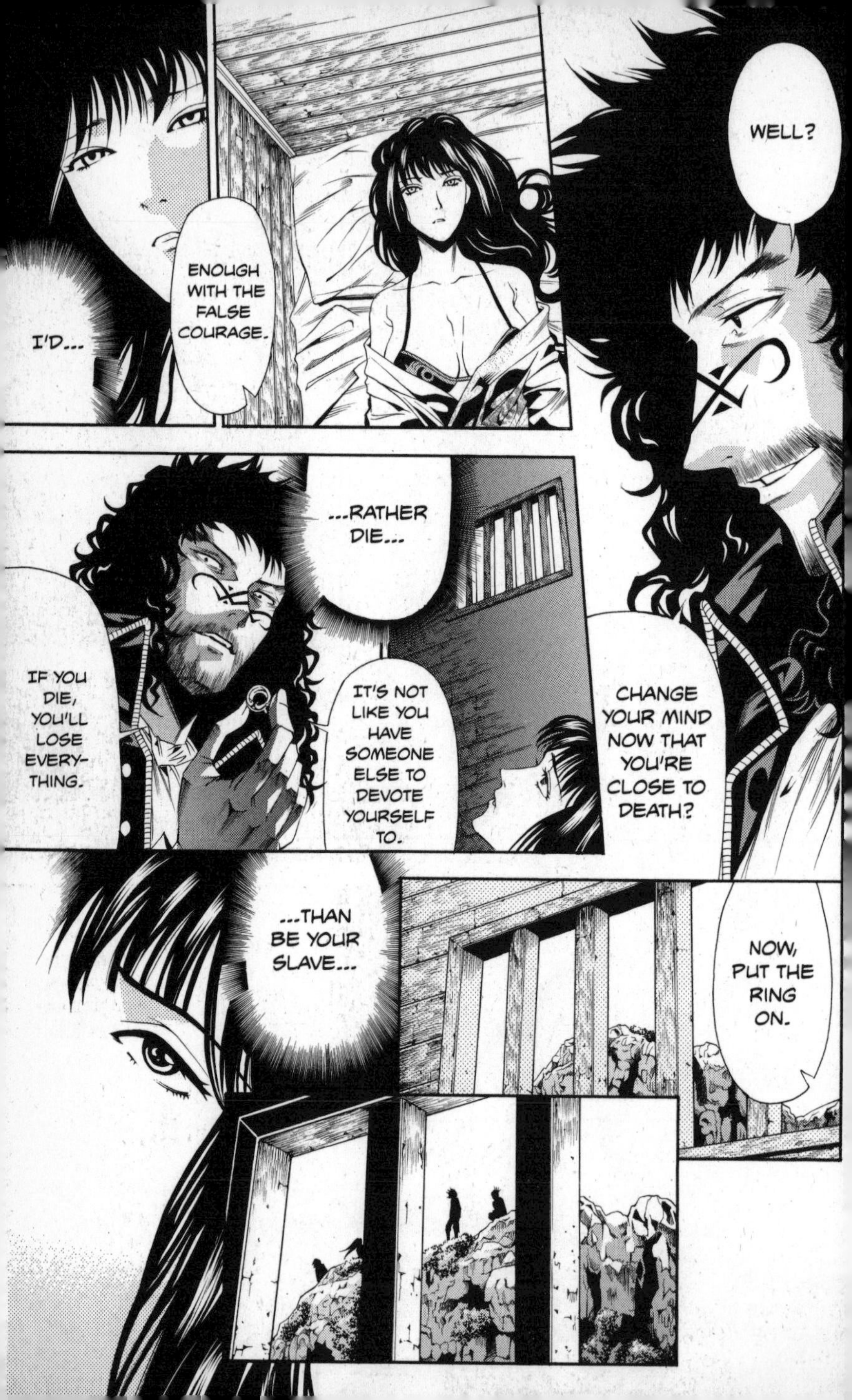
WELL?
CHANGE YOUR MIND NOW THAT YOU'RE CLOSE TO DEATH?
ENOUGH WITH THE FALSE COURAGE.
I'D...
...RATHER DIE...
IT'S NOT LIKE YOU HAVE SOMEONE ELSE TO DEVOTE YOURSELF TO.
IF YOU DIE, YOU'LL LOSE EVERY-THING.
NOW, PUT THE RING ON.
...THAN BE YOUR SLAVE...

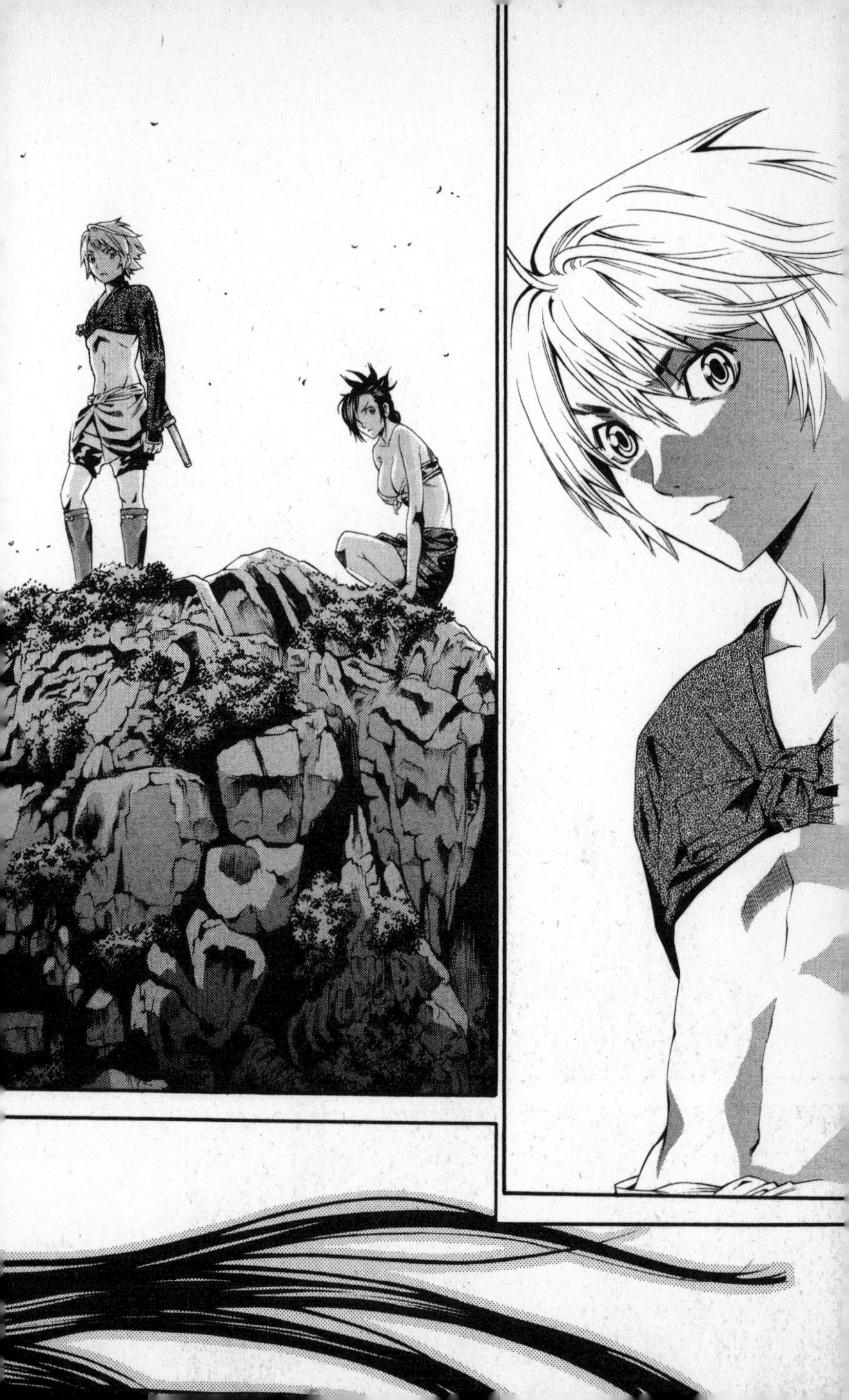

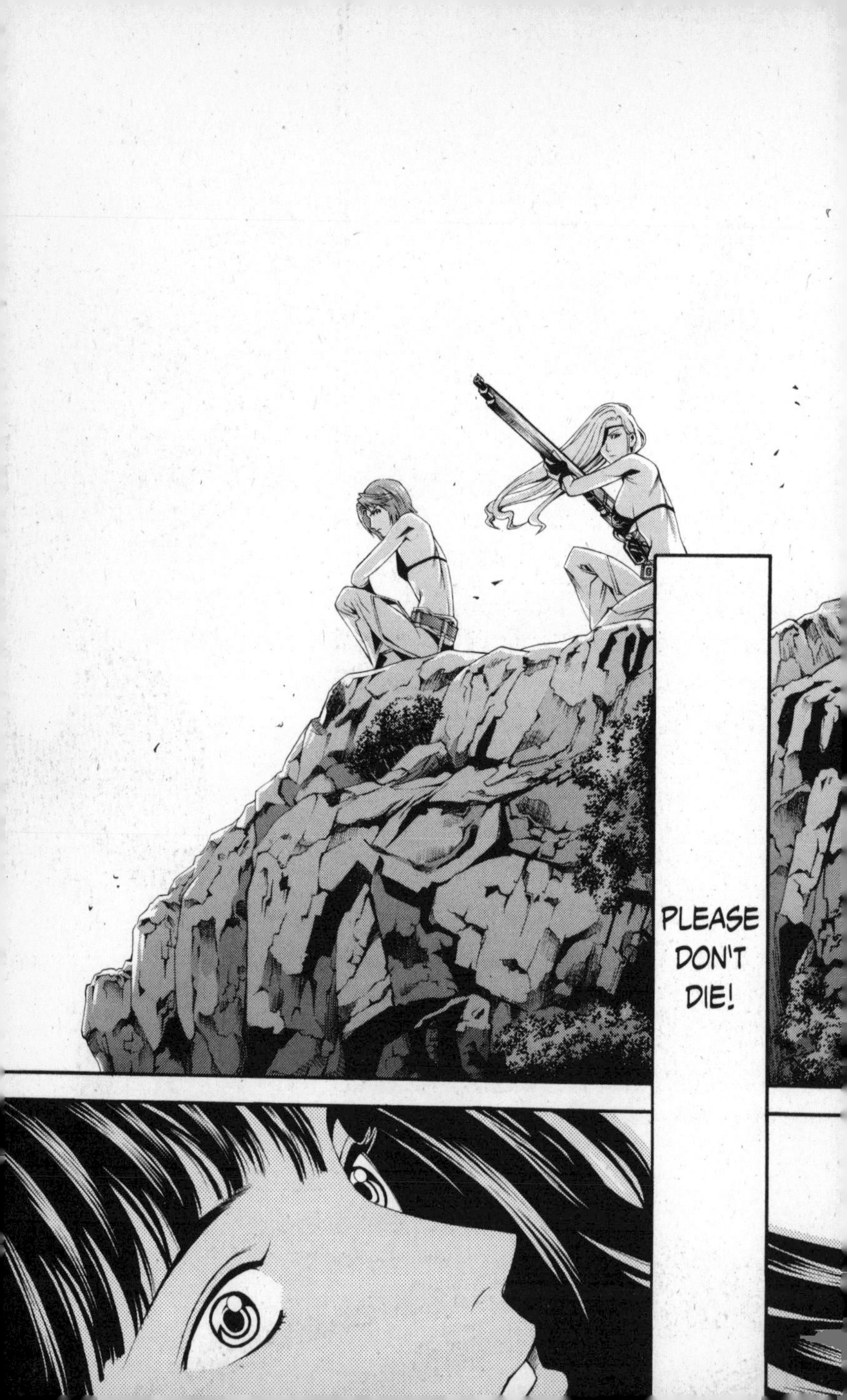
PLEASE DON'T DIE!

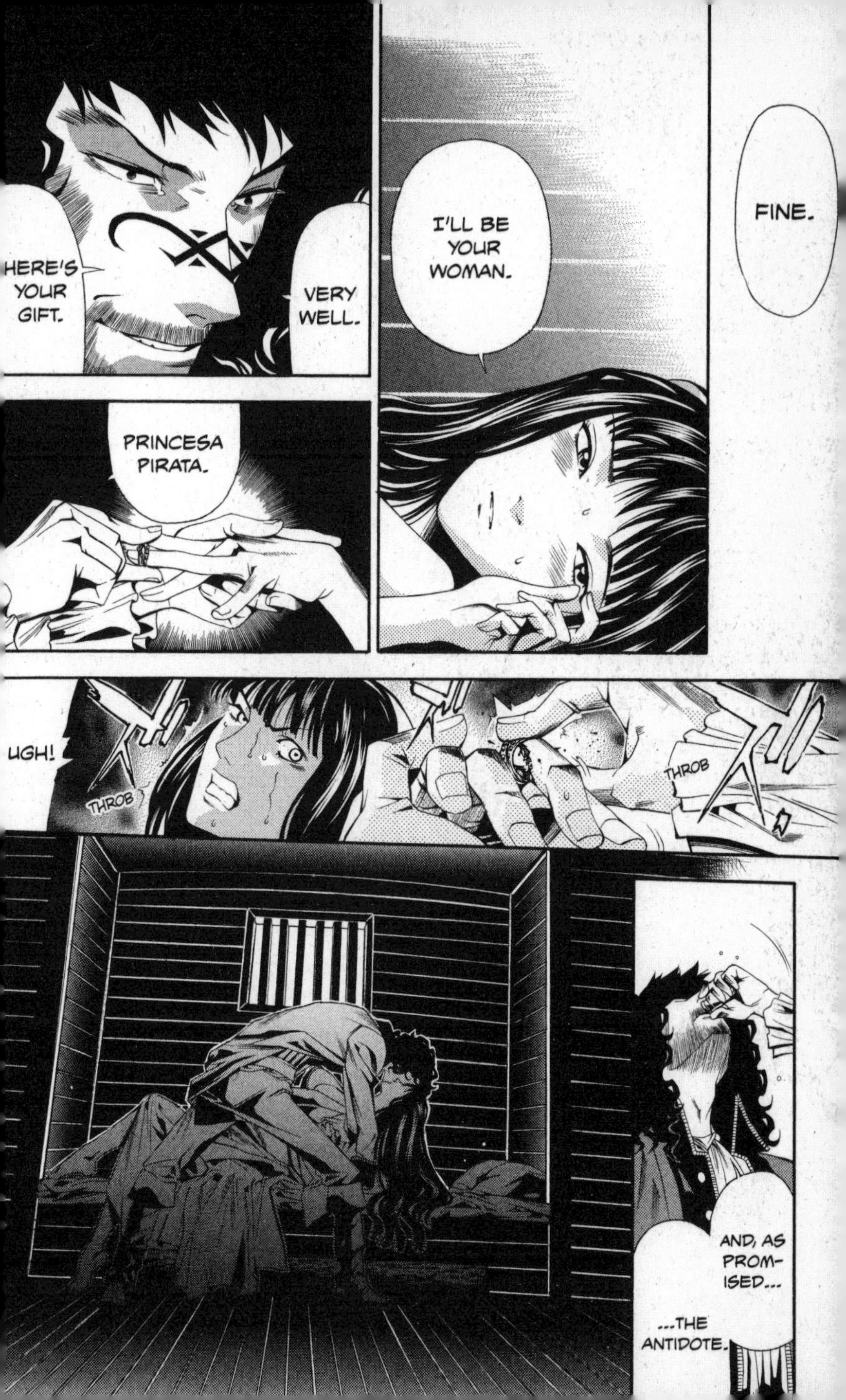
FINE.
I'LL BE YOUR WOMAN.
VERY WELL.
HERE'S YOUR GIFT.
PRINCESA PIRATA.
THROB
UGH!
THROB
AND, AS PROMISED...
...THE ANTIDOTE.

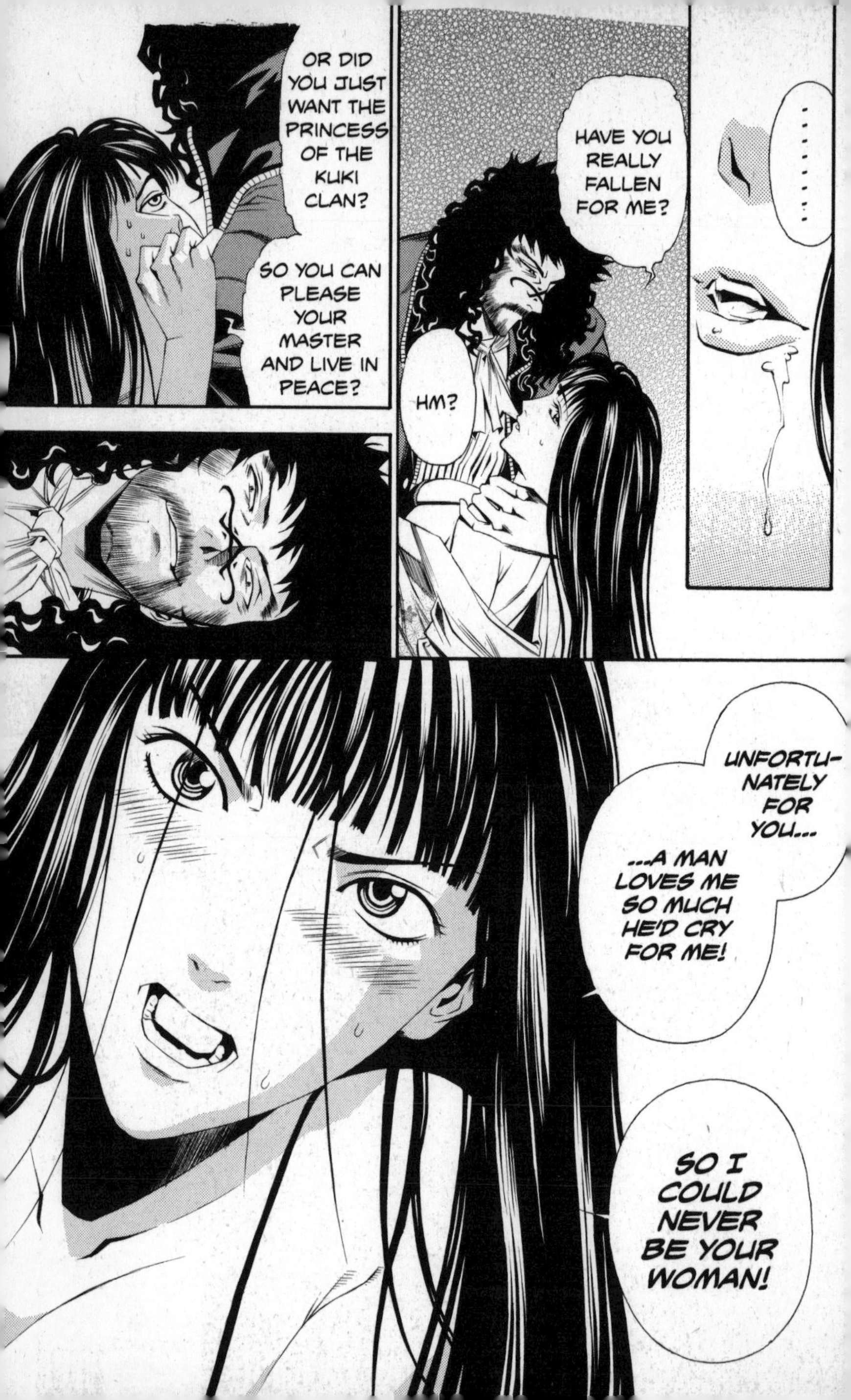
......
HAVE YOU REALLY FALLEN FOR ME?
HM?
OR DID YOU JUST WANT THE PRINCESS OF THE KUKI CLAN?
SO YOU CAN PLEASE YOUR MASTER AND LIVE IN PEACE?
UNFORTU-NATELY FOR YOU...
...A MAN LOVES ME SO MUCH HE'D CRY FOR ME!
SO I COULD NEVER BE YOUR WOMAN!

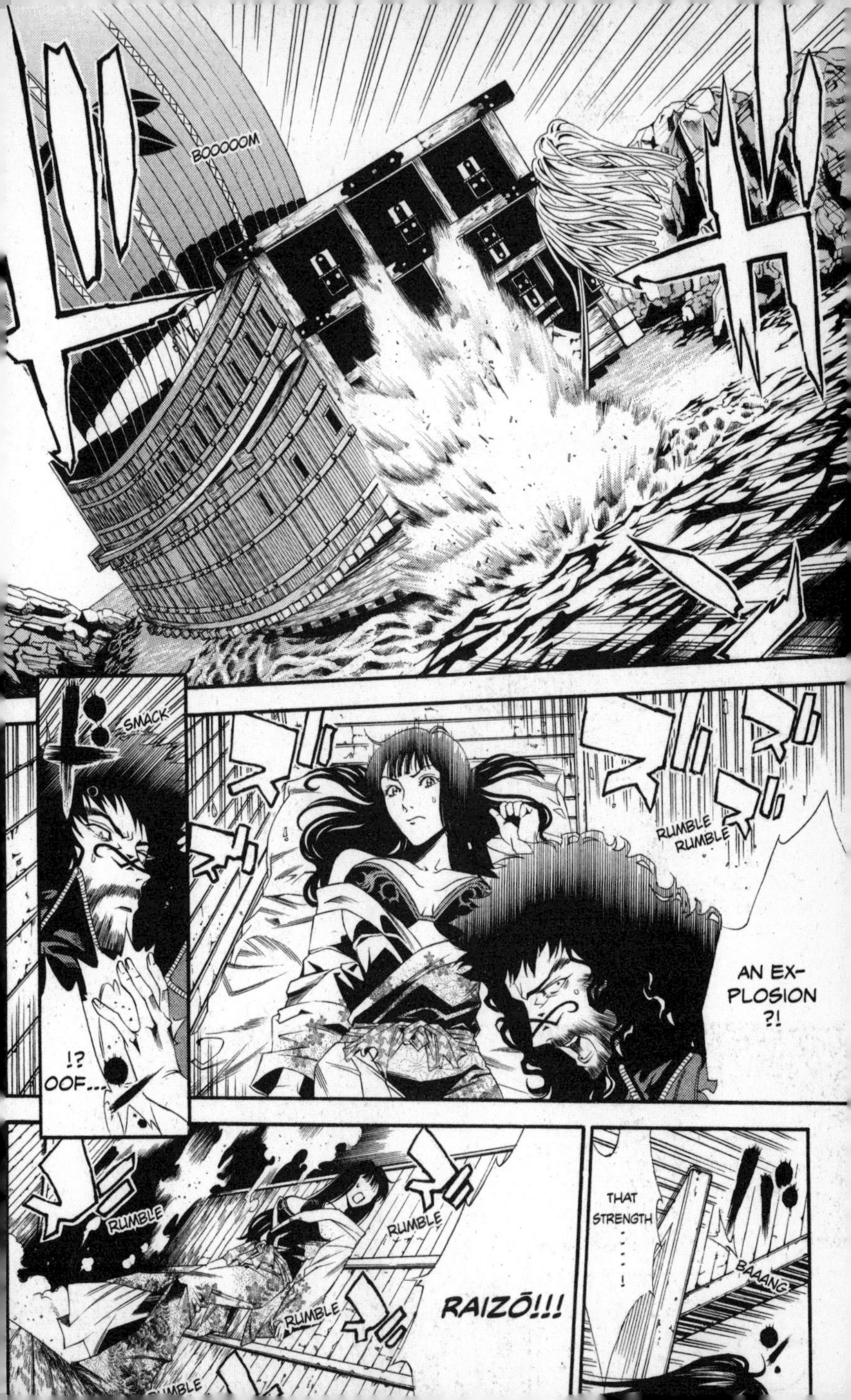
BOOOOOM
RUMBLE RUMBLE
AN EX-
PLOSION
?!
SMACK
!?
OOF...
THAT
STRENGTH
.....!
BAAANG
RUMBLE
RUMBLE
RAIZŌ!!!
RUMBLE

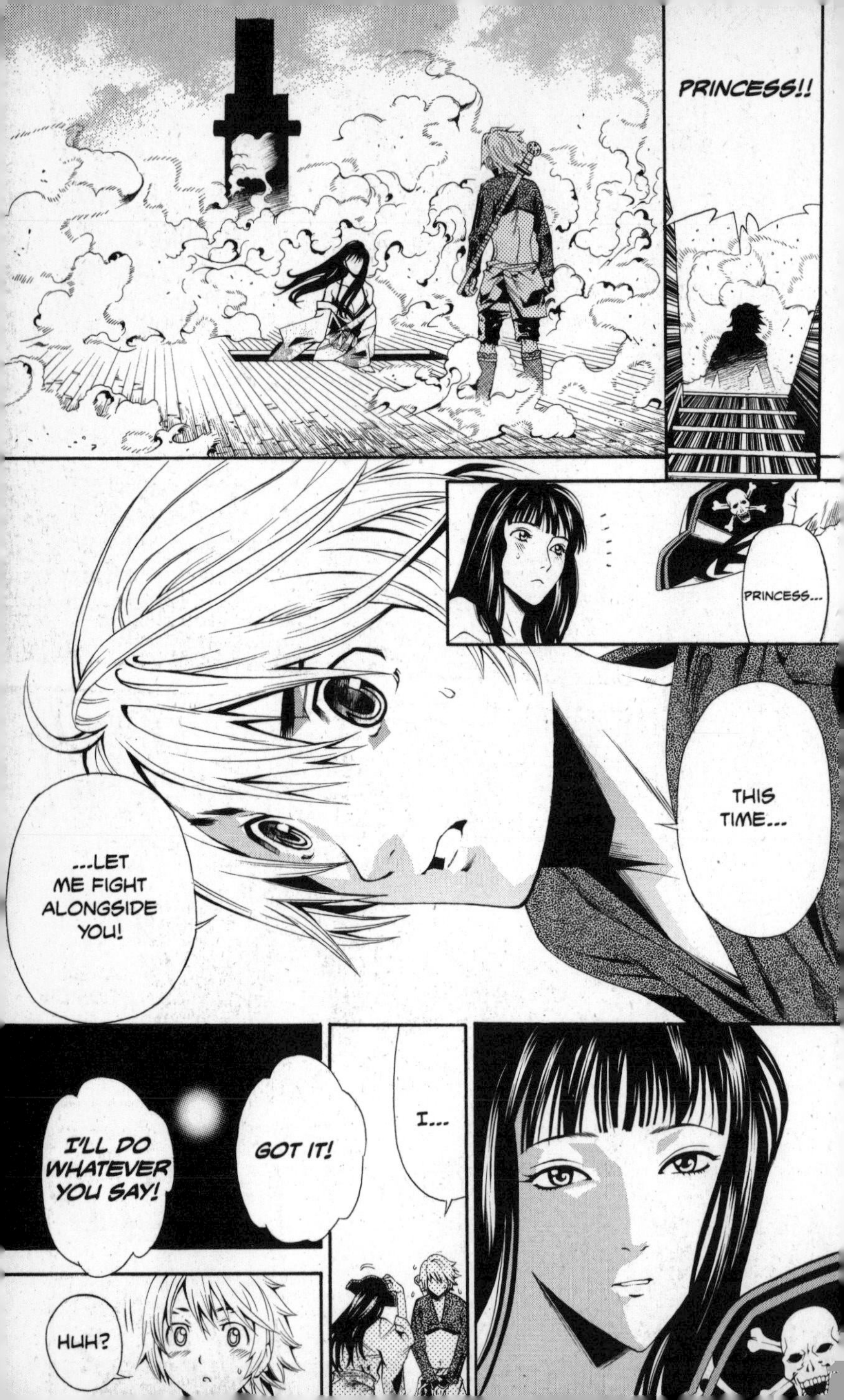
PRINCESS!!
PRINCESS...
THIS TIME...
...LET ME FIGHT ALONGSIDE YOU!
I...
GOT IT!
I'LL DO WHATEVER YOU SAY!
HUH?

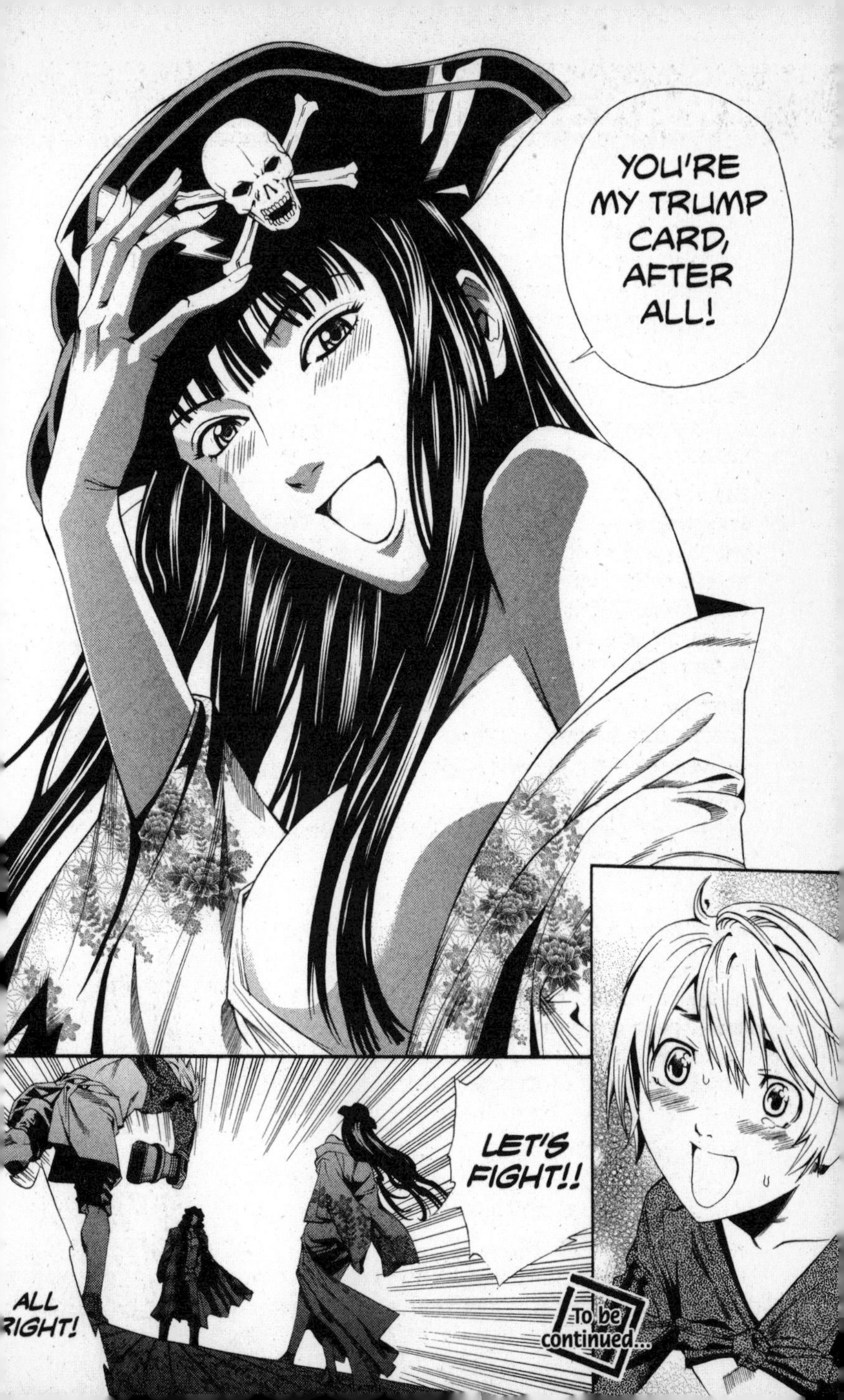
YOU'RE MY TRUMP CARD, AFTER ALL!
LET'S FIGHT!!
ALL RIGHT!
To be continued...

# TRANSLATION NOTES

Japanese is a tricky language for most Westerners, and translation is often more art than science. For your edification and reading pleasure, here are notes on some of the places where we could have gone in a different direction with our translation of the work, or where a Japanese cultural reference is used.

### Kunoichi
A *kunoichi* is a female ninja. It is written くノ一, which symbolizes the strokes necessary to write 女, "woman."

### Sengoku era
*Sengoku jidai* (Warring States Era) lasted from the mid-15th century to the beginning of the 17th century. As its name suggests, it was a time of civil war in Japan, with regional lords (*daimyo*) taking control because of a weak central government. The most famous *daimyo* were Oda Nobunaga, known for his military prowess, and Tokugawa Ieyasu, who went on to become the first shogun of Japan's final shogunate.

### shinobi
Another word for ninja. *Shinobi* was the more commonly used term for ninja until its usage declined in popularity post-World War II.

### Hime or himegimi.
*Hime* means "princess." In this case it is also used towards any female of noble lineage, i.e. the daughter of a chief.

### ninpō
*Ninpō* literally means "ninja arts" or "ninja technique."

### ihai, page 3
An *ihai* is a mortuary tablet that's often placed on a Buddhist altar to honor a deceased loved one. It's usually a wood or stone tablet that's engraved with the deceased person's posthumous name, which is given to them by the Buddhist priest who performed their funerary rites.

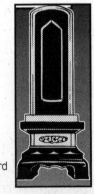

### gōshi, page 8
A *gōshi* is a "country samurai"; a samurai who lived in a rural district rather than a castle town.

### hara-kiri, page 14
Literally means "cutting stomach," it is a ritual suicide. The word is read "seppuku," but in spoken dialogue is called "hara-kiri."

### *topknot*, page 14
Traditional hairstyle of samurai in the Edo period. The top of the head was shaved, leaving a long section of hair which was oiled and pulled into a folded ponytail. Today the only ones to sport topknots are sumo wrestlers.

### *mon*, page 52
The mon was a currency used in Japan from 1336 until 1870. It was then replaced with the yen.

### *Eiroku*, page 85
A sub-era of the Warring States Era, which lasted from February 1558 through April 1570.

ROOOOAR

EIROKU 3 TAJO CASTLE, TOSHI.

RA-SEN-GAN

HM?

RASENGAN

THERE'S A SHIP.

### *Rasengan*, page 104
Kisarabi's special *ninpō* attack. It's written with the characters meaning "wizard" and "eye."

# TOMARE!

## [STOP!]

**You are going the wrong way!**

**Manga is a completely different type of reading experience.**

**To start at the *beginning*, go to the *end*!**

That's right! Authentic manga is read the traditional Japanese way—from right to left, exactly the *opposite* of how American books are read. It's easy to follow: Just go to the other end of the book, and read each page—and each panel—from the right side to the left side, starting at the top right. Now you're experiencing manga as it was meant to be.